GERMAN LITERATURE

GARLAND REFERENCE LIBRARY
OF THE HUMANITIES
(VOL. 108)

GERMAN LITERATURE
An Annotated Reference Guide

Uwe K. Faulhaber
Penrith B. Goff

GARLAND PUBLISHING, INC. • NEW YORK & LONDON
1979

Library of Congress Cataloging in Publication Data

Faulhaber, Uwe K
German literature : an annotated reference guide.

(Garland reference library of the humanities ; v. 108)
Includes index.
1. German literature—History and criticism—Bibliography. I. Goff, Penrith, joint author.
II. Title.
Z2231.F38 [PT85] 016.83 77-83349
ISBN 0-8240-9831-5

Printed on acid-free, 250-year-life paper
Manufactured in the United States of America

CONTENTS

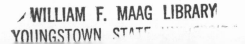

PREFACE

This annotated bibliography is designed to fill the need for an in-depth guide which can also serve as a handy volume for quick reference. It embraces the major research tools, literary criticism, and periodicals in the field of German studies. Though comprehensive enough for the established scholar and teacher, it will also be useful to the undergraduate, the comparatist, and the librarian. To this end we have given particular attention to works in English.

In general, entries are listed alphabetically according to author, editor, or title. *Forschungsberichte* and checklists of historically important literary histories and bibliographies are arranged chronologically. Each annotation describes the basic contents of the work, its range, organization, etc. In addition we have evaluated each work from the standpoint of quality, reliability, currency, and usefulness. The annotation reflects specifically the edition listed; other editions or reprints may be indicated in parentheses. Some antiquated works whose approach has fallen into disfavor are included because they contain a wealth of material not easily found elsewhere. Some works, traditionally included in bibliographies, we found to be no longer useful; this we indicated in our annotation. We have also included a selection of works which are of primarily historical value. The designations of critical method should not be seen as evaluations but as thumbnail descriptions: by "positivistic" is meant an approach which stresses the facts external to the literary work; "intellectual-historical" indicates an emphasis on the ideas in a work or its place in the context of intellectual history, rather than its aesthetic characteristics; "Marxist-socialist" loosely designates works in which the Marxist ideology is basic.

Particularly with the student researcher in mind, we have provided a substantial list of periodicals which includes all the major professional journals as well as a number of literary reviews and other periodicals which often publish material of interest to the Germanist. The entire range of periodical literature is presented; the annotations will be especially useful to those who do not have all the periodicals readily available. Finally, the annotated checklist in the last chapter refers the researcher to a broad spectrum of dictionaries, encyclopedias, and standard histories of related disciplines.

The author-title-subject index, citing item numbers only, is intended to facilitate rapid location of an item or annotation. Some items, such as major current and completed bibliographies and comprehensive literary histories, appear more than once; they are repeated in sections on genre, literary history, literature in translation, etc., to remind the researcher that they are standard works in these areas also. At the end of each such entry the item number of the complete, annotated entry is given in parentheses. Each such cross-entry is indicated by asterisks in place of an item number.

We wish to express our gratitude to Wayne State University for financial support, to Cindy Faulhaber for substantial aid in preparing the index, to Flint Purdy Librarian Kanhya Kaul and all the ever helpful library staff, but most especially to Reference Librarian George Masterton, whose interest, wit, counsel, and professional skill did so much to alleviate the tedium and frustration of our task.

U.K.F.
P.G.

ABBREVIATIONS AND ACRONYMS

Aufl.	*Auflage*, printing or edition
bibl.	bibliography
BRD	Bundesrepublik Deutschland
ca.	circa, approximately
ch.	chapter
col(s).	column(s)
Coll. Germ.	*Colloquia Germanica*
comp.	compiler
DDR	Deutsche Demokratische Republik
dir.	directed
Dt. Phil. im Aufriß	*Deutsche Philologie im Aufriß*
DU	*Deutschunterricht*
DVLG	*Deutsche Vierteljahrsschrift für Literatur-geschichte*
E	English
ed(s).	editor(s)
enl.	enlarged
F	French
fasc.	fascicle
FRG	Federal Republic of Germany
G	German
GDR	German Democratic Republic
GRM	*Germanisch-Romanische Monatshefte*
H.	*Heft*, issue
I	Italian
illus.	illustrations
irreg.	irregular, irregularly
ISBN	International Standard Book Number
JEGP	*Journal of English and Germanic Philology*

lit.	literary, literature
MHG	Middle High German
MLR	*Modern Language Review*
n.d.	no date
NF	*Neue Folge*, new series
nos.	numbers
NS	new series
OHG	Old High German
pl.	plate, plates
PMLA	*Publications of the Modern Language Association of America*
pr.	press
pt(s).	part(s)
publ.	published
R	Russian
repr.	reprint
rev.	revised
S	Spanish
suppl.	supplement
trans.	translated
u.a.	*und andere*, and others
univ., Univ.	university, *Universität*
unpubl.	unpublished
US	United States
USA	United States of America
USSR	Russia
VlB	*Verzeichnis lieferbarer Bücher*
vol(s).	volume(s)
WB	*Weimarer Beiträge*

I.
Bibliographies of Bibliographies

CONTENTS

A. GUIDES TO REFERENCE MATERIAL

1. Fleischhack, Curt, Ernst Rückert, and Günther Reichardt. *Grundriß der Bibliographie.* In collaboration with Gottfried Günther and Werner Dux. Leipzig: Harrassowitz, 1957. viii, 263 pp.

   Covers the humanities and sciences but is severely limited in scope. Contains much East European material. Each item extensively and reliably annotated. CAUTION: this book was designed for training librarians; therefore entries are most readily located by use of the author-subject index.

2. Schneider, Georg. *Handbuch der Bibliographie.* 4th rev. ed. Leipzig: Hiersemann, 1930. ix, 674 pp. (Repr. 1969)

   Introductory material on theory and history of bibliography. Includes only general bibliographies. Each entry extensively annotated. Most readily accessible through index and table of contents. Contains author-title and subject indexes.

3. Silvestri, Gerhard, et al. *Einführung in die Bibliographie. Bibliographien und Nachschlagewerke.* 3rd. rev. ed. Vienna: Österreichisches Institut für Bibliotheksforschung, 1973. vi, 88pp.

   Listings, with some annotation, of bibliographies of bibliographies, major central library catalogues, European national bibliographies, bibliographies of translations, current and completed bibliographies, dissertation indexes, biographical handbooks, and encyclopedias. Compact and reliable.

4. Totok, Wilhelm, Rolf Weitzel, and Karl-Heinz Weimann. *Handbuch der bibliographischen Nachschlagewerke.* 4th rev. ed. Frankfurt: Klostermann, 1972. xxxiv, 367pp. (^{1}1954)

   Offers an excellent selection of titles in the humanities and sciences. Organization not always apparent. Brief and clear annotations for each item. Contains author-subject-title index.

5. Walford, Albert John, ed. *Guide to Reference Material.* 3 vols. 2nd ed. London: Library Association, 1966-1970. I: "Science and Technology"; II: "Philosophy and Psychology, Religion, Social Sciences, Geography, Biography and History"; III: "Generalities, Languages, the Arts and Literature." (III, ^{1}1959)

   Extensive compendium for the librarian; III contains ca. 4,700 items. Easily accessible.

6. Winchell, Constance Mabel, ed. *Guide to Reference Books*. 8th ed. Chicago: American Library Association, 1967. xx, 741pp.

Continued by:

7. Sheehy, Eugene Paul, ed. *Guide to Reference Books*. 9th ed. Chicago: American Library Association, 1976. xviii, 1015pp. ([1]1902: *Guide to the Study and Use of Reference Books*)

The standard work for the reference librarian. Written with the student in mind. Abundant annotations, most often including the Library of Congress catalog card numbers. Includes books to 1974. Best general reference work available.

B. COMPLETED GENERAL BIBLIOGRAPHIES OF BIBLIOGRAPHIES

8. *To 1862* Petzholdt, Julius. *Bibliotheca bibliographica. Kritisches Verzeichnis der das Gesamtgebiet der Bibliographie betreffenden Literatur des In- und Auslandes in systematischer Ordnung. Mit alphabetischem Namen- und Sachregister*. Leipzig: Engelmann, 1866. xii, 939pp. (Repr. 1961)

Attempts to present a complete listing of bibliographies to 1862. Includes general, national, and subject bibliographies with extensive annotations. Clearly organized. Very useful for its period.

9. *1904-1925* "Bibliographie des Bibliotheks- und Buchwesens." 1904-1912 and 1922-1925. *Zentralblatt für Bibliothekswesen* (No. 1446), compiled in annual supplemental issues (29, 31-32, 34, 36-37, 39-40, 42, 51, 54, 56, 58).

Continued by:

10. *1904-1939* Hoecker, Rudolf, and Joris Vorstius, comps. *Internationale Bibliographie des Buch- und Bibliothekswesens mit besonderer Berücksichtigung der Bibliographie*, 1904-1912, 1922-1939. *NF* 1-15. Leipzig: Harrassowitz, 1928-1941.

Pt. 1 lists a large number of general, national, and subject bibliographies. Includes independent bibliographies and those in books. Pt. 2 continues *Bibliographie fur Buch- und Bibliothekswesen* (library science only).

11. *1930-1940* Vorstius, Joris, ed. *Internationaler Jahresbericht der Bibliographie. The Year's Work in Bibliography. Annuaire international des Bibliographies*. 11 vols. Leipzig: Harrassowitz, 1931-1941.

Annual survey with focus on general and subject bibliographies.

12. *1930-1953* *Bibliographie der versteckten Bibliographien aus deutschsprachigen Büchern und Zeitschriften der Jahre 1930-1953*. Compiled by the Deutsche Bücherei. Leipzig: Verlag für Buch- und Bibliothekswesen, 1956. 371pp.

Some 13,000 items not published separately are listed. Section XV: "Sprach- und Literaturwissenschaft," titles A-Z. Contains subject index. The coverage of this bibliography is not comprehensive. The bibliography is continued by *Bibl. der deutschen Bibliographien* (No. 19, No. 20)

13. *1939-1950* Widmann, Hans. *Bibliographien zum deutschen Schrifttum der Jahre 1939-1950*. Tübingen: Niemeyer, 1951. xii, 284pp.

Sections on international bibliographies, bibliographies in books, regional and author bibliographies. Particularly important for its focus on bibliographies published in the Third Reich.

14. *To 1950* Malclès, Louise-Noëlle. *Les sources du travail*. Geneva: Librairie Droz, 1950-1958. 3 vols. (II in 2 pts.). (Repr. 1965)

I: general bibliographies including East European; II: pts. 1 and 2: humanities; III: science and technology. Arranged according to discipline. For German literature see section: "Langue et littérature allemandes." Sparse annotations. II contains title-author index at end of pt. 2.

15. *To 1963* Bestermann, Theodore. *A World Bibliography of Bibliographies and of Bibliographical Catalogues, Calendars, Abstracts, Digests, Indexes, and the Like*. 4th rev. ed. 5 vols. Lausanne: Societas Bibliographica, 1965-1966. ([1]1939-1940)

Over 84,000 titles, arranged by subjects. Individual listings: chronological by date of publication. I-IV: subjects A-Z; V: author index, subject index, titles of serial and anonymous works, addresses of libraries and archives. Easily accessible to beginners.

16. *1964-1974* Toomey, Alice F., comp. *A World Bibliography of Bibliographies. 1964-1974. A List of Works Represented by Library of Congress Printed Catalog Cards. A Decennial Supplement to Theodore Bestermann, A World Bibliography of Bibliograpies*. 2 vols. Totowa, N.J.: Rowman & Littlefield, 1977. I, A-J. xii, 586pp.; II, K-Z. vi, pp. 587-1166.

Supplement to the 4th ed. of Bestermann (above). Format based on Bestermann, but records only bibliographies in book form. Ca. 18,000 items under 6,000 subject headings. General, author, and subject bibliographies. Quite useful.

C. CURRENT BIBLIOGRAPHIES OF BIBLIOGRAPHIES

17. *1938 to present* *Bibliographic Index. A Cumulative Bibliography of Bibliographies, 1937ff.* New York: Wilson, 1938ff.

First published quarterly, now biennially, cumulated annually. XIII for 1973 contains ca. 10,000 items: separate bibliographies, bibliographical lists in books, pamphlets, bulletins, and journals. Organized by subject index only. Books and pamphlets are listed by author, bulletins and periodicals by title. For German literature entries see: "German Language." Individual volumes not indexed. Listings for German not extensive.

18. *1959 to present* *Bibliographische Berichte. Bibliographical Bulletin.* Compiled by Erich Zimmermann, commissioned by the Deutsches Bibliographisches Kuratorium. Frankfurt: Klostermann, 1959ff. Publ. 1954-1956 in *Zeitschrift für Bibliothekswesen und Bibliographie* (No. 1447); issued 1957-1958 by that periodical as "Bibliographische Beihefte." 1954-1958 publ. quarterly; 1959ff. biyearly.

Indexes bibliographies appearing in book form or in books and periodicals. International in scope. Titles are grouped under 18 classified subjects. XV/XVI (1974) covers 8,630 items. For Germanic languages and literatures see section 11.2. Title-author list A-Z. Author bibliographies follow the general section. See also related subjects. Two separately published index vols.: 1959-1963 (1965); 1964-1968 (1970). Some annotations.

19. *1957-1965* *Bibliographie der deutschen Bibliographien. Jahresverzeichnis der selbständig erschienenen und der in deutschsprachigen Büchern und Zeitschriften enthaltenen versteckten Bibliographien.* Compiled by the Deutsche Bücherei. Leipzig: Verlag für Buch- und Bibliothekswesen, 1957ff. I. 1954 (1957)-XII. 1964-1965 (1969).

Ca. 7,700 items in XII. See index section VIII for classified subjects. An index of separately published and unpublished bibliographies, and bibliographies appearing in books and journals. Listed by subjects or authors A-Z, with a classified index consisting of 20 categories. Cooperative effort of 9 libraries and various documentation centers. This series is continued by:

20. *1966 to present* *Bibliographie der deutschen Bibliographien. Monatliches Verzeichnis der selbständigen und versteckten Bibliographien Deutschlands, der Literaturverzeichnisse deutschprachiger Veröffentlichungen des Auslandes, der im Ausland erschienenen Bibliographien über Deutschland und Personen des deutschen Sprachgebietes sowie wichtiger ungedruckter Titelzusammenstellungen.* Compiled by the Deutsche Bücherei. Leipzig: Verlag für Buch- und Bibliothekswesen, 1966ff. Jahrgang 1, Heft 1ff.

Monthly publication bound in annual volumes. International in scope. X (1975) classified according to 20 subjects (section 8: "Sprach- und Literaturwissenschaft"). Each section is subdivided into: A. bibliographies in book form; B. unprinted material; C. bibliographies in books and journals; D. current bibliographies. Information is easily accessible.

II.

General and National Bibliographies

CONTENTS

A. INDEXES AND BIBLIOGRAPHIES UP TO THE FIFTEENTH CENTURY

21. Bergmann, Rolf. *Verzeichnis der althochdeutschen und altsächsischen Glossenhandschriften. Mit Bibliographie der Glosseneditionen, der Handschriftenbeschreibungen und der Dialektbestimmungen.* Berlin, New York: de Gruyter, 1973. xxxiv, 136pp.

    Lists 1,023 items according to location, giving complete bibliographical information for each item. Indexes: holding institutions; dialect of gloss; reference numbers used by Steinmeyer and Sievers in vols. 1-5, 1879-1922. Bibliography, pp. xix-xxxiv. Excellent for the specialist.

22. *Corpus der altdeutschen Originalurkunden bis zum Jahre 1300.* Initiated by Friedrich Wilhelm, continued by Richard Newald, ed. by Helmut de Boor, Bettina Kirschstein, Diether Haacke. 6 vols. Lahr: Schauenburg, 1932ff.

    Reproductions of documents of the German language area:
    I. *1200-1282* (Nos. 1-564). 1932.
    II. *1283-1292* (Nos. 565-1657). 1943.
    III. *1293-1296* (Nos. 1658-2559). 1957.
    IV. *1297-1300* (Nos. 2560-3598). 1963.
    Supplemental vols. V and VI, 1963-1975ff. (in fascicles).

23. Mayer, Hartwig. *Althochdeutsche Glossen. Nachträge. Old High German Glosses. A Supplement.* Toronto, Buffalo: Univ. of Toronto Pr., 1974. xx, 154pp.

    Lists 160 glosses from 124 manuscripts in the US and Europe. No alphabetical word index. Introduction in German and English. A supplement to Bergmann's *Verzeichnis* (No. 21). Arranged according to location. Index: author, title.

24. Sievers, Eduard, ed. *Verzeichnis altdeutscher Handschriften.* New York: Olms, 1974. 178pp. ([1]1890)

    116 manuscripts described: location, size, binding, etc. First 2 and last 2 lines are cited. Not easily accessible. Index: first lines.

25. Vizkelety, Andras. *Beschreibendes Verzeichnis der altdeutschen Handschriften in ungarischen Bibliotheken.* 2 vols. Wiesbaden: Harrassowitz, 1969-1973. I. 222pp., 7 pl.; II. 324 pp., 7 pl.

I. *Szechenyi-Nationalbibliothek.* Each item contains descriptive heading, date, geographical origin, pages, size, first and last line, detailed description of manuscript material, including writing, binding, etc.

II. *Budapest, Debrecen, Eger, Esztergom, Györ, Kalocsa, Panonhalma, Papa, Pecs, Szombathely.*

B. INCUNABULA

26. Borchling, Conrad, and Bruno Claussen. *Niederdeutsche Bibliographie. Gesamtverzeichnis der niederdeutschen Drucke bis zum Jahre 1800.* 3 vols. Neumünster: Wachholtz, 1931-1957.

Chronologically arranged: I covers 1473-1600; II covers 1601-1800 plus addenda, corrections, indexes; III, pt. 1, addenda to I and II, and III, pt. 2, expands the coverage to include 1801-1950.

27. Brandes, Walther. *Bibliographie der niedersächsischen Frühdrucke bis zum Jahre 1600.* Baden-Baden: Heitz, 1960. 138pp.

600 items from the 15th and 16th centuries, A-Z by author/editor. Complete bibliographical information with indication of current location. Table: geographical distribution of printing activity.

28. *Einblattdrucke des xv. Jahrhunderts. Ein bibliographisches Verzeichnis.* Published by the Kommission für den Gesamtkatalog der Wiegendrucke. Halle: Karras, 1914. xix, 553pp. (Repr. 1968)

A listing of incunabula divided according to subject headings and international in scope. In addition to standard bibliographical information, list contains first and last lines of specimen, present location, etc. Indexes: owners, printers (listed by towns), subject.

29. *Gesamtkatalog der Wiegendrucke.* Published by the Kommission für den Gesamtkatalog der Wiegendrucke. 8 vols. ff.

An international index of incunabula at ca. 4,000 libraries.

I. *Abano-Alexius.* Leipzig: Hiersemann, 1925. lxiii, 682 cols.
II. *Alforabius-Arznei.* Leipzig: Hiersemann, 1926. xi, 786 cols. Index: printers and places of publication.
III. *Ascher-Bernardus Clarallensis.* Leipzig: Hiersemann, 1928. xxxii, 754 cols. Index: printers and places; pp. xxi-xxvi; commentary on method of describing incunabula employed in the *Gesamtkatalog*.
IV. *Bernardus de Cracovia-Brentius.* Leipzig: Hiersemann. viii, 694 cols. Index: printers, places.
V. *Breviaire-Byenboeck.* Leipzig: Hiersemann, 1932. x, 742 cols. and suppl. to V. Index: printers, places.

VI. *Caballus-Confessione*. Leipzig: Hiersemann, 1934, viii, 854 cols., suppl.
VII. *Coniuration-Eigenschaften*. Leipzig: Hiersemann, 1938. viii, 815 cols., suppl. Vols. I-VII also contain index of Hain numbers used.
VIII. Ed. by the Deutsche Staatsbibliothek zu Berlin. Stuttgart: Hiersemann and Berlin: Akademie, 1972ff., fasc. 1ff. 128pp. of introduction with abbreviation lists (supplanting index I).

This is an indispensible tool for the study of incunabula.

30. Panzer, Georg Wolfgang. *Annalen der älteren deutschen Literatur oder Anzeiger und Beschreibung derjenigen Bücher welche von Erfindung der Buchdruckerkunst bis MDXX in deutscher Sprache gedruckt worden sind*. 3 vols. Nuremberg (place varies): Grattenauer (publisher varies), 1788-1864. (Repr. 1961)

I. For 1470-1520. 1788. 464pp. plus suppl. for 3 vols. 1462-1520. 1802. 198pp.
II. For 1521-1526. 1802. 495 pp.
III. *Repertorium typographicum. Die deutsche Literatur im ersten Viertel des sechzehnten Jahrhunderts*. Ed. by Emil Waller. 1864. 506pp. For 1500-1526, supplements to I and II.

Combined author-title list A-Z provides title-page and bibliographical information. Index: author and subject in each volume.

31. Burger, Konrad. *Supplement zu Hain und Panzer. Beiträge zur Inkunabelbibliographie. Nummerconcordanz von Panzers lateinischen und deutschen Annalen und Ludwig Hains Repertorium bibliographicum*. Leipzig: Lokay, 1908. viii, 440pp.

A concordance to Panzer, Hain, et al. Items listed by Panzer numbers with corresponding numbers for other catalogs.

C. GENERAL TRADE CATALOGS, INDEXES, AND BIBLIOGRAPHIES (1451-1912)

32. *1451-1877* Brunet, Jacques-Charles. *Manuel du libraire et de l'amateur de livres*. 15th ed. 8 vols. Paris: Didot, 1860-1880. (Repr. 1966-1968)

Range: I-V: to 1850; suppl. VII, VIII: to 1877. I-V: list of authors/titles of anonymous works, A-Z, of ca. 47,500 rare and otherwise noteworthy books. International with particular focus on French material. Each entry provides full bibliographical information. Index: VI: short titles. VII, VIII: suppl. by Pierre Deschamps and Gustave Brunet of ca. 12,500 additional items. Continues format of main part.

33. *1450-1820* Ebert, Friedrich Adolf. *Allgemeines bibliographisches Lexikon.* 2 vols. Leipzig: Brockhaus, 1821-1830. (Repr. 1965)

Author/title list A-Z of ca. 24,280 items (modeled after Brunet, see above). Based on the holdings of the Dresden court library; international in scope. Selection focuses on literature and literary history, includes translations into German. Some annotation; no subject index.

34. *1450-1757* Georgi, Theophilus. *Allgemeines europäisches Bücherlexikon.* 5 parts and 3 supplements. Leipzig: Georgi, 1742-1758. (Repr. 1966-1967)

Author/title list A-Z. International in scope (German and Latin books emphasized). Pts. 1-4; A-Z; Pt. 5: French works A-Z; Supplements 1-3: newly edited and reissued books for the years 1739-1747, 1747-1754, and 1753-1757.

35. *1450-1855* Graesse, Jean Georges Théodore. *Trésor de livres rares et précieux; ou, Nouveau dictionnaire bibliographique contenant plus de cent mille articles de livres rares, curieux et recherchés, d'ouvrages de luxe, etc. avec les signes connus pour distinguer les éditions originales des contrefaçons qui en ont été faites, des notes sur la rareté et le mérite de livres cités et le prix que ces livres ont attaints dans les ventes les plus fameuses, et qu'ils conservent encore dans les magasins de bouquinistes les plus renommés de l'Europe.* 7 vols. Dresden: Kuntze, 1859-1869. (Repr. 1950-1951)

Author/title list A-Z based on Brunet (No. 32) with additional German literature titles. I-VI, A-Z; VII, supplement.

36. *1455-1600* Johnson, Alfred Forbes, and Victor Scholderer. *Short-Title Catalogue of Books Printed in the German-Speaking Countries and German Books Printed in Other Countries from 1455 to 1600 Now in the British Museum.* London: Trustees of the British Museum, 1962. viii, 1224pp.

A collection of ca. 24,000 items listed by subject and author A-Z. Index of printers and publishers A-Z, pp. 965-1222.

37. *1501-1520* Proctor, Robert. *An Index of German Books 1501-1520 in the British Museum.* London: The Holland Pr., 1903. 273pp. (^{2}1954)

Titles listed by place of publication A-Z, subdivided by printers A-Z. Complete bibliographical information. Provided with numerous special indexes and an appendix: illus. to the type-register.

38. *1501-1600* *Index Aureliensis. Catalogus librorum sedecimo saeculo impressorum.* Pars 1, Tomus A, vol. 1ff. Baden-Baden: Koerner, 1962ff.

To date 8 vols. have appeared. Promises to be the standard source for material between 1501-1600. Pt. 1: holdings of selected libraries; pt. 2: supplements; pt. 3: indexes, printers, locations, personal names and places. For sources, see: Wagner, Friedrich Georg. *Bibliotheka bibliographica librorum sedecimi saeculi. Bibliographisches Repertorium für die Drucke des 16. Jahrhunderts.* Baden-Baden: Heitz, 1960. 98pp. Listing of 2,033 items by author A-Z.

39. *1501-1600* *Bibliographie der deutschen Drucke des 16. Jahrhunderts.* Bad Bocklet, Vienna, Zurich, Florence: Krieg, 1960ff.

I. *Otto Bucher. Dillingen.* vii, 283pp. 1960.

40. *1501-1600* Adams, Herbert Mayow. *Catalogue of Books Printed on the Continent of Europe, 1501-1600, in Cambridge Libraries.* 2 vols. London: Cambridge Univ. Pr., 1967.

International listing by author A-Z. Many German titles. Indexes: printers, places of printing.

41. *1601-1699* Bruckner, J. *A Bibliographical Catalogue of Seventeenth Century German Books Published in Holland.* The Hague, Paris: Mouton, 1971. xxxviii, 552pp. illus.

A chronological listing of 623 numbered items with complete bibliographical information. Indexes: authors, anonymous titles, translators; editors and engravers; printers and publishers.

42. *1601-1699* Mitchell, Phillip Marshall. *A Bibliography of Seventeenth Century German Imprints in Denmark and the Duchies of Schleswig-Holstein.* 3 vols. Lawrence: Univ. of Kansas Libraries, 1969-1976.

I and II. 1969. xix, 748 pp.
III. Additions and Corrections. 1976. xi, 110pp.

A chronological listing of 3,139 items. Indexes: authors, editors, translators, engravers; printers and publishers; titles. Some annotations.

43. *1700-1892* Heinsius, Wilhelm. *Allgemeines Bücher-Lexikon oder vollständiges alphabetisches Verzeichnis aller von 1700 bis zu Ende 1892 erschienenen Bücher, welche in Deutschland und in den durch Sprache und Literatur damit verwandten Ländern gedruckt worden sind.* 19 vols. Leipzig: Brockhaus, 1812-1894. (Repr. 1962-1963)

Author/title list, A-Z, of German books with complete bibliographical information. I-IV: 1700-1810; subsequent vols. cover approximately 5-year periods.

44. *1750-1910* Kayser, Christian Gottlob. *Vollständiges Bücherlexikon. Ein Verzeichnis der seit dem Jahre 1750 im*

deutschen Buchhandel erschienenen Bücher und Landkarten. 36 parts and 6 index vols. Leipzig: Tauchnitz (publishers vary), 1834-1911. (Repr. 1961-1962)

Entries by author, title A-Z for vols. 1-6; vols. 7ff. by author, title-catchword A-Z. Entries provide complete bibliographical information. See also index vols. Wider in scope than Heinsius (above) and includes some Austrian and Swiss titles. CAUTION: index (vols. 7ff.) does not list titles by first word but only by catchword.

45. *1851-1912* *Hinrichs' Fünfjahrs-Katalog der im deutschen Buchhandel erschienenen Bücher, Zeitschriften, Landkarten, etc. Titelverzeichnis und Sachregister, 1851-1912*. 13 vols. Leipzig: Hinrichs, 1857-1913. Title and editors vary. Superseded by *Deutsches Bücherverzeichnis* (No. 51), 1911ff.

46. Thelert, Gustav. *Supplement zu Heinsius', Hinrichs' und Kaysers Bücher-Lexikon. Verzeichnis einer Anzahl Schriften, welche seit der Mitte des neunzehnten Jahrhunderts in Deutschland erschienen, in den genannten Katalogen aber gar nicht oder fehlerhaft aufgeführt sind. Mit bibliographischen Bemerkungen*. Grossenhain, Leipzig: Baumert & Runge, 1893. 405pp. (Repr. 1973)

Listing by author A-Z. Numerous dissertations listed. Annotations limited and sparse.

47. *1883-1912* Georg, Karl (Vol. 1: with Leopold Ost). *Schlagwort-Katalog Verzeichnis der im deutschen Buchhandel erschienenen Bücher und Landkarten in sachlicher Anordnung*. 7 vols. Hannover: Lemmermann, 1889-1913. Subtitle and publishers vary. Subject and key word listing. Superseded by *Deutsches Bücherverzeichnis* (No. 51), 1911ff.

D. NATIONAL AND TRADE BIBLIOGRAPHIES

1. Austria

48. *1945ff.* *Österreichische Bibliographie. Verzeichnis der österreichischen Neuerscheinungen*. 1945ff. Compiled by the Österreichische Nationalbibliothek. Vienna: Hauptverband des österreichischen Buchhandels, 1946ff. Recent vol.: 1975 (for 1974).

Frequency of publication varies; 1949ff. biweekly issues which are cumulated quarterly, annually, quinquennially. Lists in 25 broad subject categories current Austrian publications, journals, newspapers, musical scores, theses, etc. For German language and literature see sections 7, 8, 10, 11. Subject and author indexes in all cumulations.

2. Germany (General)

49. Weitzel, Rolf. *Die deutschen nationalen Bibliographien. Eine Anleitung zu ihrer Benutzung.* 3rd. ed. Frankfurt: Buchhändler-Vereinigung, 1967. 95pp. ([1]1958)

This compact but lively guide is designed to facilitate access to the national bibliographies.

50. *1911-1965* *Gesamtverzeichnis des deutschsprachigen Schrifttums (GV) 1911-1965.* Reinhard Oberschelp, ed. Munich: Dokumentation, 1976-1977ff. Vols. 1-30ff.

A comprehensive bibliography of primary and secondary material for the years 1911-1965, comparable to the *National Union Catalog.* Planned for ca. 2.5 million items culled from *Deutsches Bücherverzeichnis*, 1911-1950 (No. 51, No. 52), *Deutsche Bibliographie* (No. 58), *Deutsche Nationalbibliographie, Reihe B* (No. 55), dissertation indexes. Large index: author and key word A-Z, not always consistently organized. Includes titles of book series and materials from Austria and Switzerland. Promises to be an invaluable bibliography.

3. Germany (1911-1945)

51. *1911-1940* *Deutsches Bücherverzeichnis. Eine Zusammenstellung der im deutschen Buchhandel erschienenen Bücher, Zeitschriften und Landkarten. Nebst Stich- und Schlagwortregister.* Leipzig: Verlag des Börsenvereins der deutschen Buchhändler, 1916ff. Vol. 1ff. for the years 1911ff. Quinquennial vols. (except vol. 1 for 1911-1914) in two parts: pt. 1: author/title index; pt. 2: subject index. Supplemented and continued by No. 52 (below).

4. German Democratic Republic

52. *1941-1950* *Deutsches Bücherverzeichnis* (above), vol. 23 for the years 1941-1950.

53. *1941ff.* *Deutsches Bücherverzeichnis. Verzeichnis der in Deutschland, Österreich und der Schweiz und im übrigen Ausland herausgegebenen Verlagsschriften (Bücher, Zeitschriften und Kartenwerke) sowie die wichtigsten Veröffentlichungen außerhalb des Buchhandels.* Compiled by the Deutsche Bücherei.

Leipzig: Verlag für Buch- und Bibliothekswesen, 1953ff. Quinquennial volumes except for vol. 23 (1941-1950).

A current continuation on a more comprehensive scale of Heinsius (No. 43), Hinrichs (No. 45), and Kayser (No. 44). Vol. 45 (1975-1976) for the years 1961-1965; for more recent coverage see:

54. *1948ff.* *Jahresverzeichnis der Verlagsschriften und einer Auswahl der außerhalb des Buchhandels erschienenen Veröffentlichungen der DDR, der BRD und Westberlins sowie der deutschsprachigen Werke anderer Länder*. Compiled by the Deutsche Bücherei. Leipzig: Verlag für Buch- und Bibliothekswesen, 1974ff. (for 1968ff.) Continuation of: *Jahresverzeichnis des deutschen Schrifttums*. Compiled by the Deutsche Bücherei. Leipzig: Verlag für Buch- und Bibliothekswesen, 1948-1973. Originally: *Halbjahresverzeichnis der Neuerscheinungen des deutschen Buchhandels. Mit Voranzeigen, Verlags- und Preisänderungen, Stich- und Schlagwortregister*. Leipzig: Börsenverein der deutschen Buchhändler, 1798-1944. 292 vols.

Jahresverzeichnis is a yearly cumulation of Reihe A and B of *Deutsche Nationalbibliographie* (below) and appears in two parts: 1: *Titelverzeichnis* (A-Z by author, followed by bibliographical information), 2: *Stich- und Schlagwortregister* (organized by subject and cue-words). CAUTION: only the primary works of an author are listed in pt. 1. For works about the author, consult pt. 2. The *Jahresverzeichnis* is finally cumulated into volumes covering 5-year periods; see *Deutsches Bücherverzeichnis* (No. 53).

55. *1931ff.* *Deutsche Nationalbibliographie*. Leipzig: Börsenverein der deutschen Buchhändler, 1931-1945. Leipzig: Verlag für Buch- und Bibliothekswesen: 1946ff. 1960ff. under the title: *Deutsche Nationalbibliographie des im Ausland erschienenen deutschsprachigen Schrifttums*.

Reihe A: Neuerscheinungen des Buchhandels. Published weekly. Lists trade publications.

Reihe B: Neuerscheinungen außerhalb des Buchhandels. Published biweekly. Lists publications not available commercially (theses, institutional publications, etc.).

Reihe C: Dissertationen und Habilitationsschriften. Published monthly. 1968ff.

Supplements for the years 1933-1945:

56. *1933-1945* *Deutsche Nationalbibliographie. Ergänzung 1: Verzeichnis der Schriften, die 1933-1945 nicht angezeigt werden durften*. Leipzig: Börsenverein der Deutschen Buchhändler, 1949. 433pp.

57. *1939-1945* *Deutsche Nationalbibliographie. Ergänzung 2: Verzeichnis der Schriften, die infolge von Kriegseinwirkungen vor dem 8. Mai nicht angezeigt werden konnten.* Leipzig: Börsenverein der Deutschen Buchhändler, 1949. 662pp.

For A and B quarterly author-subject indexes are issued. Parts are divided according to disciplines. Of special interest: section 7: language and literature; section 8: belles-lettres. An easy-to-use guide to current publications. Not cumulative, however, therefore somewhat cumbersome as bibliography for larger spans of time; use *Jahresverzeichnis* (No. 54).

5. Federal Republic of Germany

58. *1945ff.* *Deutsche Bibliographie. Verzeichnis aller in Deutschland erschienenen Veröffentlichungen und der in Österreich und der Schweiz im Buchhandel erschienenen deutschsprachigen Publikationen sowie der deutschsprachigen Veröffentlichungen anderer Länder. Bücher und Karten.* Frankfurt: Buchhändlervereinigung, 1953ff. for the years 1945-1950; all subsequent vols. are quinquennial.

Quinquennial vols., each divided into 2 pts. Pt. 1: author-title index; pt. 2: subject index. Not listed are: publications by academies, musical scores. A most complete bibliography; readily accessible.

59. *1951ff.* *Deutsche Bibliographie. Halbjahresverzeichnis. Verzeichnis aller im Wöchentlichen Verzeichnis, Reihe A, angezeigten Veröffentlichungen, der eingesandten österreichischen und schweizerischen Verlagswerke sowie einer Auswahl von Erscheinungen außerhalb des Buchhandels.* Compiled by the Deutsche Bibliothek. Frankfurt: Buchhändlervereinigung, 1951ff.

2 vols. in 2 pts. per year. Pt. 1: author-title index; pt. 2: subject index. Cumulative listing of *Reihe A* (below), *Reihe B* and *C* included selectively.

60. *1947ff.* *Deutsche Bibliographie. Wöchentliches Verzeichnis. Amtsblatt der deutschen Bibliothek.* Frankfurt: Buchhändlervereinigung, 1947ff. 1965ff. divided into three series:

Reihe A: Erscheinungen des Verlagsbuchhandels. Published weekly. Lists trade publications.

Reihe B: Erscheinungen außerhalb des Verlagsbuchhandels. Published monthly. Lists theses, institute publications, and similar publications not traded.

Reihe C: Karten. Published bimonthly.

Cumulative monthly and quarterly author-subject indexes also incorporate *Österreichische Bibliographie* (No. 48), and *Das Schweizer Buch* (No. 64). 1958ff. Two supplements: "Archiv ungedruckter wissenschaftlicher Schriften. Bibliographie eingegangener Arbeiten." Lists work in progress. "Vorankündigungen zum wöchentlichen Verzeichnis." Lists forthcoming books.

Titles divided according to 25 classes of special interest: section 7. "Sprach- und Literaturwissenschaft," 8. "Schöne Literatur," 13. "Musik, Tanz, Theater, Film, Rundfunk." Readily accessible for current publications. For longer time spans use *Halbjahresverzeichnis* (No. 59) and quinquennial cumulations (No. 58).

61. *1971ff.* *Verzeichnis lieferbarer Bücher. German Books in Print. Bücherverzeichnis im Autorenalphabet kumuliert mit Titel- und Stichwortregister mit Verweisung auf den Autor. Author's Alphabet Cumulated with Title Index with Reference to the Author.* 6th ed. Frankfurt: Büchhandler-Vereinigung. 3 vols. 1976. Supplement, 1977. ([1]1971)

Content 1976/77: 237,046 titles for FRG, Austria, and Switzerland. Listed by author, titles without authors, key word and title references in one alphabet A-Z. Titles are listed according to the first title word, key words in mechanical order. Book series are listed under series titles, if so stocked (series lists are not normally found in bibliographies!). *VlB* lists all titles available at present through the official German book market, including price and national distributor. Supplement for 1977 includes appendix: index of publishers A-Z, addresses, ISBN component of publisher, and index by ISBN component of publisher.

6. Switzerland

62. *1871-1900* *Bibliographie der Schweiz. Bibliographisch-kritische Revue der neuen Erscheinungen der Schweiz.* 6 vol. Zurich: Schweizerisches Antiquariat, 1871-1900 (publisher and subtitle vary).

A monthly listing of books and articles by Swiss authors A-Z in all fields; some books are reviewed. Continued by:

63. *1901-1942* *Bibliographisches Bulletin der Schweiz. Bulletin bibliographique de la Bibliothèque Nationale Suisse.* Ed. by the Schweizerische Landesbibliothek. Bern: Benteli, 1901-1942. Vols. 1-42.

A monthly listing by author or title A-Z of books published in Switzerland, foreign books about Switzerland, and books by Swiss authors. Author/subject index at end of each volume. Continued 1943ff. as:

64. *1943ff.* *Das Schweizer Buch. Le Livre suisse. Il Libro svizzero. Bibliographisches Bulletin der Schweizerischen Landesbibliothek Bern.* Zurich: Verlag des Schweizerischen Buchhändler- und Verlegervereins, 1943ff.

Appears in 2 series: A (biweekly): *Erscheinungen des Buchhandels.* Lists books published commercially, including books about Switzerland published in other countries; B (bimonthly): *Erscheinungen außerhalb des Buchhandels.* Lists items not commercially published, as theses, institutional publications, offprints, etc. Both A and B list maps, phonograph records, new periodical titles. Contents organized by 25 subject classes.

65. *1948ff.* *Schweizer Bücherverzeichnis. Repertoire du livre suisse. Elenco del libro svizzero. Katalog der schweizerischen Landesbibliothek.* 1948/50ff. Zurich: Schweizerische Buchhändler- und Verlegerverein, 1951ff. Quinquennial cumulation.

Appears in 2 pts. Pt. 1: Titelverzeichnis. Index is a cumulation of the material in pts. A and B of *Das Schweizer Buch.* Pt. 2: listing of material by subject and cue-words. 1956ff. (for the years 1951-1955) incorporates *Das Schweizerische Zeitschriftenverzeichnis* under the new title:

66. *1951ff.* *Schweizerische Nationalbibliographie. Schweizerisches Zeitschriftenverzeichnis. Fünfjahresausgabe.* 1951/55ff. Zurich: Schweizerischer Buchhändler- und Verlegerverein, 1956ff.

Covers all material published in Switzerland in French, German, and Italian. Lists over 4,000 periodicals, government publications, almanacs, yearbooks. Excludes newspapers and club news. Titles A-Z by subject with index of titles and catchwords. Entries include complete bibliographical information.

7. The United States

67. *1872ff.* *Publishers Weekly. The Book Industry Journal, 1872ff.* New York: Bowker, 1872ff. vol. 1ff.

Subtitle and publisher vary. Lists on a weekly basis books of all publishers on all subjects. Does not include government publications, dissertations, theses, periodicals, etc.

68. *1873ff.* *Publishers Trade List Annual, 1873ff.* New York: Bowker, 1873ff.

An annual collection of publishers' catalogs, by publisher A-Z. Information provided varies greatly from catalog to catalog.

69. *1898ff.* *Cumulative Book Index. A World List of Books in the English language.* New York: Wilson, 1898ff.

Varying quarterly, annual, and multi-year cumulations. Monthly publication. Since 1957 biennial, since 1969 annual cumulation. Greatly enlarged scope since 1930. Author and subject headings A-Z. Easily accessible. Invaluable for most recent book titles in English. Supplement to:

70. *1899-1928* *United States Catalog. Books in Print.* 4th ed. New York: Wilson, 1928. (^{1}1899, ^{2}1902, ^{3}1912)

71. *1948ff.* *Books in Print. An Author-Title-Series Index to the Publishers Trade List Annual, 1948ff.* New York: Bowker, 1948ff.

Each annual volume contains an author and title index. Since 1966 authors and titles in separate volumes.

72. *1955ff.* *Paperbound Books in Print.* New York: Bowker, 1955ff.

Semiannual publication with separate subject, author-title indexes.

73. *1957ff.* *Subject Guide to Books in Print. An Index to the Publishers Trade List Annual 1957ff.* New York: Bowker, 1957ff.

Annual. Provides a subject listing A-Z.

74. *1966ff.* *Forthcoming Books. Now Including New Books in Print. A Forecast of Books to Come, 1966ff.* New York: Bowker, 1966ff. vol. 1ff.

Bimonthly.

75. *1967ff.* *Subject Guide to Forthcoming Books, 1967ff.* New York: Bowker, 1967ff. vol. 1ff.

Bimonthly

E. NATIONAL LIBRARY CATALOGS

1. France

76. Bibliothèque Nationale, Paris. *Catalogue général des livres imprimés de la Bibliothèque Nationale. Auteurs.* Paris: Imprimerie Nationale, 1897ff. vol. 1ff.

An important source for bibliographical information about French books. Listings by author A-Z. Does not include anonymous works, government and corporate authors, or periodicals. Author catalog only for books published before 1960. Works about the authors listed systematically after primary entry. Series not yet complete: vol. 223, *Will-Willi*, 1975. Supplement:

77. *Catalogue général des livres imprimés de la Bibliothèque Nationale. Auteurs, Collectivités--Auteurs, Anonymes, 1960-1964.* 12 vols. Paris: Bibliothèque Nationale, 1965-1967.

Supplements and updates the above with corporate entries, collections, anonyma, joint authors, translators, etc.

2. Germany

78. *Deutscher Gesamtkatalog.* Title, vols. 1-8: *Gesamtkatalog der preußischen Bibliotheken mit Nachweis des identischen Besitzes der bayrischen Staatsbibliothek in München und der Nationalbibliothek in Wien.* 14 vols. Berlin: Preußische Druckerei- und Verlags- Aktiengesellschaft, 1931-1939 (not continued).

Range: to 1930. Vols. 1-8 list holdings of 11 Prussian libraries plus those of the Bavarian State Library and the Austrian National Library. Vols. 9-14: scope enlarged to include some 110 German and Austrian libraries. Excellent, very complete and still useful for range: "A"-"Beethordnung."

79. *Berliner Titeldrucke.* Berlin: Preußische Druckerei und Verlags-Aktiengesellschaft, 1892-1944. Title varies: 1893-1910, *Verzeichnis der aus der neuerschienenen Literatur von der Königlichen Bibliothek zu Berlin* (added 1898: *und den Preußischen Universitäts-Bibliotheken*) *erworbenen Druckschriften.* 1910-1937, *Berliner Titeldrucke.* 1938-, *Gesamtkatalog. Neue Titel.*

Issued on a weekly basis with quarterly and annual cumulations for the years 1931-1943. Quinquennial cumulations:

80. *Berliner Titeldrucke. Fünfjahreskatalog 1930-1934.* 8 vols. Berlin: Preußische Druckerei und Verlags-Aktiengesellschaft, 1935.

81. *Deutscher Gesamtkatalog. Neue Titel. Fünfjahreskatalog 1935-1939.* 8 vols. Berlin: Preußische Druckerei und Verlags-Aktiengesellschaft, 1940. An important supplement to *Deutscher Gesamtkatalog* (No. 78).

Continuation after 1945:

82. *Berliner Titeldrucke. Neue Folge. Zugänge aus der Sowjetunion und den europäischen Ländern der Volksdemokratie. Jahreskatalog 1954-1959.* Berlin: Deutsche Staatsbibliothek, 1956-1962.

83. *Berliner Titeldrucke. Neuerwerbungen ausländischer Literatur der wissenschaftlichen Bibliotheken der Deutschen Demokratischen Republik. Reihe A, B.* Berlin: Deutsche Staatsbibliothek, 1960-1963.

84. *Berliner Titeldrucke. Neuerwerbungen ausländischer Literatur wissenschaftlicher Bibliotheken der Deutschen Demokratischen*

Republik. Jahreskatalog 1964ff. Berlin: Deutsche Staatsbibliothek, 1965ff.

85. *Namenschlüssel. Zu Pseudonymen, Doppelnamen und Namensabwandlungen. Stand vom 1. 7. 1941.* 4th ed. Hildesheim: Olms, 1968. 1019pp.

86. *Namenschlüssel. Zu Pseudonymen, Doppelnamen und Namensabwandlungen. Ergänzungen aus der Zeit vom 1. Juli bis 31. Dezember 1965.* Compiled by a collective of the Deutsche Staatsbibliothek Berlin. Hildesheim: Olms, 1968. 276pp.

Both volumes are valuable indexes to the listings of the *Deutscher Gesamtkatalog. Neue Titel* and *Berliner Titeldrucke*. The listing A-Z includes: forms of authors' names which differ from the catatlog entries, pseudonyms, parts of compound names, transliterations, etc.

3. Great Britain

87. British Museum. *Catalogue of the Printed Books in the Library of the British Museum.* 95 vols. London: Clowes, 1881-1900. (Repr. in 58 vols., 1946)

88. British Museum. *Catalogue of Printed Books. Supplement.* 10 vols. London: Clowes, 1900-1905. (Repr. 1950)

The above superseded by:

89. British Museum. *General Catalogue of Printed Books. Photolithographic Edition to 1955.* 263 vols. London: Trustees of the British Museum, 1959-1966.

90. British Museum. *General Catalogue of Printed Books. 10-Year Supplement 1956-1965.* 50 vols. London: Trustees of the British Museum, 1968.

91. British Museum. *General Catalogue of Printed Books. 5-Year Supplement 1966-1970.* 26 vols. London: Trustees of the British Museum, 1971-1972. Further quinquennial supplements planned.

4. United States

92. U.S. Library of Congress. *A Catalog of Books Represented by Library of Congress Printed Cards, Issued to July 31, 1942.* 167 vols. Ann Arbor, Mich.: Edwards, 1942-1946.

93. ———. *Supplement. Cards Issued to August 1, 1942-December 31, 1947.* 42 vols. Ann Arbor, Mich.: Edwards, 1953.

Includes all cards from 1898 to 1947. The listings for the supplement are not limited to the period 1942-1947. Books are listed regardless of their imprint date. Supplement also includes 26,000 titles for anonymous and pseudonymous works. Vol. 24, films.

94. *National Union Catalog. A Cumulative Author List Representing Library of Congress Printed Cards and Titles Reported by Other American Libraries, 1953-1957.* 28 vols. Ann Arbor, Mich.: Edwards, 1958.

Vols. 1-26, authors A-Z; vol. 27, music and records; vol. 28, films.

All listings to 1956 are superseded by:

95. *The National Union Catalog. Pre-1956 Imprints.* vol. 1ff. London, Chicago: Mansell, 1968ff. ca. 610 vols.

Includes titles of anonymous and pseudonymous works, maps, musical scores, journals and series. Does not include films and records.

96. *National Union Catalog. A Cumulative Author List Representing Library of Congress Printed Cards and Titles Reported by Other American Libraries, 1958-1962.* 54 vols. New York: Rowman & Littlefield, 1963.

Vols. 1-50, authors A-Z; vols. 51-52, music and records; vols. 53-54, films.

97. *National Union Catalog. 1956 through 1967. A Cumulative Author List Representing Library of Congress Printed Cards and Titles Reported by Other American Libraries.* 125 vols. Totowa, N.J.: Rowman & Littlefield, 1970-1972.

98. *National Union Catalog. A Cumulative Author List Representing Library of Congress Printed Cards and Titles Reported by Other American Libraries, 1968-1972.* 119 vols. Ann Arbor, Mich.: Edwards, 1973.

Continued on a current basis:

99. *National Union Catalog. A Cumulative Author List.* Washington: Library of Congress, Card Division.

A monthly listing with quarterly, annual, and quinquennial cumulations.

III.

Bibliographies of German Literature

CONTENTS

A. GUIDES TO REFERENCE MATERIAL

100. Arnold, Robert F. *Allgemeine Bücherkunde zur neueren deutschen Literaturgeschichte.* 4th ed., rev. by Herbert Jacob. Berlin: de Gruyter, 1966. ix, 395pp. ([1]1910)

Reference guide in 6 parts and 102 specialized categories: bibliography, biography, journals; world literature: literary histories, thematology, anthologies; German literature: literary histories, including local and parochial, youth literature, journals, etc.; large sections on related disciplines, including science, philology, dictionaries, religion, philosophy, pedagogy, history, law, etc. Individual sections chronologically arranged. Extremely useful for its comprehensiveness and specialized categories. Note: earlier editions use a complex system of abbreviations. Indexes: author, subject.

101. Friedrich, Wolfgang. *Einführung in die Bibliographie zur deutschen Literaturwissenschaft.* Halle: Niemeyer, 1967. 116pp.

Introductory handbook. Selected bibliographies presented in running text. Includes material on related disciplines such as pedagogy, sociology, comparative literature. Good resource book on GDR publications.

102. Geiger, Hans, Albert Klein, Jochen Vogt. *Hilfsmittel und Arbeitstechniken der Literaturwissenschaft.* 2nd rev. ed. Opladen: Westdeutscher Verlag, 1972. 100pp. ([1]1971)

A compact handbook for German literature studies with annotations on major reference works. Pt. 1: theories and methods of primary text study and editing; pt. 2: compendia, lexica, literary histories, bibliographies, techniques of writing and documenting formal papers. Index: subject. Study questions.

103. Hansel, Johannes. *Bücherkunde für Germanisten. Studienausgabe.* 6th enl. ed. rev. by Lydia Tschakert. Berlin: Schmidt, 1972. 197pp. ([1]1961)

One of the standard resource books for German studies, with introduction to research. Contents: 1. "Darstellungen zur Sprach- und Literaturwissenschaft"; 2. "Abgeschlossene Fachbibliographien"; 3. "Periodische Fachbibliographien"; 4. "Periodische Allgemeinbibliographien"; 5. "Zeitschriften"; 6. "Ausblick" (i.e. research and editions in progress). Each broad category is subdivided by subjects. Entries annotated.

Includes tables for quick reference. Indexes: author-title, subject. This bibliography is constantly being updated. The information is generally easily obtainable, particularly with the aid of the indexes.

104. Loewenthal, Fritz. *Bibliographisches Handbuch zur deutschen Philologie*. Halle: Max Niemeyer, 1932. xii, 217pp.

A reliable, selected bibliography including the Scandanavian languages and some Dutch and Old English items. Sections: 1. "Allgemeines"; 2. "Frühgeschichte, Mythologie, Volkskunde"; 3. "Sprachwissenschaft"; 4. "Literatur- und Geistesgeschichte"; 5. "Nachträge und Berichtigungen." Includes a very few authors with primary and secondary bibliography. Author-subject index. Formerly a standard resource book, now outdated, hence of limited use.

105. Raabe, Paul. *Einführung in die Quellenkunde zur neueren deutschen Literaturgeschichte. 2., umgearbeitete Auflage des darstellenden Teils der Quellenkunde zur neueren deutschen Literaturgeschichte*. Stuttgart: Metzler, 1966. viii, 95pp. ([1]1962)

A thorough introduction to primary material, including sections on archives, preparation of editions, manuscriptology, printing, etc. Bibliographical portions are annotated. Excellent handbook for students.

106. ———. *Quellenrepertorium zur neueren deutschen Literaturgeschichte. 2., umgearbeitete Auflage des quellenkundlichen Teils der Quellenkunde zur neueren deutschen Literaturgeschichte*. Stuttgart: Metzler, 1966. 112pp. ([1]1963)

Resource book to the above. Lists archives, catalogs, manuscript collections, important critical editions, documentary material, etc. Reference facilitated by thorough indexing. Material well annotated and consistently reliable.

B. FORSCHUNGSBERICHT

107. Fromm, Hans. *Germanistische Bibliographie seit 1945. Theorie und Kritik*. Stuttgart: Metzler, 1960. vii, 84pp.

2 surveys of research containing, in addition to a report on the status of bibliography, a general discussion of the theory and methodology of bibliography.

C. BIBLIOGRAPHIES TO SECONDARY LITERATURE

1. Completed Bibliographies

108. Goedeke, Karl. *Grundriß zur Geschichte der deutschen Dichtung. Aus den Quellen.* 2nd comp. rev. ed. Vols. 1-13. Düsseldorf, Dresden: Ehlermann, 1884-1953. Series being continued: XIV, XV. Berlin: Akademie, 1959-1966.

Range: beginnings to 1830. This is the most complete bibliography of German literature for the period covered. Indispensable for the researcher. Some biographical and critical annotation on authors, individual works, etc. Important for primary bibliography with exhaustive entries on editions, treatises, histories, biographical and critical articles. Detailed index at the end of each volume. CAUTION: this work is not uniformly structured. Read the following outline carefully before using. Consult *Index zu Goedeke* (No. 111).

I. *Das Mittelalter.* 1884, #1-100 (=Book 1-3)
Range: beginnings to 1515. Outdated.

II. *Das Reformationszeitalter.* 1886, #101-175 (=Book 4)
Range: 1515-1600 (Humanism and early Baroque).

III. *Vom Dreißigjährigen bis zum Siebenjährigen Kriege.* 1887, #176-200 (=Book 5)
Range: 1600-1750 (Baroque and early Enlightenment).

IV. *Vom Siebenjährigen bis zum Weltkriege* (i.e., Napoleonic Wars) *Nationale Dichtung.* 1891, #201-246 (=Book 6, Part 1)
Range: 1750-ca. 1800 (Enlightenment, Storm and Stress)
CAUTION: this volume has been extensively revised; see below.

V. (title as IV. No subtitle). 1893, #247-281 (=Book 6, Part 2)
Range: Schiller and his contemporaries.

VI. *Zeit des Weltkrieges* (i.e., Napoleonic Wars). 1898, #292-298 (=Book 7, Part 1)
Range: Romantic movement, Austrian and Swiss authors.

VII. (title as VI). 1900, #298-311 (=Book 7, Part 2)
Range: Austrian authors continued, dialect authors, translations.

VIII. *Vom Weltfrieden bis zur französischen Revolution 1830.* 1905, #312-330 (=Book 8, Part 1)
Range: journals, almanacs, authors of late Romanticism.

IX. (title as VIII). 1910, #331 (=Book 8, Part 2)
Range: regional novelists.

X. (title as VIII). 1913, #332-333 (=Book 8, Part 3)
Range: authors of popular fiction.

XI. Part 1 (title as VIII). 1951, #334 (=Book 8, Part 4)
Range: drama and theater of 1815 to ca. 1830; addenda for Book 8, Parts 1, 2, 3.

XI. Part 2 (title as VIII). 1953, #334 (=Book 8, Part 4)
Range: drama and theater of *Vormärz* (1815 to ca. 1830) in Austria.

XII. (title as VIII). 1929, #335-337 (=Book 8, Part 5)
Range: Swiss, Austrian, Bavarian authors.

XIII. (title as VIII). 1938, #338-344 (=Book 8, Part 6)
Range: west and middle German, Silesian authors.
XIV. (title as VIII) 1959, #345 (=Book 8, Part 7)
Range: northeast German authors.
XV. (title as VIII) 1969, #346-347 (=Book 8, Part 8)
Range: foreign and dialect authors.
XVI.-XVIII. in preparation.

109. Goedeke, Karl. *Grundriß zur Geschichte der deutschen Dichtung. Aus den Quellen*. 3rd rev. ed. IV, Parts 1-4. Dresden: Ehlermann, 1910-1916. Continued: IV, Part 5. Berlin: Akademie Verlag, 1960.

IV. *Vom Siebenjährigen bis zum Weltkriege* (i.e., Napoleonic Wars)

Part 1. 1916, #201-232 (=Book 6, Part 1)
Range: Enlightenment, Storm and Stress.

Part 2. 1910, #233-234 (=Book 6, Part 1)
Range: Goethe biography, literature about Goethe.

Part 3. 1912, #235-246 (=Book 6, Part 1)
Range: Goethe's works; secondary literature. Goethe bibliography continued in Part 5.

Part 4. 1913, #233-246 (=Book 6, Part 1)
Range: addenda, corrections, and indexes for Parts 2-4.

Part 5. 1960.
Range: Goethe bibliography 1912-1950 (continues Part 3).

110. *Goedekes Grundriß zur Geschichte der deutschen Dichtung. Neue Folge. Fortführung von 1830 bis 1880*. Ed. by the Deutsche Akademie der Wissenschaften zu Berlin. Ed. Leopold Magon. I. by Georg Minde-Pouet and Eva Rothe. Berlin: Akademie, 1962. 733pp.

The "Neue Folge" is to include ca. 10,000 authors; I contains author bibliographies: Abbenseth, Diedrich--Ayßlinger, Daniel. This promises to be a standard work for the period. NOTE: writers given detailed treatment in the 2nd ed. (see above) are not included.

111. Rambaldo, Hartmut. *Index zu Goedeke*. Nendeln/Liechtenstein: Kraus-Thomson, 1975. 393pp.

A cumulated index of authors A-Z based on the 2nd ed. of *Goedeke* (1884-1966), the 3rd ed. of vol. 4, and part of vol. 1 of *Goedeke, Neue Folge*. Has increased the usefulness and accessibility of *Goedeke* immensely.

112. *Jahresberichte über die Erscheinungen auf dem Gebiete der germanischen Philologie*. Ed. Gesellschaft für deutsche Philologie. Vols. 1-42. Berlin: Calvary, 1880-1923.

Range: 1879-1920.

113. ———. *NF*. Vols. 1-15. Berlin: de Gruyter, 1924-1939.

Range: 1921-1935.

114. ———. *NF*. Vols. 16-19 (in one vol.). Ed. Deutsche Akademie der Wissenschaften zu Berlin. Berlin: de Gruyter, 1954. xxiii, 1052pp.

Range: 1936-1939

Comprehensive bibliography of monographs, critical editions, articles on German language and literature from the beginnings to the end of the Middle Ages. Coverage varies significantly: vol. 41 to 1770, vol. 42 to 1832, *NF* vol. 1 to 1700, etc. In the original series vols. are in 2 parts: 1. extensive text; 2. bibliography. *NF* is in 1 part; annotations range from brief descriptions to reviews of important publications. Vol. 16-19 is divided into 2 parts: "Sprachlich--sachlicher Teil" and "Literarhistorischer Teil," and provides little more than a title list. Indexes: author-reviewer, subject at the end of each vol.

115. *Jahresberichte für neuere deutsche Literaturgeschichte*. Ed. Julius Elias et al. Vols. 1-26, No. 1. Stuttgart, Berlin-Steglitz (place of publication varies): Behr, 1892-1919.

Range: 1890-1915

A comprehensive annual survey of monographs, critical editions, theses and articles on German literature from the mid-15th century to the present (range varies). Vols. 1-12 (1890-1901) contain a research and publication report organized by subject categories with bibliographical citations in the footnotes. NOTE: for specific information consult the indexes: author, subject. Vols. 13-26, No. 1 (1902-1915) are divided into 2 parts: 1. bibliography; 2. text, with cross references to the bibliography. Comprehensive and informative. Series continued:

116. *Jahresbericht über die wissenschaftlichen Erscheinungen auf dem Gebiet der neueren deutschen Literatur*. Ed. Literaturarchiv-Gesellschaft in Berlin. *Neue Folge*. Vols. 1-15. Berlin, Leipzig: de Gruyter, 1924-1939. Series ceased publication and was completed as:

117. ———. *NF* 16/19. Ed. Deutsche Akademie der Wissenschaften zu Berlin. Berlin: de Gruyter, 1956. xix, 689pp.

Range: 1921-1939

Annual survey of monographs, critical editions, theses, and articles on German literature from the mid-15th century to the present (range varies). Organized into broad subject categories. For the most part a bibliographical tabulation; some annotations for important items. Indexes: author/reviewer, subject. Continued as:

118. *Jahresbericht für deutsche Sprache und Literatur*. Ed. Deutsche Akademie der Wissenschaften zu Berlin. Institut für deutsche Sprache und Literatur. Compiled under the direction of Gerhard Marx. Berlin: Akademie-Verlag, Aufbau, 1960-1966.

I. *1960*. xxv, 979pp. For the years 1940-1945.
II. *1966*. xxxvi. 1193pp. For the years 1946-1950.

Combines the organization and scope of the *Jahresberichte über die wissenschaftlichen Erscheinungen auf dem Gebiet der neueren deutschen Literatur* (No. 116) and the *Jahresbericht über die Erscheinungen auf dem Gebiete der germanischen Philologie* (No. 112). Each vol. has 4 sections: A: "Allgemeiner Teil (deutsche Philologie, Bibliographie, Enzyklopädie)," B: "Sprachlicher Teil," C. "Literaturwissenschaftlicher Teil," D. "Ergänzungen." Offers an extensive bibliography of monographs, theses, articles, etc. Frequent annotations on content, no critical commentary. Indexes: authors and reviewers; titles; subject. Easily accessible.

119. Körner, Josef. *Bibliographisches Handbuch des deutschen Schrifttums*. 3rd completely rev. and enl. ed. Bern: Francke, 1949. 644pp. (Repr. 1966)

Range: Beginnings to 1948. Bibliography of editions and secondary literature. Work disproportionately divided into 4 parts: 1. general (bibliographies, literary histories, journals, editions, etc.), 2. German literature before Goethe, 3. literature of the Goethe period, 4. literature after Goethe. Organization of these sections varies according to historical intra-literary, and geographical considerations. NOTE: for specific periods see table of contents, pp. 641-644, and subject and author indexes, pp. 547-640. Completeness and accuracy of entries vary. Individual items not set off for easy reference; sections designed to be read in entirety. Despite these drawbacks, still particularly useful for Goethe, Romanticism, and for the period to 1948.

120. Olzien, Otto. *Bibliographie zur deutschen Literaturgeschichte*. Stuttgart: Metzler, 1953. 156pp. *Nachträge 1953-54. Mit Ergänzungen und Berichtigungen*. Stuttgart: Metzler, 1955. 24pp.

Range: beginnings - 1954.

An extremely abbreviated, uneven, error-prone supplement to Körner (above). Divided into 4 parts: 1. general (bibliographies, literary histories, etc.), 2. literary history by periods, 3. individual authors, 4. supplement to index of *Annalen der deutschen Literatur* (No. 448).

121. *Handbuch der deutschen Literaturgeschichte. 2. Abteilung. Bibliographien*. Paul Stapf, ed. Bern, Munich: Francke.

I. Kratz, Henry. *Frühes Mittelalter. Vor- und Frühgeschichte des deutschen Schrifttums*. 1970. 287pp. (No. 447)
II. Batts, Michael. *Hohes Mittelalter*. 1969. 112pp. (No. 475)
III. Jones, George F. *Spätes Mittelalter (1300-1450)*. 1971. 124pp. (No. 476)
IV. Engel, James E. *Renaissance, Humanismus, Reformation*. 1969. 80pp. (No. 534)
V. Merkel, Ingrid. *Barock*. 1971. 113pp. (No. 538)
VI. Grotegut, Eugene K., and G.F. Leneaux. *Das Zeitalter der Aufklärung*. 1974. 76pp. (No. 577)
VII. Tentative title: *Goethezeit*. Has not appeared.
VIII. Osborne, John. *Romantik*. 1971, 166pp. (No. 626)
IX. Cowen, Roy C. *Neunzehntes Jahrhundert (1830-1880)*. 1970. 216pp. (No. 659)

X. Goff, Penrith. *Wilhelminisches Zeitalter.* 1971. 216pp. (No. 712)

XI. Pickar, Gertrud B. *Deutsches Schrifttum zwischen den beiden Weltkriegen (1918-1945).* 1974. 139pp. (No. 715)

XII. Glenn, Jerry. *Deutsches Schrifttum der Gegenwart (ab 1945).* 1971. 128pp. (No. 795)

122. Albrecht, Günter, and Günther Dahlke, eds. *Internationale Bibliographie zur Geschichte der deutschen Literatur von den Anfängen bis zur Gegenwart.* Complied by German, Soviet, Bulgarian, Yugoslavian, Polish, Rumanian, Czechoslovakian, and Hungarian scholars. 3 parts in 4 vols. Munich-Pullach: Dokumentation, Berlin: Volk und Wissen, 1969-1977.

Pt. 1. *Von den Anfängen bis 1789.* 1969. 1045pp.
Pt. 2. 1. *Von 1789 bis zur Gegenwart.* 1971. 1031pp.
Pt. 2. 2. *Von 1789 bis zur Gegenwart. Personal-Bibliographie 20. Jahrhundert. Nachträge zur Gesamtbibliographie.* 1972. 1126pp.
Pt. 3. *Sachregister. Personen-Werk-Register.* 1977. 377pp.

Range: 1: to 1967; 2,1: to 1969; 2,2: to 1970. Very comprehensive. Includes materials from socialist countries normally not listed. Poets listed by country of origin (Austrian, German, Swiss). Abundant use of symbols and abbreviations make use somewhat laborious; page layout makes for difficult reading. Excellent bibliography.

123. Köttelwesch, Clemens, ed. *Bibliographisches Handbuch der deutschen Literaturwissenschaft 1945-1969.* I. *Von den Anfängen bis zur Romantik.* Frankfurt: Klostermann, 1973. xxxii, 2398 cols. Range: material up to 1969.

124. ———. *Bibliographisches Handbuch der deutschen Literaturwissenschaft 1945-1972.* II. *1830 bis zur Gegenwart.* Frankfurt: Klostermann, 1976. xliii, 1996 cols. Range: material to 1972.

Ca. 200,000 monographs, articles, reviews, with complete bibliographical listing. Subsections are chronologically organized. Volumes are a handy adaptation of *Bibliographie der deutschen Literaturwissenschaft* (No. 129). Lists *Forschungsberichte*, *Sammelwerke*, and encyclopedic references, author bibliographies, etc.

2. Current Bibliographies

125. Modern Language Association of America. *MLA International Bibliography of Books and Articles on the Modern Languages and Literatures.* New York: Modern Language Association of America, 1922ff. Appears annually.

Title varies:
1922-1956: "MLA American Bibliography" (for the years 1921-

1955) published as regular issue of *Publications of the Modern Language Association of America* (*PMLA*) (Repr. 8 unnumbered vols., New York: Kraus, 1964).

Bibliography of "American writers of books and articles" on language and literature. Bibliography for 1955 includes general sections on literature, language, and folklore, language and literature sections for English, American, French, Italian, Spanish and Portuguese, Germanic, East European, Yiddish. Author index.

1957-1963: "Annual Bibliography" (for the years 1956-1962) published as a regular issue of *PMLA* (repr. under the title: *MLA International Bibliography*. 7 unnumbered vols. New York: Kraus, 1964). Scope greatly enlarged to include "Books and articles written in English, French, German, Spanish, Italian, Portuguese, Scandinavian, and Dutch." 1957 issue based on a master list of 1000 items regularly indexed. Section on Oriental language and literature added.

1964ff.: *MLA International Bibliography of Books and Articles on the Modern Languages and Literatures* (for the years 1963ff.).

The organization of the bibliography from 1922ff. has remained the same. Each section is divided by country or languages, subdivided by national literatures, then chronologically arranged by centuries with individual authors A-Z. For German literature see "Germanic Language and Literature, section German Language and Literature." The scope of the bibliography has been continually enlarged: bibliography for 1967 includes 1300 journals, collections, *Festschriften*, dissertations. Bibliography for 1969ff. issued as a 4 volume supplement to *PMLA* (also published as a one-volume annual "Library Edition"). Master list includes 1500 journals, collections, *Festschriften*, dissertations.

I: sections on General, English, American, Asian, African, and Latin-American literatures.
II: sections on General Romance, French, Italian, Spanish, Portuguese, and Brazilian, Romanian, General Germanic, German, Netherlandic, Scandinavian, Modern Greek, Oriental, African, and East European literatures.
III: linguistics.
IV: sections on pedagogy in the modern foreign languages, arranged by subject from a master list of some 300 items compiled under the auspices of the American Council on the Teaching of Foreign Languages (ACTFL).

126. *MLA Abstracts*. 1970-1975. 3 vols. ("Library Edition" publ. in one vol.) published 1972-1977 as suppl. to corresponding vols. I-III of *MLA International Bibliography*. Contents: 200-word abstracts of journal articles; to be used in conjunction with the bibliography, in which an asterisk preceding an item number indicates the item is abstracted in the corresponding vol. of *MLA Abstracts*. Easily accessible. Discontinued after 1975.

The MLA bibliography series is the most comprehensive current bibliography available in English. Entries are quite reliable. Publication is often tardy.

127. *The Year's Work in Modern Language Studies.* Ed. by the Modern Humanities Research Association. Vol. 1ff. London: Cambridge Univ. Pr., 1930ff. Editors and organization of material vary.

An annual, critical survey of research published during the previous year. Includes reviews of major articles, monographs, studies, and editions. Focus on English scholarship. Quality generally high, information accurate though not always complete. Affords an excellent, limited view of materials published recently in the field. No longer current. Easily accessible.

128. *Beiträge zur Literaturkunde. Bibliographie ausgewählter Zeitungs- und Zeitschriftenbeiträge.* 1945ff. Vol. 1, 1945-1951, appeared as supplement to the journal *Der Bibliothekar.* 1952-1965, Leipzig: Verlag für Buch- und Bibliothekswesen; 1966ff., Leipzig: Bibliographisches Institut.

Biyearly bibliography of primary and secondary literature (includes world literature), listing articles, reviews, books, speeches from important journals and newspapers in the GDR and German socialist publications in foreign countries. Organization: I. "Literaturwissenschaftliche Probleme" (or: "Allgemeine und grundlegende Fragen der Literatur"), II: "Literatur der Völker" (arranged geographically), III: "Schriftsteller und Werke" (A-Z; includes title list of anthologies of GDR authors). For 1972 a new section: "Allgemeine und grundlegende Fragen der Kulturpolitik." Valuable bibliography for Marxist-Socialist criticism.

129. *Bibliographie der deutschen Literaturwissenschaft.* Hanns W. Eppelsheimer, ed. Vols. 1-8 for 1945-1968. Frankfurt: Klostermann, 1957-1969. Appeared biennially. Continued as:

Bibliographie der deutschen Sprach- und Literaturwissenschaft. Clemens Köttelwesch, ed. Vol. 9ff. for 1969ff. Frankfurt: Klostermann, 1970ff. Publ. annually.

Organized by large subject groupings, then A-Z or chronologically. Includes secondary literature, bibliographies, *Forschungsberichte*, primary works, editions, letters, biographies, some reviews. CAUTION: sections on the periods of German literature list major authors first, then minor figures. Introductory material includes journals used, anthologies, collected essays by single authors, hints for usage, abbreviations. Indexes: subject, author, in each vol. NOTE: XVI (1976)ff. name, subject. Index of names includes names of literary figures as well as authors of secondary literature. Most reliable and comprehensive current bibliography available. Has been continually enlarged; early vols. contain little material from GDR; vol. 9ff. linguistics included. The vols. for 1945-1969 have been reworked: see No. 123, No. 124.

130. *Germanistik. Internationales Referatenorgan mit bibliographischen Hinweisen.* Ed. by Tilman Krömer. Vol. 1ff. Tubingen: Niemeyer, 1960ff.

Comprehensive bibliographical quarterly of German studies with annual cumulation. International in scope, lists articles, dissertations, books, editions, parts of books. Attempts to be as exhaustive as possible with philological and literary items pertaining specifically to German studies. Entries provide complete bibliographical information. Monographs, studies, editions are briefly reviewed. Organized by subject areas; use table of contents and annual index of names and authors at the end of each volume. This bibliography has grown rapidly from 2,424 numbered items in 1960 to 6,165 in 1976. Special feature: "Editionsvorhaben zu mittelalterlichen Texten," 4 (1963)-17(1976)ff., reporting usually in the 1st and 3rd quarters. This bibliography is the most valuable source available to German scholars for keeping abreast of developments in the field.

131. *Referatendienst zur Germanistischen Literaturwissenschaft. Literaturwissenschaftliche Information und Dokumentation.* Publ. by the Zentralinstitut für Literaturgeschichte. Deutsche Akademie der Wissenschaften zu Berlin. Vol. 1ff. (8 fasc.), 1970ff. Bimonthly, annual indexes. 1975ff. quarterly. 1970ff.: new title: *Referatendienst zur Literaturwissenschaft.*

Provides reviews of the latest books published in the GDR, reviews of significant journal articles. Includes some major articles and contributions from other socialist countries. Affords the scholar a limited opportunity to appraise the most recent publications in his field of interest. Arranged by subject categories, entries on literary history 15th to 20th century. Indexes: authors of books, A-Z; authors of articles, A-Z; reviewers, A-Z. Extremely selective.

D. BIBLIOGRAPHIES OF PRIMARY LITERATURE

1. First Editions

132. Brieger, Lothar, with collab. of Hans Bloesch. *Ein Jahrhundert deutscher Erstausgaben. Die wichtigsten Erst- und Originalausgaben von etwa 1750 bis 1880.* Stuttgart: Hoffmann, 1925. iii, 200pp.

A-Z listing by author of some 2,635 of the most important first editions and collected works. Detailed bibliographical information. Listing is selective; for a more complete listing see item X.

133. Hirschberg, Leopold. *Der Taschengoedeke. Bibliographie deutscher Erstausgaben.* 2 vols. Stuttgart: Deutscher Taschenbuch Verlag, 1961. (^{1}1924)

Lists first editions of German literature from 1650 to 1870's, a limited number of foreign authors in translation to 1900, plus philosophy, the arts, and music. Listing by author A-Z. Includes references to *Goedeke* (No. 108), records anonyms and pseudonyms.

134. Wilpert, Gero von, and Adolf Gühring. *Erstausgaben deutscher Dichtung. Eine Bibliographie zur deutschen Literatur 1600-1960*. Stuttgart: Kröner, 1967. x, 1468pp.

Approximately 47,000 editions for 1360 authors of belles-lettres. Bibliographical entries uniformly complete and usually reliable. First editions published after 1960 may be located in *Deutsche Bibliographie* (No. 58).

2. Manuscripts

135. Frels, Wilhelm. *Deutsche Dichterhandschriften von 1400 bis 1900. Gesamtkatalog der eigenhändigen Handschriften deutscher Dichter in den Bibliotheken und Archiven Deutschlands, Österreichs, der Schweiz und der ČSR*. Leipzig: Hiersemann, 1934. xiv, 382pp. (Repr. 1970) Two listings: by author A-Z, by location A-Z. Very exhaustive compilation.

3. Archivology

136. Folter, Ronald. *Deutsche Dichter- und Germanistenbibliotheken. Eine kritische Bibliographie ihrer Kataloge*. Stuttgart: Eggert, 1975. 262pp.

847 listings of special library collections of German authors and scholars of German literature. Appendices: auction catalogs, manuscripts; catalogs limited to one author; public library holdings; auction-bookseller catalogs with a foreword by an author. Indexes: book auction houses, catalogs. International in scope; information not always reliable.

137. *Nachlässe und Sammlungen in der Handschriftenabteilung des Schiller-Nationalmuseums und des Deutschen Literaturarchivs. Ein Verzeichnis*. Marbach: Deutsches Literaturarchiv, 1972. 93pp.

Range: 18th and 19th centuries. Holdings of the archive listed by author A-Z with brief descriptive commentary. For further information on archival holdings see *Jahrbuch der Deutschen Schiller-Gesellschaft*, 1ff. (No. 1586)

138. Schuder, Werner, ed. *Archive. Archive im deutschsprachigen Raum*. 2nd ed. 2 vols. Berlin, New York: de Gruyter, 1974. (^{1}1932) I, A-N. xv, 736pp.; II. O-Z. pp. 737-1418.

Lists ca. 8,000 A-Z by location. Includes public and private holdings. Provides descriptions of holdings, history of the collection, address, hours, etc. Indexes: location, subject.

E. BIBLIOGRAPHIES OF REPRINTS AND *FESTSCHRIFTEN*

139. Leistner, Otto, ed. *Internationale Bibliographie der Festschriften mit Sachregister. International Bibliography of Festschriften with Subject Index.* Osnabrück: Biblio, 1976. 893pp.

Range: 1850-1974. "List of Festschriften arranged by name of the personality or institution honoured," pp. 1-753; listings include complete bibliographical information. Index: subject, pp. 757-868, does not analyze the complete content of each *Festschrift*; glossary of frequently used foreign terms with German and English equivalents, pp. 869-889.

140. Ostwald, Renate. *Nachdruckverzeichnis vos Einzelwerken, Serien und Zeitschriften aus allen Wissensgebieten.* 2 vols. Wiesbaden: Nobis, 1965, 1969. xviii, 748 cols., 6pp.; xiii, 1964 cols., 39pp.

Range: I. 1945-1964; II. 1965-1968. Lists by author A-Z available reprints of monographs, series, periodicals. Listing includes original place of publication, year, reprinting press. NOTE: year of reprint frequently omitted. Does not include first facsimile printings of manuscripts. Very comprehensive listing.

141. *Guide to Reprints*. Ed. by the Information Handling Services. Englewood, Colo.: Indianhead, 1967ff. (formerly Washington: Microcard Eds.)

Annual cumulation of books and journals published in the US, listed by author A-Z. For 1976 557pp.; contains German titles.

F. INDEXES TO ANONYMS AND PSEUDONYMS

142. Holzmann, Michael, and Hanns Bohatta. *Deutsches Anonymen-Lexikon, 1501-1926. Aus den Quellen bearbeitet.* 7 vols. Leipzig: Breitkopf & Härtel, 1902-1928. (Repr. 1961)
I-IV (1908) 51,743 entries for 1501-1850; V (1910) 10,811 entries for 1851-1908; VI (1911) 8,508 for 1501-1910 plus addenda and corrections; VII (1928) 11,978 entries for 1501-1926 plus addenda and corrections. Listing by title A-Z. International in scope, lists many translations into German. Invaluable source.

143. ———. *Deutsches Pseudonymen-Lexikon. Aus den Quellen bearbeitet.* Vienna: Akademie, 1906. xxiv, 323pp. (Repr. 1961) Lists 19,000 pseudonyms A-Z and gives real name and source. No titles cited.

144. Taylor, Archer, and Frederic J. Mosher. *The Bibliographical History of Anonyma and Pseudonyma.* Chicago: University of Chicago Pr., 1951. ix, 288pp.

Surveys homonyms, Latinized names, pseudepigrapha, anonyma, and pseudonyma. Valuable bibliography of books and articles containing lists of anonyma and pseudonyma. International listings. Classified guide to dictionaries. Valuable source book.

G. TITLE INDEXES

145. Schneider, Max. *Deutsches Titelbuch. Ein Hilfsmittel zum Nachweis von Verfassern deutscher Literaturwerke.* 2nd rev. and enl. ed. Berlin: Peschke, 1927. viii, 799pp. (^{1}1907-1909, *Von wem ist es doch?*)

Listing by title. See foreword for specific cataloging. Indexes: pseudonyms, subjects. Easily accessible.

146. Ahnert, Heinz-Jörg. *Deutsches Titelbuch 2. Ein Hilfsmittel zum Nachweis von Verfassern deutscher Literaturwerke 1915-1965 mit Nachträgen und Berichtigungen zum deutschen Titelbuch 1 für die Zeit von 1900 bis 1914.* Berlin: Haude & Spenersche Verlagsbuchhandlung, 1966. xii, 636pp.

Contains ca. 24,000 titles. Each title followed by genre designation, author's name, year of publication. Lists only publications in book form, no song or poem titles or first lines, as *Titelbuch 1* (above). Basis for selection: literary significance, historical importance, commercial success. Subject index. Note: titles alphabetized by the particle beginning the title or by the first noun in the nominative case.

147 Dühmert, Anneliese. *Von wem ist das Gedicht? Eine bibliographische Zusammenstellung aus 50 deutschsprachigen Anthologien.* Berlin: Haude & Spenersche Verlagsbuchhandlung, 1969. viii, 564pp.

Contains information on 1,100 poems from 50 anthologies (1850's-1960's) by authors born 1500-1899. Not included: Goethe, Schiller, dialect poetry, riddles, children's rhymes, poems of less than 5 lines. List of anthologies, pp. i-iv; index of first lines by first word A-Z, pp. 2-256; titles of poems A-Z, pp. 257-478; authors A-Z, pp. 479-499; historical personal names mentioned in poems A-Z, pp. 500-527; geographical terms A-Z, pp. 528-564. This volume is designed to aid the user in finding author or title of a poem with which he is only partially familiar.

IV.

Dissertations

Abstracts, Bibliographies, Indexes

CONTENTS

A. AUSTRIA

148. *Gesamtverzeichnis österreichischer Dissertationen*. Vol. 1ff. Vienna: Verband der wissenschaftlichen Verbände Österreichs, 1967ff.

A listing of dissertations by universities, subdivided by colleges within each. Vol. 1 contains a bibliography of dissertation indexes from 1872 to 1962.

B. FRANCE

149. *Catalogue des thèses de doctorat soutenues devant les universités françaises. Nouvelle série* 1959ff. Paris: Cercle de la Librairie, 1960ff.

Yearly listings of theses and dissertations at French universities. For language and literature see section VI. "Lettres." Each subject heading is subdivided by universities, further subdivided by type of doctorate and alphabetized by author's name. Author index at the end of each volume.

For French theses prior to 1958 see:

150. *Catalogue des thèses et écrits académiques,* 1884/85ff. Paris: Cercle de la Librairie, 1885-1958.

Listings organized by university until 1913; from 1914ff. divided by subject.

For current listings of French dissertations see:

151. *Journal. Bibliographie de la France ou Journal général de l'imprimerie et de la librairie*. Paris: Cercle de la Librairie, 1811ff. Vol. 1ff.

Published weekly. From 1930ff. supplement D: "Thèses, classement par facultés et universités" to *Bibliographie officielle* contains current listings of theses.

C. GERMANY

*** *Deutsche Bibliographie. Wöchentliches Verzeichnis. Amtsblatt der deutschen Bibliothek.* Frankfurt: Buchhändlervereinigung, 1947ff.

Reihe B: Erscheinungen außerhalb des Verlagsbuchhandels. Lists theses, institutional publications and similar non-traded publications. Published monthly. (No. 60)

*** *Deutsche Nationalbibliographie.* Leipzig: Börsenverein der deutschen Buchhändler, 1931-1945. Leipzig: Verlag für Buch- und Bibliothekswesen, 1946ff.

Reihe B: Neuerscheinungen außerhalb des Buchhandels. Published biweekly. Lists theses, institutional publications, etc. (No. 55)

Reihe C: Dissertationen und Habilitationsschriften. Published monthly. (No. 55)

152. *Germanistische Dissertationen in Kurzfassung. Jahrbuch für Internationale Germanistik. Reihe B.* vol. 1ff. Bern, Frankfurt: Lang, 1975ff.

A selection of dissertation abstracts from all fields of German language and literature. International in scope. Presentations are of varying length. Vol. 1, 267pp. 1-39 dissertations; vol. 2, 1976, 244pp. 40-77 dissertations; vol. 3, 1976, 252pp. 78-119 dissertations.

*** *Gesamtverzeichnis des deutschsprachigen Schrifttums* (GV) 1911-1965. Reinhard Oberschelp, ed. Munich: Dokumentation, 1976-1977ff. vols. 1-30ff. (See No. 50)

153. *Jahresverzeichnis der deutschen Hochschulschriften.* Vol. 1ff. (1885/86). Berlin, Leipzig, 1887ff. Publisher changed frequently; currently: Leipzig: Verlag für Buch- und Bibliothekswesen. Title for the years 1924-1935: *Jahresverzeichnis der an den deutschen Universitäten und Hochschulen erschienenen Schriften.*

Standard official list of theses and dissertations accepted by German institutions of higher learning. Organized by institutions, subdivided by faculties, and listed alphabetically by author. For specific works see indexes: author, subject at the end of each vol.

154. Rojek, Hans J. *Bibliographie der deutschsprachigen Hochschulschriften zur Theaterwissenschaft von 1953 bis 1960.* Berlin: Selbstverlag der Gesellschaft für Theatergeschichte, 1962. xvii, 170pp.

Listings on drama and playwrights. Sections: general, geographical-general, historical-geographical, subdivided by epochs and listed A-Z. A useful supplement to standard bibliographies. Indexes: author, subject. For years prior to 1953 see:

155. Schwanbeck, Gisela. *Bibliographie der deutschsprachigen Hochschulschriften zur Theaterwissenschaft von 1885 bis 1952.* Berlin: Selbstverlag der Gesellschaft für Theatergeschichte, 1956. xiv, 563pp.

Some 3309 items dealing with European theater. Format similar to the above.

156. "Verzeichnis der germanistischen Dissertationsvorhaben. Liste 11. Stand der Meldungen vom 29. Februar 1972." Georg Bangen, comp. *Jahrbuch für Internationale Germanistik* 2 (1970), 2. 257pp.

Contains 4256 numbered items. Lists dissertations in progress in 7 large categories for German language and literature. Continued:

157. "Verzeichnis der germanistischen Dissertationsvorhaben. Liste 12. Meldungen vom 1. März 1972 bis 28. Februar 1975." Georg Bangen, comp. *Jahrbuch für Internationale Germanistik* 6 (1974), 2, 167-199. To be continued.

Same principles of inclusion and listing as above. Lists 1-10 (1958-1968) were available only in hectographed form.

D. GREAT BRITAIN

158. *Index to Theses Accepted for Higher Degrees by the Universities of Great Britain and Ireland and the "Council for National Academic Awards."* Vol. 1, 1950/51ff. London: Aslib, 1953ff.

Annual listing divided according to broad subjects and subdivided by institution (including some foreign institutions) and author. Indexes: author, subject at the end of each volume; index includes many cross references. Information contained is easily accessible.

159. Norman, Frederick. *Theses in German Studies. A Catalogue of Theses and Dissertations in the Field of Germanic Studies (Excluding English) Approved for Higher Degrees in the Universities of Great Britain and Ireland between 1903 and 1961.* London: Univ. of London, Institute of Germanic Languages, 1962, viii, 46pp.

Lists 455 theses by author A-Z, giving title, degree awarded, university, and year. Subject index.

E. UNITED STATES AND CANADA

160. *Canadian Theses. Thèses canadiennes.* 1952ff. Ottowa: National Library of Canada, 1953ff.

Title listing of graduate theses (A.M. and Ph.D.) classified according to subject, subdivided by university. Each vol. contains author index.

161. *Comprehensive Dissertation Index, 1861-1972.* 37 vols. Ann Arbor: Xerox University Microfilms, 1973.

Lists the titles of virtually all Ph.D. dissertations accepted at US institutions during the years 1861-1972. Includes some major foreign institutions for the years 1969-1972. Gives complete bibliographical information for each title. (For a summary of dissertation content see item X.) I-XXXII divided according to subject: "Language and Literature," XXIX-XXX. Author index: XXXIII-XXXVII. Caution: the subject index is divided according to broad categories, such as authors, genres, epochs, and key words in titles. Information is not easily accessible. Continued in annual cumulations.

162. *Dissertation Abstracts. A Guide to Dissertations and Monographs Available in Microform.* Ann Arbor, Mich.: University Microfilms, 1952ff., vol. 12ff. Vols. 1-11, 1938-1951, appear under the title *Microfilm Abstracts*.

Monthly compilation (with annual cumulation) of informative summaries of dissertations submitted to University Microfilms by virtually all the major institutions of higher learning in the US. Each entry gives the bibliographical information for and a concise summary of the dissertation. Listing divided according to disciplines. Each issue has author and subject indexes which are cumulated yearly as *Index to American Doctoral Dissertations*, after 1964/65 as *Dissertation Abstracts* (including Canadian dissertations). *Dissertation Abstracts*, beginning with vol. 27, no. 1, 1966, is divided into two sections: A. "The Humanities and Social Sciences"; B. "The Sciences and Engineering." With vol. 30, no. 1, 1969 title changed to *Dissertation Abstracts International*. Listings currently include some major foreign institutions.

163. *Doctoral Dissertations Accepted by American Universities, 1933/34-1954/55.* 22 nos. New York: Wilson, 1934-1956.

164. *A List of American Doctoral Dissertations Printed in 1912-1938.* 26 vols. Washington: Government Printing Office, 1913-1940.

Author list A-Z and subject index. Items carry Library of Congress catalog number. Items in this series are also listed in No. 161.

165. Palfrey, Thomas R., and Henry E. Coleman, Jr. *Guide to Bibliographies of Theses. United States and Canada.* Chicago: American Library Association, 1936. 48pp.

Bibliographies of theses and abstracts listed under 3 headings: general, special fields, institutions. Superseded by *Comprehensive Dissertation Index* (No. 161)

V.

Biography and Bio-Bibliography

CONTENTS

A. INTERNATIONAL BIOGRAPHY

1. Bibliography

166. Arnim, Max. *Internationale Personalbibliographie*. 2nd rev. ed. 3 vols. Stuttgart: Hiersemann, 1952 (I,II), 1963 (III). ([1]1936)

Range: I (A-K) and II (L-Z): 1800-1943; III: 1944-1959 plus supplement by Gerhard Bock and Franz Hodes for I and II (e.g., Heine, omitted earlier, is included in III). 2nd ed. omits some names included in 1st. Indexes bibliographies from Goedeke, Kürschner, books, periodicals, biographical dictionaries, *Festschriften*, etc. for approximately 90,000 scholars and authors. Includes biographical data with each entry. Emphasis on German writers.

167. Bohatta, Hanns, and Franz Hodes. *Internationale Bibliographie der Bibliographien. Ein Nachschlagewerk unter Mitwirkung von Walter Funke*. Frankfurt: Klostermann, 1950. 652pp.

Approximately 16,000 titles. Extensive listings in the humanities and sciences, subdivided by disciplines. CAUTION: entries alphabetized inconsistently by title, author, or country; user should start with author, title, and subject indexes. Work includes no personal bibliographies. Authors intended it as a supplement to Max Arnim: *Internationale Personalbibliographie*.

168. *Index Bibliographicus Notorum Hominum (IBN)*. Ed. by Jean-Pierre Lobies and François-Pierre Lobies Adiuvante. Osnabrück: Biblio, 1973ff.

Promises to be the most comprehensive international bio-bibliographical reference work available. Planned in 5 parts:

Pars A. *Allgemeine Einführung. General Introduction.*
Pars B. *Liste der ausgewerteten bio-bibliographischen Werke. List of the Evaluated Bio-bibliographical Works.* 1973. 884pp.
The majority of sources based on Slocum (below). Biographical reference works organized according to geographical, historical, or linguistic principles.
Pars C. *Corpus Alphabeticum. Sectio generalis.* vol. 1ff. 1974ff.
Listing of persons A-Z with reference numbers to Pars B.
Pars D. *Supplementum.*
Pars E. *Gesamtregister der Verweisungen. General Index of References.*

169. Slocum, Robert B. *Biographical Dictionaries and Related Works. An International Bibliography of Collective Biographies, Bio-Bibliographies, Collections of Epitaphs, Selected Geneological Works, Dictionaries of Anonyms and Pseudonyms, Historical and Specialized Dictionaries, Biographical Materials in Government Manuals, Bibliographies of Bibliography, Biographical Indexes, and Selected Portrait Catalogs.* Detroit: Gale Research, 1967. xxiii, 1056pp. Contains 4829 numbered items.

170. ———. *Supplement.* Detroit: Gale Research, 1972, xiii, 852pp. Adds 3400 new items.

Both volumes have extensive author, title, subject indexes. Does not contain biographies of individuals.

2. Dictionaries and Indexes

171. *Biography Index. A Cumulative Index to Biographical Material in Books and Magazines.* vol. 1ff. New York: Wilson, 1949ff.

Quarterly with annual and three-year cumulations. Contains names A-Z listing all kinds of biographical materials, including autobiography, letters, diaries, memoirs, journals, fiction, drama, poetry, juvenile literature, etc. from books, periodicals, *Festschriften*, etc. Index by profession and occupation.

172. Hennicke, Karl August. *Beiträge zur Ergänzung und Berichtigung des Jöcherschen Allgemeinen Gelehrten Lexikons und des Meuselschen Lexikons der von 1750 bis 1800 verstorbenen teutschen Schriftsteller.* Leipzig: Vogel, 1811-1812. iv, 122pp. (Repr. 1969)

Supplement to Jöcher (below) and Meusel (No. 206) for the years 1750-1800 supplying omitted authors and items. Very confusingly compiled.

173. *The International Who's Who.* 1st ed. London: Europa Publications, 1935ff. Annual publication. Short biographies only.

174. Jöcher, Christian Gottlieb. *Allgemeines Gelehrten Lexikon. Darinne die Gelehrten aller Stände sowohl männlichen als weiblichen Geschlechts, welche vom Anfange der Welt bis auf jetzige Zeit gelebt, und sich der gelehrten Welt bekannt gemacht, nach ihrer Geburt, Leben, merkwürdigen Geschichten, Absterben und Schriften aus den glaubwürdigsten Skribenten in alphabetischer Ordnung beschrieben wurden.* 4 vols. Leipzig: Gleditsch, 1750-1751.

175. ———. *Allgemeines Gelehrten Lexikon-Fortsetzung und Ergänzungen.* Leipzig: Gleditsch, 1784-1787; Delmenhorst: Jötzen, 1810; Bremen: Heyse, 1813-1819; Leipzig: Selbstverlag der Deutschen Gesellschaft, 1897. 7 vols. I and II by J.C. Adelung; III-VI by H.W. Rotermund; VII by O. Günther. (Repr. 1960-1961). A comprehensive international lexicon of published authors A-Z from the beginnings to 1750.

B. NATIONAL BIOGRAPHIES

1. Austria

176. *Neue österreichische Biographie, ab 1815.* Begun by Anton Bettelheim, August Fournier, Heinrich Friedjung, et al., dir. by A. Bettelheim. 8 vols. Vienna: Almathea, 1923-1935.

177. ———. IX-XVII. Vienna, Munich, Zurich: Almathea, 1956-1968.

Pt. 1: I-VIII, biographical articles for ca. 132 major figures, not alphabetically arranged. Index in VIII. Pt. 2: bibliography of Austrian biography, including biographical dictionaries. Listing in 2 pts.: subject or specialty, geographic location.

178. *Österreichisches Biographisches Lexikon 1815-1950.* Ed. Österreichische Akademie der Wissenschaften. Vol. 1ff. Graz, Cologne: Böhlau, 1957ff. Lieferung 27 (1974) "Marko-Mehoffer."

Continues Wurzbach (No. 181). Brief biographical sketches of persons in the arts, politics, and sciences who died prior to 1951. Limited to the territory of the Austro-Hungarian Empire and the succeeding Austrian state. Short primary and secondary bibliographies.

179. Pollak, Walter, ed. *Tausend Jahre Österreich. Eine biographische Chronik.* 3 vols. Vienna, Munich: Jugend und Volk, 1973-1974. Illus.

I. *Von den Babenbergern zum Wiener Kongreß.* 432pp.
II. *Vom Biedermeier bis zur Gründung der modernen Parteien.* 430pp.
III. *Der Parlementarismus und die beiden Republiken.* 527pp.

Short essays on major figures from all areas of Austrian cultural history; III contains a chronological table: 899-1974. On the whole this is a handy survey. Entries on literary figures are too brief to be of value.

180. *Who's Who in Austria. A Biographical Dictionary Containing about 4000 Biographies of Prominent Personalities from and in Austria.* vol. 1ff. Montreal: International Book and Publishing Co., 1955ff. Place of publication, subtitle vary. 9th ed. by Otto J. Groeg, 1977.

Biennial volumes. Brief biographical sketches with brief bibliographies. Contains a directory of organizations, institutes, learned societies, and enterprises.

181. Wurzbach, Constant von. *Biographisches Lexikon des Kaiserthums Österreich, enthaltend die Lebensskizzen der denkwürdigen Personen, welche seit 1750 in den österreichischen Kronländern geboren wurden oder darin gelebt und gewirkt haben.* 60 vols. Vienna: Hof- und Staatsdruckerei, 1856-1891. Subtitle varies.

Contains biographies for 24,254 prominent figures of the Austrian Empire. Articles also provide some bibliography. Standard for its field.

182. ———. *Register zu den Nachträgen in Wurzbachs Biographischem Lexikon des Kaiserthums Österreich*. Vienna: Gilhofer & Ranschburg, 1923. 16pp.

2. Germany

183. *Allgemeine Deutsche Biographie*. Ed. by Historische Kommission bei der Königlichen Akademie der Wissenschaften. 56 vols. Leipzig: Duncker & Humblot, 1875-1912. I-XLV, A-Z; XLIV-LV, *Nachträge bis 1899*, Andr-Z (A-Ad is included in XLV); LVI, *Generalregister.*

An outstanding biographical dictionary of figures of national significance who died before 1900. Entries include biographical information, primary and secondary bibliographical material. CAUTION: since there are supplemental sections in many volumes, use the general index (LVI) to locate information more quickly. Contains ca. 26,000 biographies.

184. *Biographisches Jahrbuch und Deutscher Nekrolog*. Ed. by Anton Bettelheim. 18 vols. and 1 index vol. Berlin: Reimer, 1897-1917.

Continues *Allgemeine Deutsche Biographie* (above). Annual publication with biographical articles on prominent people who died during the year reported on. Separate necrology list with bibliography to death notices. Index vol. covers I-X (1896-1905).

185. *Deutsches Biographisches Jahrbuch*. Ed. by the Verband der Deutschen Akademien. 7 vols. Stuttgart, Berlin, Leipzig: Deutsche Verlagsanstalt, 1925-1932.

I. 1914-1916; II. 1917-1920; III. 1921; IV. 1922; V. 1923; X. 1928; XI. 1929.

Biographies of varying length with bibliography. Necrology lists. Continues Bettelheim, *Biographisches Jahrbuch* (above).

186. Heimpel, H., Theodor Heuss, Benno Reifenberg. *Die großen Deutschen*. 5 vols. Berlin: Propyläen Verlag, 1956-1957. (^{1}1935-1936; 4 vols.)

Essays on selected outstanding Germans and occasionally non-Germans. Good detailed biography and appraisal. V has list of names treated in all volumes and index of names for all volumes.

187. *Kürschners Deutscher Gelehrten-Kalender*. 11th ed. 2 vols. Berlin: de Gruyter, 1970/71ff. (^{1}1925, has appeared irregularly in subsequent editions.)

I. *A-M*; II. *N-Z, Register*
An offshoot of *Kürschners Deutscher Literatur-Kalender* (No. 215). Bio-bibliographical sketches of some 20,000 living scholars and professionals in non-literary fields. Indexes: necrology, birthdays, scholars by discipline, publishing houses in Austria, Germany, and Switzerland.

188. *Neue Deutsche Biographie*. Ed. by the Historische Kommission bei der Bayrischen Akademie der Wissenschaften. Vol. 1ff. Berlin: Duncker & Humblot, 1953ff. 12 vols. planned.

Biographical dictionary of leading German figures or foreigners who lived for a time in Germany and had a significant impact on German history or culture. Compact articles in 4 pts.: 1. dates and profession, 2. lineage, 3. biography, 4. bibliography (archives, portraits, etc.). Includes authors living up to 1962.

189. *Wer ist's? Eine Sammlung von rund 18000 Biographien mit Angaben über Herkunft, Familie, Lebenslauf, Veröffentlichungen und Werke, Lieblingsbeschäftigung, Mitgliedschaft bei Gesellschaften, Anschrift und Mitteilungen von allgemeinem Interesse. Auflösungen von ca. 5000 Pseudonymen*. 10th ed. by Herrmann A.L. Degener. Berlin: Degener, 1935 (^{1}1905). International in scope; after 1918 increasingly national in orientation. Continued as:

190. *Wer ist wer? Das deutsche Who's who. XI. Ausgabe von Degeners Wer ist's?* Berlin: arani, 1955ff. (^{19}1977) Place of publication and publisher vary. Since 1962 issued in 2 vols., one each for the GDR and the FRG.

191. *Who's Who in Germany. A Biographical Dictionary Containing about 12,000 Biographies of Prominent People in Germany and 2400 Organizations*. Ed. by Horst G. Kliemann and Stephen S. Taylor. 3rd ed. 2 vols. Munich: Oldenbourg, 1964. (^{1}1956)

Short biographical sketches. Limited to the Federal Republic of Germany. Contains lists of organizations, associations, institutions.

3. Switzerland

192. *Historisch-Biographisches Lexikon der Schweiz*. 7 vols. + 2 supplements. Neuchâtel: Attinger, 1921-1934.

An encyclopedia of Switzerland which includes history, geography, leading figures, etc. Many biographical articles with brief bibliography.

193. *Who's Who in Switzerland Including the Principality of Liechtenstein. A Biographical Dictionary Containing More Than 4000 Biographies of Prominent People in and from Switzerland (Including the Principality of Liechtenstein)*. 10th ed. Geneva: Nagel, 1975. 749pp.

Range: 1974/75. Biographical dictionary with brief entries on contemporary notables from all walks of life. Gives current address, bibliography, distinctions, etc.

C. GERMAN AUTHORS

1. Author Bibliographies

194. Hansel, Johannes. *Personalbibliographie zur deutschen Literaturgeschichte. Studienausgabe.* Berlin: Schmidt, 1967. 175pp.

Lists bibliographical information for 300 authors. Each entry provides references to completed bibliographies, completed partial author bibliographies with indication as to primary or secondary literature, location of literary remains, *Forschungsberichte*, literary societies. Index: authors of bibliographies, subject. Reliable, invaluable tool.

195. ———. *Personalbibliographie zur deutschen Literaturgeschichte. Studienausgabe.* Neubearbeitung und Fortführung von 1966 bis auf den jüngsten Stand von Carl Paschek. 2nd rev. ed. Berlin: Schmidt, 1974. 258pp.

Adds 43 twentieth-century authors to those included in the 1st ed. Indexes: authors of bibliographies, subjects.

196. Stock, Karl F., Rudolf Heiliger, Marylene Stock. *Personalbibliographien österreichischer Dichter und Schriftsteller. Von den Anfängen bis zur Gegenwart. Mit Auswahl einschlägiger Bibliographien, Literaturgeschichten und Anthologien.* Munich-Pullach: Dokumentation, 1972. xxiii, 703pp.

Lists some 6,000 items. Pt. A: bibliographies, standard reference works with emphasis on Austrian material; pt. B: bibliographies of authors A-Z who were born or died in Austria, major works, and authors who wrote in Austria or in the area of the Austro-Hungarian empire. Listings include primary and secondary bibliographies, literary histories, articles, dissertations, bibliographies, and handbooks. Includes a supplement; index: author and subject.

197. Wiesner, Herbert, Irena Živsa, Christoph Stoll. *Bibliographie der Personalbibliographien zur deutschen Gegenwartsliteratur.* Munich: Nymphenburger Verlagshandlung, 1970. 359pp.

Contains both primary and secondary bibliographies for ca. 500 authors and scholars. In addition: biography, evaluations of research, and archival information. Excellent reference work.

2. Bio-Bibliographical Handbooks and Dictionaries

a. *General*

See also "B. National Biographies. 2. Germany."

*** Adling, Wilfried, et al., eds. *Lexikon sozialistischer deutscher Literatur. Von den Anfängen bis 1945. Monographisch-historische Darstellungen.* Gießen: Polit-Buchvertrieb, 1973. 592pp. (see No. 722)

198. Albrecht, Günter, Kurt Böttcher, Herbert Greiner-Mai, Paul Günter Krohn. *Lexikon deutschsprachiger Schriftsteller von den Anfängen bis zur Gegenwart.* 2 vols. Leipzig: Bibliographisches Institut, 1967, 1968. 820pp.; 799pp. and 16 photos. (1st-5th editions under the title *Deutsches Schriftstellerlexikon*, 1960-1964.)

Range: to the 1960's. Alphabetically arranged. Biographies and commentary on most important works. Primary bibliographical information only. Emphasis on East German writers. Quite reliable.

*** Garland, Henry, and Mary. *The Oxford Companion to German Literature.* Oxford: Clarendon Pr., 1976. vii, 977pp. (see No. 1287)

199. Giebisch, Hans, and Gustav Gugitz. *Bio-Bibliographisches Literaturlexikon Österreichs. Von den Anfängen bis zur Gegenwart.* Vienna: Hollineck, 1964. viii, 517pp.

Authors, A-Z, writing in the German language from the Middle Ages to 1963, including folklorists, literary scholars born in the Austro-Hungarian Empire before ca. 1900 and authors currently living in Austria. Does not include politicians, journalists, historians, philosophers. Listing: name, pseudonym, short biography, primary bibliography, secondary literature. Bibliographical information somewhat spotty. Includes many minor Austrian poets and authors. Index: pseudonyms, pp. 505-517. Excellent source of information on relatively unknown authors.

200. Kosch, Wilhelm. *Deutsches Literatur-Lexikon. Biographisches und bibliographisches Handbuch.* 2nd comp. rev. and enl. ed. 4 vols. Bern: Francke, 1949-1958. (^{1}1927-1930, 2 vols.)

Compendium of terminology, themes, motifs, titles, authors, philosophers, critics, and historians. Contains primary and secondary bibliography on writers. Bibliographical material not always reliable and generally too brief. Well suited for quick orientation. The following edition in progress promises to be an excellent revision:

201. ———. *Deutsches Literatur-Lexikon. Biographisch-bibliographisches Handbuch.* Originated by Wilhelm Kosch. 3rd completely rev. ed. by Bruno Berger and Heinz Rupp (editors change). Bern, Munich: Francke, 1968ff.

I. *Aal-Bremeneck*. 1968. xii, 1024 cols.
II. *Bremer-Davidis*. 1969. viii, 1024 cols.
III. *Davidis-Eichendorff*. 1971. viii, 1048 cols.
IV. *Eichenhorst-Filchner*. 1972. x, 1024 cols.
V. *Filex-Fux*. 1978. x, 926 cols.
VI. *Gaa-Gysin*. 1978. xiii, 1092 cols.

Concentrates on authors but also includes theologians, philosophers, historians, etc. Comprehensive primary and selected secondary bibliography expanded and brought up to date. Excellent presentation.

*** Rüdiger, Horst, and Erwin Koppen, eds. *Kleines literarisches Lexikon*. 4th rev. ed. 3 vols. in 4 pts. Bern, Munich: Francke, 1966 (III), 1969 (I,II). ([1]1947 ed. Wolfgang Kayser)

I. *Autoren. Von den Anfängen bis zum 19. Jahrhundert*. 840pp. (to 1863)
II. *Autoren II. 20. Jahrhundert. Erster Teil: A-K*. 449pp. *Autoren II. 20. Jahrhundert. Zweiter Teil: L-Z*. 550pp. (see No. 1296)

202. Wilpert, Gero von. *Deutsches Dichterlexikon. Biographisch-bibliographisches Handwörterbuch zur deutschen Literaturgeschichte*. Stuttgart: Kröner, 1963. xi, 657pp.

Range: beginnings to the 1960's. Alphabetical listing of ca. 2,000 authors (for anonymous works: titles) whose major contribution was made in German or while living in a German-speaking area. Each entry contains a biographical sketch, appraisal of achievement, and a bibliography of works followed by secondary literature. Extremely reliable; an excellent resource book.

b. Periods Prior to the Twentieth Century

203. Brümmer, Franz. *Lexikon der deutschen Dichter und Prosaisten vom Beginn des 19. Jahrhunderts bis zur Gegenwart*. 6th rev. and enl. ed. 8 vols. Leipzig: Reclam, 1913. ([1]1885)

Contains ca. 9,900 biographies. Addendum in VIII to 1912. Brief biographical sketches, little primary bibliography.

204. Friedrichs, Elisabeth. *Literarische Lokalgrößen 1700-1900. Verzeichnis der in regionalen Lexika und Sammelbänden aufgeführten Schriftsteller*. Stuttgart: Metzler, 1967. x, 439pp.

Excellent source book for minor poets (also scholars, clergymen, etc., who published belles-lettres) not usually included in bibliographies. Alphabetical listing by name, pseudonym with bio-bibliographical information.

205. *Das gelehrte Teutschland oder Lexikon der jetzt lebenden Schriftsteller*. Begun by Georg Christoph Hamberger, continued by Johann Georg Meusel. 5th ed. 23 vols. Lemgo: Meyersche Hofbuchhandlung, 1796-1834. (Repr. 1965-1966)

A-Z listing includes all writers of German in Germany and abroad, foreigners residing in Germany or German-speaking areas, living in 1795ff. Individual listings: biographical information, book publications in chronological order with complete bibliographical data, some secondary literature. Work supplements Goedeke (No. 108). XXIII of the reprint contains a table of contents: see "Einführung" by Paul Raabe at the end of the vol. Raabe also supplies information on the work and its editors as well as hints for its use. No indexes.

206. Meusel, Johann Georg. *Lexikon der vom Jahr 1750-1800 verstorbenen teutschen Schriftsteller.* 15 vols. Leipzig: Fleischer, 1802-1816. Complements Hamberger-Meusel (above).

*** Natan, Alex, ed. *German Men of Letters. Twelve Literary Essays.* 5 vols. London: Wolff, 1961-1969. (see No. 734)

207. Pataky, Sophie. *Lexikon deutscher Frauen der Feder. Eine Zusammenstellung der seit dem Jahre 1840 erschienenen Werke weiblicher Autoren, nebst Biographien der lebenden und einem Verzeichnis der Pseudonyme.* 2 vols. Berlin: Pataky, 1898. 527pp. 545pp.

Range: 1840-1898. Listing by last name A-Z. Includes women writers in all fields. Particularly exhaustive for the years 1866-1898. Supplement: II, pp. 469-543. Index of pseudonyms in II. Includes women writers not found in other reference works.

*** Stammler, Wolfgang, ed. (I,II) and Karl Langosch, ed. (III, IV). *Die deutsche Literatur des Mittelalters. Verfasserlexikon.* 5 vols. Berlin: de Gruyter, 1933-1955.

I. *Aalen-Futerer.* 1933. xiii, 786 cols.
II. *Der von Gabelstein-Kyeser.* 1936. 992 cols.
III. *Laber-Rynsteten.* 1943. 1166 cols.
IV. *Saarburg-Zwinger.* 1953. 1172 cols.
V. *Nachtragsband.* 1955. 1150 cols. (see No. 484)

*** Wiese, Benno von, ed. *Deutsche Dichter der Romantik. Ihr Leben und Werk.* Berlin: Schmidt, 1971. 530pp. (see No. 645)

*** ———, ed. *Deutsche Dichter des 19. Jahrhunderts. Ihr Leben und Werk.* Berlin: Schmidt, 1969. 600pp. (see No. 676)

c. *The Twentieth Century*

i. General

*** Fleischmann, Wolfgang Bernard. *Encyclopedia of World Literature in the 20th Century in Three Volumes. An Enlarged and Updated Edition of the Herder Lexikon der Weltliteratur im 20. Jahrhundert.* New York: Ungar, 1967-1971. I. *A-F.* xxiv, 425pp.; II. *G-N.* xxiv, 469pp.; III. *O-Z*, xxvii, 591pp.; IV. *Supplement and Index.* Ed. Frederick Ungar and Lina Mainiero. 1975. xvii, 462pp. (see No. 1284)

*** Kunisch, Hermann, ed. *Handbuch der deutschen Gegenwartsliteratur. Unter Mitwirkung zahlreicher Fachgelehrter.* 2nd rev. ed. 3 vols. Munich: Nymphenburger Verlagshandlung, 1969-1970. (^{1}1965) (see No. 732)

208 ———, ed. *Kleines Handbuch der deutschen Gegenwartsliteratur. 116 Autoren und ihr Werk in Einzeldarstellungen.* 2nd rev. ed. Munich: Nymphenburger Verlagshandlung, 1969. 631pp. (^{1}1967)

Range: 20th century. This is a handy reduction of the above. The selection includes a few notable essayists, scholars, psychologists and philosophers in addition to authors. Listed by last name A-Z, each entry includes biographical information, major contribution, and primary bibliography.

*** *Lexikon der Weltliteratur im 20. Jahrhundert.* 2 vols. Freiburg, Basel, Vienna: Herder, ^{3}1965-1966. I. *A-J.* 1096 cols.; II. *K-Z.* 1326 cols. + 24pp. indexes.

*** Mann, Otto, ed. *Christliche Dichter im 20. Jahrhundert. Beiträge zur europäischen Literatur.* 2nd rev. ed. Bern, Munich: Francke, 1968. 506pp. (^{1}1955) (see No. 733)

209. Olles, Helmut. *Literaturlexikon 20. Jahrhundert.* Reinbek: Rowohlt, 1971. 850pp.

Range: 1900-1970. International in scope with emphasis on German language authors and literature after 1945. 2,000 biographical sketches listed A-Z, including primary and secondary bibliography; for major figures a critical appraisal is given. Includes poets, writers, essayists, literary scholars, psychologists, philosophers.

210. Stern, Desider. *Werke von Autoren jüdischer Herkunft in deutscher Sprache. Eine Bio-Bibliographie.* 3rd ed. Vienna: Stern, 1970. 455pp. (^{1}1967)

Range: 19th and 20th centuries. Authors (A-Z) include important figures from all disciplines. For each entry: biography, primary bibliography, archival and literary remains with addresses. Also includes book lists on exile, lyric, and prose publications in Yiddish, German reference materials on Judaica. First published for the book exhibit of the B'nai B'rith in Vienna, 1967. Unique and useful.

211. Ungar, Frederick, ed. *Handbook of Austrian Literature.* New York: Ungar, 1973. xvi, 296pp.

Range: predominantly 20th century. Bio-bibliographical entries for 80 Austrian authors and notables (including Buber, Freud, Friedell, Lukács, Wittgenstein) with appraisal of major works followed by primary and selected secondary bibliography. Based for the most part on H. Kunisch, *Handbuch der deutschen Gegenwartsliteratur* (No. 732)

*** Wiese, Benno von, ed. *Deutsche Dichter der Moderne. Ihr Leben und ihr Werk.* 3rd rev. ed. Berlin: Schmidt, 1975. 624pp. (^{1}1965) (see No. 741)

ii. 1900-1945

*** Friedmann, Hermann, and Otto Mann, eds. *Expressionismus. Gestalten einer Literaturbewegung.* Heidelberg: Rothe, 1956. 375pp. (No. 758)

*** Klein, Alfred. *Im Auftrag ihrer Klasse. Weg und Leistung der deutschen Arbeiterschriftsteller 1918-1933.* Berlin, Weimar: Aufbau, 1972. 854 pp. (see No. 772)

*** Soergel, Albert. *Dichtung und Dichter der Zeit. Eine Schilderung der deutschen Literatur der letzten Jahrzehnte.* 20th ed. Leipzig: Voigtländer, 1928. xii, 1062pp. ([1]1911) (No. 736)

*** ———. *Dichtung und Dichter der Zeit. Neue Folge. Im Banne des Expressionismus.* Leipzig: Voigtländer, 1925. xi, 904pp. (No. 737)

*** ———. *Dichter aus deutschem Volkstum. Dichtung und Dichter der Zeit. Dritte Folge.* Leipzig: Voigtländer, 1934. 231pp. (No. 738)

*** ———, and Curt Hohoff. *Dichtung und Dichter der Zeit. Vom Naturalismus bis zur Gegenwart.* 2 vols. Düsseldorf: Bagel, 1961-1963. 896pp., 893pp. (No. 739)

*** Spalek, John M., and Joseph Strelka, eds. *Deutsche Exilliteratur seit 1933. Band 1. Kalifornien. Teil 1.* Bern, Munich: Francke, 1976. 868pp. (see No. 785)

*** Sternfeld, Wilhelm, and Eva Tiedemann. *Deutsche Exil-Literatur 1933-1945. Eine Bio-Bibliographie.* 2nd rev. and enl. ed. Heidelberg: Lambert Schneider, 1970. 606pp. ([1]1962) (see No. 787)

iii. Contemporary

212. Albrecht, Günter, Kurt Böttcher, Herbert Greiner-Mai, and Paul Günter Krohn. *Schriftsteller der DDR.* 2nd ed. Leipzig: Bibliographisches Institut, 1975. 656pp. ([1]1974)

A lexicon of some 700 authors, critics, essayists, biographers, and editors. Each entry lists general biography, appraisal of achievement, primary bibliography. Appendix: literary prizes and their recipients, pp. 642-656. This is the most useful of the GDR author lexica.

213. Endres, Elisabeth. *Autorenlexikon der deutschen Gegenwartsliteratur 1945-1975.* Frankfurt: Fischer Taschenbuch, 1975. 202pp.

A. Compact outline history; B. 350 contemporary authors A-Z. Entries include biography, primary bibliography, appraisal of major works. Primary bibliography, pp. 47-51. Some recent minor authors included.

*** Geerdts, Hans Jürgen, ed. *Literatur der DDR. Einzeldarstellungen.* Stuttgart: Kröner, 1974. xxiv, 571pp. (see No. 824)

214. Kay, Ernest, ed. *The International Authors and Writers Who's Who.* 7th ed. Cambridge, Engl.: Melrose Pr., 1976. xiv, 676pp. ([1]1934)

A geographical listing of literati, critics, scholars, scientists, professionals, and professors. Does not include one-book authors, pamphleteers, highly technical and specialized writers. Each entry: place and date of birth, education and profession, short bibliography, honors, memberships, current address. Index: literary agents, pseudonyms. Of limited usefulness for German-speaking countries.

215. *Kürschners Deutscher Literatur-Kalender.* Vol. 1ff. Berlin: de Gruyter, 1879ff. Appears irregularly. Beginning with XLII, 1925, issued in 2 series: *Literatur-Kalender* and *Kürschners deutscher Gelehrten-Kalender* (see No. 187).

This is the Who's Who of living Austrian, German and Swiss and German-language authors living abroad, A-Z. Each item: brief biography, prizes, current address, primary bibliography of first editions; secondary bibliography infrequent and scanty. Appendices: 1. Necrology, 2. Calendar of birthdays by month and day, 3. List of translators, 4. List of leading publishers by country, 5. German-language journals with address, editor, and frequency of publication, 6. List of organizations by country, 7. Literary societies by country, 8. Literary prizes and distinctions, 9. List of geographical locations and authors who represent them. A first source for current biographical information.

216. *Nekrolog zu Kürschners Literatur-Kalender 1901-1935.* Ed. Gerhard Lüdtke. Berlin, Leipzig: de Gruyter, 1936. vii, 976 cols.

Attempts to list all German-language authors (A-Z) who died 1901-1935. Each entry gives a brief biography and primary bibliography. Listings are based on a supplemental necrology of *Kürschners Deutscher Literatur Kalender* (above). Index of authors by date of birth and index of authors by date of death. Continued as:

Kürschners Deutscher Literatur-Kalender. Nekrolog 1936-1970. Ed. by Werner Schuder. Berlin, New York: de Gruyter, 1973. xiv, 871pp.

Format as above with addition of some secondary bibliography. Ca. 5,200 authors listed.

VI.

Literary Criticism, Methodology, Theory

CONTENTS

A. GUIDES TO LITERARY CRITICISM, METHODOLOGY, AND THEORY

217. Baesecke, Georg. *Deutsche Philologie*. Gotha: Perthes, 1919. xi, 132pp.

General handbook with bibliography incorporated into the text. Good survey of research.

218. Conrady, Karl Otto. *Einführung in die neuere deutsche Literaturwissenschaft. Mit Beiträgen von Horst Rüdiger und Peter Szondi und Textbeispielen zur Geschichte der deutschen Philologie*. Reinbek: Rowohlt, 1966. 246pp.

Introduction to the study of German literature as a discipline, its aims and curriculum. Contains basic reading list for students, pp. 111-133. Appendix: H. Rüdiger, "Zwischen Interpretation und Geistesgeschichte. Zur gegenwärtigen Situation der deutschen Literaturwissenschaft," pp. 137-154; P. Szondi, "Zur Erkenntnisproblematik in der Literaturwissenschaft (Auszug)," pp. 155-162; collection of 16 brief excerpts: "Textbeispiele zur Geschichte der deutschen Philologie," covers 1865 to 1965. Index: names, subjects. Excellent, somewhat conservative introduction for the serious beginner.

219. Krauss, Werner. *Grundprobleme der Literaturwissenschaft. Zur Interpretation literarischer Werke. Mit einem Textanhang*. Reinbek: Rowohlt, 1968. 254pp.

A general introduction to literature, its definition and interpretation. Discusses genre, major components of literary works, various critical approaches (idealistic-materialistic, linguistic, national-comparative), problems of translation, literary history, etc. Not limited to German literature; examples also drawn from French and Spanish literature. Includes primary texts. Index: author and subject. Glossary of literary terms, pp. 237-242. Bibliography.

220. Kuhn, Hugo. "Germanistische Handbücher." *DVLG* 29 (1955), 122-130.

221. Newald, Richard. *Einführung in die Wissenschaft der deutschen Sprache und Literatur*. 2nd rev. ed. Lahr: Schauenburg, 1949. 227pp. ([1]1947)

Introduction to the study of German language and literature. List of terminology, pp. 161-227, covers a broad range of the discipline. Extensive bibliography in each section.

222. Ruttkowski, Wolfgang, and Eberhard Reichmann, eds. *Das Studium der deutschen Literatur. Eine Einführung für amerikanische Studierende.* Philadelphia: National Carl Schurz Foundation, 1974. vii, 227pp.

A compact, comprehensive introduction to the study of German literature. Chapters by various experts: (1) genre, basic concepts, (2) prosody, (3) style, structure, (4) outline history of German literature, (5) interpretation. Appendix: questions and exercises (by chapters), pp. 184-200. Index: texts cited (author A-Z); index of literary terminology (German, French, English) with page references to occurrence in the text, pp. 206-227. An excellent introduction, filled with useful, generally reliable information.

223. Stroh, Fritz. *Handbuch der germanischen Philologie.* Berlin: de Gruyter, 1952. xx, 820pp.

Compendium for the student. Includes a history of the discipline, pp. 38-165, material on folklore, culture, mythology, customs, ethics, law, art, settlements, etc. Primary and secondary literature covered, pp. 519-638.

224. Wehrli, Max. *Allgemeine Literaturwissenschaft.* 2nd ed. Bern: Francke, 1969. 168pp. (^{1}1951)

A general introduction to the discipline with critical appraisals of major contributions analyzed chronologically. Not a guide but an overview of research (not limited to German literature). Somewhat outdated but still useful for the beginner.

225. Zelewitz, Klaus. *Einführung in das literaturwissenschaftliche Arbeiten.* Stuttgart, Berlin, Cologne, Mainz: Kohlhammer, 1974. 137pp.

A compact handbook intended for the beginning university student. Material treated in 5 subject categories: 1. the primary text (first editions, critical composite editions, authorized editions, libraries, catalogues, etc.); 2. bibliography, research in primary and secondary material; 3. interpreting literature; 4. the form of the research paper; 5. supplementary material for the study of literature. Also discusses French and English literature studies at the German university. Bibliography, pp. 123-134. Index: subject. Glossary of abbreviations. Useful as a basic introduction.

B. BIBLIOGRAPHIES

1. Completed Bibliographies

*** *Bibliographisches Handbuch der deutschen Literaturwissenschaft 1945-1969* (No. 123): see section I. "Allgemeine Literatur-

wissenschaft. A. Theorie und Geschichte. B. Systematik der Literaturwissenschaft," and II. "Literatur und literarisches Leben." Selected cumulation of (No. 129) to 1969.
II: see section XII. "Deutschsprachige Literatur des 20. Jahrhunderts. D. Systematik der Literaturwissenschaft. E. Literatur und literarisches Leben. K. Deutsche Literaturwissenschaft nach dem 2. Weltkrieg." Selected cumulation of (No. 129) to 1972.

*** *Internationale Bibliographie zur Geschichte der deutschen Literatur* (No. 122) I: see section "Literaturwissenschaft. Literarische Wertung/Literaturkritik. Theorie der Literatur/Poetik." Selected cumulation to 1969. Marxist-socialist criticism well represented.

2. Current Bibliographies

*** *Bibliographie der deutschen Sprach- und Literaturwissenschaft* (No. 129): see section V. "Allgemeine Literaturwissenschaft. Theorie, Geschichte, Systematik. Ästhetik, Poetik. Rhetorik, Stilistik. Literatursoziologie. Literatur und Politik. Literarisches Leben." 1 (1945)-16 (1976)ff. Most reliable and comprehensive current bibliography available. Editions and secondary material listed. Publ. annually.

*** *Germanistik* (No. 130): see section XVII, "Allgemeines zur Literaturwissenschaft. Systematik und Methodenlehre--Periodisierung--Kategorien. Ästhetik, Wertung, Literaturkritik. Poetik: Allgemeines, Literaturtheorie. Literatur und Gesellschaft," 1 (1960)-17 (1976)ff. Comprehensive quarterly, up to date. Lists editions and secondary material, reviews books.

*** *MLA International Bibliography* (No. 125), I: see section "General Literature and Related Topics. 1. Esthetics. 2. Literary Criticism and Literary Theory."
II: see section "German Literature. 1. General and Miscellaneous. 2. Themes, Types, and Special Topics," 1921-1975ff. Annual cumulation. Lists editions and secondary material. Extensive and reliable.

*** *Referatendienst zur Literaturwissenschaft* (No. 131): see section "Literaturtheorie/Poetik. Funktion, Gegenstand und Methode der Literatur," 1 (1969)-6 (1975)ff. Marxist-socialist quarterly review of books. Limited in scope.

C. HISTORY OF CRITICISM

1. Literary Criticism to 1950

a. Forschungsberichte

226. May, Kurt. "Über die gegenwärtige Situation einer deutschen Literaturwissenschaft." *Trivium* 5 (1947), 293-303.

227. Storz, Gerhard. "Wendung zur Poetik. Ein Literaturbericht." *DU* 5 (1952), 69-83.

228. Majut, Rudolf. "Englische Arbeiten 1940-1951 zur deutschen Literaturgeschichte vom Realismus bis zur Gegenwart." *GRM, NF* 3 (1953), 38-50.

229. Seidler, Herbert. "Deutsche Dichtungswissenschaft in den letzten Jahren. 1946-1962." *DU* 15 (1963), 3, Beilage.

b. General Histories

230. Behrend, Fritz. *Geschichte der deutschen Philologie in Bildern. Eine Ergänzung zu dem Deutschen Literaturatlas von Könnecke-Behrend.* Marburg: Elwert, 1927. xii, 78pp.

Portraits of leading critics from Gottsched to Könnecke; sample pages of handwriting included.

231. Bruford, Walter Horace. *Literary Interpretation in Germany.* Cambridge: Cambridge Univ. Pr., 1952. 47pp.

Rather general assessment; takes the European context into account.

232. Cramer, Thomas, and Horst Wenzel, eds. *Literaturwissenschaft und Literaturgeschichte. Ein Lesebuch zur Fachgeschichte der Germanistik.* Munich: Fink, 1975. 510pp.

A collection of articles and excerpts from the writings of Gervinus, Scherer, Dilthey, Peterson, Schücking, Merker, Unger, Benjamin, Löwenthal, Cysarz, Kutzbach, Nadler, Muschg, Lukács, Viëtor, Wehrli, Wellek and Warren, W. Krauss, Hass, Sengle, Goldmann, Jauß, Weimann. Excellent choices for an overview.

233. Dünninger, Josef. "Geschichte der deutschen Philologie." *Dt. Phil. im Aufriß* (No. 1283), I, 83-222.

234. Bartel, Klaus J. *German Literary History 1777-1835. An Annotated Bibliography.* Bern, Frankfurt: Lang, 1976. 229pp.

Pt. 1 lists 44 literary histories; pt. 2 analyzes these (methodology, presentation of material). Appendices: 1. location of sources in US; 2. bibliography of works. Of very limited usefulness.

235. Frank, Horst Joachim. *Geschichte des Deutschunterrichts. Von den Anfängen bis 1945.* Munich: Hanser, 1973. 996pp.

A survey of the teaching of German and German literature from the beginnings in monastery schools, focusing on the 19th and 20th centuries and the achievements in this period. Indexes: names, places. Bibliography, pp. 966-981, extensive. Author wishes to provide historical background to the current discussions on future directions of the teaching of German.

236. Gress, Franz. *Germanistik und Politik. Kritische Beiträge zur Geschichte einer nationalen Wissenschaft.* Stuttgart-Bad Canstatt: Fromann, Holzboog, 1971. 184pp.

This examination of the relationships between German literary criticism and national politics includes brief analyses of the works of Scherer, Sauer, Nadler, and Hildebrand. Extensive bibliography, pp. 160-181.

237. Lempicki, Sigmund von. *Geschichte der deutschen Literaturwissenschaft bis zum Ende des 18. Jahrhunderts.* 2nd enl. ed. Göttingen: Vandenhoeck & Ruprecht, 1968. xii, 507pp. (^{1}1920)

Still the most important history of criticism from the Middle Ages to ca. 1816. Chronological table, pp. 492-507.

238. Mahrholz, Werner. *Literaturgeschichte und Literaturwissenschaft.* 2nd rev. and enl. ed. by Franz Schultz. Leipzig: Kröner, 1932. xi, 244pp. (^{1}1923)

A brief history of German literary criticism with focus on the literary histories and major editions. Chronological table, pp. 221-227. Appendix: F. Schultz, "Winke für das Studium der neueren deutschen Literaturgeschichte," pp. 228-237. Index: names.

239. Markwardt, Bruno. *Geschichte der deutschen Poetik.* 5 vols. Berlin: de Gruyter, 1937-1967.

I. *Barock und Frühaufklärung.* 1937. xii, 457pp.
II. *Aufklärung, Rokoko, Sturm und Drang.* 1956. vii, 692pp.
III. *Klassik und Romantik.* 1958. 730pp.
IV. *Das neunzehnte Jahrhundert.* 1959. vii, 750pp.
V. *Das zwanzigste Jahrhundert.* 1967. 1032pp.

A very readable summary of the views of literature of the major, and a large number of minor writers. These are extrapolated in detail from the writer's theoretical and literary works. Each writer's views and achievement are appraised and placed into the context of the times. Attempts to be objective; appraisal conservative. Each volume contains an extensive section of notes, an extensive, carefully subdivided index of concepts, catchwords and phrases, and index of names. This is a monumental work but in view of the broad range covered can serve only as an introduction to the views of any given writer. The index of concepts and catchwords is of particular value as a reference aid.

240. Marsch, Edgar, ed. *Über Literaturgeschichtsschreibung. Die historisierende Methode des 19. Jahrhunderts in Programm und Kritik.* Darmstadt: Wissenschaftliche Buchgesellschaft, 1975. xv, 508pp.

Introduction with brief historical survey. A good collection of 50 otherwise not easily accessible articles and excerpts by critics and authors 1708 to 1900. Material not limited to German literature. Indexes: names, subjects.

241. Milch, Werner. "Literaturkritik und Literaturgeschichte. Prolegomena zu einer Geschichte der Rezension." *GRM* 18 (1930), 1-15.

242. ———. "Die Anfänge der literarischen Kritik in Deutschland." *Zeitungswissenschaft* 6 (1931), 8-16.

Both essays also contained in: Milch, Werner. *Kleine Schriften zur Literatur- und Geistesgeschichte. Mit einem Nachwort von Max Rychner.* Ed. by Gerhard Burkhardt. Heidelberg, Darmstadt: Lambert Schneider, 1957, pp. 9-24 and 25-37.

243. Neumann, Friedrich. *Studien zur Geschichte der deutschen Philologie. Aus der Sicht eines alten Germanisten.* Berlin: Schmidt, 1971. 155pp.

A historical survey of German literary criticism from its beginnings to Wolfgang Kayser, with emphasis on 19th- and 20th-century critics. Author index.

244. Pollmann, Leo. *Literaturwissenschaft und Methode.* 2 vols. Frankfurt: Athenäum, 1971.

I. *Theoretischer Teil und Methodengeschichtlicher Überblick.* 164pp. Pt. 1: the nature and function of literature; pt. 2: the history of criticism (1800-1950). Bibliography, pp. 161-164.
II. *Gegenwartsbezogener systematisch-kritischer Teil.* 155pp. Appraisal of contemporary schools of criticism, including structuralism, New Criticism, sociological methods. Bibliography, pp. 138-141. Indexes for I, II: author, subject.

Both volumes are international in scope but emphasize the contribution of Romance scholarship.

245. Raumer, Rudolf von. *Geschichte der germanischen Philologie, vorzugsweise in Deutschland.* Munich: Oldenbourg, 1870. xii, 743pp.

Survey of literary criticism from the Reformation to the 1860's. Takes the European scene into account. A study of historical significance.

246. Salm, Peter. *Three Modes of Criticism. The Literary Theories of Scherer, Walzel, and Staiger.* Cleveland: The Press of Case Western Reserve Univ., 1968. xiv, 127pp.

A lucid, straightforward summary. One chapter on each critic with an ample bibliography at the end of each chapter. Index: names, subject.

247. Wellek, René. *A History of Modern Criticism: 1750-1950*. New Haven: Yale University Pr., 1955ff.

I. *The Later Eighteenth Century*. 1955, vii, 358pp.
II. *The Romantic Age*. 1955. v, 459pp.
III. *The Age of Transition*. 1965, xvi, 389pp.
IV. *The Later Nineteenth Century*. 1965, v, 671pp.
V. *The Twentieth Century*. (in prep.)

A compendious international history of criticism with excellent outline summaries of major critics. Each volume contains an extensive section: bibliography and notes (organized by chapters) and a brief chronological table of works (by countries). Indexes: names; topics and terms.

2. Literary Criticism since 1950

a. *Forschungsberichte*

248. Closs, August. "Forschungsbericht über Germanistik auf englischem Sprachgebiet." *Euphorion* 45 (1950), 249-256; 46 (1952), 217-223; 47 (1953), 421-430; 48 (1954), 466-471; 50 (1956), 428-442.

249. Bernd, Clifford. "Die Leistungen der amerikanischen neueren Germanistik während des letzten Jahrzehnts (1951-1961)." *Wirkendes Wort* 17 (1965), 343-350.

250. Daemmrich, Horst S. "Die Germanistik in den Vereinigten Staaten. Studium und Forschung." *Coll. Germ.* 3 (1969), 316-332.

b. *Bibliography*

251. Herfurth, Gisela, Jörg Hennig, Lutz Huth. *Topographie Germanistik. Standortsbestimmungen 1966-1971. Eine Bibliographie*. Berlin: Schmidt, 1971. 143pp.

A wide-ranging bibliography of materials pertinent to the recent re-examination of German studies in Germany and abroad. Sections are included on the universities, secondary schools, educational policy, symposia, etc. The bibliography includes newspaper articles and unpublished material.

c. *Assessments of Current Trends*

252. Demetz, Peter. "Zur Situation der Germanistik. Tradition und aktuelle Probleme." In: Durzak, Manfred, ed. *Die deutsche Literatur der Gegenwart. Aspekte und Tendenzen*. Stuttgart:

Reclam, 1971, pp. 322-336. (No. 805). Also in: Grimm, Reinhold, J. Hermand. *Methodenfragen* (No. 299), pp. 162-184.

253. Duroche, L.L. *Aspects of Criticism. Literary Study in Present-Day Germany*. The Hague, Paris: Mouton, 1967. 213pp.

An introduction, particularly well suited to English readers, to the tradition of literary criticism (academic and journalistic) in Germany and its differences from English criticism. Deals with major figures and currents in contemporary criticism but does not include Marxist-socialist approaches. Bibliography.

254. Hernadi, Paul. *Beyond Genre. New Directions in Literary Classification*. Ithaca, London: Cornell Univ. Pr., 1972. ix, 224pp.

Range: 19th century to the 1960's. An examination of some 60 critics. Chapters are arranged by subject. Lukács and Frye are afforded special attention but in most cases little more than a general statement of a critic's ideas is provided. A useful introduction. Index: author and subject. Bibliography, pp. 207-217.

255. Ingold, Felix Philipp, ed. *Literaturwissenschaft und Literaturkritik im 20. Jahrhundert*. Bern: Kandelaber, 1970. 186pp.

Five essays: Wehrli, "Deutsche Literaturwissenschaft"; Bosonnet, "Anglo-amerikanische Literaturkritik"; Kopp, "Französische Literaturwissenschaft"; Bonalumi, "Italienische Literaturkritik"; Ingold, "Sowjetische Literaturwissenschaft." Index: names. Extensive and carefully selected bibliography at the end of each section. Contributions on the whole excellent.

256. Jurgensen, Manfred. *Deutsche Literaturtheorie der Gegenwart. Georg Lukács, Hans Mayer, Emil Staiger, Fritz Strich*. Munich: Francke, 1973. 205pp.

An analysis of the methodology of four leading literary critics with particular attention to their theories of literature and history. A valuable introduction.

257. Klein, Albert, and Jochen Vogt. *Methoden der Literaturwissenschaft. 1: Literaturgeschichte und Interpretation*. Düsseldorf: Bertelsmann, 1971. 135pp.

A succinct survey of German literary criticism from the 19th century to the 1960's. Pp. 71-132: documentation and illustrations from German criticism. Index: authors; study questions. Socialist theories and the sociological approach to literature not included. Often a bit too brief in its descriptive part; definitions sparse.

258. Kolbe, Jürgen, ed. *Ansichten einer künftigen Germanistik*. 5th ed. Munich: Hanser, 1971. 224pp. ([1]1969)

16 essays on the status and trends of German studies. Discussions concerned with developments in Germany. Much of the

volume focuses on the need for reform and on the future direction of the discipline.

259. ———, ed. *Neue Ansichten einer künftigen Germanistik.* Munich: Hanser, 1973. 357pp.

15 essays on new directions in German literary studies. Focuses on the interrelationship between literature and sociology, linguistics, speech and communication. Individual essays give excellent insight into the current status of the discipline and its future. A sequel volume to the above.

260. Lange, Victor, ed. *Modern Literature II. Italian, Spanish, German, Russian, and Oriental Literature.* Englewood Cliffs, N.J.: Prentice Hall, 1968. ix, 297pp.

A brief commentary and analysis of US scholarship in German literature since the 1920's. Report by John R. Frey, pp. 123-183, is, however, too succinct to offer more than a broad overview.

261. Mulot, Arno. "Zur Neubesinnung der Literaturwissenschaft." *GRM NF* 1 (1950/51), 172-177.

262. Rüdiger, Horst. "Zwischen Interpretation und Geistesgeschichte. Zur gegenwärtigen Situation der deutschen Literaturwissenschaft." *Euphorion* 57 (1963), 227-244. Also in: Conrady, Karl Otto, *Einführung in die neuere deutsche Literaturwissenschaft* (No. 218), pp. 137-154, and in: R. Grimm, J. Hermand. *Methodenfragen* (No. 299), pp. 101-124.

D. AESTHETICS

1. Bibliographies

263. *Jahrbuch für Aesthetik und allgemeine Kunstwissenschaft* 1 (1951), 233-414. "Bibliographie für Aesthetik und allgemeine Kunstwissenschaft 1944-1949." 2 (1952/54), 191-200. "Bibliographie 1950." Not continued.

264. *Journal of Aesthetics and Art Criticism* 4 (1946)-31 (1973). "A Selective Current Bibliography for Aesthetics and Related Fields." Not continued.

2. Studies

265. Bense, Max. *Aesthetica. Metaphysische Beobachtungen am Schönen.* Stuttgart: Deutsche Verlags-Anstalt, 1954. 178pp.

Informal discussion of ca. 30 elements of aesthetics with focus on literary aspects. Good introduction.

266. Emrich, Wilhelm. "Zur Ästhetik der modernen Dichtung." *Akzente* 1 (1954), 371-387.

267. Henckmann, Wolfhart. "Ästhetik." *Handlexikon* (No. 1290), pp. 17-22.

268. Kainz, Friedrich. *Vorlesungen über Ästhetik*. Vienna: Sexl, 1948. 664pp.

English ed.: *Vorlesungen über Ästhetik. Aesthetics, the Science*. Trans. with an introduction by Herbert A. Schueller. Detroit: Wayne State Univ. Pr., 1962, xxx, 549pp. A general introduction to aesthetics (not confined to literature).

269. Markwardt, Bruno. "Geschmack." *Reallexikon* (No. 1288), I, 556-569.

270. Nohl, Hermann. *Die ästhetische Wirklichkeit. Eine Einführung*. Frankfurt: Schulte-Blumke, 1935. 216pp.

Introduction to aesthetics with specific reference to literary epochs; survey of aesthetics in German literary criticism.

271. Renner, Rolf Günter. "Schöne Literatur." *Die Literatur* (No. 1281), pp. 34-66.

272. Wehrli, Max. "Literatur und Ästhetik." *Reallexikon* (No. 1288), II, 79-82.

E. EVALUATION OF LITERATURE

273. Kayser, Wolfgang. "Vom Werten in der Dichtung." *Wirkendes Wort* 2 (1951-1952), 350-357. Pedagogical focus.

274. ———. "Literarische Wertung und Interpretation." *DU* 5 (1952), 13-27.

275. Kuhnert, Reinhard. "Die literarische Wertung." *Die Literatur* (No. 1281), pp. 417-431.

276. Müller-Seidel, Walter. *Probleme der literarischen Wertung. Über die Wissenschaftlichkeit eines unwissenschaftlichen Themas*. 2nd ed. Stuttgart: Metzler, 1969. xxi, 194pp. (^{1}1965)

Theoretical analysis of the problems of evaluative literary criticism. Thorough, provocative, and demanding treatment of a complex subject.

277. Schulte-Sasse, Jochen. *Literarische Wertung*. Stuttgart: Metzler, 1971. ix, 79pp.

A compact introduction to literary evaluation. Includes a historical survey but focuses on current problems and theories of evaluation. Bibliography at the end of each section of text. Indexes: author, subject.

F. STYLISTICS

278. Lausberg, Heinrich. *Handbuch der literarischen Rhetorik. Eine Grundlegung der Literaturwissenschaft.* Munich: Hueber, 1960. 957pp.

A comprehensive presentation of rhetoric from definition and history to individual techniques. Based on Latin and Greek sample material. II: *Registerband*, bibliography, pp. 605-638, terminology A-Z.

279. Michel, Georg, et al., eds. *Einführung in die Methodik der Stiluntersuchung. Ein Lehr- und Übungsbuch für Studierende.* Berlin: Volk und Wissen, 1968. 219pp.

A textbook with a concise introduction to the theory of stylistics and stylistic analysis, followed by numerous examples, study questions, and exercises. Specimens drawn mainly from GDR literature. Bibliography, pp. 215-219. Useful for self-study.

280. Reiners, Ludwig. *Stilkunst. Ein Lehrbuch deutscher Prosa.* Munich: Beck, 1961. xv, 784pp. ([1]1943)

A lively introduction to prose style with questions and exercises in the text. The 6 chapters cover a broad range of subjects from syntax to the use of wit and irony.

281. Seidler, Herbert. *Allgemeine Stilistik.* Göttingen: Vandenhoeck & Ruprecht, 1953. 366pp.

A thorough systematic discussion of major aspects of style with examples drawn from German literature. Clear definitions, helpful hints regarding interpretation, lucid presentation. Indexes: names, subjects.

282. Thieberger, Richard. "Stil." *Die Literatur* (No. 1281), pp. 250-263.

G. THEORY OF LITERATURE

283. Daemmrich, Horst S. *Literaturkritik in Theorie und Praxis.* Munich: Francke, 1974. 228pp.

Introduction to the study of literature, including an appraisal of various methods of criticism, clearly illustrated definitions of major literary terminology. Emphasis on the literary work as an intricate system of structural and thematic relationships, their tension and resolution. Index: authors; notes. An excellent introduction, clearly organized for easy access.

284. Hamburger, Käte. *Die Logik der Dichtung*. 2nd rev. ed. Stuttgart: Klett, 1968. 284pp. ([1]1957) English ed.: *The Logic of Literature*. 2nd rev. ed. trans. by Marilynn J. Rose. Bloomington, London: Indiana Univ. Pr., 1973. x, 369pp.

An elaboration of the logic of literature as the relationship of literature to the general system of language: 1. foundations in theory of language, 2. fictional or mimetic genres (epic, dramatic), 3. the lyric genre, 4. special forms (ballad, *Ich-Erzählung*), 5. the question of symbol in literature. Demanding reading; has become a standard work.

285. Ingarden, Roman. *Das literarische Kunstwerk. Mit einem Anhang von den Funktionen der Sprache im Theaterschauspiel*. Tübingen: Niemeyer, 1965. xxiii, 431pp. ([1]1931)

A phenomenology of the literary work: 1. mode of existence, definition; 2. aspects of structure and levels of meaning; 3. addenda, consequences, borderline cases, the life of the literary work, the ontological position of the literary work. A standard work of criticism which has been very influential on the development of literary aesthetics.

286. ———. *Vom Erkennen des literarischen Kunstwerks*. Tübingen: Niemeyer, 1968. 440pp. English ed.: *The Cognition of the Literary Work of Art*. Trans. by Ruth Ann Crowley and Kenneth R. Olson. Evanston: Northwestern Univ. Pr., 1973. xxx, 436pp.

An epistemological inquiry into the nature of the aesthetic experience of literature and the nature of a literary work. Basic reading for an understanding of current developments in criticism.

287. Kayser, Wolfgang. *Das sprachliche Kunstwerk. Eine Einführung in die Literaturwissenschaft*. 3rd ed. Bern: Francke, 1954. 444pp. ([1]1948)

A comprehensive, readable introduction to literary criticism which concentrates on the nature of the literary work of art as a linguistic structure. Pt. 1: basic concepts of analysis (content, prosody, linguistic forms, structure); pt. 2: basic concepts of synthesis (content, rhythm, style, genre structure). Indexes: author, subject. Bibliography, pp. 391-424. This has deservedly become a standard work.

288. Petersen, Julius. *Die Wissenschaft von der Dichtung. System und Methodenlehre der Literaturwissenschaft. Band 1. Werk und Dichtung*. 2nd ed. with material from the *Nachlaß*, ed. by Erich Trunz. Berlin: Junker & Dünnhaupt, 1944. xx, 663pp. ([1]1939; vol. 2 never published)

A comprehensive, lucid, and systematic presentation in four books (books 3 and 4 incomplete at time of author's death):

1. the work: tradition, text and author, analysis, interpretation and evaluation; 2. the poet: life, psychological life, creative process, poet's existence; 3. and 4. (fragmentary): synthetic criticism, genre history, types of poets, literary generations. Notes (by chapter), pp. 586-645. This work exerted great influence on the school of *Geistesgeschichte*.

289. Seidler, Herbert. *Die Dichtung. Wesen. Form, Dasein.* 2nd rev. ed. Stuttgart: Kröner, 1965. xii, 714pp. (^{1}1959)

A thorough discussion of all aspects of the literary work taking current research into account, and including evaluation: definition of literature, reality and man in literature, literature as form, the unfolding of poetic potential, literature in historical reality. Index: subject. Extensive bibliography organized by chapters, pp. 691-706.

290. Staiger, Emil. *Grundbegriffe der Poetik.* 8th ed. Zurich, Freiburg: Atlantis, 1968. 256pp. (^{1}1946)

A poetics grounded in the view that genre distinctions arise from the poet's temperament. 3 main chapters: lyrical style (recollection), epic style (imagination), dramatic style (tension), with an afterword on the development of the concept poetics. A standard work.

291. ———. "Die Kunst der Interpretation." *Neophilologus* 13 (1951), 1-15.

292. Wellek, René, and Austin Warren. *Theory of Literature.* 3rd ed. New York: Harcourt, Brace & World, 1962. 375pp. (^{1}1948)

An excellent presentation which assumes some knowledge of basic concepts and terminology. Takes previous scholarship and theory into account. International in scope. Contents: pt. 1: definitions and distinctions (nature of literature and literary criticism), pt. 2: preliminary operations (the ordering and establishing of evidence), pt. 3: extrinsic approach (via biography, psychology, society, ideas, other arts), pt. 4: intrinsic approach (mode of existence, euphony, rhythm, meter, style, image, literary genres, evaluation literary history). Extensive notes, pp. 273-313. Index: author-subject. Comprehensive bibliography, pp. 317-357. Standard work.

293. Walzel, Oskar. *Gehalt und Gestalt im Kunstwerk des Dichters.* Berlin-Neubabelberg: Athenaion, 1923. 408pp. illus.

Introduction to literature and its components. Indexes: names, subjects. An opulent volume. Fundamental for the method of *Geistesgeschichte*.

H. METHODOLOGY OF CRITICISM

294. Arnold, Heinz Ludwig, and Volker Sinemus, eds. *Grundzüge der Literatur- und Sprachwissenschaft*. I. *Literaturwissenschaft*. Munich: Deutscher Taschenbuch Verlag, 1973. 566pp. (^{3}1975)

An anthology of essays embracing 9 major areas of literary criticism. Including editing, methods of analysis, and popular literature; systematic, compact coverage with careful attention to definitions. Glossary of terms, pp. 459-502, excellent. Bibliography, pp. 503-553. A substantial presentation.

295. Burger, Heinz Otto. "Methodische Probleme der Interpretation." *GRM NF* 1 (1950/51), 81-92.

296. Bürger, Peter. *Theorie der Avantgarde*. Frankfurt: Suhrkamp, 1974. 138pp.

Four essays on the avantgarde and society with emphasis on Benjamin's theory of art and the Adorno-Lukács debate. Bibliography of titles cited.

297. Flemming, Willi. "Analyse und Synthese und die Funktion der Norm." *Studium Generale* 7 (1954), 352-363.

298. Glinz, Hans. *Textanalyse und Verstehenstheorie*. I: *Methodenbegründung, soziale Dimensionen, Wahrheitsfragen. 8 ausgeführte Beispiele*. Frankfurt: Athenäum, 1973. 325pp.

Textbook for the analysis of prose texts, primarily for students of literature, but the methodology is applicable to any prose text. Appendix: texts used, with commentary. Bibliography, pp. 319-322.

299. Grimm, Reinhold, and Jost Hermand, eds. *Methodenfragen der deutschen Literaturwissenschaft*. Darmstadt: Wissenschaftliche Buchgesellschaft, 1973. xi, 553pp.

An important collection of 23 essays published between 1955-1965 by specialists, reflecting the major methodological concerns in criticism; does not include material on linguistic, and structuralist methodology. Index: names.

300. Hass, Hans-Egon. "Literatur und Geschichte." *Neue Deutsche Hefte* 6 (1958-1959), 307-318. Also in: R. Grimm, J. Hermand, *Methodenfragen* (above), pp. 358-374.

301. Hauff, Jürgen, Albrecht Heller, Bernd Hüppauf, Lothar Köhn, Klaus-Peter Philippi. *Methodendiskussion*. 2 vols. Frankfurt: Athenäum, 1971. vii, 183pp.; 235pp.

A student handbook of methods and theories of literary criticism. Covers positivism, formalism, structuralism, hermeneutics, Marxist-socialist criticism. Each discussion is accompanied by definitions, example excerpts, questions, self-testing exercises. Index: author, II. Bibliography, I pp. 174-179, II pp. 219-227. Well organized, elementary introduction, valuable for its self-teaching aids.

302. Hermand, Jost. *Synthetisches Interpretieren. Zur Methodik der Literaturwissenschaft.* Munich: Nymphenburger Verlagsbuchhandlung, 1968. 269pp.

Pt. 1. "Methodenpluralismus seit 1900," is a historical survey of 7 recent approaches to literary criticism; pt. 2. "Möglichkeit einer neuen Synthese," proposes a new unified approach on the basis of a historical-dialectic method. Somewhat polemic but excellent for beginners. Author index.

303. ——— and Evelyn Torton Beck. *Interpretative Synthesis. The Task of Literary Scholarship.* New York: Ungar, 1975. vii, 232pp.

A revised and enlarged version of the above. Bibliography, pp. 221-224.

304. Kaiser, Herbert. *Materialien zur Theorie der Literaturdidaktik. Quellen- und Arbeitstexte mit einer kommentierenden Einleitung.* Munich: Fink, 1973. 361pp.

This extensive introduction, designed for students and teachers of German literature, analyzes hermeneutics, dialectics, and Marxist literary theory, and compares all three. A special section discusses teaching German literature. Pp. 141-339: primary texts by critics, authors, etc. Bibliography. Somewhat spotty in quality.

305. Kimpel, Dieter, and Beate Pinkerneil, eds. *Methodische Praxis der Literaturwissenschaft. Modelle der Interpretation.* Kronberg: Scriptor, 1975. x, 323pp.

Eight essays embracing criticism since 1967 deal with hermeneutics, Marxist-socialist and sociological criticism, reception of art, formalism, structuralism, semiotics. Each essay is comprised of 2 sections: 1. theory, methodology; 2. interpretations applying method outlined. Of uneven quality.

306. Maren-Grisebach, Manon. *Methoden der Literaturwissenschaft.* 2nd rev. ed. Munich: Francke, 1972. 117pp. (^{1}1970)

A succinct, clearly organized outline of terminology, assumptions, methods, and limitations of the basic approaches to literature: positivistic, intellectual-historical, phenomenological, existential, morphological, sociological, and statistical. Excellent for quick orientation with selected bibliography for each chapter, pp. 111-116, and notes, pp. 101-110.

307. Martini, Fritz. "Poetik." *Dt. Phil. im Aufriß* (No. 1283), I, 223-280.

308. Lunding, Erik. *Wege zur Kunstinterpretation.* Aarhus: Universitetsforlaget, 1952. 93pp.

A general survey in 4 parts: "Das Verstehen der Dichtung als Dichtung," "Interpretation," "Wege zur Kunstinterpretation," "Ausblick." Commentary on problems inherent in genre. Not a methodology.

309. ———. *Strömungen und Strebungen der modernen Literaturwissenschaft*. Copenhagen: Munksgaard, 1952. 89pp.

A superb appraisal of recent methodologies.

310. Oppel, Horst. "Methodenlehre der Literaturwissenschaft." *Dt. Phil. im Aufriß* (No. 1283), I, 39-82.

311. Sengle, Friedrich. "Zur Einheit von Literaturgeschichte und Literaturkritik," *DVLG* 34 (1960), 327-337. Also in: R. Grimm, J. Hermand. *Methodenfragen* (No. 299), pp. 47-61.

312. ———. "Aufgaben und Schwierigkeiten der heutigen Literaturgeschichtsschreibung. Ein Vortrag." *Archiv für das Studium der neueren Sprachen und Literaturen* 200 (1963), 241-264. Also in: R. Grimm, J. Hermand. *Methodenfragen* (No. 299), pp. 375-401.

313. Söring, Jürgen. *Literaturgeschichte und Theorie. Ein kategorialer Grundriß*. Stuttgart, Berlin, Cologne, Mainz: Kohlhammer, 1976. 188pp.

A theoretical introduction to the problems and the writing of literary history. Numerous philosophies and methodologies are examined. Too compact and encyclopedic for the beginner. Bibliography, pp. 181-188; extensive notes.

314. Wehrli, Max. "Zum Problem der Historie in der Literaturwissenschaft." *Trivium* 7 (1949), 44-59. Argues for the retention of history in literary criticism.

315. Žmegač, Viktor, ed. *Methoden der deutschen Literaturwissenschaft. Eine Dokumentation*. Frankfurt: Athenäum, 1971. 383pp.

A collection of 24 essays on German literary criticism during the last 100 years. Focuses on the pluralistic aspects of criticism; includes essays by Scherer, Walzel, Spitzer, Unger, Muschg, Müller, Staiger, Viëtor, Curtius, Kuhn, Weimann, among others. Index: names, subjects; bibliography. An important anthology.

316. ———, and Zdenko Škreb, eds. *Zur Kritik literaturwissenschaftlicher Methodologie*. Frankfurt: Athenäum Fischer Taschenbuchverlag, 1973. 293pp.

A collection of 11 historical-critical appraisals by leading literary critics of positivism, *Geistesgeschichte*, interdisciplinary approaches, formalism, structuralism, New Criticism, and psychoanalytic, materialistic, linguistic, and sociological methodologies. Indexes: author, subject. A good introduction to the complexities of literary theory.

I. METHODOLOGIES

1. Geistesgeschichte

317. Böckman, Paul. "Von den Aufgaben einer geisteswissenschaftlichen Literaturbetrachtung." *DVLG* 9 (1931), 448-471.

318. Cysarz, Herbert. *Literaturgeschichte als Geistesgeschichte. Kritik und System.* Halle/Saale: Niemeyer, 1926. 304pp.

Extensive, somewhat unwieldy introduction; appendix, pp. 264-304: "Hauptfragen einer geisteswissenschaftlichen Dramaturgie."

319. Ermatinger, Emil. "Zeitstil und Persönlichkeitsstil." *DVLG* 4 (1926), 615-650.

320. Haeckel, Hanns. "Das Problem von Wesen, Möglichkeiten und Grenzen des Verstehens für den Literaturhistoriker." *DVLG* 27 (1953), 431-447.

321. Kluckhohn, Paul. "Geistesgeschichte." *Reallexikon* (No. 1288), I, 537-540.

322. Petersen, Julius. *Literaturgeschichte als Wissenschaft.* Heidelberg: Winter, 1914. 71pp. A concise lecture.

*** ———. *Die Wissenschaft von der Dichtung. System und Methodenlehre der Literaturwissenschaft. Band 1. Werk und Dichtung.* Berlin: Junker & Dünnhaupt, 1944. xx, 663pp. (No. 288)

323. Richter, Werner. "Strömungen und Stimmungen in den Literaturwissenschaften von heute." *Germanic Review* 21 (1946), 81-113. An assessment of the state of literary criticism and *Geistesgeschichte*.

324. Unger, Rudolf. "Literaturgeschichte und Geistesgeschichte." *DVLG* 4 (1926), 177-192. Also in:

325. ———. *Aufsätze zur Prinzipienlehre der Literaturgeschichte. Gesammelte Schriften, I.* Berlin: Dunker & Dünnhaupt, 1929. 231pp. A collection of 9 essays published 1908-1926.

326. Viëtor, Karl. "Deutsche Literaturgeschichte als Geistesgeschichte. Ein Rückblick." *PMLA* 60 (1945), 899-916. A superb review of the method.

327. Walzel, Oskar. *Die wechselseitige Erhellung der Künste. Ein Beitrag zur Würdigung kunstgeschichtlicher Begriffe.* Berlin: Reuther & Reichard, 1917. 92pp. A lecture on the use of art and art history in literary criticism; fundamental for comparative art criticism.

*** ———. *Gehalt und Gestalt im Kunstwerk des Dichters.* Berlin-Neubabelberg: Athenaion, 1923. 408pp. (No. 293)

328. Wiese, Benno von. "Zur Kritik des geistesgeschichtlichen Epochenbegriffes." *DVLG* 11 (1933), 130-144.

329. ———. "Geistesgeschichte oder Interpretation? Bemerkungen zur Lage der zeitgenössichen deutschen Literaturwissenschaft." In: *Die Wissenschaft von deutscher Sprache und Dichtung. Methoden, Probleme, Aufgaben. Festschrift für Friedrich Maurer.* Stuttgart: Klett, 1963, pp. 239-261. Also in: R. Grimm, J. Hermand. *Methodenfragen* (No. 299), pp. 79-100.

2. Existentialist Criticism

330. Dehn, Fritz. "Existentielle Literaturwissenschaft als Entscheidung." *Dichtung und Volkstum* 38 (1937), 29-43.

331. ———. "Anmerkungen zur Frage einer existentiellen Literaturbetrachtung." *Orbis litterarum* 13 (1958), Suppl. 2, 48-58.

332. Oppel, Horst. "Kierkegaard und die existentielle Literaturwissenschaft." *Dichtung und Volkstum* 38 (1937), 18-29.

333. Lunding, Erik. *Adalbert Stifter. Mit einem Anhang über Kierkegaard und die existentielle Literaturwissenschaft.* Copenhagen: Nyt nordisk forlag, 1946. 163pp. Appendix, pp. 133-150.

A compact assessment of existential methodology and ideology.

334. Pfeiffer, Johannes. "Zu Heideggers Deutung der Dichtung." *DU* 5 (1952), 57-68.

335. Pongs, Hermann. "Neue Aufgaben der Literaturwissenschaft." *Dichtung und Volkstum* 38 (1937), 1-17.

3. Phenomenological Criticism

*** Ingarden, Roman. *Das literarische Kunstwerk. Mit einem Anhang von den Funktionen der Sprache im Theaterschauspiel.* Tübingen: Niemeyer, 1965. xxiii, 431pp. (No. 285)

*** ———. *Vom Erkennen des literarischen Kunstwerks.* Tübingen: Niemeyer, 1968. 440pp. (No. 286)

336. Konstantinović, Zoran. *Phänomenologie und Literaturwissenschaft. Skizzen zu einer wissenschaftstheoretischen Begründung.* Munich: Kist, 1973. 245pp.

An introduction to various schools of literary phenomenology. Pursues the examination of the relation between phenomenology and literature. Includes a discussion of Marxism and phenomenology. Indexes: author, subject; notes.

337. Szondi, Peter. "Über philologische Erkenntnis." *Die Neue Rundschau* 73 (1962), 146-165. Also in: R. Grimm, J. Hermand. *Methodenfragen* (No. 299), pp. 232-254.

338. ———. "Zur Erkenntnisproblematik in der Literaturwissenschaft." *Die Neue Rundschau* 73 (1962), 146-165. In abbreviated form in: Karl Otto Conrady, *Einführung in die neuere deutsche Literaturwissenschaft* (No. 218), pp. 155-162.

339. Wolff, Ernst Georg. *Ästhetik der Dichtkunst. Systematik auf erkenntniskritischer Grundlage.* Zurich: Schulthess, 1944. vii, 671pp.

Presentation somewhat cumbersome and inaccessible.

4. Psychological Criticism

a. Forschungsbericht

340. Goldstein, Melvin. "Literature and Psychology 1948-1968. A Commentary." *Literature and Psychology* 17 (1967), 159-176.

b. Bibliographies

341. *Literature and Psychology* 1 (1951)-23 (1972). "Current Bibliography."

342. Kiell, Norman. *Psychoanalysis. Psychology and Literature. A Bibliography.* Madison: Univ. of Wisconsin Pr., 1963. v, 225pp. Lists 4460 titles.

c. Studies

343. Beutin, Wolfgang, ed. *Literatur und Psychoanalyse. Ansätze zu einer psychoanalytischen Textinterpretation. Dreizehn Aufsätze.* Munich: Nymphenburger Verlagshandlung, 1972. 320pp.

A collection of essays by specialists including Rank, Sachs, Jung, Freud, Hoffmann, Lesser. Index: author and subject. Bibliography, pp. 300-314 for 1913-1957.

344. Cremerius, Johannes. *Neurose und Genialität.* Frankfurt: Fischer, 1971. 291pp.

Extensive bibliography, "Verzeichnis der internationalen psychoanalytisch-biographischen Publikationen von 1907 bis 1960," pp. 275-289. Lists sections on authors, painters and sculptors, composers, politicians, religious leaders, scholars.

345. Groeben, Norbert. *Literaturpsychologie. Literaturwissenschaft zwischen Hermeneutik und Empirie.* Stuttgart, Cologne, Mainz: Kohlhammer, 1972. 269pp.

Excellent, thorough coverage, including the psychology of creativity, reception, and interpretation. Index: author, subject. Glossary. Bibliography, pp. 222-242.

346. Kaplan, Morton, and Robert Kloss. *The Unspoken Motive. A Guide to Psychoanalytic Criticism.* New York: The Free Press, 1973. xi, 323pp.

Pt. 1: introduction to the major elements of theory; pt. 2: 6 essays on psychoanalytic criticism and application of theory; pt. 3: historical and critical review of leading psychoanalytical critics. Appendix: "The Dissenting Schools." Index: names, subjects. Bibliography, pp. 281-286. A sound basic introduction with illustrations drawn from world literature.

347. Matt, Peter von. *Literaturwissenschaft und Psychoanalyse. Eine Einführung.* Freiburg: Rombach, 1972. 114pp.

This series of lectures held at the University of Zurich provides a good basic introduction to the fundamentals of psychoanalytical interpretation. Copious analyses and brief examples are included. Indexes: names, subjects; notes.

348. Muschg, Walter. "Psychoanalyse und Literaturwissenschaft." In: W.M., *Pamphlet und Bekenntnis.* Olten, Freiburg: Walter, 1968, pp. 111-135. ([1]1930)

349. Schrey, Gisela. *Literaturästhetik der Psychoanalyse und ihre Rezeption in der deutschen Germanistik vor 1933.* Frankfurt: Athenaion, 1975. 188pp.

Three-part survey: 1. psychoanalysis and literature; 2. literary criticism and psychoanalysis; 3. developments after 1945 (very brief). Bibliography, pp. 177-188. A solid history.

350. Urban, Bernd, ed. *Psychoanalyse und Literaturwissenschaft. Texte zur Geschichte ihrer Beziehungen.* Tübingen: Niemeyer, 1973. xlvi, 299pp.

A collection of 12 important contributions to this field published 1909-1933, including articles by Stekel, Reik, Jung, Walzel, Muschg, and Pongs. Indexes: author, subject. Bibliography for further reading, pp. 262-272.

5. Morphological Criticism

351. Böckmann, Paul. *Formgeschichte der deutschen Dichtung. I. Von der Sinnbildsprache zur Ausdruckssprache. Der Wandel der literarischen Formensprache vom Mittelalter zur Neuzeit.* Hamburg: Hoffmann & Campe, 1949. xvi, 700pp.

Range: 1150-1785 (courtly epic to Storm and Stress). Not a descriptive literary history but a series of studies applying a morphological approach. The characteristic stance of each epoch is determined and the literary forms which gave it expression are shown to be symptomatic. Demanding reading.

352. ———. "Die Interpretation der literarischen Formensprache." *Studium Generale* 7 (1954), 341-351.

353. Friedmann, Hermann. *Die Welt der Formen. System eines morphologischen Idealismus.* 2nd rev. and enl. ed. Munich: Beck, 1930. xxii, 519pp. ([1]1925)

An outline philosophical basis for morphology which takes full account of earlier work. No direct application to literature. Interesting reading for the advanced student.

*** Müller, Günther. *Geschichte des deutschen Liedes vom Zeitalter des Barock bis zur Gegenwart.* Munich: Drei Masken, 1925. x, 335pp. (No. 1221)

354. ———. "Über die Seinsweise von Dichtung." *DVLG* 17 (1939), 137-152.

355. ———. "Morphologische Poetik," *Hélicon* 5 (1943), 1-22.

356. ———. *Die Gestaltfrage in der Literaturwissenschaft und Goethes Morphologie.* Halle: Niemeyer, 1944. 84pp. Also in:

357. ———. *Morphologische Poetik. Gesammelte Aufsätze.* Ed. by Elena Müller. Tubingen: Niemeyer, 1968, pp. 146-224. Volume contains a reprinting of 18 essays.

358. Oppel, Horst. *Die Literaturwissenschaft in der Gegenwart. Methodologie und Wissenschaftslehre.* Stuttgart: Metzler, 1939. xvi, 182pp.

A critical history of literary theory with emphasis on phenomenological and existential views. Indexes: names, concepts.

359. ———. *Morphologische Literaturwissenschaft. Goethes Ansicht und Methode.* Mainz: Kirchheim, 1947. 120pp. (Repr. 1967)

Based on Goethe's tenets of morphology with focus on the idea of *Gestalt*, unity, and metamorphosis. A critical attempt is made to define the limits of this approach.

*** Viëtor, Karl. *Geschichte der deutschen Ode.* Munich: Drei Masken, 1923. vii, 198pp. (No. 1247)

6. National Socialist Criticism

360. Bartels, Adolf. *Geschichte der deutschen Literatur.* 2 vols. Leipzig: Avenarius, 1901-1902. ([19]1943)

Chronological survey of German literature. Evaluation of literature based on racial criteria. Important document for the aesthetics of National Socialist criticism. Treats a large number of minor figures.

361. Conrady, Karl Otto. "Deutsche Literatur und Drittes Reich." In: *Nationalismus in Germanistik und Dichtung. Dokumentation des Germanistentages in München vom 17. - 22. Oktober 1966.* Ed. by Benno von Wiese and Rudolf Heuß. Berlin: Schmidt, 1967, pp. 37-60.

362. Geißler, Rolf. "Form und Methoden der nationalsozialistischen Literaturkritik." *Neophilologus* 51 (1967), 262-277.

363. Gilman, Sander L. *NS-Literaturtheorie. Eine Dokumentation. Mit einer Einleitung von Cornelius Schnauber.* Frankfurt: Athenäum, 1971. xxii, 264pp.

A collection of 23 articles and excerpts from the period. 1. literary theory: a. ethnic perspective (Nadler, Langenbucher, Kindermann), b. racial perspective (Alt, Petersen, Büttner), c. existential perspective (Pongs, Dahn, Oppel); 2. the genres (Wanderscheck, Kolbenheyer, Wähler); 3. the re-appraisal of German literature. These essays, together with the compact introduction, provide a good overview of the period.

*** Ketelsen, Uwe-K. *Völkisch-nationale und nationalsozialistische Literatur in Deutschland 1890-1945.* Stuttgart: Metzler, 1976. ix, 116pp. (No. 781)

364. Kluckhohn, Paul. "Die konservative Revolution in der Dichtung der Gegenwart." *Zeitschrift für deutsche Bildung* 9 (1933), 177-190.

365. Koch, Franz. "Der Weg zur volkhaften Dichtung der Gegenwart." *Zeitschrift für Deutschkunde* 51 (1937), 1-14 and 98-113.

*** Nadler, Josef. *Literaturgeschichte des deutschen Volkes. Dichtung und Schrifttum der deutschen Stämme und Landschaften.* 4th rev. ed. 4 vols. Berlin: Propyläen, 1938-1941. ([1]1912-1918) (No. 438)

366. Vondung, Klaus. *Völkisch-nationale und nationalsozialistische Literaturtheorie.* Munich: List, 1973. 247pp.

Pt. 1. Anthology of original texts, pp. 25-102; pt. 2. survey of research and criticism during the period 1933-1945 and the reevaluation after 1945. Short biographies, pp. 214-225. Index: names. Bibliography, pp. 220-241. An interesting introduction.

7. Sociological Criticism

a. Bibliographies

367. Becker, Eva D. and Manfred Dehn. *Literarisches Leben. Eine Bibliographie. Auswahlverzeichnis von Literatur zum deutschsprachigen literarischen Leben von der Mitte des 18. Jahrhunderts bis zur Gegenwart.* Hamburg: Verlag für Buchmarkt-Forschung, 1968. 254pp.

A selected bibliography in 5 parts including sections covering the influences on the creation of a literary work, its distribution, reception, literary public, and selection (by publishing houses, libraries, critics). Detailed descriptions, sometimes with annotations. Does not include titles on individual works. Appendix: references. Indexes: author, subject.

368. Carter, Paul J., and George K. Smart. *Literature and Society 1961-1965. A Selective Bibliography.* Coral Gables, Fla.: Univ. of Miami Pr., 1967. vii, 160pp.

Contains 691 annotated titles of articles and books. Selection based on *MLA International Bibliography* (No. 125). Subject index.

369. Duncan, Hugh Dalziel. *Language and Literature in Society. A Sociological Essay on Theory and Method in the Interpretation of Linguistic Symbols, with a Bibliographical Guide to the Sociology of Literature.* Chicago: Univ. of Chicago Pr., 1953. xv, 262pp. Bibliography, pp. 141-214, mainly English titles.

b. Studies

370. Bark, Joachim, ed. *Literatursoziologie.* Stuttgart, Cologne, Berlin, Mainz: Kohlhammer, 1974. 2 vols.

I. *Begriff und Methodik.* 170pp. A representative collection of 13 previously published essays which are intended to demonstrate the many-faceted sociological view of literature; includes essays by P. Stöcklein, T. Adorno, U. Jaeggi, L. Goldmann, H.N. Fügen.

II. *Beiträge zur Praxis.* 195pp. 11 essays focusing on literature, society, and economics. Includes 5 essays of interpretation.

371. Burns, Elisabeth and Tom Burns, eds. *Sociology of Literature and Drama. Selected Readings.* Harmondsworth, Middlesex: Penguin, 1973. 506pp.

An anthology of 33 essays previously published by internationally known scholars and writers. Topics are divided into 4 sections: 1. the social perspective, 2. the critical perspective, 3. the fictive and the social world, 4. social processes and individual strategies, 5. readers and audiences. Index: author. Bibliography, pp. 489-497. This collection is of excellent quality.

372. Braem, Helmut M. "Der Autor." *Die Literatur* (No. 1281), pp. 115-145.

Includes sections: "Abriß der Sozialgeschichte des Autors," "Akademien--Dichterkreise--Interessenverbände," "Literaturpreise," and "Schutz geistigen Eigentums."

373. Fügen, Hans Norbert. *Die Hauptrichtungen der Literatursoziologie und ihre Methoden. Ein Beitrag zur literatursoziologischen Theorie.* 2nd ed. Bonn: Bouvier, 1966. viii, 215pp.

Four introductory essays on the interdependence and application of sociology and literary criticism. An examination of Marxist criticism is included. Somewhat outdated but still useful as an introduction. Bibliography, pp. 193-215.

374. ———. *Wege der Literatursoziologie*. Neuwied am Rhein, Berlin: Luchterhand, 1968. 479pp.

26 essays on literature and sociology covering a broad range of background material such as sociological literary criticism on the 19th century, Marxist criticism, the role and status of the author, reception of literary works, the role of institutions. The essays, mostly by eminent scholars, provide basic background for current discussions of these topics. Indexes: author, subject. Bibliography, pp. 439-451.

375. Hauser, Arnold. *Sozialgeschichte der Kunst und Literatur*. 2 vols. Munich: Beck, 1953. xi, 536pp.; viii, 586pp. (Repr. in one vol. 1969) English ed.: *The Social History of Art*. Trans. in collaboration with the author by Stanley Godman. New York: Knopf, 1951. 2 vols. 1022pp.; New York: Vintage, 1958. 4 vols.

History of the arts from an anthropological and sociological point of view. Contents (Vintage ed.): 1. Prehistoric to Middle Ages; 2. Renaissance to Baroque; 3. Rococo, Classicism, Romanticism; 4. Naturalism to the Film Age. Bibliographical information in footnotes. Good outline history, though at times too general.

376. ———. *Soziologie der Kunst*. Munich: Beck, 1974. xvi, 818pp.

An in-depth treatment of art from the sociological perspective, beginning with the materialistic aesthetics of Marx and Engels and including the relationship between art and society, dialectics, author and reading public, etc. Excellent introduction to the whole school of thought. No bibliography.

377. Kuhn, Hugo. "Dichtungswissenschaft und Soziologie." *Studium Generale* 3 (1950), 622-626.

378. Kuttenkeuler, Wolfgand, ed. *Poesie und Politik. Zur Situation der Literatur in Deutschland*. Stuttgart, Berlin, Cologne, Mainz: Kohlhammer, 1973. 410pp.

Pt. 1: 11 essays by specialists on various aspects of literature and politics in all three genres ranging from literature as a mass medium to the literary situation in the GDR. Pt. 2: specimen texts, pp. 284-403. Index: authors. Bibliography. Of uneven quality.

379. *Literaturwissenschaft und Sozialwissenschaften. Grundlagen und Modellanalysen. Mit Beiträgen von Horst Albert Glaser, Peter Hahn, Olaf Hansen, Helmut Hartwig, Thomas W.H. Metscher, G. Karin Pallowski, Michael Pehlke, Bernd Jürgen Warneken*. Stuttgart: Metzler, 1971. 448pp.

8 essays treating Hegel, modern theories of literature and sociology, the relationship of art to ideology, documentary art, the situation of art in the US, the proletarian theater. Bibliography, pp. 435-448.

380. Philippi, Klaus-Peter. "Methodologische Probleme der Literatursoziologie. Kritische Bemerkungen zu einer fragwürdigen Situation." *Wirkendes Wort* 20 (1970), 217-230. Also in: R. Grimm, J. Hermand. *Methodenfragen* (No. 299), pp. 508-530.

381. Ragotzky, Hedda. "Literatursoziologie." *Handlexikon* (No. 1290), pp. 266-270.

382. Schücking, Levin Ludwig. "Literaturgeschichte und Geschmacksgeschichte." *GRM* 5 (1913), 561-577.

383. ———. *Die Soziologie der literarischen Geschmacksbildung.* Munich: Rösl, 1923. 151pp. English ed.: *The Sociology of Literary Taste.* Trans. by E.W. Dickes. New York: Oxford Univ. Pr., 1945. v, 78pp.

A compact examination of the extra-literary influences on literature: contemporary taste, sociological forces, social position of writer, etc. Somewhat outdated but one of the first treatments of the subject.

384. Strelka, Joseph. *Die gelenkten Musen. Dichtung und Gesellschaft.* Vienna, Frankfurt, Zurich: Europa, 1971. 414pp.

A broad, detailed introduction to a sociology of literature: 1. origins of the literary work (the artist, reading public, historical and social milieu); 2. aspects of the work (content, structure, form, style); 3. the effect of the work (reception, literary influence, aspects of evaluation). Material is not limited to German literature but is international in scope. Index: author; notes. A valuable contribution to the field.

8. Marxist Criticism

385. Bogdal, Klaus-Michael, Burkhardt Lindner, Gerhard Plumpe, eds. *Arbeitsfeld. Materialistische Literaturtheorie. Beiträge zu ihrer Gegenstandsbestimmung.* Wiesbaden: Athenaion, 1975. 287pp.

8 essays on literary theory and avantgarde literature with the focus generally on Lasalle, Mehring, and Brecht. Contributes little new material to the field. Useful annotated bibliography, pp. 269-285.

386. Demetz, Peter. *Marx, Engels und die Dichter. Zur Grundlagenforschung des Marxismus.* Stuttgart: Deutsche Verlags-Anstalt, 1959. 342pp. illus. English ed.: *Marx, Engels, and the Poets. Origins of Marxist Literary Criticism.* Rev. and enl. by the author and trans. by Jeffrey L. Sammons. Chicago, London: Univ. of Chicago Pr., 1967. x, 278pp.

Excellent examination of the beginnings of "Marxist-socialist" criticism in the 19th century, focusing on Marx and Engels. Bibliography (international), pp. 319-332. Index: names.

387. ———. "Wandlungen der marxistischen Literaturkritik: Hans Mayer, Ernst Fischer, Lucien Goldmann." In: Wolfgang Paulsen, ed. *Der Dichter und seine Zeit. Politik im Spiegel der Literatur. 3. Amherster Kolloquium zur modernen deutschen Literatur 1969.* Heidelberg: Stiehm, 1970, pp. 13-32.

388. Goldmann, Lucien. "Dialektischer Materialismus und Literaturgeschichte." *Die neue Rundschau* 75 (1964), 214-229. Also in: R. Grimm, J. Hermand. *Methodenfragen* (No. 299), pp. 487-507.

389. LeRoy, Gaylord C., and Ursula Beitz, eds. *Preserve and Create. Essays in Marxist Literary Criticism.* New York: Humanities Pr., 1973. iv, 276pp.

A collection of 13 essays previously published by Marxist critics. Pt. 1: current directions of Marxist criticism, theory of modernism; pt. 2: humanism and late capitalism; pt. 3: revolutionary-socialist literature. Index: names. A substantial introduction to Marxist criticism by eminent GDR and Soviet critics.

390. Lukács, Georg. *Schriften zur Literatursoziologie.* Ed. by Peter Ludz. Neuwied: Luchterhand, 1961. 568pp.

A collection of 30 previously published essays (1909-1956); bibliography of Lukács' writings and secondary material, pp. 503-531, containing 425 items. Indexes: names, subjects. An important collection.

391. Maren-Grisebach, Manon. *Theorie und Praxis literarischer Wertung.* Munich: Francke, 1974. 126pp.

A brief presentation of Marxist and National Socialist systems of literary evaluation and a comparison of the two. Clearly organized into compact subsections. Excellent introduction to the field. Notes.

392. Simons, Elisabeth. "Nächste Aufgabe der Literaturgeschichtsschreibung in der Deutschen Demokratischen Republik." *Einheit* 19 (1964), 72-86.

393. Vassen, Florian. *Methoden der Literaturwissenschaft II. Marxistische Literaturtheorie und Literatursoziologie.* Dusseldorf: Bertelsmann, 1972. 186pp.

A compact introduction for students. Contains abundant specimen texts (pp. 63-165) for analysis. Somewhat too encyclopedic to serve as more than a first introduction. Index: authors. Study questions (pp. 178-184). Bibliography.

394. Weiland, Werner. "Materialistische Literaturwissenschaft." *Handlexikon* (No. 1290), pp. 281-286.

395. Weimann, Robert. *Literaturgeschichte und Mythologie. Methodologische und historische Studien.* Berlin, Weimar: Aufbau, 1974. 515pp.

Previously published essays reprinted here in revised form offer critical appraisals of the possibilities and limitations of literary history from a Marxist point of view. Very clearly formulated and presented, with emphasis on English studies. Appendix: summary of theories: "Past Significance and Present Meaning in Literary History," pp. 431-452. Index: names.

396. Žmegač, Viktor, ed. *Marxistische Literaturkritik.* Bad Homburg: Athenäum, 1970. 441pp.

20 previously published essays by leading Marxist scholars and theorists on the methodology and practice of Marxist literary criticism. Focuses on the multi-faceted aspects of Marxist criticism.

397. *Zur Theorie des sozialistischen Realismus.* Ed. by the Institut für Gesellschaftswissenschaften beim ZK der SED. 2nd ed. Berlin: Dietz, 1975. 913pp.

A collection of 13 essays by a single author or by a collective, which provides an overview of the nature, principal concerns, theory and methodologies of socialist realism. Includes a survey of socialist realism in the GDR, Marxist-Leninist theory concerning the artist and artistic technique, the function and effect of socialist art, the theory of artistic progress, the unity of socialist art, ideology and art, art in the GDR and the world. This anthology is invaluable for its official definition and explication of socialist art.

9. Literary Reception

398. Grimm, Günther, ed. *Literatur und Leser. Theorien und Modelle zur Rezeption literarischer Werke.* Stuttgart: Reclam, 1975. 444pp.

A collection of 14 essays on the theory and methodology of literary reception. Pt. 1: survey of research to 1973, aspects of theory; pt. 2: practical application of method to literary texts ranging from medieval to 20th-century popular literature. Attention given to the pedagogical application of the methodology. Index: names. Extensive bibliography, pp. 343-358.

399. Hohendahl, Peter Uwe. *Literaturkritik und Öffentlichkeit.* Munich: Piper, 1974. 235pp.

A collection of previously published essays on Heine's criticism of Romanticism, the criticism of Young Germany, criticism in the age of the mass media, the production and the reception of the best seller. Focuses on the impact of literary criticism on the reading public, the relationship between literary criticism and mass media, and the phenomenon of the best seller. Outstanding volume.

400. ———, ed. *Sozialgeschichte und Wirkungsästhetik. Dokumente zur empirischen und marxistischen Rezeptionsforschung*. Frankfurt: Athenäum, 1974. 310pp.

A collection of 13 essays on the various methodologies, theories, and problems of literary reception. Focus on the most recent developments. Index: names. Bibliography, pp. 297-301. Excellent introduction.

401. Jauß, Hans Robert. *Literaturgeschichte als Provokation*. Frankfurt: Suhrkamp, 1970. 251pp.

A collection of revised, previously published essays. A basic volume for the recently established critical method of the reception of literature, and the social and aesthetic impact of a literary work of art. Particularly important is essay 4: "Literaturgeschichte als Provokation der Literaturwissenschaft," which elaborates 7 major theses of the new direction of criticism. Notes.

402. Klein, Ulrich. "Rezeption." *Handlexikon* (No. 1290), pp. 409-413.

403. Link, Hannelore. *Rezeptionsforschung. Eine Einführung in Methoden und Probleme*. Stuttgart, Berlin, Cologne, Mainz: Kohlhammer, 1976. 186pp.

An examination of the relationship between the work of art, its author and its reader. Includes an introduction to written communication, research, theoretical models, and various schools of thought. Index: author. Bibliography, pp. 172-180. Excellent as a first introduction.

404. Naumann, Manfred, et al. *Gesellschaft, Literatur, Lesen. Literaturrezeption in theoretischer Sicht*. Berlin, Weimar: Aufbau, 1973. 584pp.

A close analysis of literary reception and aesthetics from a Marxist-socialist point of view; description of major schools of criticism in East and West; problems of reading and the reader; 3 practical demonstrations; the productive function of literature. Extensive and clearly presented theoretical discussion. Index: author; notes.

10. Literature and the Arts

a. Bibliography

405. *Bibliography on the Relations of Literature and the Other Arts 1952-1967*. Ed. Modern Language Association. New York: AMS, 1968. Pagination varies.

A selective checklist: 1. theory and general, 2. music and literature, 3. visual arts and literature. Sections 2 and 3 chronologically arranged. Lack of indexes makes access to contents difficult.

b. Studies

406. Bebermeyer, Gustav. "Literatur und bildende Kunst." *Reallexikon* (No. 1288), II, pp. 82-103.

407. Berger, Kurt. "Die Dichtung im Zusammenhang der Künste." *DVLG* 21 (1943), 229-251.

408. Hermand, Jost. *Literaturwissenschaft und Kunstwissenschaft. Methodische Wechselbeziehungen seit 1900.* Stuttgart: Metzler, 1965. 76pp.

A very compact historical outline of the interrelationships between literary and art criticism from 1900 to the 1960's. Each chapter clearly organized and subdivided. Abundant bibliographical references at the end of each subsection. Index: names.

409. Ingarden, Roman. *Untersuchungen zur Ontologie der Kunst. Musikwerk, Bild, Architektur, Film.* Tübingen: Niemeyer, 1962. ix, 341pp.

Examination from a phenomenological point of view. Little on the interrelationships of art and literature. Of limited use.

410. Just, Klaus Günther. "Musik und Dichtung." *Dt. Phil. im Aufriß* (No. 1283), III, 699-750.

411. Martini, Fritz. "Literatur und Film." *Reallexikon* (No. 1288), II, 103-111.

412. Reichert, Georg. "Literatur und Musik." *Reallexikon* (No. 1288), II, 143-163.

413. ———. "Oper." *Reallexikon* (No. 1288), II, 767-781.

414. Staiger, Emil. *Musik und Dichtung.* 3rd ed. Zurich: Atlantis, 1966. 138pp. (^{1}1947)

Collection of 6 lectures and 1 essay on Bach, Gluck, Goethe, and Mozart, Romanticism in literature and music, *Rosenkavalier*, Schoeck, Honegger. Of limited, general interest.

415. Stammler, Wolfgang. "Schrifttum und Bildkunst im deutschen Mittelalter." *Dt. Phil. im Aufriß* (No. 1283), III, 613-698.

416. Wais, Kurt. *Symbiose der Künste. Forschungsgrundlagen zur Wechselberührung zwischen Dichtung, Bild- und Tonkunst.* Stuttgart: Kohlhammer, 1936. 35pp.

Lecture on various approaches to the study of the interrelationships of the arts. Still valuable for its succinct delineation of methodologies.

11. Literature and Other Disciplines

a. *Bibliographies*

417. Dudley, Fred A., ed. *The Relations of Literature and Science. A Select Bibliography 1930-1949.* Washington: Pullman, 1949. 59pp. Lists 647 titles. Continued as:

418. "Relations of Literature and Science. Selected Bibliography for 1950ff." *Symposium* 5 (1951)-21 (1967). Not continued.

b. *Studies*

419. Emrich, Berthold. "Literatur und Geschichte." *Reallexikon* (No. 1288), II, 111-142.

420. Hoppe, Karl. "Philosophie und Dichtung." *Dt. Phil. im Aufriß* (No. 1283), III, 751-1098.

421. Ihwe, Jens, ed. *Literaturwissenschaft und Linguistik. Eine Auswahl zur Theorie der Literaturwissenschaft. Ergebnisse und Perspektiven.* 3 vols. in 4 pts. Frankfurt: Athenäum, 1971-1972.

     I. *Grundlagen und Voraussetzungen.* xiv, 387pp.
     II. *Zur linguistischen Basis der Literatur* I, pts. 1 and 2. xiv, 616pp.
     III. *Zur linguistischen Basis der Literatur* II. 474pp.

     A collection of 61 essays by international experts on structuralism, transformational grammar, linguistic and literary theory, theory of verse, prosody, semantics, etc. Index: subject, III. Wide-ranging, demanding introduction. Excellent survey of research to the 1970's.

422. Kanzog, Klaus. "Literatur und Recht." *Reallexikon* (No. 1288), II, 164-195.

423. Kreuzer, Helmut, and Rul Gunzenhäuser, eds. *Mathematik und Dichtung. Versuche zur Frage einer exakten Literaturwissenschaft.* 3rd ed. Munich: Nymphenburger Verlagshandlung, 1970. 363pp. ([1]1965)

     21 essays by eminent scholars on the use of such procedures as mathematical linguistics, statistics, etc. for the analysis of literary texts. Bibliography pp. 347-357. Somewhat demanding for the beginner.

424. Zeltner, Hermann. "Philosophie und Dichtung." *Reallexikon* (No. 1288), III, 83-103.

VII.

History of German Literature

CONTENTS

A. SURVEYS OF GERMAN LITERATURE

For a more comprehensive listing see Arnold, Robert F., *Allgemeine Bücherkunde* (No. 100), pp. 111-119.

1. Surveys of Interest to Literary Historians

Although the following histories have been superseded by subsequent scholarship, they are included here because of their historical significance. The date to the left is that of the first edition.

425. *1827* Koberstein, August. *Grundriß der Geschichte der deutschen Nationalliteratur*. 5th rev. ed. Karl Bartsch, ed. 5 vols. Leipzig: Vogel, 1872-1873. (Repr. 1974)

426. *1835-1842* Gervinus, Georg Gottfried. *Geschichte der poetischen National-Literatur der Deutschen*. 5 vols. Leipzig: Engelmann. 5th rev. ed. Karl Bartsch, ed., under the title *Geschichte der deutschen Dichtung*. 5 vols. Leipzig: Engelmann, 1871-1874.

427. *1839-1840* Laube, Heinrich. *Geschichte der deutschen Literatur*. 4 vols. Stuttgart: Hallberger, 1839-1840.

428. *1845* Vilmar, August Friedrich Christian. *Vorlesungen über die Geschichte der deutschen Nationalliteratur*. 2nd ed. Marburg: Elwert, 1847. x, 714pp. 3rd enl. ed.: *Geschichte der deutschen Nationalliteratur*. 2 vols. Marburg: Elwert, 1848. xvi, 888pp. (^{13}1870)

429. *1851-1859* Kurz, Heinrich. *Geschichte der deutschen Literatur mit ausgewählten Stücken aus den Werken der vorzüglichsten Schriftsteller*. 8th ed. 4 vols. Leipzig: Teubner, 1887-1894.

430. *1854-1856* Cholevius, Johannes Carl Leo. *Geschichte der deutschen Poesie nach ihren antiken Elementen*. 2 vols. Leipzig: Brockhaus, 1854-1856.

431. *1857* Eichendorff, Joseph von. *Geschichte der poetischen Literatur Deutschlands*. 2 vols. Paderborn: Schöningh, 1857.

432. *1901-1902* Bartels, Adolf. *Geschichte der deutschen Literatur.* 2 vols. Leipzig: Avenarius, ^{19}1943.

433. *1937* Koch, Franz. *Geschichte deutscher Dichtung.* Hamburg: Hanseatische Verlagsanstalt, 1937. 362pp.

434. *1941* Fricke, Gerhard, Franz Koch, and Klemens Lugowski, eds. *Von deutscher Art in Sprache und Dichtung.* 5 vols. Stuttgart, Berlin: Kohlhammer, 1941.

I. Maurer, Friedrich, ed. *Die Sprache.* ix, 222pp.
II. Hoefler, Otto, ed. "Frühzeit" and Wolff, Ludwig, ed. "Mittelalterliche Dichtung." 319pp.
III. Quint, Josef, ed. "Durchbruch deutscher Glaubenskräfte" and Wiese, Benno von, ed. "Bildungsdichtung und ihr Gegenspiel." 269pp.
IV. Obenauer, Karl Justus, ed., "Die schöpferische Selbstverwirklichung in der Goethezeit" and Kindermann, Heinz, ed. "Gefährdung und Selbstbehauptung im Kampf um die Wirklichkeit." 435pp.
V. Koch, Franz, ed. "Dichtungsformen" and "Mächte und Ideen." 467pp.

2. Surveys of General Interest

The date to the left is that of the first edition.

435. *1883* Scherer, Wilhelm. *Geschichte der deutschen Literatur.* Berlin: Knaur, n.d. 831pp.

Range: Earliest records of Germanic literature--Goethe's death. This prestigious work is the prototype of histories of German literature. Strict positivistic approach: particular emphasis on Germanic literature, Middle High German literature, and Goethe. Trans. by Mrs. F.C. Conybeare, ed. by F. Max Müller 2 vols. New York: Scribners, 1899.

436. *1899-1937* Nagl, Johann Willibald, Jakob Zeidler, and Eduard Castle, eds. *Deutsch-österreichische Literaturgeschichte. Ein Handbuch zur Geschichte der Dichtung in Österreich-Ungarn.* 4 vols. Vienna: Fromme, 1899-1937. illus.

Range: Beginnings to 1918. Positivistic approach. A huge, valuable literary history of Austria containing extensive summaries of individual works.

437. *1902* Robertson, J.G. *A History of German Literature.* 6th ed. by Dorothy Reich with the assistance of W.I. Lucas, M. O'C. Walshe, and James Lynn. Edinburgh, London: Blackwood, 1970. xviii, 817pp.

Range: Gothic period--German drama of the 1960's. Positivistic approach: strict chronological organization with excellent summaries of individual works. Works often inadequately integrated into their epoch. Cue-words in margin facilitate quick reference. Extensive bibliography. Chronological table relates development of German history and literature to the European scene.

438. *1912-1918* Nadler, Josef. *Literaturgeschichte des deutschen Volkes. Dichtung und Schrifttum der deutschen Stämme und Landschaften.* 4th rev. ed. 4 vols. Berlin: Propyläen, 1938-1941.

I. *Volk (800-1740).* xxii, 710pp.
II. *Geist (1740-1813).* xviii, 687pp.
III. *Staat (1814-1914).* xvi, 707pp.
IV. *Reich (1914-1940).* xviii, 689pp.

Ethno-geographic approach: reader should be mindful of the biases inherent in a history of literature in terms of authors' regional and ancestral origins. Contains abundant material on regional minor poets usually not treated in literary histories. Richly illustrated. Extensively indexed.

439. *1932* Nadler, Josef. *Literaturgeschichte der deutschen Schweiz.* Leipzig, Zurich: Grethlein, 1932. 542pp.

Range: 800-1930. Chronological survey of literature, organized geographically. No analysis of works. Despite rather biased point of view, useful for its wealth of descriptive detail.

440. *1934-1935* Stockum, Theodor Cornelius van, and Jan van Dam. *Geschichte der deutschen Literatur.* 2 vols. Groningen: J.B. Wolters. (^{3}1961)

I. *Von den Anfängen bis zum 18. Jahrhundert.* xii, 315pp.
II. *Vom 18. Jahrhundert bis zur Gegenwart.* viii, 343pp.

An historical survey emphasizing the social, economic, and philosophical background. Individual authors viewed as reflecting the intellectual climate of their period. Clearly organized, often too compact. Indexes: author, title.

441. *1946* Boesch, Bruno, ed. *Deutsche Literatur in Grundzügen. Die Epochen deutscher Dichtung in Darstellungen von L. Beriger (u.a.).* 3rd rev. ed. Bern, Munich: Francke, 1967. 500pp.

Range: Old High German literature--contemporary literature. Chronological surveys of German literature with emphasis on masterpieces. No analyses of literary works. Orientation that of intellectual history. Contents: H. Rupp, "Die Literatur der Karolingerzeit" and "Die Literatur bis zum Beginn der höfischen Dichtung (900-1170)"; F. Ranke, "Die höfisch-ritterliche Dichtung (1160-1250)"; B. Boesch, "Die Literatur des Spätmittelalters (1250-1500)"; L. Beriger, "Das Zeitalter des Humanismus und der Reformation"; G. Weydt, "Barock"; M. Wehrli, "Das Zeitalter der Aufklärung"; W. Kohlschmidt, "Sturm und Drang," "Die Klassik," and "Die Romantik"; K. Fehr, "Der Realismus (1830-1885)"; A. Bettex, "Die moderne Literatur (von 1885 bis zur Gegenwart)." Brief bibliography follows each essay. Indexes: author, subject. Too compact for a beginner.

442. *1948* Friedrich, Werner P., with the collaboration of Oskar Seidlin and Philipp A. Shelley. *History of German Literature*. 2nd ed. New York: Barnes & Noble, 1961. vi, 356pp. College Outline Series.

Range: Old High German Literature--contemporary literature. Designed as a reference work. Introduces discussions of epochs with outline of European developments. Summaries often too sketchy, labelling too rigid. Each chapter followed by a bibliography of translations. A chronological table relates German history and literature to Western literature. Contains extensive bibliography.

443. *1948* Muschg, Walter. *Tragische Literaturgeschichte*. 3rd rev. ed. Bern: Francke, 1957. 639pp.

Not a literary history but an examination of the artist and his outer and inner world. Divided according to major themes. Conclusions reached are subjective. Index: names. Not meant as an introduction.

444. *1948* Nadler, Josef. *Literaturgeschichte Österreichs*. Linz: Österreichischer Verlag für Belletristik und Wissenschaft, 1948. 516pp.

Range: ca. 1000 to 1918. A strictly chronological survey with emphasis on Austrian contributions to German literature. Bibliography, pp. 482-502.

445. *1949* Fricke, Gerhard. *Geschichte der deutschen Literatur*. 3rd ed. Basel: Schwabe, 1951. 391pp.

Range: Old High German--Expressionism. Excellent orientation for the beginner. Does not attempt to incorporate most recent scholarship. Most detailed treatment: nineteenth-century realism and literature after the turn of the century. Discussion of early German literature very brief.

446. *1949* Martini, Fritz. *Deutsche Literaturgeschichte von den Anfängen bis zur Gegenwart*. 15th ed. Stuttgart: Kröner, 1968. 697pp.

Range: Old High German literature--contemporary literature. A most useful introduction. See especially the treatment of the 18th and 19th centuries. Somewhat challenging stylistically for undergraduates. Contains extensive bibliography.

447. *1949-1950* Schneider, Hermann. *Geschichte der deutschen Dichtung. Nach ihren Epochen dargestellt*. 2 vols. Bonn: Athenäum. I, 1949. Pp. 1-347; II, 1950. Pp. 348-776.

Range: Beginnings--ca. 1914. Divides the history of literature into 12 thematic periods with special emphasis on two "classical" periods (MHG, Classicism). Little discussion of 20th century. Conservative, intellectual-historical approach. The focus is on epochs rather than individual works. Of little use to a beginner. Extensive bibliography in II.

*** *1951* Hauser, Arnold. *Sozialgeschichte der Kunst und Literatur.* 2 vols. Munich: Beck, 1953. xi, 536pp.; viii, 586pp. (Repr. in 1 vol. 1969) English ed.: *The Social History of Art.* Trans. in collaboration with the author by Stanley Godman. New York: Knopf, 1951. 2 vols. 1022pp.; New York: Vintage, 1958. 4 vols. (see No. 375)

448. *1952* *Annalen der deutschen Literatur. Eine Gemeinschaft zahlreicher Fachgelehrter.* Ed. by Heinz Otto Burger. 2nd rev. ed. Stuttgart: Metzler, 1971. 838pp.

Range: 2000 B.C.--1900 A.D. Strictly chronological survey of major works, which are summarized briefly. Information on individual poets is dispersed and thus not readily accessible. Contents: Felix Genzmer, "Vorgeschichte und frühgeschichtliche Zeit (2000-770)" pp. 1-36; Helmut de Boor, "Von der Karolingischen zur Cluniazensischen Periode (770-1170)," pp. 37-97; Hugo Kuhn, "Die Klassik des Rittertums in der Stauferzeit (1170-1230)," pp. 99-177; Friedrich Ranke, "Von der ritterlichen zur bürgerlichen Dichtung (1230-1430)," pp. 179-253; Siegfried Beyschlag, "Städte, Höfe, Gelehrte (1430-1490)," pp. 255-286; Richard Newald, "Humanismus und Reformation (1490-1600)," pp. 287-338; Willi Flemming, "Das Jahrhundert des Barock (1600-1700)," pp. 339-404; Fritz Martini, "Von der Aufklärung zum Sturm und Drang (1700-1775)," pp. 405-463; Wolfdietrich Rasch, "Die Zeit der Klassik und frühen Romantik (1775-1805)," pp. 465-550; Wolfgang Baumgart, "Die Zeit des alten Goethe (1805-1832)," pp. 551-619; Heinz Otto Burger, "Der plurale Realismus des 19. Jahrhunderts (1832-1888)," pp. 621-718; Karl Riha, "Naturalismus und Antinaturalismus (1889-1900)," pp. 719-760. Chronological table by Kurt Halbach, pp. 761-810. An excellent survey of the various epochs and developments within them, including philosophy and the fine arts.

449. *1953* Grabert, Willy, and Arno Mulot. *Geschichte der deutschen Literatur.* Munich: Bayrischer Schulbuch Verlag, ^{13}1969. 497pp.

Range: Beginnings--1950. A chronological textbook history providing concise definitions of periods, summaries of major works, text specimens, and illustrations. Excellent for beginners. Annotated glossary of works.

450. *1960* Rose, Ernst A. *A History of German Literature.* New York: New York Univ. Pr., 1960. xiii, 353pp.

Range: Origins of German culture--20th century (disassociative and surrealistic style). Intended as an introduction for students of European culture. Little or no concentration on individual authors. Despite its summary (dogmatic) approach, valuable for quick orientation in philosophical and aesthetic trends. Select bibliography of translations appended.

451. *1964* Mann, Otto. *Deutsche Literaturgeschichte. Von der germanischen Dichtung bis zur Gegenwart.* Gütersloh: Bertelsmann, 1964. 639pp.

Range: Old High German literature--contemporary literature. A readable general introduction with emphasis on intellectual currents before 1900. Treatment of 20th-century literature extremely conservative with strong Christian orientation.

452. *1965* Geerdts, Hans Jürgen, ed. *Deutsche Literaturgeschichte in einem Band*. Berlin: Volk und Wissen, [4]1970. 768pp.

Range: 750-1964. A chronological survey using the Marxist-socialist approach; periods seen against historical and socialist background, important figures are analyzed in detail. Emphasis in the treatment of the 20th century is on GDR literature. A solid general introduction, except for the section on the 20th century.

453. *1966-1969* Ritchie, James M., ed. *Periods in German Literature*. 2 vols. London: Wolff. I, 1966. viii, 320pp.; II, *Texts and Contexts*, 1969. x, 266pp.

I. A collection of 12 essays: R.B. Farrell, "Problems of Periods and Movements"; J.H. Tisch-Wackernagel, "Baroque"; R.H. Samuel, "Rococo"; J.D. Stowell, "Enlightenment and Storm and Stress"; R.B. Farrell, "Classicism"; L. Ryan, "Romanticism"; M.J. Norst, "Biedermeier"; J.M. Ritchie, "Realism"; G. Schulz, "Naturalism"; B. Coghlan, "The Turn of the Century"; H. Maclean, "Expressionism"; R. Livingstone, "German Literature from 1945." Indexes: author and subject, titles. Limited bibliographies at the end of each chapter. Outstanding introduction for beginner.
II. For each movement, a representative work is chosen and analyzed in terms of the whole period: Grimmelshausen, Wieland, Lessing, Lenz, Goethe, Novalis, Stifter, Fontane, Holz and Schlaf, T. Mann, Kaiser. Short bibliographies at the end of each section. Analyses on the whole excellent.

454. *1968* Kranz, Gisbert. *Europas christliche Literatur von 500 bis 1500*. Munich, Paderborn, Vienna: Schöningh, 1968. 525pp.

A chronological history divided according to genre and centered about major figures of the era. Although focus is on religious writings, secular literature is included. Chronological table: title, author, language, pp. 448-451; Indexes: subject, names. Extensive bibliography, pp. 452-501.

455. *1968* ———. *Europas christliche Literatur von 1500 bis heute*. 2nd enl. ed. Munich, Paderborn, Vienna: Schöningh, 1968. 656pp.

A chronological survey of authors who wrote from a Christian point of view. Chronological tables: works, pp. 539-543; authors, pp. 544-548. Indexes: subjects, names. Extensive bibliography, pp. 550-634.

456. *1971* Boesch, Bruno, ed. *German Literature. A Critical Survey*. Trans. Ronald Taylor. London: Methuen, 1971. vii, 375pp.

Range: 800-1940's. 12 essays on major epochs in German literature. Approaches to interpretation vary. Individual works seldom analyzed. Indexes: names, subject; bibliography.

457. *1971* Daemmrich, Horst S., and Diether H. Haenicke, eds. *The Challenge of German Literature*. Detroit: Wayne State Univ. Pr., 1971. 432pp.

Range: Middle High German literature to contemporary literature. Storm and Stress not covered. Addressed to the beginning student: specific works are analyzed to show the development of individual authors and to integrate them in their era. See especially: chapters on Classicism, Impressionism and Expressionism, and literature after 1933. Also includes the chapters: "The Establishment of Standard Modern Literary German"; "The Eighteenth Century: Foundation and Development of Literary Criticism."

458. *1971* Garland, Henry B. *Concise Survey of German Literature*. Coral Gables: Univ. of Miami Pr., 1971. 125pp.

Range: 700-1960's. Thumbnail sketch. Index: author and subject. No analysis of literary works. Too encyclopedic: names, works, dates.

459. *1972* Salzer, Anselm, and Eduard von Trunk. *Geschichte der deutschen Literatur in 3 Bänden*. 3rd enl. ed. Zurich: Stauffacher, 1972. (^{1}1912)

I. *Von den Anfängen bis zum Sturm und Drang*. 596pp. illus.
II. *Von der Klassik bis zum Naturalismus*. 655pp. illus.
III. *Das 20. Jahrhundert*. 605pp. illus.

An attractive, richly illustrated historical survey of major authors and works; some summaries included. Indexes: III, author and subject. Of value to the general reader.

460. *1974* Magill, Charles P. *German Literature*. London, Oxford, New York: Oxford Univ. Pr., 1974. 190pp.

Range: 12th century--1970's. A very compact outline with little general literary history or background; touches only upon major works; focus is on the 18th and 19th centuries, other periods being unevenly treated. Too brief even for the general reader. Bibliography, pp. 179-184. Quotations are in English.

461. *1974* Weimar, Karl S., ed. *German Language and Literature. Seven Essays*. Englewood Cliffs: Prentice-Hall, 1974. xii, 367pp.

Range: 4th century B.C.--1966. Essays vary in approach and quality. Focus is on major figures: the German language (Moulton), German literature to Goethe (Schulz-Behrend), the age of Goethe (Leppmann), Hölderlin (Hamburger), the Romantics (Weimar), realism (Stern), modern German literature 1900-1966 (Klarmann). Many text specimens with English translation. Bibliographies at the end of each section; annotated bibliography, pp. 355-359. Index: author and subject. A solid introduction for the general reader.

B. MEDIEVAL LITERATURE (770-1480)

1. Forschungsberichte

462. Frings, Theodor. "Erforschung des Mittelalters." *Beiträge zur Geschichte der deutschen Sprache und Literatur, Halle,* 87 (1965), 1-39; first published in *Forschungen und Fortschritt* 26 (1950), 9-16 and 39-43.

463. Kuhn, Hugo. "Vom neuen Bild des Mittelalters." *DVLG* 24 (1950), 530-544.

464. Horacek, Blanka. "Zur Dichtung der mittelhochdeutschen Blütezeit." *Wissenschaft und Weltbild* 7 (1954), 153-158 and 227-229.

465. Ruh, Kurt. "Altdeutsche Mystik." *Wirkendes Wort* 7 (1956/57), 135-146 and 212-231.

466. Fischer, Hanns. "Neue Forschungen zur deutschen Dichtung des Spätmittelalters (1230-1500)." *DVLG* 31 (1957), 303-345.

467. ———. "Probleme und Aufgaben der Literaturforschung zum deutschen Spätmittelalter." *GRM* 40, NF 9 (1959), 217-227.

468. Rupp, Heinz. "Neue Forschung zu Form und Bau mittelalterlicher Dichtung." *DU* 11 (1959), 2, 117-124.

469. ———. "Forschung zur althochdeutschen Literatur. 1945-1962." *DVLG* 38 (1964), Sonderheft, 1-67.

470. ———. *Forschung zur althochdeutschen Literatur. 1945-1962.* Stuttgart: Metzler, 1965. 77pp.

471. Fischer, John H., ed. *The Medieval Literature of Western Europe. A Review of Research, Mainly 1930-1960.* New York, London: New York Univ. Pr., 1966. xvi, 432pp.

Resource book: survey of recent scholarship in the areas of Latin, Old English, French, German, Old Norse, Italian, Spanish, Catalan, Portuguese, Celtic literatures. See: W.T.H. Jackson, "Medieval German Literature," pp. 191-254: detailed evaluation of literary histories, treatment of genres and authors. Covers secondary and primary material.

472. Messerer, Wilhelm. "Der Stil in der karolingischen Kunst. Zum Stand der Forschung." *DVLG* 41 (1967), 117-166.

473. Janota, Johannes. "Neue Forschungen zur deutschen Dichtung des Spätmittelalters (1230-1500). 1957-1968." *DVLG* 45 (1971), Sonderheft, 1-242.

474. Naumann, Heinrich. "Mittellateinische Literatur. Forschungsbericht." *Wirkendes Wort* 21 (1971), 343-350.

2. Bibliographies

a. Completed Bibliographies

475. Batts, Michael. *Hohes Mittelalter.* Bern, Munich: Francke, 1969. 112pp.

A brief, easily accessible guide to text editions and research on the period, with emphasis on publications from 1950-1965: general, pre-courtly, courtly, late courtly literature. Index: author, subject.

*** *Bibliographisches Handbuch der deutschen Literaturwissenschaft 1945-1969.* (No. 123), I: see section V. "Mittelalter." Selected cumulation of (No. 129) to 1969.

*** *Internationale Bibliographie zur Geschichte der deutschen Literatur* (No. 122), I: see sections "Deutsche Literatur von den Anfängen bis 1050," "Deutsche Literatur von 1050 bis 1160," "Deutsche Literatur von 1160 bis 1230," and "Deutsche Literatur von 1230 bis 1480." Selected cumulation to 1967. Marxist-socialist scholarship well represented.

476. Jones, George F. *Spätes Mittelalter (1300-1450).* Bern, Munich: Francke, 1971. 124pp.

Pt. 1: general material, history, the arts, language, literary history; pt. 2: didactic poetry; pt. 3: narrative prose; pt. 4: drama; pt. 5: lyric poetry; pt. 6: prose. For author entries, editions and secondary literature listed. Indexes: author and title, subject. A handy volume for quick reference.

477. Kratz, Henry. *Frühes Mittelalter. Vor- und Frühgeschichte des deutschen Schrifttums.* Bern, Munich: Francke, 1970. 287pp.

Range: Indo-European period to Latin Middle Ages; covers research to 1965. Pt. 1: Indo-European, the Germanic tribes from the beginnings to the Old High German period; pt. 2: Old High German period. Editions and secondary literature listed. Indexes: author, subject. Particularly noteworthy: bibliography of Middle Latin literature in Germany during the OHG period, pp. 210-225. An excellent and very handy compilation.

478. Maurer, Friedrich, et al. "Bibliographie zur deutschen Philologie." *Archiv für das Studium der neueren Sprachen* 193 (1956/57)-195 (1958/59). Bibliography mainly to the end of the Middle Ages.

b. Current Bibliographies

*** *Bibliographie der deutschen Sprach- und Literaturwissenschaft* (No. 129): see section IX. "Mittelalter," 1 (1945-1953)-16 (1976)ff. Most reliable and comprehensive current bibliography available. Editions and secondary literature. Publ. annually.

*** *Germanistik* (No. 130): see section XXII. "Von den Anfängen bis zum Beginn der höfischen Dichtung (770-1170)." XXIII. "Hochmittelalter (1170-1250)," and XXXIV. "Spätmittelalter (1250-1450)," 1 (1960)-17 (1976)ff. Comprehensive quarterly, generally up to date. Editions and secondary material. Books are reviewed.

*** *MLA International Bibliography* (No. 125): see section "German Literature. III. Literature before 1500," 1921-1975ff. Annual cumulation. Editions and secondary material. Extensive and generally reliable.

*** *Referatendienst zur Literaturwissenschaft* (No. 131): see section "Allgemeine und vergleichende Literaturgeschichte" and "Geschichte der Nationalliteraturen. Deutsche Literatur," 1 (1969)-6 (1975)ff. Marxist-socialist quarterly review of books. Limited in scope.

*** *The Year's Work in Modern Language Studies* (No. 127): see section "Medieval Literature," 1 (1930)-37 (1975)ff. Covers primary and secondary publications for the previous year. Annotated.

3. Literary Histories

a. Entire Period (770-1480)

479. Ehrismann, Gustav. *Geschichte der deutschen Literatur bis zum Ausgang des Mittelalters*. 2 parts in 4 vols. Munich: Beck, 1918-1935.

Range: Old High German period to late Middle Ages. Introduction to Old High German literature (pt. 1) and Middle High German literature (pt. 2). Early Middle Ages (pt. 2, I), high Middle Ages (pt. 2, II, III), late Middle Ages (pt. 2, III). Subject-author index in each volume. Clearly organized text with extensive bibliography. Indispensable.

*** Genzmer, Felix, Helmut de Boor, Hugo Kuhn, Friedrich Ranke, Siegfried Beyschlag. *Geschichte der deutschen Literatur von den Anfängen bis zum Ende des Spätmittelalters (1490)*. Stuttgart: Metzler, 1962. viii, 294pp. Identical to No. 448, pp. 1-286.

480. Golther, Wolfgang. *Die deutsche Dichtung im Mittelalter. 800 bis 1500*. 2nd ed. Stuttgart: Metzler, 1922. iii, 572pp.

A survey organized by genre and divided into 4 chapters covering Old High German, early Middle High German, and Middle High German literature, and the literature of the 14th and 15th centuries. Reflects the research of its day. Often provides little more than plot summaries. Some centuries completely neglected. Index: names, subjects.

481. Jackson, William Thomas Hobdell. *The Literature of the Middle Ages*. New York: Columbia Univ. Pr., 1960. xiii, 432pp.

An introductory history of 12th and 13th-century literature, with its focus on German and French contributions. Chapters include discussions on influences, the audience, romance, *chanson de geste*, Germanic epic, lyric, drama, beast epic. Solid analyses.

482. Salmon, Paul. *Literature in Medieval Germany*. New York: Barnes & Noble, 1968. xxi, 284pp.

Range: 8th-15th century. A compact first introduction for the general reader. Emphasis is on major works. Contains plot summaries. All examples translated. Extensive bibliography, pp. 171-267, with focus on materials in English translation. An excellent introduction for those who do not read German.

483. Schmitt, Ludwig Erich, ed. *Kurzer Grundriß der germanischen Philologie bis 1500*. 3 vols. Berlin: de Gruyter, 1970ff.

I. *Sprachgeschichte*. 1970. x, 440pp.
Range: beginnings to ca. 1500. Well organized, extremely reliable and informative essays on the Germanic family of languages: F. Coetsen, "Zur Entwicklung der germanischen Grundsprache"; J.W. Marchand, "Gotisch"; H. Kuhn, "Altnordisch"; H. Pilch, "Altenglisch"; W. Krogmann, "Altfriesisch"; W. Krogmann, "Altsächsisch und Mittelniederdeutsch"; A. von Loey, "Altniederländisch und Mittelniederländisch"; S. Sonderegger, "Althochdeutsche Sprache"; G. Schieb, "Mittelhochdeutsch"; J. Erben, "Frühneuhochdeutsch."

II. *Literaturgeschichte*. 1971. viii, 665pp.
Range: beginnings to ca. 1500. Compact surveys of German literature with emphasis on developments in Germany. Selections are excellent general introductions to their subjects: G. Zink, "Heldensage"; P. Scardigli, "Gotische Literatur"; D. Hofmann, "Altnordische Literatur: Edda und Skalden"; G. Turville-Petre, "Altnordische Literatur: Saga"; F. Norman, "Altenglische Literatur"; W. Krogman, "Altfriesische Literatur"; C.C. de Bruin, "Mittelniederländische Literatur"; J. Rathofer, "Altsächsische Literatur"; W. Krogmann, "Mittelniederländische Literatur"; S. Sonderegger, H. Burger, "Althochdeutsche Literatur"; W. Brandt, "Mittelhochdeutsche Literatur: Epik"; H. Schottmann, "Mittelhochdeutsche Literatur: Lyrik"; G. Eis, "Mittelhochdeutsche Literatur: Fachprosa"; W.F. Michael, "Deutsche Literatur bis 1500: Drama"; F. Neumann, "Deutsche Literatur bis 1500: Versgeschichte (Metrik)."

III. *Sach- und Kulturgeschichte*. *Namen- und Sachregister*. In preparation.

484. Stammler, Wolfgang, ed. (I, II) and Karl Langosch, ed. (III, IV). *Die deutsche Literatur des Mittelalters. Verfasserlexikon.* 5 vols. Berlin: de Gruyter, 1933-1955.

I. *Aalen-Futerer.* 1933. xiii, 786 cols.
II. *Der von Gabelstein-Kyeser.* 1936, 992 cols.
III. *Laber-Rynsteten.* 1943. 1166 cols.
IV. *Saarburg-Zwinger.* 1953. 1172 cols.
V. *Nachtragsband.* 1955. 1150 cols.

Range: 8th to 15th century. Invaluable author lexicon (A-Z). Includes writers in the fields of literature, history, philosophy, theology, law, medicine, and science as well as titles of anonymous works, and authors who wrote in medieval Latin and were important to German literature. Entries include bibliographical and biographical information and an evaluation of the writer's work. Exhaustive bibliographies are supplemented by V to ca. 1954. Continued by: Kurt Ruhm and Gundolf Keil, Werner Schröder and Burghart Wachinger, eds. *Die deutsche Literatur des Mittelalters. Verfasserlexikon.* 2nd completely rev. ed. Berlin: de Gruyter, 1976ff., fasc. 1ff. 6 vols. planned.

*** ———. "Schrifttum und Bildkunst im deutschen Mittelalter." *Dt. Phil. im Aufriß* (No. 1283), III, 613-698 (No. 415).

485. Walshe, Maurice O'Connell. *Medieval German Literature. A Survey.* Cambridge: Harvard Univ. Pr., 1962. xiv, 421pp.

Range: 8th to 16th century. A chronological survey by genre with major emphasis on the epic. Primary texts translated, major works summarized. Late medieval literature not covered in detail. Extensive bibliography and notes. Introduction: research problems. Chronological table and map. A basic introduction.

486. Wapnewski, Peter. *Deutsche Literatur des Mittelalters. Ein Abriß.* Göttingen: Vandenhoeck & Ruprecht, 1960. 127pp.

Range: 750 to 1500. Chronological outline history with most important works and authors of the period included. Especially informative for beginners. Chronological table of works and authors mentioned in text. Selected bibliography of standard works on period.

b. Old High German, Pre-Courtly, and Courtly Literature (770-1250)

487. Bertau, Karl. *Deutsche Literatur im europäischen Mittelalter.* 2 vols. Munich: Beck, 1972, 1973. I. xxi, 765pp.; II. xiii, pp. 769-1432. illus.

Range: 800-1200. A chronological survey of German literature against the backdrop of European history with literature viewed as an expression of sociological and cultural developments. Major literary contributions are summarized and analyzed. An excellent work, though demanding. Index: proper names in II. Chronological table, pp. 1238-1381. Bibliography and abbreviations, pp. 1175-1224.

488. Bostock, J. Knight. *A Handbook on Old High German Literature.* 2nd ed. by K.C. King and D.R. McLintock. Oxford: Oxford Univ. Pr., 1976. xv, 344pp. ([1]1955)

A compact chronological survey of the early documents of German literature (5th to 11th century) with emphasis on the literary aspects. Extensive analyses of the *Merseburg Charms*, the *Lay of Hildebrand*, the *Wessobrunn Prayer* and the *Muspilli*, the *Ludwigslied*, *Waltharius*, and *Ruodlieb*. Conclusions are based on the most recent research. Appendix: Old Saxon and Old High German meter, maps. Selected bibliography, pp. 332-336. Index: author, subject. Superb introductory survey.

489. de Boor, Helmut. *Die deutsche Literatur von Karl dem Großen bis zum Beginn der höfischen Dichtung 770-1170.* 8th ed. (= 4th rev. ed.) with bibliographical appendix by Dieter Haacke. Munich: Beck, 1971. viii, 295pp. ([1]1949)

An excellent introduction with special emphasis on individual works and authors. Structured chronologically. Does not attempt to incorporate most recent scholarship or methodology. Selected bibliography at end of each chapter. Appendix: extensive bibliography carefully organized for further reading; chronological table of important works and historical events.

490. ———. *Die höfische Literatur. Vorbereitung, Blüte, Ausklang 1170-1250.* 8th ed. (= 4th ed.) with bibliographical appendix by Dieter Haacke. Munich: Beck, 1970. viii, 464pp. ([1]1953)

Treats the development of epic, lyric, religious, and didactic literature separately. Emphasis on individual works and authors. Bibliography and chronological table, similar to above.

491. Erb, Ewald. *Geschichte der deutschen Literatur von den Anfängen bis 1160.* 2 Halbbände. Berlin: Volk und Wissen, 1963, 1964. I, xvi, 448pp.; II. vii, 452-1157pp.

Vol. I of the official Marxist-socialist history of German literature in the GDR. I: the language and literature of Germanic society, the early feudal period (6th to 8th century) and the early high feudal period (8th to 11th century); II: feudal society to the middle of the 13th century; the Middle High German language, religious literature 1000-1200, the pre-courtly epic. Social and historical background are stressed throughout. Index: II, subject, title. Bibliography at the end of each section; addenda to bibliography, II, pp. 1024-1040.

492. Pickering, F.P. *Literature and Art in the Middle Ages.* Coral Gables, Fla.: Univ. of Miami Pr., 1970. xii, 362pp. German ed.: *Literatur und Kunst im Mittelalter.* Berlin: Schmidt, 1966.

Various aspects of medieval literature and art, including major themes represented and the relation between words and images. Chapter 6 is a guide to medieval art for students of literature. Indexes: author, subject. Biblical quotations.

493. Schneider, Hermann. *Heldendichtung, Geistlichendichtung, Ritterdichtung.* 2nd rev. ed. Heidelberg: Winter, 1943. xvi, 604pp. ([1]1925)

Range: 3rd century to 1300. Intellectual-historical approach with emphasis on heroic, religious, and courtly literature. Much cultural material. Little analysis of individual works. Suitable as advanced background reading.

494. ——— and Wolfgang Mohr. "Mittelhochdeutsche Dichtung." *Reallexikon* (No. 1288), II, 314-335.

495. Schwietering, Julius. *Die deutsche Dichtung des Mittelalters.* Bad Homburg: Gentner, 1957. 313pp. ([1]1941)

Range: ca. 770-1250. Emphasizes the development of literary genres. Selective presentation of works and authors with interpretations of representative works. Outstanding in treatment of the epic. Excellent introduction for beginners.

496. Trier, Jost. *Der deutsche Wortschatz im Sinnbezirk des Verstandes. Die Geschichte eines sprachlichen Feldes.* I. *Von den Anfängen bis zu Beginn des 13. Jahrhunderts.* Heidelberg: Winter, 1931. 347pp. (Repr. 1973)

Provides tables and comparative analyses of usage and meanings. An excellent aid for study of the literature of the period.

497. Unwerth, Wolf von, Theodor Siebs. *Geschichte der deutschen Literatur bis zur Mitte des 11. Jahrhunderts.* Berlin: de Gruyter, 1920. ix, 261pp.

A thorough, positivistic survey of literature with emphasis on individual works and their analysis. Index: author, subject. Bibliography in the text. Excellent for the beginner despite its age.

498. Vogt, Friedrich. *Geschichte der mittelhochdeutschen Literatur.* I. Teil. *Frühmittelhochdeutsche Zeit. Blütezeit.* II. *Das höfische Epos bis zu Gottfried von Straßburg.* 3rd rev. ed. Berlin, Leipzig: de Gruyter, 1922. x, 363pp.

Range: 1050 to 1300. I: early Middle High German religious and secular literature with emphasis on individual works. Summaries and some interpretation. II: courtly epic, focusing on H. v. Veldeke, H. v. Aue, W. v. Eschenbach, G. v. Straßburg. Short bibliographies at the beginning of each section. Very informative despite its age.

499. Wentzlaff-Eggebert, Friedrich Wilhelm. *Kreuzzugsdichtung des Mittelalters. Studien zu ihrer geschichtlichen und dichterischen Wirklichkeit.* Berlin: de Gruyter, 1960. xix, 404pp.

Range: 12th and 13th centuries. An extensive survey which includes history and analyses of literature. Focus is on the major themes and motifs of the genre; copious text specimens provided. Latin and French literature taken into account. Primary and secondary bibliography, pp. 372-402. Notes. Standard work.

c. Late Medieval Literature, Mysticism (1250-1480)

500. Clark, James M. *The Great German Mystics. Eckhart, Tauler and Suso.* Oxford, Blackwell, 1949. vii, 121pp.

A compact study of the major exponents of mysticism in the 14th century. Includes Eckhart, Tauler, Suso, Merswin, and the Franciscans. Index: names, titles. Well selected bibliography, pp. 110-117. Excellent as a first introduction.

501. de Boor, Helmut. *Die deutsche Literatur im späten Mittelalter. Zerfall und Neubeginn 1250-1400.* Pt. 1. *1250-1350.* 4th ed. (= 1st ed.) Munich: Beck, 1973. xi, 590pp. ([1]1962)

Quality and format similar to No. 489 and No. 490.

502. Quint, Josef. "Mystik." *Reallexikon* (No. 1288), I, 693-727.

503. Ruh, Kurt, ed. *Altdeutsche und altniederländische Mystik.* Darmstadt: Wissenschaftliche Buchgesellschaft, 1964. xii, 501pp.

A collection of 1 original and 15 previously publ. essays (1922-1963) by specialists including G. Müller, Quint, Schwietering, Ruh, Stammler. Indexes: names. Offers a good overview of research.

504. Wentzlaff-Eggebert, Friedrich Wilhelm. *Deutsche Mystik zwischen Mittelalter und Neuzeit. Einheit und Wandlung ihrer Erscheinungsformen.* 3rd enl. ed. Berlin: de Gruyter, 1969. xx, 397pp. ([1]1944)

Range: 1100-1800. The first general study of the field. Establishes the unity of mystical writings with definitions and summary of the elements of mysticism. A standard history.

505. ——— and Erika. *Deutsche Literatur im späten Mittelalter 1250-1450.* 3 vols. Reinbek: Rowohlt, 1971.

I. *Rittertum und Bürgertum.* 281pp.
II. *Kirche.* 242pp.
III. *Neue Sprache aus neuer Welterfahrung.* 243pp.

Each volume is introduced by a brief, chronologically arranged, thematically oriented discussion of the period. Two-thirds of each volume comprised of specimen texts from the period. Annotations too sparse for the non-native reader.

d. Medieval Latin Literature

506. Curtius, Ernst Robert. *Europäische Literatur und lateinisches Mittelalter.* Bern: Francke, [7]1969. 608pp. ([1]1948) English ed.: *European Literature and the Latin Middle Ages.* Trans. by Willard R. Trask. New York: Pantheon, 1953. xv, 662pp..

Still a standard work in the field. Wide-ranging essays on the era show the relationship between the literatures of antiquity, Middle Latin and European literature. A wealth of material is presented. Outstanding also for beginners.

507. Hauck, Karl. "Mittellateinische Literatur." *Dt. Phil. im Aufriß* (No. 1283), II, 2555-2624.

508. Langosch, Karl. "Mittellateinische Dichtung in Deutschland." *Reallexikon* (No. 1288), II, 335-391.

509. ———. *Lateinisches Mittelalter. Einleitung in Sprache und Literatur.* Darmstadt: Wissenschaftliche Buchgesellschaft, ^{3}1969. 96pp. (^{1}1963)

Range: ca. 500-1500. A resource book for the language and literature of the Latin Middle Ages, including an in-depth review of major research, editions, anthologies, etc.

510. Mantius, Max. *Geschichte der lateinischen Literatur des Mittelalters.* 3 vols. Munich: Beck.

I. *Von Justinian bis zur Mitte des zehnten Jahrhunderts.* 1911. xiii, 766pp.
II. *Von der Mitte des zehnten Jahrhunderts bis zum Ausbruch des Kampfes zwischen Kirche und Staat.* 1923. xii, 873pp. Includes supplement to I and indexes for I and II.
III. *Vom Ausbruch des Kirchenstreites bis zum Ende des zwölften Jahrhunderts.* With Paul Lehmann. 1931. xiii, 1164pp. Includes supplement to II.

Range: 6th to 12th century. An elaborate positivistic history of writers in Latin, subdivided according to subjects and individual writers. Each volume contains chronological tables, indexes.

511. Szöverffy, Josef. *Weltliche Dichtungen des lateinischen Mittelalters. Von den Anfängen bis zum Ende der Karolingerzeit.* Berlin: Schmidt, 1970. 771pp.

1. A general introduction to medieval Latin, medieval literature; 2. transition from Roman antiquity to the Middle Ages; 3. literature in the time of the Merovingians; 4. literature during the Carolingian Renaissance. Divided into compact, substantive sections. Extensive listings of primary material in the text. Index: author, subject, Latin first lines. Structured as a handbook. Most extensive survey of this material available.

C. SIXTEENTH AND SEVENTEENTH CENTURIES

1. Forschungsberichte

a. Neo-Latin Literature

512. Conrady, Karl Otto. "Die Erforschung der neulateinischen Literatur. Probleme und Aufgaben." *Euphorion* 49 (1955), 413-445.

b. Renaissance, Humanism, Reformation

513. Rupprich, Hans. "Deutsche Literatur im Zeitalter des Humanismus und der Reformation." *DVLG* 17 (1939), Referatenheft, 83-133.

514. Newald, Richard. "Deutsche Literatur im Zeitalter des Humanismus. Ein Literaturbericht." *DVLG* 27 (1953), 309-326 (covers 1939-1952).

515. Liebing, Hans. "Reformationsgeschichtliche Literatur 1945-1954." *DVLG* 28 (1954), 516-537.

516. Stupperich, Robert. "Vom Humanismus zur Reformation." *Archiv für Kunstgeschichte* 36 (1954), 388-401.

517. Edighoffer, Roland. "De l'Humanisme au Frühbarock." *Etudes germaniques* 19 (1964), 461-466.

518. Lefebvre, Joel. "De Brant à Moscherosch. Quelques publications récentes." *Etudes germaniques* 22 (1967), 63-74.

519. Wuttke, Dieter. *Deutsche Germanistik und Renaissanceforschung. Ein Vortrag zur Forschungslage.* Bad Homburg, Berlin, Zurich: Gehlen, 1968. 46pp.

 A survey of recent Renaissance research (to 1967) in German literature with bibliographical references in the text. Index: names.

520. Schmidt, Josef. "Bücher im Umkreis des 16. Jahrhunderts. Forschungsbericht." *Wirkendes Wort* 23 (1973), 129-136.

521. Herding, Otto. "Über einige Richtlinien in der Erforschung des deutschen Humanismus seit etwa 1950." In: *Humanismusforschung seit 1945. Ein Bericht aus interdisziplinärer Sicht.* Bonn, Bad Godesberg: Deutsche Forschungsgemeinschaft, 1975. 197pp.

c. Baroque

522. Trunz, Erich. "Die Erforschung der deutschen Barockdichtung." *DVLG* 18 (1940), Suppl., 1-101.

523. Lunding, Erik. "Stand und Aufgaben der deutschen Barockforschung." *Orbis litterarum* 8 (1950), 27-91.

524. ———. "Die deutsche Barockforschung. Ergebnisse und Probleme." *Wirkendes Wort* 2 (1951-1952), 298-306.

525. Peuckert, Will-Erich. "Die zweite Mystik. Ein Forschungsbericht." *DVLG* 32 (1958), 286-304.

526. Müller-Schwefe, Gerhard. "The European Approach to Baroque." *Philological Quarterly* 45 (1966), 419-433.

527. de Capua, Angelo George. "Baroque and Mannerism. Reassessment 1965." *Coll. Germ.* 1 (1967), 101-110.

528. Brauneck, Manfred. "Barockforschung. Ein Literaturbericht." In: *Das 17. Jahrhundert in neuer Sicht. Beiträge von Peter Jentzsche, Manfred Brauneck, Ernst Eugen Starke.* Stuttgart: Klett, 1969, 93-120.

529. Grimm, Reinhold. "Bild und Bildlichkeit. Zu einigen neueren Arbeiten." *GRM*, *NF* 19 (1969), 379-412.

530. Brauneck, Manfred. "Deutsche Literatur des 17. Jahrhunderts. Revision eines Epochenbildes. Ein Forschungsbericht 1945-1970." *DVLG* 45 (1971). Sonderheft, 378-468.

531. Zeman, Herbert. "Deutsche Barockliteratur." *Wissenschaft und Weltbild* 22 (1969), 139-152 and 33 (1970), 68-78.

532. Lindberg, John D. "Internationale Bibliographie der deutschen Barockliteratur." *Coll. Germ.* 4 (1970), 110-120.

533. ———. "Die internationale Bibliographie der deutschen Barockliteratur. Ein 2. Bericht." *Jahrbuch für internationale Germanistik* 4 (1972), 2, 12-15.

2. Bibliographies

a. Completed Bibliographies

*** *Bibliographisches Handbuch der deutschen Literaturwissenschaft 1945-1969* (No. 123), I: see section VI. "Renaissance, Humanismus, Reformation" and VII. "Zeitalter des Barock." Selected cumulation of (No. 129) to 1969.

534. Engel, James. *Renaissance, Humanismus, Reformation.* Bern, Munich: Francke, 1969. 80pp.

A brief, handy bibliography listing text editions and secondary literature for the period, with emphasis on research from 1950-1965. Index: author, subject.

*** *Internationale Bibliographie zur Geschichte der deutschen Literatur* (No. 122). I: see section "Deutsche Literatur von 1480 bis 1680." Selected cumulation to 1967. Marxist-socialist criticism well represented.

535. Jantz, Harold. *German Baroque Literature. A Descriptive Catalogue of the Collection Harold Jantz and a Guide to the Collection on Microfilm.* 2 vols. New Haven: Research Publications, 1974. I. xxviii, 258pp.; II. Pp. 259-550.

Lists 317 early Baroque, 3169 Baroque, and 144 post-Baroque works by author, title, and various subject categories, A-Z. Indexes: names, subject; various specialized indexes plus reel index to microfilm collection with cross references to the Faber du Faur collection.

536. Kemp, Friedhelm. "Bibliographien zur deutschen Barockliteratur. Versuch einer Übersicht und einer Kritik." *Börsenblatt* (Frankfurt) 28 (1972), A40-A44.

537. "Literature of the Renaissance." *Studies in Philology* 42 (1945)-66 (1969).

538. Merkel, Ingrid. *Barock*. Bern, Munich: Francke, 1971. 113pp.

Focus on research published 1950-1967. General literature, bibliography, history; 13 chapters on the various genres, epochs, literary schools. Author entries include primary (selected) and secondary literature. Indexes: names, subjects.

539. Pyritz, Hans. "Bibliographie der deutschen Barockliteratur." In: Paul Hankamer, *Deutsche Gegenreformation und deutsches Barock* (No. 557), pp. 478-512.

540. Schottenloher, Karl. *Bibliographies zur deutschen Geschichte im Zeitalter der Glaubensspaltung 1517-1585*. 2nd ed. 6 vols. Stuttgart: Hiersemann, 1956-1958. ([1]1933-1940) Includes titles to the mid-1930's. Continued by: Ulrich Thürauf. *Bibliographie ... Das Schrifttum von 1938-1960*. VII. Stuttgart: Hiersemann, 1966. viii, 691pp. See especially I, II, VI, VII.

b. Current Bibliographies

*** *Bibliographie der deutschen Sprach- und Literaturwissenschaft* (No. 129): see section X. "16. Jahrhundert" and XI. "17. Jahrhundert." 1 (1945-1953)-16 (1976)ff. Most reliable and comprehensive current bibliography available. Editions and secondary material. Publ. annually.

541. *Bibliographie internationale de l'humanisme et de la renaissance*. Ed. by the Fédération internationale des sociétés et instituts pour l'étude de la renaissance. Geneva: Librairie Droz, 1966ff.

5 vols. covering the years 1965-1969. 1969 vol. lists 6,193 items. Annual cumulations listed by author A-Z. Includes 15th and 16th-century literature, history, science, philosophy, and religion. Useful because it is indeed international in scope.

*** *Germanistik* (No. 130): see section XXV. "Vom deutschen Frühhumanismus bis zum Einsetzen der Reformation (1450-1520)," XXVI. "Das Zeitalter der Reformation (1520-1580)," and XXVII. "Barock (1580-1700)." 1 (1960)-17 (1976)ff. Comprehensive quarterly, up to date. Editions and secondary material. Books are reviewed.

*** *MLA International Bibliography* (No. 125) II: see section "German Literature. IV. Sixteenth and Seventeenth Centuries."

1921-1975ff. Annual cumulation. Editions and secondary material. Extensive and generally reliable.

*** *Referatendienst zur Literaturwissenschaft* (No. 131): see section "Allgemeine und vergleichende Literaturwissenschaft" and "Geschichte der Nationalliteraturen. Deutsche Literatur." 1 (1969)-7 (1976)ff. Marxist-socialist quarterly review of books. Limited in scope.

*** *Wolfenbütteler Barock-Nachrichten* (No. 1551): see section 2 "Bibliographische Information. A. Textausgaben, Reprints und Forschungsliteratur. B. Rezensionen. C. Selbstanzeigen" and "e. Addenda zu Barockbibliographien." 1 (1974)-4 (1977)ff. Up-to-date quarterly. Comprehensive listing. No annotation. Best available.

*** *The Year's Work in Modern Language Studies* (No. 127): see section "The Sixteenth Century" and "The Seventeenth Century." 20 (1958)-37 (1975)ff. Covers primary and secondary publications for the previous year. Annotated.

3. Literary Histories

a. Entire Period (1490-1700)

542. Buck, August, ed. *Renaissance und Barock*. 2 vols. Frankfurt: Athenaion, 1972. ix, 328pp., 79 illus.; x, 375pp., 87 illus.

20 essays on various European aspects of the era. Not a chronological history but a treatment of the high points of national literatures. Includes material on social and cultural background. Richly illustrated, intended for the general reader. Bibliography at the end of each chapter. Index: authors, with bio-biblio. information.

543. Gaede, Friedrich. *Humanismus, Barock, Aufklärung. Geschichte der deutschen Literatur vom 16. bis zum 18. Jahrhundert*. Bern, Munich: Francke, 1971. 347pp.

A chronological history. Each part clearly subdivided into sections covering background (history, philosophical developments of the period), the genres, and the major representatives of the epoch. Good, basic introduction, well organized. Index: authors. No bibliography.

544. Kohlschmidt, Werner. *Geschichte der deutschen Literatur vom Barock bis zur Klassik*. Stuttgart: Reclam, 1965. 956pp., 112 illus.

A chronological history. Compact, simply and clearly written, work analyses, particularly of lyric poetry. Attention to major figures in each period. A good introduction. Index: names, subjects. Bibliography (by period and by author), pp. 895-930.

545. Müller, Günther. *Geschichte der deutschen Seele. Vom Faustbuch zu Goethes Faust.* Freiburg: Herder, 1939. 494pp. (Repr. 1962)

Intellectual-historical approach: traces the concept of *Humanität* from the Faust chapbook to Brentano. Methodology and subject matter interesting for advanced students.

546. ———. *Deutsche Dichtung von der Renaissance bis zum Ausgang des Barock.* Wildpart-Potsdam: Athenaion, 1927. 263pp. illus. (Repr. 1957)

A compact presentation of the period with selective summaries of works. Lavishly illustrated with reproductions of manuscripts, title pages, woodcuts, etc.

*** Newald, Richard, Willi Flemming, Fritz Martini, Wolfdietrich Rasch, Wolfgang Baumgart. *Geschichte der deutschen Literatur vom Humanismus bis zu Goethes Tod (1490-1832).* Stuttgart: Metzler, 1962. viii, 344pp. (No. 448, pp. 287-619)

b. Renaissance, Humanism, Reformation (1360-1570)

547. Bebermeyer, Gustav. "Frühneuhochdeutsche Literatur." *Reallexikon* (No. 1288), I, 507-521.

548. Burger, Heinz Otto. *Renaissance, Humanismus, Reformation. Deutsche Literatur im europäischen Kontext.* Bad Homburg, Berlin, Zurich: Gehlen, 1969. 510pp. illus.

Detailed chronological history of periods with little literary analysis. Major works are summarized. Extensive quotations from primary material included. Focus on the German humanists with ample history and biography. Index: names. Very informative.

549. Boeckh, Joachim G., Günther Albrecht, Kurt Böttcher, Klaus Gysi, Paul Günter Krohn. *Geschichte der deutschen Literatur von 1480 bis 1600.* Vierter Band. 2nd ed. Berlin: Volk und Wissen, 1961. xi, 541pp., illus.

Vol. IV of the official Marxist-socialist history of German literature in the GDR. Includes extensive material on the economic and social conditions, the literary genres, Humanism, social satire, Reformation and the anti-feudal forces, mysticism, bourgeois authors. Indexes: author, subject. Bibliography at the end of each section.

550. Könneker, Barbara. *Die deutsche Literatur der Reformationszeit. Kommentar zu einer Epoche.* Munich: Winkler, 1975. 284pp.

Introductory survey, followed by a chronological table 1517-1555, then compact analyses of 12 major works of the period. Extensive bibliography, pp. 184-269. Indexes: names; titles. A valuable introduction.

551. Roloff, Hans-Gert. "Reformationsliteratur." *Reallexikon* (No. 1288), III, pp. 365-403.

552. Rupprich, Hans. *Die deutsche Literatur vom späten Mittelalter bis zum Barock.* Pt. 1 and pt. 2. Munich: Beck, 1970-1973.

Pt. 1: *Das ausgehende Mittelalter, Humanismus und Renaissance* (1360-1520). 1970. xii, 835pp.
A chronological history organized by genre. The material is extensively covered with many individual interpretations and summaries. Comprehensive bibliography, pp. 733-800.

Pt. 2: *Das Zeitalter der Reformation* (1520-1570). 1973. xii, 554pp.
Chronological history divided by genre. Vast amount of material well organized. Many detailed analyses and chronological table of era. Extensive bibliography, pp. 458-513.

553. Stammler, Wolfgang. *Von der Mystik zum Barock 1400-1600.* Stuttgart: Metzler, 1927. 554pp. (Repr. 1950)

Intellectual-historical approach: evaluates era in entirety: contains no summaries of works. Excellent evaluation of period for the advanced reader. Table: cultural-historical and literary data.

c. Baroque (1600-1700)

554. Alewyn, Richard, ed. *Deutsche Barockforschung. Dokumentation einer Epoche.* 2nd ed. Berlin, Cologne: Kiepenheuer & Witsch, 1970. 472pp. (^{1}1965)

A collection of essays by various scholars on aspects of Baroque literature. Not a systematic coverage from a unified point of view.

555. Barner, Wilfried, ed. *Der literarische Barockbegriff.* Darmstadt: Wissenschaftliche Buchgesellschaft, 1975. vii, 597ff.

A collection of 25 essays published from 1888-1970 by eminent scholars including Wölfflin, Strich, Cysarz, Croce, Walzel, Curtius, Spitzer, Hatzfeld, Pranz, and Szyrocki. Essays not confined to German literature. Excellent introduction to most important contributions to research of the period.

556. Boeckh, Joachim G., Günter Albrecht, Kurt Böttcher, Klaus Gysi, Paul Günter Krohn, Hermann Strohbach. *Geschichte der deutschen Literatur. Fünfter Band. Von 1600 bis 1700. Mit einem Abriss der Geschichte der sorbischen Literatur.* Erster Teil. Berlin: Volk und Wissen, 1962. xiii, 592pp., illus.

Vol. V of the official Marxist-socialist history of German literature of the GDR. Extensive background material on economic and social developments, the literary genres, mystical and feudal literature. An historical survey of Sorbian literature to 1880. Indexes: author, subject. Bibliography at the end of each section.

557. Hankamer, Paul. *Deutsche Gegenreformation und deutsches Barock. Die deutsche Literatur im Zeitraum des 17. Jahrhunderts.* 2nd ed. Stuttgart: Metzler, 1947. ix, 543pp. (^{1}1935)

Pt. 1: social and religious background; pt. 2: literary forms: lyric, drama, prose. Quite perceptive in its attention to social structure and mores of the period and their influence on literary production. Not an introduction; reader should be acquainted with the literature of the period. Index: names and subject. Chronological table: pp. 513-530. Extensive and important bibliography of material to the early 1930's: Hans Pyritz, "Bibliographie der deutschen Barockliteratur," pp. 478-512. Bibliography omitted in 3rd ed., 1964.

558. Newald, Richard. *Die deutsche Literatur vom Späthumanismus zur Empfindsamkeit 1570-1750*. Munich: Beck, 1951. vii, 556pp.

A clearly organized history with extensive summaries of important works. Chronological table of important works and historical events. Selected bibliography at the end of each chapter.

559. Pascal, Roy. *German Literature in the Sixteenth and Seventeenth Centuries. Renaissance, Reformation, Baroque*. New York: Barnes & Noble, 1968. xix, 274pp.

A general introduction. Pt. 1: political, religious, intellectual and linguistic background; pt. 2: literature of the 16th century, literature of the 17th century. Surveyed chronologically by genre. Extensive bibliography, pp. 151-245. Appendix: essay on German painting of the period. Superb for beginners.

560. Szyrocki, Marion. *Die deutsche Literatur des Barock. Eine Einführung*. Reinbek: Rowohlt, 1968. 269pp.

A chronological survey by genre. Introduction contains extensive background material; text incorporates many sample passages and thorough intrinsic analyses. Good bibliography. One of the best introductions to the Baroque.

561. Tisch-Wackernagel, J.H. "*Barock*." In: *Periods in German Literature* (No. 453), pp. 17-39. A definition of the Baroque literary period.

562. Wentzlaff-Eggebert, Friedrich-Wilhelm. *Der Triumphierende und der Besiegte. Tod in der Wort- und Bildkunst des Barock*. Berlin, New York: de Gruyter, 1975. x, 203pp., 66 illus.

Pt. 1: chronological survey of the theme; pt. 2: thematic analysis of works by Cats, Gryphius, Balde, Schönborn. Index: names. Bibliography. Appendix: specimen texts, pp. 180-195. An important study of a major theme of Baroque literature.

d. Neo-Latin Literature (15th-17th Centuries)

563. Ellinger, Georg. *Geschichte der neulateinischen Literatur Deutschlands im 16. Jahrhundert*. 3 vols. Berlin, Leipzig: de Gruyter, 1929-1933.

I. *Italien und der deutsche Humanismus in der neulateinischen Lyrik*. 1929. xxiii, 516pp.

Pt. 1: the development of Italian poetry of the 15th and 16th centuries; pt. 2: the poetry of the German humanists to the end of the 15th century.

II. *Die neulateinische Lyrik Deutschlands in der ersten Hälfte des sechzehnten Jahrhunderts.* 1929. vi, 420pp.

Pt. 3: lyric poetry from the beginning of the 16th century to 1560.

III. Pt. 1: *Geschichte der neulateinischen Lyrik in den Niederlanden vom Ausgang des fünfzehnten bis zum Beginn des siebzehnten Jahrhunderts.* 1933. viii, 334pp.

III. Pt. 2: never published.

A positivistic history of the lyric poets of the era, embracing many minor talents. Chapters are divided according to individual authors. There is little interpretation. Still valuable for its wealth of detailed information. Index: proper names.

564. ——— and Brigitte Ristow. "Neulateinische Dichtung." *Reallexikon* (No. 1288), II, pp. 620-645.

D. EIGHTEENTH CENTURY

1. Forschungsberichte

565. Schumann, Detlev W. "Neuorientierung im 18. Jahrhundert." *MLR* 9 (1948), 54-73 and 135-145.

566. Prang, Helmut. "Literaturbericht zur deutschen Vorklassik." *Wirkendes Wort* 2 (1951-1952), 231-238.

567. Schumann, Detlev W. "Germany in the 18th Century. Some New Publications." *JEGP* 51 (1952), 259-275 and 434-450.

568. David, Claude C. "L'âge d'or de l'Allemagne." *Critique* 84 (1954), 421-440.

569. Schumann, Detlev W. "New Studies in German Literature of the Eighteenth Century." *JEGP* 54 (1955), 705-726.

570. Rasch, Wolfdietrich. "Die Literatur der Aufklärungszeit." *DVLG* 30 (1956), 533-600.

571. Skalweit, Stephan. "Das Zeitalter des Absolutismus als Forschungsproblem." *DVLG* 35 (1961), 298-315.

572. Anger, Alfred. "Deutsche Rokoko-Dichtung. Ein Forschungsbericht." *DVLG* 36 (1962), 430-479 and 614-648.

573. Namowicz, Tadeusz. "Pietismus in der deutschen Kultur des 18. Jahrhunderts. Bemerkungen zur Pietismusforschung." *WB* 13 (1967), 469-480.

2. Bibliographies

a. Completed Bibliographies

574. "Bibliographie deutschsprachiger Bücher und Zeitschriftenaufsätze zur deutschen Literatur von der Aufklärung bis zur bürgerlichen Revolution von 1848/49." Ed. by Gottfried Wilhelm. *WB* 1 (1955)-4 (1958). Coverage from Jan. 1, 1954. Continued in enlarged form as:

575. "Internationale Bibliographie zur deutschen Klassik. 1750-1850." Ed. by Klaus Hammer (to 1961), Hans Henning and Siegfried Seifert. Folge 1 and 2 to Folge 5 and 6 in: *Zeitschrift für deutsche Literaturgeschichte* 6 (1960)-8 (1962); Folge 7-10 in: *WB* 9 (1963)-10 (1964).

Published in book form: Henning, Hans, and Siegfried Seifert. *Internationale Bibliographie zur deutschen Klassik. 1750-1850.* Folge 11/12. 1964-1965. Weimar: Nationale Forschungs- und Gedenkstätten der klassischen deutschen Dichtung, 1970. 277pp. Continued:

Folge 13. 1970. 336pp. For 1966.
Folge 14. 1970. 385pp. For 1967.
Folge 15. 1971. 395pp. For 1968.
Folge 16. 1971. 310pp. For 1969.
Folge 17, 2 vols.: I, 1971, 251pp; II, 1972, 259pp. For 1970.

Most comprehensive and reliable bibliography available for the reporting period 1960-1970.

*** *Bibliographisches Handbuch der deutschen Literaturwissenschaft 1945-1969* (No. 123), I: see section VIII. "18. Jahrhundert" and IX. "Zeitalter der Klassik und Romantik." Selected cumulation of (item X) to 1969.

576. "The Eighteenth Century. A Current Bibliography." *Philological Quarterly* 50 (1971)-54 (1975). Extensive international bibliography. Excellent for German literature. Not to be continued.

577. Grotegut, Eugene K. and G.F. Leneaux. *Das Zeitalter der Aufklärung.* Bern, Munich: Francke, 1974. 76pp.

Selective bibliography in 2 parts: 1: bibliographies, related subjects, aesthetics, themes and motifs, foreign influences, genres; 2: 131 authors A-Z, editions and secondary material to 1965. Does not include Storm and Stress, *Göttinger Hain.* Excellent for the beginner; information easily located.

*** *Internationale Bibliographie zur Geschichte der deutschen Literatur* (No. 122), I: see section "Deutschsprachige Literatur von 1680 bis 1789." Selected cumulation to 1967. Marxist-socialist criticism well represented.

578. Julius, Werner. "Bibliographie deutscher Hochschulschriften zur deutschen Literatur von der Aufklärung bis zur bürgerlichen Revolution 1848-1849, die in den Jahren 1945-1953 erschienen sind." *WB* 3 (1957), 134-183.

b. Current Bibliographies

*** Bibliographie der deutschen Sprach- und Literaturwissenschaft (No. 129): see section XII. "18. Jahrhundert," "Goethezeit," and XIV. "Goethes Zeitgenossen," 1 (1945-1953)-15 (1975)ff. Most reliable and comprehensive bibliography available. Editions and secondary material. Publ. annually.

*** *Germanistik* (No. 130): see section XXVIII "Aufklärung, Empfindsamkeit und Vorklassik (1700-1770)" and XXIX "Goethezeit (1770-1830)," 1 (1960)-17 (1976)ff. Comprehensive quarterly, up to date. Lists editions and secondary material. Books are reviewed.

*** *MLA International Bibliography* (No. 125), II: see section "German Literature. V. Eighteenth and Early Nineteenth Centuries," 1921-1975ff. Annual cumulation. Editions and secondary material. Extensive and generally reliable.

*** *Referatendienst zur Literaturwissenschaft* (No. 131): see section "Geschichte der Nationalliteraturen. Deutsche Literatur (1690-1770)," 1 (1969)-6 (1975)ff. Marxist-socialist quarterly review of books. Limited in scope.

*** *The Year's Work in Modern Language Studies* (No. 127): see section "The Classical Era," 1 (1930)-37 (1975)ff. Covers primary and secondary publ. for the previous year. Annotated.

3. Literary Histories

a. Entire Period (1700-1805)

579. Benz, Richard. *Deutsches Barock. Kultur des achtzehnten Jahrhunderts. Erster Teil.* Stuttgart: Reclam, 1949. 560pp.

580. ———. *Die Zeit der deutschen Klassik. Kultur des achtzehnten Jahrhunderts, 1750-1800.* Stuttgart: Reclam, 1953. 612pp.

Both parts focus on the philosophical and artistic currents of the 18th century. Valuable background reading, especially for the material on the non-literary arts.

581. Bruford, Walter Horace. *Germany in the Eighteenth Century. The Social Background of the Literary Revival.* Cambridge: Cambridge Univ. Pr., 1935. x, 354pp. Maps. (Repr. 1959)

A survey of the social, economic, and political structure of Germany with information on the religious, ethical, and cultural life in the period. The situation of the writer in

Germany and England is compared in detail. Appendices: German money, weights and measures; statistics of Germany prior to the Napoleonic Wars. Bibliography of writers of memoirs, diaries, etc. Good introductory reading.

582. Butler, Eliza Marian. *The Tyranny of Greece over Germany. A Study of the Influence Exercised by Greek Art over the Great German Writers of the Eighteenth, Nineteenth and Twentieth Centuries.* Cambridge: Cambridge Univ. Pr., 1935. xi, 351pp.

Chapters on Winckelmann, Lessing and Herder, Goethe, Schiller, Hölderlin, Heine. Written in a lively style, somewhat polemical. Index: authors, titles. Despite its age this study is well worth reading.

583. Dilthey, Wilhelm. *Das Erlebnis und die Dichtung. Lessing, Goethe, Novalis, Hölderlin.* 15th ed. Göttingen: Vandenhoeck & Ruprecht, 1970. 335pp. ([1]1905)

A classic model of intellectual-historical methodology: analyzes the achievements and personalities of four literary giants in whom the cultural and intellectual trends of the age are summed up. Presumes knowledge of these authors' major works.

584. Farrell, R.B. "Classicism." *Periods in German Literature* (No. 453), pp. 99-120.

585. Guthke, Karl S. *Literarisches Leben im achtzehnten Jahrhundert in Deutschland und in der Schweiz.* Bern, Munich: Francke, 1975. 423pp.

Analysis of various elements of the literary scene of the 18th century including critical trends, the reception of literature, the stage and drama. Particular attention to Albrecht von Haller. Index: names. Good background reading.

586. Hettner, Hermann. *Geschichte der deutschen Literatur im achtzehnten Jahrhundert.* Ed. by Georg Witkowski. 4 Pts. in 1 vol. Leipzig: List, 1929. ([1]1864-1872; reedited several times, repr. 1961)

Pt. 1. *Vom Westfälischen Frieden bis zur Thronbesteigung Friedrichs des Großen 1648-1720.* 261pp.
Pt. 2. *Das Zeitalter Friedrichs des Großen.* 373pp.
Pt. 3. *Das Klassische Zeitalter der deutschen Literatur I: Sturm und Drang.* 246pp.
Pt. 4. *Das klassische Zeitalter der deutschen Literatur II: Das Ideal der Humanität.* 359pp.

An extensive survey emphasizing political history and the history of ideas. Literature and the other arts are viewed in the context of 18th-century culture. Little interpretation of individual works. A valuable in-depth examination of the period. Index of proper names, see pt. 4.

587. Hinck, Walter, ed. *Europäische Aufklärung (I. Teil).* Frankfurt: Athenaion, 1974. 223pp. 50 illus.

11 essays on social background, aesthetic theory, major genres. Emphasis on European developments. Well selected bibliographies at the end of each chapter. Essays on the whole are superb. Includes Storm and Stress. Two additional volumes are planned for the major authors.

*** Kohlschmidt, Werner. *Geschichte der deutschen Literatur vom Barock bis zur Klassik.* (No. 544)

588. Mason, Gabriel R. *From Gottsched to Hebbel.* London: Harrap, 1961. 268pp. illus.

Range: 1720-1850. Superb introduction written expressly for students. Crisp, succinct discussion of the major figures and their contribution. Index: authors, titles. Excellent for the beginner.

589. Mayer, Hans. *Von Lessing bis Thomas Mann. Wandlungen in der bürgerlichen Literatur in Deutschland.* Pfullingen: Neske, 1959. 414pp.

A collection of 15 previously published essays, including discussions of Schnabel, Lessing, Bräker, Schiller, Goethe, E.T.A. Hoffmann, the German novel in the 19th century, Meyer, G. Hauptmann, T. Mann. Not a survey. Interesting for its Marxist approach.

590. Menhennet, Alan. *Order and Freedom. Literature and Society in Germany from 1720 to 1805.* London: Weidenfeld & Nicolson, 1973. ix, 270pp.

Examines the interaction of the arts and the educated classes of the period, exploring the social and political background in particular. The Age of Enlightenment is presented as the age of order, Storm and Stress as the epoch of freedom, and Weimar Classicism as the synthesis of both. Very little literary analysis, some oversimplification for the sake of the scheme. Somewhat too subjective. Index: authors. Bibliography, pp. 257-264.

*** Newald, Richard, Willi Flemming, Fritz Martini, Wolfdietrich Rasch, Wolfgang Baumgart. *Geschichte der deutschen Literatur vom Humanismus bis zu Goethes Tod (1490-1832).* Stuttgart: Metzler, 1962. viii, 344pp. (No. 448), pp. 287-619)

591. Stahl, E.L., and W.E. Yuill. *German Literature of the Eighteenth and Nineteenth Centuries.* New York: Barnes & Noble, 1970. xxiv, 510pp.

Pt. 1: basic and thorough introduction chronologically arranged by movements from Rationalism to Realism; pt. 2: biographical and primary/secondary bibliographical information on major authors. Appendix: chapters on painting, architecture, and sculpture. Excellent for beginners.

592. Viëtor, Karl. *Deutsches Dichten und Denken von der Aufklärung bis zum Realismus. Deutsche Literaturgeschichte von 1700-1890.* Berlin: de Gruyter, 1936. 156pp. (^{3}1959)

Intellectual-historical approach: emphasizes the importance of philosophy, theology, science, etc. for each period discussed. Discussions of literature too summary.

593. Walzel, Oskar. *Deutsche Dichtung von Gottsched bis zur Gegenwart*. 2 vols. Wildpark-Potsdam: Athenaion, 1930.

Conservative intellectual-historical approach with references to contemporary psychology. Important authors and works extensively treated. Literary history not viewed in terms of periods but as uninterrupted flux. I: German Classicism (Gottsched to Goethe); II: post-Classicism (Romanticism, Young Germany, Realism, Naturalism, Impressionism, post-1914). Lavishly illustrated. Good as introduction. Somewhat arbitrary use of standard terminology confusing for beginners.

b. Enlightenment, Empfindsamkeit, Rococo (1700-1770)

594. Anger, Alfred. *Literarisches Rokoko*. Stuttgart: Metzler, 1968. x, 115pp. ([1]1962)

Excellent resource book: a critical survey of the research on the epoch in the form of condensed literary history. Not meant as an introduction to the literature of the period but as a guide to further study. Comprehensive bibliography following each section.

595. Blackall, Eric A. *The Emergence of German as a Literary Language 1700-1775*. Cambridge: Cambridge Univ. Pr., 1959. xi, 539pp.

Important study tracing development of literary German by careful linguistic and stylistic analysis of literary texts with important references to foreign literatures. Extremely valuable for background material on the period. Selected bibliography.

596. Kaiser, Gerhard. *Pietismus und Patriotismus im literarischen Deutschland. Ein Beitrag zum Problem der Säkularisation*. 2nd rev. ed. Frankfurt: Athenäum, 1973. xxxvi, 367pp. ([1]1960)

A history of German Pietism. Index: author and subject. Bibliography, pp. 346-356.

597. ———. *Von der Aufklärung bis zum Sturm und Drang*. Gütersloh: Mohn, 1966. 142pp.

Brief, compact chronological history with focus on major authors and the standard descriptions of epochs: Enlightenment, *Empfindsamkeit*, *Anakreontik*, Storm and Stress, Klopstock, Lessing, Wieland. Bibliography. Excellent introduction.

598. Newald, Richard. *Von Klopstock bis zu Goethes Tod 1750-1832. Erster Teil. Ende der Aufklärung und Vorbereitung der Klassik 1750-1786*. Munich: Beck, 1957. 438pp. ([5]1967)

Clearly structured according to major authors. Individual works summarized. Biographical data also on minor poets. Section 1: break with classicistic tradition; 2: Storm and Stress; 3: the rise of Weimar. Bibliography at the end of each chapter. An excellent introduction to the period.

599. Sauder, Gerhard. *Empfindsamkeit*. I. *Voraussetzungen und Elemente*. Stuttgart: Metzler, 1974. xx, 341pp.

Not a literary history but an introduction to the background of the period. Definition and history of the term "Empfindsamkeit." Survey of criticism. Historical and cultural developments. Indexes: author, subject; bibliography, pp. 301-328. Superb background study for the period.

600. Schneider, Ferdinand Josef. *Die deutsche Dichtung der Aufklärungszeit*. 2nd ed. Stuttgart: Metzler, 1948. 368pp.

Intellectual-historical approach: emphasis on literary genres and epoch-making works. Individual chapters brief and compact. Good introductory history although evaluations of individual works sometimes questionable.

601. Schöffler, Herbert. *Deutsches Geistesleben zwischen Reformation und Aufklärung. Von Martin Opitz zu Christian Wolff*. 2nd ed. Frankfurt: Klostermann, 1956. xiv, 245pp. ([1]1940)

A survey of intellectual life in Silesia and Prussia during the 17th and 18th centuries. Index: names. A good discussion of literary interrelationships between Catholics and Protestants.

602. Stowell, J.D. "Enlightenment and Storm and Stress." *Periods in German Literature* (No. 453), pp. 67-95.

603. Unger, Rudolf. *Hamann und die Aufklärung. Studien zur Vorgeschichte des romantischen Geistes im 18. Jahrhundert*. 2 vols. 4th ed. Tübingen: Niemeyer, 1968. ([1]1911)

Intellectual-historical approach. Somewhat ponderous examination of Hamann and his time. I, sections 1, 2: philosophical and aesthetic background of Enlightenment; sections 3, 4: psychological bases of Hamann's aesthetics; II, footnotes, specimen texts, Hamann bibliography. Cumbersome reading.

604. Zeman, Herbert. *Die deutsche anakreontische Dichtung. Ein Versuch zur Erfassung ihrer ästhetischen und literaturhistorischen Erscheinungsformen im 18. Jahrhundert*. Stuttgart: Metzler, 1972. vii, 386pp.

A positivistic survey of anacreontic poetry in European literature with emphasis on the 18th century. Index: authors, notes. Few new insights; a good introduction.

c. Storm and Stress (1770-1780)

605. Kahn, Ludwig. *Social Ideals in German Literature 1770-1830*. New York: Columbia Univ. Pr., 1938. 108pp. (Repr. 1969)

A discussion of social attitudes reflected in the literature of Storm and Stress, Classicism, and Romanticism. Compact and clearly presented.

606. Pascal, Roy. *The German Sturm und Drang*. Manchester: Manchester Univ. Pr., 1953. xvi, 347pp.

A general introduction to the period: cultural, social, political contexts with a solidly written survey of literature: aesthetics, idea of nature and history, achievements of the period. Examples are given in English. Index: names. Outstanding survey for the non-German reader.

607. Runge, Edith Amelie. *Primitivism and Related Ideas in Sturm und Drang Literature*. Baltimore: Johns Hopkins, 1946. xii, 303pp.

Extensive analysis of the concept of nature and its applications by authors of the period. Bibliography. Index: names. Of limited usefulness.

608. Schneider, Ferdinand Josef. *Die deutsche Dichtung der Geniezeit*. Stuttgart: Metzler, 1952. viii, 367pp.

Approach: same as No. 600. Organized by individual works. Includes lesser known poets. Excellent introductory study.

d. Classicism (1786-1805)

609. Burger, Heinz Otto, ed. *Begriffsbestimmung der Klassik und des Klassischen*. Darmstadt: Wissenschaftliche Buchgesellschaft, 1972. xvii, 483pp.

An anthology of important essays published 1926-1970 by foremost scholars. Pt 1: general treatment, definition, literary expression, historical position; pt. 2: specific literary phenomena. Excellent introduction to fundamental aspects of the period.

610. Ermatinger, Emil. *Deutsche Dichter (1750-1900). Eine Geistesgeschichte in Lebensbildern. Überarbeitet mit Bildern und Bildtexten versehen von Jörn Görres*. 2nd ed. Bonn, Frankfurt: Athenäum, 1961. 855pp. ([1]1948-1949)

Intellectual-historical approach: emphasis on cultural and sociological factors of the time as they relate to the development of individual authors. Particularly valuable sections: Klopstock, Wieland, Lessing, Goethe, Schiller, Hölderlin, Jean Paul, Grillparzer, Hebbel. Good background material.

611. Hettner, Hermann. *Literaturgeschichte der Goethezeit*. Ed. by Johannes Anderegg. Munich: Beck, 1970. xii, 800pp. (Repr. of *Literaturgeschichte des achtzehnten Jahrhunderts*, III, 3rd rev. ed. 1876)

A highly detailed and well organized historical survey. The work of art is viewed both as an organic whole and in the context of its time. Pt. 1: Storm and Stress: Herder, Gerstenberg, early Goethe, Lenz, Klinger, Wagner, Maler Müller, Heinse, Hamann, Jacobi, the Pietists, Göttinger Hainbund, Schiller to 1787; pt. 2: Weimar Classicism: Kant, Goethe, Schiller, Forster, Klinger, Jean Paul, the beginnings of Romanticism, the arts, music, Goethe 1806-1832. Afterword by J. Anderegg on Hettner's work and methodology, pp. 709-738. Chronology. Primary and secondary bibliography. Index: authors and titles. A standard work which is still of value.

612. Kohlschmidt, Werner. *A History of German Literature, 1760-1805*. Trans, by Ian Hilton. New York: Holmes and Meier, 1975. viii, 406pp.

Translation of W.K., *Vom Barock zur Klassik*, pt. 3 (No. 544). Superb chronological survey with excellent work analyses and background material. Focus on Schiller and Goethe. Text samples translated. Bibliography, chronological table (history, literature), glossary, pp. 389-390. A very fine introduction for beginners and comparatists.

613. Korff, Hermann August. *Geist der Goethezeit. Versuch einer ideellen Entwicklung der klassisch-romantischer Literaturgeschichte*. 4 vols., + index vol. Leipzig: Weber (I, II), Koehler und Amelung (III, IV), 1923-1953; Koehler und Amelung, (index volume) 1958. (Repr. 1966)

Intellectual-historical approach; traces the recurring rhythm of rising and waning ideas with particular emphasis on the dichotomy irrationalism/rationalism. Excellent study of epochs: I, Storm and Stress; II, Classicism; III, early Romanticism; IV, late Romanticism. The wealth of detail in these volumes is made readily accessible by the systematically organized index volume.

614. Mayer, Hans. *Zur deutschen Klassik und Romantik*. Pfullingen: Neske, 1963. 365pp.

A collection of previously published essays on Wieland, Goethe, Schiller, Kleist, Jean Paul, R. Wagner; "Fragen der Romantikforschung," pp. 263-305. Marxist point of view.

615. Schultz, Franz. *Klassik und Romantik der Deutschen*. 2 vols. 3rd ed. Stuttgart: Metzler, 1959. ([1]1935-1940)

Intellectual-historical approach: I: "Die Grundlagen der klassisch-romantischen Literatur": emphasis on the interrelationships of the two periods. II: "Wesen und Form der klassisch-romantischen Literatur": interrelationships demonstrated on a morphological basis. Useful for advanced study.

616. Storz, Gerhard. *Klassik und Romantik. Eine stilgeschichtliche Darstellung*. Mannheim, Vienna, Zurich: Bibliographisches Institut, 1972. 247pp.

Using an intrinsic approach, oriented specifically on the interpretation of individual works, this study surveys the development of poetic style as a reflection of the aesthetic principles of each epoch. Index; author and subject. A substantial examination.

617. Strich, Fritz. *Deutsche Klassik und Romantik oder Vollendung und Unendlichkeit. Ein Vergleich.* 5th ed. Bern, Munich: Francke, 1962. 374pp. ([1]1923)

Rigid intellectual-historical attempt to apply Wölfflin's categories to literature. Category "style" is the unity of a work, a personality, a time, a nation. Operates within the polarity: classic style (*Vollendung*) vs. romantic style (*Unendlichkeit*). Little discussion of individual works and authors; assumes a broad knowledge of literary works of the period.

E. ROMANTICISM (1798-1835)

1. Forschungsberichte

618. Wiese, Benno von. "Forschungsbericht zur Romantik." *Dichtung und Volkstum* 38 (1937), 65-85.

619. Ruprecht, Erich. "Romantikforschung und Romantikprobleme." *Universitas* 3 (1948), 1447-1456.

620. Körner, Josef. "Zur Romantikforschung 1938-1946." In: J.K., *Marginalien. Kritische Beiträge zur geistesgeschichtlichen Forschung.* Frankfurt: Schult-Bulmke, 1950. 91pp.

621. Mayer, Hans. "Fragen der Romantikforschung." In: H.M., *Zur deutschen Klassik und Romantik*, 1963 (No. 614), pp. 263-305.

622. Müller, Joachim. "Romantikforschung." *DU* 15 (1963), 4, Beilage; 17 (1965), 5, Beilage; 20 (1968), 2, Beilage; 24 (1972), 5, Beilage.

623. Roisch, Ursula. "Analyse einiger Tendenzen der westdeutschen bürgerlichen Romantikforschung seit 1945." *WB* 16 (1970), 2, 52-81.

624. Heintz, Günter. "Neue Arbeiten zur Literatur zwischen 1815 und 1848." *Literatur in Wissenschaft und Unterricht* 5 (1972), 154-170.

2. Bibliographies

a. Completed Bibliographies

*** Bibliographie deutschsprachiger Bücher und Zeitschriftenaufsätze zur deutschen Literatur von der Aufklärung bis zur bürgerlichen Revolution 1848/49." And: "Internationale Bibliographie zur deutschen Klassik. 1750-1850." Coverage: 1955-1970; see (No. 575).

*** *Bibliographisches Handbuch der deutschen Literaturwissenschaft 1945-1969* (No. 123), I: see section IX, "Zeitalter der Klassik und Romantik," selected cumulation of (No. 129) to 1969.

625. Elkins, Jr., A.C., and L.J. Forstner, eds. *The Romantic Movement. Bibliography 1936-1970. A Master Cumulation from ELH, Philological Quarterly, and English Language Notes.* 7 vols. Ann Arbor: The Pierian Pr., 1973. 3289pp.

A selective and critical reprint of the periodical bibliographies on Romanticism published in *English Literary History* 4 (1937)-16 (1949), continued in *Philological Quarterly* 29 (1950)-43 (1964), continued in *English Language Notes* 3 Suppl. (1965)-9 Suppl. (1971). Vol. 7 contains indexes: author, main entry, reviewer, personal names, subject. Recent bibliographies quite extensive with numerous annotations. Excellent German section by various editors. Continued by *English Language Notes* (No. 627).

*** *Internationale Bibliographie zur Geschichte der deutschen Literatur* (No. 122), II, 1: see section "Deutschsprachige Literatur von 1789 bis 1830." Selected cumulation to 1969. Marxist-socialist criticism well represented.

626. Osborne, John. *Romantik.* Bern, Munich: Francke, 1971. 166pp.

Material on research in Romanticism, definition, background and history, relationship of the other arts, aesthetics and criticism, relationship to world literature; early Romanticism; Heidelberg circle; Berlin circle; smaller circles of Romanticism elsewhere in Germany. For each author entry: author bibliography, editions, letters and documents, biographies, studies. Indexes: names and subjects; authors. Clearly organized; easy to use.

b. Current Bibliographies

*** *Bibliographie der deutschen Sprach- und Literaturwissenschaft* (No. 129): see section XV, "Romantik," 1 (1945-1953)-16 (1976)ff. Most reliable and comprehensive current bibliography available. Editions and secondary material. Annual publication.

627. *English Language Notes.* "The Romantic Movement. A Selective and Critical Bibliography." 10 (1972) Suppl., 215pp.; 11 (1973) Suppl., 179pp.; 12 (1974) Suppl., 177pp.; 13 (1975) Suppl., 210pp.; 14 (1976), 155pp. Being continued. Exhaustive international bibliography.

*** *Germanistik* (No. 130): see section XXIX. "Goethezeit (1770-1830)," 1 (1960)-17 (1976)ff. Comprehensive quarterly, up to date. Editions and secondary material. Books are reviewed.

*** *MLA International Bibliography* (No. 125), II: see section "German Literature. Eighteenth and Early Nineteenth Centuries," 1921-1975ff. Annual cumulation. Editions and secondary material. Extensive and reliable.

*** *Referatendienst zur Literaturwissenschaft* (No. 131): see section "Geschichte der Nationalliteraturen. Deutsche Literatur (1770-1848)," 1 (1969)-6 (1975)ff. Marxist-socialist quarterly review of books. Limited in scope.

*** *The Year's Work in Modern Language Studies* (No. 127): see section "The Romantic Era," 16 (1954)-37 (1975)ff. Covers primary and secondary material for the previous year. Annotated.

3. Literary Histories

628. Benz, Richard. *Die deutsche Romantik. Geschichte einer geistigen Bewegung*. Stuttgart: Reclam, 1937. 487pp.

Presentation of a profile of Romanticism from a philosophical, psychological point of view. Little interpretation of literature. Good background reading. Assumes some knowledge of the movement.

629. Eichner, Hans, ed. *"Romantic" and Its Cognates. The European History of a Word*. Toronto, Buffalo: Univ. of Toronto Pr., 1972. 536pp.

A superb collection of 10 essays on the concept of Romanticism in Germany, England, France, Italy, Spain, and the Scandinavian countries. Of particular interest: R. Immerwahr, "'Romantic' and Its Cognates in England, Germany, and France," pp. 17-97; H. Eichner, "Germany/Romantisch-Romantik-Romantiker," pp. 98-156; H.H.H. Remak, "Trends of Recent Research on West European Romanticism," pp. 475-500. Chronological table, pp. 501-513. Index: proper names. A useful introduction to the period.

*** Ermatinger, Emil. *Deutsche Dichter (1750-1900). Eine Geistesgeschichte in Bildern*. 2nd ed. Bonn, Frankfurt: Athenäum, 1961. 855pp. (No. 610)

630. Furst, Lilian R. *Romanticism*. 2nd enl. ed. London: Methuen, 1976. viii, 84pp.

A compact introduction providing definitions and a chronological survey. Bibliography.

631. ———. *Romanticism in Perspective. A Comparative Study of Aspects of the Romantic Movements in England, France, and Germany*. London: Macmillan, New York: St. Martin's Pr., 1969. 366pp.

A three-pronged presentation of the era under the headings "Individualism," "Imagination," "Feeling." Chronological table 1720-1839. Index: names, titles. Annotated bibliography, pp. 351-357. A solid introduction.

632. Haym, Rudolf. *Die romantische Schule. Ein Beitrag zur Geschichte des deutschen Geistes*. 5th ed. Berlin: Weidmann, 1928. xii, 1004pp. ([1]1870; repr. 1961)

Intellectual-historical approach; excellent analysis of Romantic philosophy concentrating on a few major figures: Tieck, the Schlegels, Novalis, Schleiermacher, Schelling. Standard work on Romanticism; still valuable for basic insights. Edition of 1928 contains extensive bibliography by Josef Körner.. Useful feature of index: brief definitions of important terms. Difficult reading.

633. Immerwahr, Raymond. *Romantisch. Genese und Tradition einer Denkform.* Frankfurt: Athenäum, 1972, 211pp.

A detailed introduction to the concept "romantic" in English, French, and German literature. Index: names. An outstanding volume.

634. Kluckhohn, Paul. *Die deutsche Romantik.* Bielefeld, Leipzig: Velhagen & Klasing, 1924. ix, 286pp.

An in-depth survey of the period from an intellectual-historical point of view. Portions of the study are still useful for background reading.

635. Kohlschmidt, Werner. *Geschichte der deutschen Literatur von der Romantik bis zum späten Goethe.* Stuttgart: Reclam, 1974. 764pp. illus.

Discussion based on the analysis of major literary works, including early Romanticism, Hölderlin, Jean Paul, Hebel, E.T.A. Hoffmann, Kleist, Eichendorff, the late Goethe; not a diachronic survey but an examination of primary work. Index: names. Bibliography, pp. 723-745. A superb presentation.

*** Korff, Hermann August. *Geist der Goethezeit. Versuch einer ideellen Entwicklung der klassisch-romantischen Literaturgeschichte.* 4 vols. Leipzig: Weber, Koehler und Amelung, 1923-1958. (No. 613)

*** Mason, Gabriel R. *From Gottsched to Hebbel.* London: Harrap, 1961. 268pp. illus. (No. 588)

*** Newald, Richard, Willi Flemming, Fritz Martini, Wolfdietrich Rasch, Wolfgang Baumgart. *Geschichte der deutschen Literatur vom Humanismus bis zu Goethes Tod (1490-1832).* Stuttgart: Metzler, 1962. viii, 344pp. (No. 448)

636. Prang, Helmut, ed. *Begriffsbestimmung der Romantik.* Darmstadt: Wissenschaftliche Buchgesellschaft, 1968. vi, 441pp.

An anthology of 22 essays published by leading scholars from 1911-1968. A solid introduction to important aspects of research in Romanticism. Notes.

637. Prawer, Siegbert, ed. *The Romantic Period in Germany. Essays by Members of the London University.* London: Weidenfeld and Nicolson, 1970. 343pp.

A general introduction: historical background, definitions, favored literary genres, the visual arts, music, and philosophy.

A wide-ranging survey of the period, designed for the general reader. Bibliography at the end of each section.

638. Reimann, Paul. *Hauptströmungen der deutschen Literatur, 1750-1848. Beiträge zu ihrer Geschichte und Kritik.* Berlin: Dietz, 1956. 856pp.

Historical survey from a militant, Marxist-socialist point of view. Index: names. Bibliography, pp. 825-834. A bit too dogmatic.

639. Robson-Scott, William D. *The Literary Background of the Gothic Revival in Germany. A Chapter in the History of Taste.* London: Oxford Univ. Pr., 1965. xiii, 334pp.

Background material on the period covering the influence of France and England, Storm and Stress, Romanticism and the revival of German medieval architecture. Individual chapters grouped around major authors, architects, art historians, critics, archeologists, engravers. Indexes: author, subject.

640. Ryan, Lawrence. "Romanticism," *Periods in German Literature* (No. 453), pp. 123-143.

*** Schultz, Franz. *Klassik und Romantik der Deutschen.* 2 vols. 3rd ed. Stuttgart: Metzler, 1959. (No. 615)

641. ——— and Hans Jürg Lüthi. "Romantik." *Reallexikon* (No. 1288), III, pp. 578-594.

*** Stahl, E.L., and W.E. Yuill. *German Literature of the Eighteenth and Nineteenth Centuries.* New York: Barnes & Noble, 1970. xxiv, 510pp. (No. 591)

*** Storz, Gerhard. *Klassik und Romantik. Eine stilgeschichtliche Darstellung.* Mannheim, Vienna, Zurich: Bibliographisches Institut, 1972. 247pp. (No. 616)

*** Strich, Fritz. *Deutsche Klassik und Romantik oder Vollendung und Unendlichkeit. Ein Vergleich.* 5th ed. Bern, Munich: Francke, 1962. 374pp. (No. 617)

642. Tymms, Ralph. *German Romantic Literature.* London: Methuen, 1955. vii, 405pp.

Chronological treatment of major authors, with particular attention to ideas and motifs recurring throughout the period. Extensive discussions of individual works. Excellent for its accumulative manner of presentation.

*** Viëtor, Karl. *Deutsches Dichten und Denken von der Aufklärung bis zum Realismus. Deutsche Literaturgeschichte von 1700-1890.* Berlin: de Gruyter, 1936. 156pp. (No. 592)

*** Walzel, Oskar. *Deutsche Dichtung von Gottsched bis zur Gegenwart.* 2 vols. Wildpark-Potsdam: Athenaion, 1930. (No. 593)

643. Wellek, René. *Concepts of Criticism.* New Haven, London: Yale Univ. Pr., 1963. xv, 403pp.

A collection of 14 superb essays on a variety of topics of literary history. See especially: "The Concept of Romanticism in Literary History," pp. 128-198, and "Romanticism Re-examined," pp. 199-221. Comparative in scope.

644. ———. *Confrontations. Studies in the Intellectual and Literary Relations between Germany, England, and the United States during the Nineteenth Century.* Princeton: Princeton Univ. Pr., 1965. vi, 221pp.

See: "English and German Romanticism," pp. 3-33, and "Carlyle and German Romanticism," pp. 34-81.

645. Wiese, Benno von, ed. *Deutsche Dichter der Romantik. Ihr Leben und Werk.* Berlin: Schmidt, 1971. 530pp.

Substantial essays on the leading figures of Romanticism: Achim and Bettina von Arnim, C. Brentano, Chamisso, Eichendorff, Görres, Hauff, Hebel, Hoffmann, Jean Paul, Kleist, Mörike, Novalis, A.W. Schlegel, F. Schlegel, Tieck, Uhland, Wackenroder. Each essay discusses the author's artistic development and literary achievements. Primary/secondary bibliography for each chapter. Excellent appraisals.

646. Willoughby, Leonard A. *The Romantic Movement in Germany.* Cambridge: Oxford Univ. Pr., 1930. vi, 192ff. (Repr. 1966)

A compact survey of the Romantic movement, Kleist, Grillparzer, and Young Germany, which presents the main ideas in capsule form; individual works are scarcely mentioned. A number of minor writers are included. Index: authors, subjects. Bibliography, pp. 182-186, has not been updated in the reprint. The study has some merit as an introduction.

F. LITERATURE 1830-1880

1. Forschungsberichte

647. Martini, Fritz. "Ergebnisse und Aufgaben der Dichtungsgeschichte des 19. Jahrhunderts. Ein Literaturbericht." *Dichtung und Volkstum* 38 (1937), 86-102.

648. ———. "Neue Forschungen zur Dichtungsgeschichte des 19. Jahrhunderts." *Dichtung und Volkstum* 40 (1939), 342-363.

649. Stuckert, Franz. "Zur Dichtung des Realismus und des Jahrhundertendes." *DVLG* 19 (1941), Suppl., 79-136.

650. Weydt, Günther. "Biedermeier und Junges Deutschland. Eine Literatur- und Problemschau." *DVLG* 25 (1951), 506-521.

651. Meyer, Herbert. "Das literarische Biedermeier." *DU* 4 (1952), 2, Beilage.

652. Hock, Erich. "Ausgaben deutscher Dichter." *Wirkendes Wort* 6 (1955-1956), 25-41 and 92-105.

653. Martini, Fritz. "Deutsche Literatur in der Zeit des 'bürgerlichen Realismus.' Ein Literaturbericht." *DVLG* 34 (1960), 581-666.

654. ———. *Forschungsbericht zur deutschen Literatur in der Zeit des Realismus.* Stuttgart: Metzler, 1962. 92pp.

655. Stein, Peter. "'Vormärz'als literaturgeschichtliche Epochenbezeichnung." *Wirkendes Wort* 22 (1972), 411-426.

656. Kahrmann, Bernd and Cordula. "Bürgerlicher Realismus." *Wirkendes Wort* 23 (1973), 53-68.

657. ———. "Bürgerlicher Realismus II. Keller, Fontane, Raabe." *Wirkendes Wort* 24 (1974), 339-356.

658. ———, Heinrich Rickartz, Barbara Steinberg. "Bürgerlicher Realismus III. Stifter, Hebbel, Otto Ludwig." *Wirkendes Wort* 26 (1976), 356-381.

2. Bibliographies

a. Completed Bibliographies

*** *Bibliographisches Handbuch der deutschen Literaturwissenschaft 1945-1972* (No. 124), II: see section X: "Neunzehntes Jahrhundert: 1830-1880." Selected cumulation of (No. 129) to 1972.

659. Cowen, Roy C. *Neunzehntes Jahrhundert (1830-1880)*. Bern, Munich: Francke, 1970. 216pp.

1. General background material, history, culture, philosophy; 2. literary histories; 3. drama; 4. reaction against Goethe and Classicism; 5. influence of Romanticism; 6. prose; 7. comedy; 8. Renaissance literature; 9. Wagner and Nietzsche. Indexes: author, subject. Reliable and handy for quick reference.

*** *Internationale Bibliographie zur Geschichte der deutschen Literatur* (No. 122), II, 1: see section "Deutschsprachige Literatur von 1830 bis 1900." Selected cumulation to 1969. Marxist-socialist criticism well represented.

b. Current Bibliographies

*** *Bibliographie der deutschen Sprach- und Literaturwissenschaft* (No. 129): see section XVI. "19. Jahrhundert. 1830-1880," 1

(1945-1953)-16 (1976)ff. Most comprehensive and reliable current bibliography available; editions and secondary material. Publ. annually.

*** *Germanistik* (No. 130): see section XXX, "Von der Spätromantik bis zum Realismus (1830-1880)," 1 (1960)-17 (1976)ff. Comprehensive quarterly, up to date. Editions and secondary material. Books are reviewed.

*** *MLA International Bibliography* (No. 125), II: see section "German Literature. VI. Nineteenth and Early Twentieth Centuries," 1921-1975ff. Annual cumulation. Editions and secondary material. Extensive and generally reliable.

*** *Referatendienst zur Literaturwissenschaft* (No. 131): see section "Geschichte der Nationalliteraturen. Deutsche Literatur (1848-1900)," 1 (1969)-6 (1975)ff. Marxist-socialist quarterly review of books. Limited in scope.

*** *The Year's Work in Modern Language Studies* (No. 127): see section "Literature, 1830-1880," 5 (1934)-37 (1975)ff. Covers primary and secondary material for the previous year. Annotated.

3. Literary Histories

a. Entire Period (1830-1880)

660. Alker, Ernst. *Die deutsche Literatur im 19. Jahrhundert (1832-1914).* 2nd rev. ed. Stuttgart: Kröner, 1961. 943pp. Same as following except that the 2nd and 3rd editions are revised to include the twentieth century.

661. ———. *Geschichte der deutschen Literatur von Goethes Tod bis zur Gegenwart.* 2 vols. Stuttgart: Cotta, 1949-1950. 453pp.; 525pp.

Morphological approach: treats individual authors under genre headings. Includes many minor authors. Volumes contain a wealth of facts; written in a journalistic rather than a scholarly vein.

662. Boeschenstein, Hermann. *German Literature of the Nineteenth Century.* New York: St. Martin's Press, 1969. vi, 170pp.

Concise treatment of the cultural and aesthetic achievements of the period from Immermann to Heyse. Despite the flaws inherent in its focus on "modernistic" features of the era, the book is an excellent introduction. Good bibliography stressing English contributions to research.

663. Böttcher, Kurt, Rainer Rosenberg, Helmut Richter, Kurt Krolop. *Geschichte der deutschen Literatur. Achter Band. Von 1830 bis*

zum Ausgang des 19. Jahrhunderts. Erster Halbband. 1830-1870. Berlin: Volk und Wissen, 1975. 708pp. illus.

Part 1 of VIII of the official Marxist-socialist history of German literature of the GDR. Provides extensive social and economic background for the periods 1830-1840, 1849-1870. Particular focus on the development of early proletarian literature and workers' literature. Index in vol. 8, pt. 2.

664. Bramstead, Ernest K. *Aristocracy and the Middle-Classes in Germany. Social Types in German Literature 1830-1900.* 2nd rev. ed. Chicago, London: Univ. of Chicago Pr., 1964. xxiv, 364pp. ([1]1937)

An examination of literature from a sociological and historical point of view in two parts: 1. "Aristocracy and the Middle-Class 1830-1900"; 2. "The Place of the German Writer in German Society 1830-1900." Emphasis is on the novel. Still one of the better studies available in English. Bibliography. Indexes: author, subject.

665. Bruford, Walter Horace. *The German Tradition of Self-Cultivation. "Bildung" from Humboldt to Thomas Mann.* London, New York: Cambridge Univ. Pr., 1975. 290pp.

Chapters on W. v. Humboldt, Goethe, Schleiermacher, Schopenhauer, Stifter, Vischer, Nietzsche, Fontane, and T. Mann. Bibliography. Index: names. Not meant as an introduction.

666. David, Claude. *Zwischen Romantik und Symbolismus 1820-1885.* Gütersloh: Mohn, 1966. 222pp.

Chronological survey of the period by genre, covering major figures. Intellectual-historical orientation. Good introduction.

*** Ermatinger, Emil. *Deutsche Dichter (1750-1900). Eine Geistesgeschichte in Lebensbildern.* 2nd ed. Bonn, Frankfurt: Athenäum, 1961. 855pp. (No. 610)

667. Field, G. Wallis. *A Literary History of Germany. The Nineteenth Century, 1830-1890.* London, Tonbridge: Benn, 1975. xv, 214pp.

A compact survey with background material in capsule form. Covers drama, prose, Heine, poetry, philosophical currents (Nietzsche), Poetic Realism, Fontane and the social novel. Summaries and major themes at times too encyclopedic. Index: names. Bibliography, pp. 185-202. Useful as a first introduction.

668. Fuerst, Norbert. *The Victorian Age of German Literature. 8 Essays.* Univ. Park, London: Penn. State Univ., Pr., 1966. 206pp.

Loosely connected essays on major events and literary figures of the epoch. Focuses on the reception of German literature abroad with articles on Grillparzer, Young Germany, Heine,

Keller, and on the history and philosophy of the period. Judgments highly subjective; of limited value.

669. Koch, Franz. *Idee und Wirklichkeit. Deutsche Dichtung zwischen Romantik und Naturalismus.* 2 vols. Düsseldorf: Ehlermann, 1956. 327pp., 467pp.

Presentation concentrates on the most important figures and their contribution to German literature. Although the emphasis is on the development of ideas, this book is an excellent source of factual information. Treats drama and prose fully, lyric poetry superficially. Extensive bibliography at end of II.

670. Lublinski, Samuel. *Literatur und Gesellschaft im neunzehnten Jahrhundert.* 4 vols. Berlin: Cronbach, 1899-1900.

I. *Die Frühzeit der Romantik.* 1899. viii, 152pp.
II. *Romantik und Historizismus.* 1899. 154pp.
III. *Das junge Deutschland.* 1900. 180pp.
IV. *Blüte, Epigonentum und Wiedergeburt.* 1900. 186pp.

A readable history of the social aspect of literature centered around poets. Some analysis of individual works. No indexes.

*** Mayer, Hans. *Von Lessing bis Thomas Mann. Wandlungen in der bürgerlichen Literatur in Deutschland.* Pfullingen: Neske, 1959. 414pp. (No. 589)

671. Mühlher, Robert. *Österreichische Dichter seit Grillparzer. Gesammelte Aufsätze.* Vienna, Stuttgart: Braumüller, 1973. 451pp.

A collection of previously published essays on Grillparzer, Nestroy, Stifter, Lenau, and others. Index: authors. Notes. Somewhat diffuse in thrust; valuable studies on the whole.

*** Natan, Alex, ed. *German Men of Letters. Twelve Literary Essays.* 5 vols. London: Wolff, 1961-1969. (No. 734)

For 19th century see: I. 1961. viii, 273pp.: Droste-Hülshoff, Eichendorff, Fontane, Grillparzer, Hauptmann, Hebbel, Herder, Hofmannsthal, Keller, Meyer, Storm, Tieck; V. 1969. 319pp.: C. Brentano, Gotthelf, Grabbe, Hoffmann, Jean Paul, Lenau, Nestroy, Platen, Raabe, Spitteler, Stifter.

672. Sagarra, Eda. *Tradition and Revolution. German Literature and Society 1830-1890.* New York: Basic Books, 1971. 348pp.

Not a history of literature but a study of the interrelationship between art and society. Emphasis is on the sociological and intellectual context of the literature of the period. Written with the beginner in mind but often oversimplified and subjective in judgment. Satisfactory as background reading.

673. Schmidt, Adalbert. *Dichtung und Dichter Österreichs im 19. und 20. Jahrhundert.* 2 vols. Salzburg, Stuttgart: Verlag Das Bergland Buch, 1964. 464pp., 460pp.

Chronological discussion of over 500 authors and their work.

Lengthy quotations from primary works. Somewhat impressionistic; often too brief and summary. II: bio-bibliographical section, pp. 367-452. Index: names. Handy as a first introduction.

*** Stahl, E.L., and W.E. Yuill. *German Literature of the Eighteenth and Nineteenth Centuries.* New York: Barnes & Noble, 1970. xxiv, 510pp. (No. 591)

674. Stern, J.P. *Idylls and Realities. Studies in 19th Century Literature.* New York: Ungar, 1971. 232pp.

General introductory essay followed by examination of authors who characterize the age: Grillparzer, Hebbel, Büchner, Heine, Mörike, Stifter, Keller, Raabe, Fontane, Nietzsche. Discussion includes copious text specimens. Focus on the contrast between the "idyllic" literary output and the social and political "realities" of the time; somewhat polemic on the failure of German liberalism. Index: authors. Selected bibliography.

*** Viëtor, Karl. *Deutsches Dichten und Denken von der Aufklärung bis zum Realismus. Deutsche Literaturgeschichte von 1700-1890.* Berlin: de Gruyter, 1936. 156pp. (No. 592)

675. Walzel, Oskar. *Die deutsche Dichtung seit Goethes Tod.* 2nd ed. Berlin: Askanischer Verlag, 1920. xiv, 527pp.

Range: 1830-1918. An extensive and important survey.

*** ———. *Deutsche Dichtung von Gottsched bis zur Gegenwart.* 2 vols. Wildpark-Potsdam: Athenaion, 1930. (No. 593)

676. Wiese, Benno von, ed. *Deutsche Dichter des 19. Jahrhunderts. Ihr Leben und Werk.* Berlin: Schmidt, 1969. 600pp.

Substantial essays on: Tieck, Rückert, Platen, Immermann, Börne, Heine, Grabbe, Büchner, Droste-Hülshoff, Gotthelf, Grillparzer, Raimund, Nestroy, Lenau, Stifter, Hebbel, Reuter, Keller, Meyer, Storm, Liliencron, Raabe, Fontane. Each essay details the author's artistic development and literary achievements. Primary/secondary bibliography (brief). Excellent appraisals.

b. Biedermeier, Young Germany, Vormärz (1815-1848)

677. Behrens, Wolfgang W., Gerhard Bott, Hans-Wolf Jäger, Ulrich Schmid, Johannes Weber, Peter Werbick. *Der literarische Vormärz.* Munich: List, 1973. 359pp.

An introduction to the period from a sociological point of view. Pt. 1: specimen texts from the epoch, pp. 35-158; pt. 2: criticism and survey of research, focus on the critical reception of the era 1850-1945 in the FRG and the GDR. Includes a short biography of authors in the period, pp. 279-284. Index: author and subject. Bibliography, pp. 285-299. Background material to *Vormärz* literature.

678\. Dietze, Walter. *Junges Deutschland und deutsche Klassik. Zur Ästhetik und Literaturtheorie des Vormärz.* Berlin: Rütten & Loening, 1957. 393pp.

Range: 1820-1848. A substantial history of the Young Germany movement in the context of its literary tradition. Major figures, themes, and developments are examined in detail. Evaluation from a Marxist point of view. Very extensive bibliography, pp. 352-378. Index: names. A valuable study.

679\. Greiner, Martin. *Zwischen Biedermeier und Bourgeoisie. Ein Kapitel deutscher Literaturgeschichte.* Göttingen: Vandenhoeck & Ruprecht, 1953. 339pp.

Three parts: 1. "Das Erbe und der Verwalter," 2. "Die Epigonen und der Weg ins Idyll," 3. "Die Zerrissenen und die Flucht ins Exil." Focus on Heinrich Heine, with discussions of Nestroy, Grillparzer, Immermann, Platen, Droste-Hülshoff, Mörike, Grabbe, Büchner, and Young Germany poets. Not meant as a reference work.

680\. Hermand, Jost, and Manfred Windfuhr, eds. *Zur Literatur der Restaurationsepoche 1815-1848. Forschungsreferate und Aufsätze. Friedrich Sengle zum 60. Geburtstag von seinen Schülern.* Stuttgart: Metzler, 1970. viii, 599pp.

The essays are in two parts: 1. surveys of research: problems of the epoch, Lenau, Platen, Droste-Hülshoff, Grabbe, Tieck, Gotthelf, Sealsfield; 2. essays on specific literary aspects of the period. A good critical survey with extensive notes at the end of each essay. Index: names.

681\. Höllerer, Walter. *Zwischen Klassik und Moderne. Lachen und Weinen in der Dichtung einer Übergangszeit.* Stuttgart: Klett, 1958. 503pp.

Transitional period from Goethe's death to Heine's death seen as anticipation of the twentieth century. Concentrates on meticulous interpretation of specimen texts from individual works as characteristic expression of the period. Major authors treated in terms of the important themes in their works. Selected bibliography; separate bibliography on "Biedermeier controversy."

682\. Houben, Heinrich Hubert. *Jungdeutscher Sturm und Drang.* Leipzig: Brockhaus, 1911. 704pp. (Repr. 1974)

A comprehensive positivistic survey with its focus on the contributions of major literary figures: Börne, Heine, Wienbarg, Laube, Mundt, Gutzkow, Varnhagen von Ense, G. Schlesier, G. Kühne, A. Jung. Many text samples and documents of the time. Index: names and subjects.

683\. Kainz, Friedrich, and Werner Kohlschmidt. "Junges Deutschland." *Reallexikon* (No. 1288), I, pp. 781-797.

684\. Neubuhr, Elfriede, ed. *Begriffsbestimmung des literarischen Biedermeier.* Darmstadt: Wissenschaftliche Buchgesellschaft, 1974. vi, 386pp.

A collection of 13 of the most important articles on the subject, published 1930's-1970's. An excellent introduction to the field.

*** Mason, Gabriel R. *From Gottsched to Hebbel.* London: Harrap, 1961. 268pp. illus. (No. 588)

685. Norst, M.J. "Biedermeier." *Periods in German Literature* (No. 453), pp. 147-168.

*** Reimann, Paul. *Hauptströmungen der deutschen Literatur, 1750-1848. Beiträge zu ihrer Geschichte und Kritik.* Berlin: Dietz, 1956. 856pp. (No. 638)

686. Sengle, Friedrich. *Biedermeierzeit. Deutsche Literatur im Spannungsfeld zwischen Restauration und Revolution 1815-1848.* Stuttgart: Metzler, 1971- .

I. *Allgemeine Voraussetzungen, Richtungen, Darstellungsmittel.* 1971. xix, 725pp.
II. *Die Formenwelt.* 1972. xvi, 1152pp.
III. (in preparation)

This promises to be the standard work on the Biedermeier period. I: historical-cultural background, methodology, aesthetics of the period. II: 7 chapters: 1. the literary scene, including the emerging theory of genre, the question of verse vs. prose, the problem of translation; 2. functional subgenres such as didactic poetry, epigram, aphorism, parable, fable, travelogue; 3. drama and the theater, tragedy, comedy, and farce; 4. lyric poetry, themes, motifs, forms; 5. epic poetry; 6. the idyll; 7. prose, its themes, motifs, forms. Extensive index: terms, names, place names, and subdivision of individual chapters makes contents easily accessible for use as a reference work.

687. Stein, Peter. *Epochenproblem Vormärz. 1815-1848.* Stuttgart: Metzler, 1974. 115pp.

An extensive survey of research with emphasis on publications from 1945-1970's; evaluates theories and methods of periodization in literary history from a socialist point of view; reports on the major critical and historical analyses of the period. Bibliography at the end of each section. Important works enumerated, pp. 102-112. Index: authors.

c. Realism (1848-1898)

688. Brinkmann, Richard, ed. *Begriffsbestimmung des literarischen Realismus.* Darmstadt: Wissenschaftliche Buchgesellschaft, 1969. xvi, 496pp.

Introduction plus 17 essays previously published by specialists from East and West Germany, including Auerbach, Lukács, Iwastschenko, Adorno, H. Mayer, Martini, Wellek, Preisendanz. Articles are not limited to German literature. Includes some analysis of individual works. Provides an excellent overview of the research from 1946-1966.

689. Martini, Fritz. *Deutsche Literatur im bürgerlichen Realismus 1848-1898*. Stuttgart: Metzler, 1962. xvi, 908pp.

Morphological approach: drama, lyric, prose treated separately. Extremely thorough presentation of philosophical and social background combined with detailed discussion of major authors. See especially sections on: Hebbel, Ludwig, Stifter, Keller, Storm, Raabe, Fontane. Extensive bibliography. Table: chronology relating German developments to European context. Indispensable.

690. ———. "Realismus." *Reallexikon* (No. 1288), III, pp. 343-365.

691. Ritchie, James M. "Realism." *Periods in German Literature* (No. 453), pp. 171-195.

G. LITERATURE 1880-1945

1. Forschungsberichte

a. Entire Period

692. Martini, Fritz. "Deutsche Literatur zwischen 1880 und 1950." *DVLG* 26 (1952), 478-535.

b. Naturalism, Impressionism, Jugendstil

693. Hermand, Jost. "Jugendstil. Ein Forschungsbericht 1918-1962." *DVLG* 38 (1964), 70-110 and 273-315.

694. ———. *Jugendstil. Ein Forschungsbericht 1918-1964*. Stuttgart: Metzler, 1965. 91pp.

695. Stroka, Anna. "Der Impressionismus der deutschen Literatur." *Germanica Wratislaviensia* 10 (1966), 141-161.

696. Hoefert, Sigfried. "Zum Stand der Naturalismusforschung." *Akten des V. Internationalen Germanisten-Kongresses* (1976), 3, 300-308.

c. Expressionism

697. Schneider, Karl L. "Neuere Literatur zur Dichtung des deutschen Expressionismus." *Euphorion* 47 (1953), 99-110.

698. Konrad, Gustav. "Expressionismus." *Wirkendes Wort* 7 (1956/57), 351-365.

699. Brinkmann, Richard. "Expressionismus-Probleme. Die Forschung der Jahre 1952-1958." *DVLG* 33 (1959), 104-181.

700. ———. "Neue Literatur zum Expressionismus." *DVLG* 34 (1960), 306-322. (Covers literature to 1960.)

701. ———. *Expressionismus. Forschungsprobleme 1952-1960.* Stuttgart: Metzler, 1961. 98pp.

702. Chiarini, Paolo. "Recenti studi null'espressionismo." *Studi Germanici*, NS 2 (1964), 2, 104-116.

703. Raabe, Paul. "Expressionismus. Eine Literaturübersicht." *DU* 16 (1964), 2, Beilage.

704. Ritchie, James M. "The Expressionist Revival." *Seminar* 2 (1966), 37-49.

d. Exile Literature

705. Spalek, John M. "Exilliteratur und Exilforschung in den USA." *Coll. Germ.* (1971), 157-166.

706. Arnold, Heinz Ludwig, and Hans-Albert Walter. "Die Exil-Literatur und ihre Erforschung." *Akzente* 20 (1973), 481-508.

707. Hans, Jan, and Werner Röder. "Emigrationsforschung." *Akzente* 20 (1973), 580-591.

708. Herz, Ulrich. *Literatur und Politik im Exil. Eine Bestandsaufnahme der internationalen Emigrationsforschung.* Stockholm: Stockholmer Koordinationsstelle zur Erforschung der deutschsprachigen Exil-Literatur, 1973. 30pp.

709. Laemmle, Peter. "Vorschläge für eine Revision der Exilforschung." *Akzente* 20 (1973), 509-519.

710. Roloff, Gerhard. *Die Erforschung der deutschen Exilliteratur. Stand, Probleme, Aufgaben.* Hamburg: Arbeitsstelle für Deutsche Exilliteratur, 1973. 180pp.

2. Bibliographies

a. Completed Bibliographies

711. Berthold, Werner. *Exil-Literatur 1933-1945. Eine Ausstellung aus Beständen der Deutschen Bibliothek.* Frankfurt am Main. 3rd rev. ed. Frankfurt: Deutsche Bibliothek, 1967. 352pp. ([1]1965)

Exhibition catalog: 362 publications are grouped under broad subject headings. Annotations include brief author biographies and some primary bibliography. Listing of exile journals, pp. 288-309. Appendix: scientists in exile. Individual items are best located through the indexes: names, newspapers and journals, organizations, institutions, publishing houses.

*** *Bibliographisches Handbuch der deutschen Literaturwissenschaft 1945-1972* (No. 124), II: see section XI. "19. Jahrhundert. Ende und Übergang zum 20. (1880-1914)" and XII. "Deutschsprachige Literatur des 20. Jahrhunderts. A. Vom Ende des 1. Weltkrieges bis 1945." Selected cumulation of (No. 129) to 1972.

712. Goff, Penrith. *Wilhelminisches Zeitalter.* Bern, Munich: Francke, 1971. 216pp.

Range: authors who first published between 1888-1918. General, historical and cultural background material; literary history, genres, movements of the period; 112 authors, A-Z. Each author entry lists primary and secondary literature. Indexes: author, subject. Easy to use.

*** *Internationale Bibliographie zur Geschichte der deutschen Literatur* (No. 122), II, 1: see section "Deutschsprachige Literatur von 1900 bis zur Gegenwart." Selected cumulation to 1969. Marxist-socialist criticism well represented.

713. Jacob, Walter. "A Bibliography of Novels and Short Stories by German Jewish Authors 1800-1914." *Studies in Bibliography and Booklore* 6 (1962/63), 75-92. Listing by author A-Z.

714. Melzwig, Brigitte. *Deutsche sozialistische Literatur 1918-1945. Bibliographie der Buchveröffentlichungen.* Berlin, Weimar: Aufbau, 1975. 617pp.

Lists 1001 first editions (1918-1945), reprints and translations (1918-1969) for 97 authors, journalists, and important foreign-born authors, A-Z. Indexes: chronology, titles, names, anthologies. Substantial primary bibliography. Reliable.

715. Pickar, Gertrud B. *Deutsches Schrifttum zwischen den beiden Weltkriegen (1918-1945).* Bern, Munich: Francke, 1974. 139pp.

Range: authors who first published between 1918-1945. Selected bibliography to 1965. Divided into 2 parts: 1: bibliographies, lexica, literature of the Twenties, the Third Reich, emigration, themes and genres; 2: 204 authors A-Z (Brecht at the end of the alphabet), editions, documents, and secondary literature for each author. Index: authors. Very easy to use.

716. Raabe, Paul. *Index Expressionismus. Bibliographie der Beiträge in den Zeitschriften und Jahrbüchern des literarischen Expressionismus 1910-1925.* 18 vols. Nendeln, Liechtenstein: Kraus-Thomson, 1972.

Serie A. Alphabetischer Index. 4 vols. Authors A-Z.
Serie B. Systematischer Index. 5 vols. Subjects.
Serie C. Index nach Zeitschriften. 5 vols.
Serie D. Titelregister. 2 vols.
Serie E. Gattungsregister. 2 vols.

An exhaustive bibliographical analysis of 100 journals and 5 yearbooks. Reliable and easy to use.

717. Soffke, Günther. *Deutsches Schrifttum im Exil 1933-1950. Ein Bestandsverzeichnis.* Bonn: Bouvier, 1965. 64pp.

Author list A-Z; includes literature, history, politics, anthologies, translations, editions, journals. Of limited usefulness.

718. *Veröffentlichungen deutscher sozialistischer Schriftsteller in der revolutionären und demokratischen Presse 1918-1945. Bibliographie.* Ed. by the Deutsche Akademie der Künste zu Berlin: Sektion der Dichtkunst und Sprachpflege. Abt. Geschichte der sozialistischen Literatur. 2nd ed. Berlin, Weimar: Aufbau, 1969. xvi, 657pp. ([1]1966)

Lists ca. 12,000 publications of 109 authors, critics, and important foreign authors in journals and newspapers, A-Z. Index: newspapers and journals. CAUTION: major authors (e.g., Brecht, F. Wolf), for whom author bibliographies are available, are not included.

719. *Veröffentlichungen der Stockholmer Koordinationsstelle zur Erforschung der deutschsprachigen Exil-Literatur.* Stockholm: Deutsches Institut.

Bericht I. 1970. 158pp.	*Bericht VI.* 1973. 87pp.
Bericht II. 1971. 118pp.	*Bericht VII.* 1974. 135pp.
Bericht III. 1972. 112pp.	*Bericht VIII.* 1974. 108pp.
Bericht IV. 1972. 97pp.	*Bericht IX.* 1975. 106pp.
Bericht V. 1973. 102pp.	*Bericht X.* 1975. 104pp.

Includes bibliography on primary and secondary material. Very comprehensive; reports on proposed research projects. Will not be continued.

b. Current Bibliographies

*** *Bibliographie der deutschen Sprach- und Literaturwissenschaft* (No. 129): see section XVII, "19. Jahrhundert. 1880-1914," and XVIII, "20. Jahrhundert. 1914-1945," 1 (1945-1953)-16 (1976)ff. Most comprehensive and reliable current bibliography available. Editions and secondary material. Published annually.

720. "Bibliography." *Journal of Modern Literature.* 1 (1970/71), Suppl., 644-985; 3 (1973/74), 351-886; 4 (1974/75), 169-525; 4 (1975), Suppl., 892-1177; 5 (1976), 545-887. To be continued.

Annual bibliography of books, including editions, dissertations, symposia, special numbers, articles on 20th-century literature. Some reviews of books. Focus on English titles.

*** *Germanistik* (No. 130): see section XXXI, "Vom Naturalismus bis zur Gegenwart," 1 (1960)-17 (1976)ff. Comprehensive quarterly, up to date. Editions and secondary material. Books are reviewed.

*** *MLA International Bibliography* (No. 125), II: see section "German Literature. VI. Nineteenth and Early Twentieth Centuries" and "VII. Recent Literature," 1921-1975ff. Annual cumulations. Editions and secondary material. Extensive and generally reliable.

*** *Referatendienst zur Literaturwissenschaft* (No. 131): see section "Geschichte der Nationalliteraturen. Deutsche Literatur (1900-Gegenwart)." 1 (1969)-6 (1975)ff. Marxist-socialist quarterly review of books. Limited in scope.

721. *Twentieth Century Literature* 1 (1955)-22 (1976)ff.: see section "Current Bibliography." Quarterly for modern literature; each issue contains an annotated review of articles (only!). Some German titles included. Up to date.

*** *The Year's Work in Modern Language Studies* (No. 127): see section "German Literature, 1880 to the Present Day," 4 (1933)-37 (1975)ff. Covers primary and secondary material for the previous year. Annotated.

3. Literary Histories

a. Entire Period (1880-1945)

722. Adling, Wilfried, et al., eds. *Lexikon sozialistischer deutscher Literatur. Von den Anfängen bis 1945. Monographisch-historische Darstellungen*. Gießen: Polit-Buchvertrieb, 1973. 592pp.

Introduction presents a brief history of socialist literature 1844-1945; lexicon (A-Z) of forerunners and figures of socialist literature, including authors, publicists, theoreticians, publishing houses, journals, organizations, etc.: for figures chiefly an appraisal of social contributions; lists some relatively unknown material. Indexes: names, historic events and personages encountered in literature. Bibliography a part of each entry.

723. Alker, Ernst. *Profile und Gestalten der deutschen Literatur nach 1914. Mit einem Kapitel über den Expressionismus von Zoran Konstantinović*. Ed. by Eugen Thurnher. Stuttgart: Kröner, 1977. xvi, 880pp.

Compiled from the literary remains of Alker. A survey of hundreds of authors from 1914 to the 1960's. Valuable for its commentary on many minor authors. Includes much on Austrian and Swiss literature. Index: names. At times too encyclopedic.

724. Bithell, Jethro. *Modern German Literature, 1880-1950*. 3rd rev. ed. London: Methuen, 1959. xii, 584pp. ([1]1939)

Extensive summaries of individual works with excerpts as examples of style characterising author and work. Bithell's approach, stressing national character and the geographical origin of the author, is somewhat outdated; therefore criticism is often inadequate and subjective. Comprehensive bibliography.

725. Friedmann, Hermann, and Otto Mann (eds.). *Deutsche Literatur im 20. Jahrhundert. Strukturen und Gestalten.* 2 vols. 4th rev. ed. Heidelberg: Rothe, 1961. 332pp., 383pp. ([1]1954)

Essays by eminent scholars. I. *Strukturen*: chapters on genres, individual periods, intellectual development. II. *Gestalten*: chapters on individual writers, presenting evaluation of their achievements and critical reception. Some appraisals have been superseded by more recent scholarship.

726. Gray, Ronald. *The German Tradition in Literature 1871-1945.* Cambridge: Cambridge Univ. Pr., 1965. viii, 384pp.

Traces the tradition of polarity and synthesis in literature. Chapters on the writer and politics, Thomas Mann, Rilke, Hofmannsthal. Bibliography.

727. Günther, Werner. *Dichter der neueren Schweiz.* 2 vols. Munich, Bern: Francke, 1963, 1968. 543pp., 663pp.

Extensive biographical essays and assessment of literary contribution, followed by a short biography and selected bibliography. I: Gotthelf, Dranmor, Frey, Leuthold, Ott, Spitteler, Bosshart, v. Tavel, Pfander, Wirz, Waser, Zollinger; II: Keller, Widmann, Hardung, Kaeslin, Reinhart, Hesse, R. Walser, P. Haller, Ullmann, Pulver, Stamm. Index: names and titles. An introduction for the non-specialist.

728. Hamburger, Michael. *Contraries. Studies in German Literature.* New York: Dutton, 1970. viii, 367pp.

Focuses on the artist and society, and the resulting tensions. Chapters on Hölderlin, Novalis, Kleist, Heine, Büchner, Nietzsche, T. Mann, Expressionist poetry, Trakl, Benn. Somewhat diffuse.

729. Hatfield, Henry. *Modern German Literature. The Major Figures in Context.* New York: St. Martin's Pr., 1967. viii, 167pp.

Range: 1880-1960. Compact literary history with focus on major figures and genres. Numerous factual errors. Index: author and subject. Bibliography.

730. Just, Klaus G. *Von der Gründerzeit bis zur Gegenwart. Geschichte der deutschen Literatur seit 1871.* Bern, Munich: Francke, 1973. 702pp.

A chronological history in 6 periods from the age of Bismarck to post-1945. Each chapter sketches cultural and political background and examines the literary achievement in the three genres. Index: authors. Notes. Presentation is often merely an enumeration of authors and works.

731. Kindermann, Heinz. *Wegweiser durch die moderne Literatur in Österreich.* Innsbruck: Österreichische Verlagsanstalt, 1954. 127pp. illus.

A compact lexicon of 20th-century authors grouped according to preferred genre and major themes. Brief biographies accompanied by author bibliographies. Adequate for quick orientation.

732. Kunisch, Hermann, ed. *Handbuch der deutschen Gegenwartsliteratur. Unter Mitwirkung zahlreicher Fachgelehrter.* 2nd rev. ed. 3 vols. Munich: Nymphenburger Verlagshandlung, 1969-1970. ([1]1965)

Range 20th century. Lexicon of authors, providing lengthy articles with biographical information and primary bibliography (not in chronological order); listings quite reliable. I. *A-K*, 1969. 410pp.; II. *L-Z, Rahmenartikel*, 1970. 477pp. II includes articles on Expressionism (No. 757), exile literature (No. 776), inner emigration (No. 790), the Third Reich (No. 778), postwar German literature (No. 812), literature in the GDR; index of proper names. III: *Bibliographie der Personalbibliographien zur deutschen Gegenwartsliteratur.* Ed. by H. Wiesner, I. Živsa, C. Stoll. 1970. 160pp. (1970 paperback). A compilation of ca. 1500 author bibliographies (A-Z) with some annotation. Entries are chronological and include surveys of research and archival information. Indexes: authors, editors, translators.

733. Mann, Otto, ed. *Christliche Dichter im 20. Jahrhundert. Beiträge zur europäischen Literatur.* 2nd rev. ed. Bern, Munich: Francke, 1968. 506pp. ([1]1955)

Introduction (O. Mann) on religion and literature; appraisal of 8 French, 6 English, 14 German authors (Barlach, Derleth, von le Fort, R.A. Schröder, K. Weiß, Seidel, Wiechert, Werfel, Bergengruen, R. Schneider, Klepper, Andres, Schaper, Böll). Short biographies and extensive secondary bibliographies for authors covered, pp. 465-500. Index: authors.

*** Mayer, Hans. *Von Lessing bis Thomas Mann. Wandlungen in der bürgerlichen Literatur in Deutschland.* Pfullingen: Neske, 1959. 414pp. (No. 589)

734. Natan, Alex, ed. *German Men of Letters. Twelve Literary Essays.* 5 vols. London: Wolff, 1961-1969.

Range: mainly 19th, 20th century. Substantial articles by various contributors. Each essay is devoted to a single author, his artistic development and literary achievement, and followed by a brief biography.

I. 1961. vii, 273pp.: Droste-Hülshoff, Eichendorff, Fontane, Grillparzer, Hauptmann, Hebbel, Herder, Hofmannsthal, Keller, Meyer, Storm, Tieck.
II. 1963. v, 298pp.: Hesse, Kaiser, le Fort, H. Mann, Morgenstern, Nietzsche, Schnitzler, Sternheim, Sudermann, R. Walser, S. Zweig.
III. 1964. 343pp.: Barlach, Benn, Borchert, Dürrenmatt, Feuchtwanger, Frisch, Kokoschka, Musil, Toller, Unruh, Werfel, Zuckmayer.
IV. *Essays on Contemporary German Literature.* 1969. 289pp.: "East German Literature," Bachmann, Böll, Celan, Eich,

Enzensberger, Gaiser, Grass, Kasack, Lehmann, Nossack.
V. 1969. 319pp.: C. Brentano, Gotthelf, Grabbe, Hoffmann, Jean Paul, Lenau, Nestroy, Mörike, Platen, Raabe, Spitteler, Stifter.

735. ———, ed. *Swiss Men of Letters. Twelve Literary Essays.* London: Wolff, 1970. 288pp.

Range: 19th-20th century. Articles on French, Italian, and Rhaeto-Romanic literature in Switzerland plus essays on H.-F. Amiel, C.-F. Ramuz, Gotthelf, Keller, Meyer, Spitteler, R. Walser, Frisch, Dürrenmatt. Brief bibliography follows each section. Good surveys.

*** Schmidt, Adalbert. *Dichtung und Dichter Österreichs im 19. und 20. Jahrhundert.* 2 vols. Salzburg, Stuttgart: Verlag Das Bergland Buch, 1964. 464pp., 460pp. (No. 673)

736. Soergel, Albert. *Dichtung und Dichter der Zeit. Eine Schilderung der deutschen Literatur der letzten Jahrzehnte.* 20th ed. Leipzig: Voigtländer, 1928. xii, 1062pp. ([1]1911)

737. ———. *Dichtung und Dichter der Zeit. NF. Im Banne des Expressionismus.* Leipzig: Voigtländer, 1925. xi, 904pp.

738. ———. *Dichter aus deutschem Volkstum. Dichtung und Dichter der Zeit. Dritte Folge.* Leipzig: Voigtländer, 1934. 231pp.

Range: 1880-1930. Very detailed, abundantly illustrated discussion of individual authors, including summaries of plot, major themes, often lengthy excerpts from texts. Excellent resource book.

739. ——— and Curt Hohoff. *Dichtung und Dichter der Zeit. Vom Naturalismus bis zur Gegenwart.* 2 vols. Düsseldorf: Bagel, 1961-1963. 896pp., 893pp.

Range: 1880-1950. Revised and updated edition of Soergel's work, particularly Expressionism and major figures who had appeared in the earlier work only in their earlier phases. Soergel's format retained. Provides an excellent orientation.

740. Van Abbé, Derek M. *Image of a People. The Germans and Their Creative Writing under and since Bismarck.* New York: Barnes & Noble, 1964. ix, 246pp. illus.

Not a literary history but a compact analysis of the cultural context of German literature with emphasis on German intellectuals and politics, religious life, education and literary taste. A knowledge of literary history is assumed. Selected bibliography.

741. Wiese, Benno von, ed. *Deutsche Dichter der Moderne. Ihr Leben und ihr Werk.* 3rd rev. ed. Berlin: Schmidt, 1975. 624pp. ([1]1965)

Range: ca. 1850-1960. 27 substantial articles. Each essay devoted to a single author, his artistic development and literary achievements. Bibliographies brief. Excellent appraisals. Articles on: Barlach, Benn, Borchardt, Brecht, Broch, Däubler, Döblin, George, Hauptmann, Hesse, Heym, Hofmannsthal, Horváth, Kafka, Kaiser, H. Mann, T. Mann, Musil, Nietzsche, Rilke, Schnitzler, Lasker-Schüler, Sternheim, Trakl, R. Walser, Wedekind, Werfel.

b. Naturalism, Impressionism, Jugendstil (1880-1914)

742. Böttcher, Kurt, Paul Günter Krohn, Peter Wruck. *Geschichte der deutschen Literatur. Achter Band. Von 1830 bis zum Ausgang des 19. Jahrhunderts. Zweiter Halbband. 1871-1900.* Berlin: Volk und Wissen, 1975. xi, 711-1274pp. illus.

Part 2 of VIII of the official Marxist-socialist history of German literature in the GDR provides extensive background material on economic and social developments. Focus on the beginnings of socialist literature and social criticism. Developments in Austria taken into account. Index: author and title.

743. Cowen, Roy C. *Der Naturalismus. Kommentar zu einer Epoche.* Munich: Winkler, 1973. 301pp.

Extensive introduction, pp. 7-110, followed by chronological table (1880-1914), and brief commentaries on Naturalist works by Kretzer, Hauptmann, Holz, Schlaf, Sudermann, Halbe, Polenz. Index: authors, works. Extensive bibliography, pp. 225-287. Not a historical overview but a presentation of characteristic features of the movement.

744. Duwe, Wilhelm. *Deutsche Dichter des XX. Jahrhunderts vom Naturalismus zum Surrealismus.* 2 vols. Zurich: Füssli, 1962. 512pp.; 488pp.

Range: 1885-1920. Literary history organized by genre; authors treated in pertinent sections. I: lyric poetry from Naturalism to late Expressionism; prose from Naturalism to Expressionism. II: prose continued to late Expressionism; drama from Naturalism to late Expressionism. Each vol. contains copious, lengthy text samples and numerous illustrations.

745. Furst, Lilian R., and Peter N. Skrine. *Naturalism.* London: Methuen, 1971. vi, 81pp.

Definition of epoch and survey of European literature. Index: authors, titles. A compact introduction.

746. Hamann, Richard, and Jost Hermand. *Deutsche Kunst und Kultur von der Gründerzeit bis zum Expressionismus.* 5 vols. Berlin: Akademie Verlag, 1965-1975.

I. *Gründerzeit.* 1965. 288pp.
II. *Naturalismus.* 1959. 336pp.
III. *Impressionismus.* 1960. 414pp.
IV. *Stilkunst um 1900.* 1967. 560pp.
V. *Expressionismus.* 1975. 309pp.

Paperback edition under the title: *Epochen deutscher Kultur von 1870 bis zur Gegenwart*. 5 vols. Munich: Nymphenburger Verlagshandlung, 1971-1976.

A cultural profile of each period as it emerges from the art produced, particularly painting and literature. Thematically organized. Volumes are not intended as histories. Lively, often polemic style. Covers a wealth of material, at times superficially; discussions of literature frequently misleading. On the whole valuable background reading for students of the period. For each vol., index: names.

747. Heller, Erich. *The Disinherited Mind. Essays in Modern German Literature and Thought*. 4th expanded ed. New York, London: Harcourt, Brace, Jovanovich, 1975. xvii, 358pp. ([1]1952)

11 essays on a wide range of topics, 19th and 20th century, focusing on the impact of Goethe and Nietzsche on the development of German thought and art. A popular and durable introduction to German literature and philosophy.

748. Hermand, Jost, ed. *Jugendstil*. Darmstadt: Wissenschaftliche Buchgesellschaft, 1971. xvi, 507pp. illus.

A general survey of the genesis and meaning of *Jugendstil* in the arts and literature; a reprinting of essays (1914-1969) by eminent scholars provides an excellent panorama of the period. Demanding reading.

749. Kaufmann, Hans, and Sylvia Schlenstedt. *Geschichte der deutschen Literatur. Neunter Band. Vom Ausgang des 19. Jahrhunderts bis 1917*. Berlin: Volk und Wissen, 1974. 600pp. illus.

Vol. IX of the official Marxist-socialist history of German literature of the GDR. Provides extensive background on imperialism and the pre-proletarianism revolutionary period. 2 sections: 1900-1910, the genres; 1900-1917, the genres. Index: author and title.

750. Koppen, Erwin. *Dekadenter Wagnerismus. Studien zur europäischen Literatur des Fin de siècle*. Berlin, New York: de Gruyter, 1973. 386pp.

Pt. A: a definition and history of the term; pt. B: the European scene, including the work of Beardsley, Mann, d'Annunzio, and others. Bibliography, pp. 343-376, includes a list of primary "decadent" literature and secondary works.

751. Kreuzer, Helmut, ed. *Jahrhundertende-Jahrhundertwende*. I. Teil. Wiesbaden: Athenaion, 1976. 475pp. illus.

Range: ca. 1870-1915. General introduction and 15 essays by leading scholars on Realism, Naturalism, Impressionism, and Symbolism in Rumanian, French and Italian, Scandinavian, German, Dutch, Hungarian, Yiddish, Slavic, English, American literature. Compact bibliographies at the end of each section. On the whole, superbly presented.

752. Mahal, Günther. *Naturalismus.* Munich: Fink, 1975. 260pp.

General introduction to the era, divided into compact chapters including definition, periodization, philosophical and social background, foreign and domestic development of the arts, genres, topics, aesthetics, etc. Section "Analysen": interpretations by A. Holz, A. Holz and J. Schlaf, and G. Hauptmann. Bibliography, pp. 235-254 (361 items). Index: names. Presents a large number of quotations, slogans, listings of facts, references to the bibliography. Presentation and access somewhat cumbersome.

753. Pascal, Roy. *From Naturalism to Expressionism. German Literature and Society 1880-1918.* London: Weidenfeld & Nicolson, 1973. ix, 349pp.

Analysis of the main areas of contact between literature and society in Germany and Austria. Discussion centered around incisive themes: philosophy, politics, the church, cultural developments, the family, etc. Bibliography, pp. 315-336, structured according to the chapters, includes material on the women's movement, autobiographies, memoirs. A thoroughly readable, superb introduction to the period.

754. Scheuer, Helmut, ed. *Naturalismus. Bürgerliche Dichtung und soziales Engagement.* Stuttgart, Berlin, Cologne, Mainz: Kohlhammer, 1974. 264pp.

A collection of 9 essays of differing quality on specific aspects of Naturalism, including lyric poetry, drama, novel, censorship, the women's movement, and studies of the background of the movement. Notes only.

755. Schulz, G. "Naturalism," *Periods in German Literature* (No. 453), pp. 199-225.

*** Walzel, Oskar. *Die deutsche Dichtung seit Goethes Tod.* 2nd ed. Berlin: Askanischer Verlag, 1920. xiv, 527pp. (No. 675)

c. Expressionism, Dadaism (1910-1924)

756. Bigsby, C.W.E. *Dada and Surrealism.* London: Methuen, 1972. viii, 91pp.

Compact definition followed by historical survey. Index: names, titles. A first introduction only.

757. Erken, Günther. "Der Expressionimus - Anreger, Herausgeber, Verleger." *Handbuch der deutschen Gegenwartsliteratur* (No. 732), pp. 335-364.

758. Friedman, Hermann, and Otto Mann, eds. *Expressionismus. Gestalten einer Literaturbewegung.* Heidelberg: Rothe, 1956. 375pp.

Essays by eminent scholars on important Expressionist authors. Pt. 1: lyric poetry (Stadler, Heym, Trakl, Stramm, Werfel, Lasker-Schüler, Loerke, Benn, Becher, Goll, Schickele). Pt. 2:

drama (Wedekind, Kaiser, Sternheim, Barlach, Jahnn). Appendices: essay on Dada; bio-bibliographical information on the authors treated; table relating Expressionist works to other contemporary literary works.

759. Furness, R.S. *Expressionism.* London: Methuen, 1973. vi, 105pp.

A compact survey of Expressionism concentrating upon poetry, drama, and film in Germany but with reference to the European and US scene. Text specimens are in English translation. Index: author and subject. Bibliography, pp. 97-101, annotated. Inadequate except as a first introduction.

760. Hamann, Richard, and Jost Hermand. *Deutsche Kunst und Kultur von der Gründerzeit bis zum Expressionismus.* V. *Expressionismus.* Berlin: Akademie Verlag, 1975. 309pp. (No. 746)

A provocative and critical examination of the themes, goals, and underlying attitudes of Expressionism with abundant parallels between literature and art. Not a history. Index: names.

761. Hinterhäuser, Hans, ed. *Jahrhundertende-Jahrhundertwende. II. Teil.* Wiesbaden: Athenaion, 1976. 493pp. illus.

Range: ca. 1900-1918. A collection of 16 essays by specialists on *Jugendstil*, Expressionism, Futurism, Dada, Modernism in American, French, Spanish, Spanish-American, Portuguese, Italian, German, Scandinavian, English, Hungarian, Rumanian, and Slavic literature. Index: author, title. Bibliographies at the end of each section. On the whole, superbly presented.

762. Kemper, Hans-Georg. *Vom Expressionismus zum Dadaismus. Eine Einführung in die dadaistische Literatur.* Kronberg: Scriptor, 1974. 242pp.

An examination of major themes and trends, subdivided according to the genre and theme. Proceeds from individual examples as typical for the era. Bibliography, pp. 236-242. A good, non-diachronic introduction.

763. Rothe, Wolfgang, ed. *Expressionismus als Literatur. Gesammelte Studien.* Bern, Munich: Francke, 1969. 797pp.

Basically an updated version of No. 758. Pt. 1: background (Impressionism, *Jugendstil*), genres (lyric poetry, drama, prose); pt. 2: lyric poets; pt. 3: dramatists; pt. 4: prose writers; pt. 5: Dada. In pts. 2-5: essays by eminent scholars on individual authors outlining artistic development and contribution of each. Each chapter concluded with a bio-bibliographical sketch. Excellent reappraisal of Expressionism.

764. Rötzer, Hans Gerd. *Begriffsbestimmung des literarischen Expressionismus.* Darmstadt: Wissenschaftliche Buchgesellschaft, 1976. vii, 511pp.

A collection of 20 previously published essays. Pt. 1: "Die Expressionismusdebatte"; pt. 2: assessments of the whole period

(Martini, Emrich, Pörtner, Paulsen, Raabe, Mayer); pt. 3: special aspects (Sokel, Ziegler, Motekat, Gruber, Kohlschmidt, Eykman, Viviani). Selected bibliography, pp. 507-511 (85 items).

765. Samuel, Richard, and R. Hinton Thomas. *Expressionism in German Life, Literature and the Theatre (1900-1924)*. Cambridge: Heffer, 1939. viii, 203pp. (Repr. 1971)

An historical survey of Expressionism from a social perspective. Includes a discussion of style. Bibliography. Still valuable reading.

766. Sokel, Walter H. *The Writer in Extremis. Expressionism in Twentieth-Century Literature*. Stanford: Stanford Univ. Pr., 1959. 251p. (German ed. 1960)

Excellent introduction to Expressionism. Pt. 1: "The New Form"; pt. 2: "The New Man"; epilogue: "The Parting of the Ways." Emphasis on basic themes and aspects of the period shown in the works of individual authors. A standard work on Expressionism.

767. Vietta, Silvio, and Hans-Georg Kemper. *Expressionismus*. Munich: Fink, 1975. 389pp.

A survey of German literary Expressionism buttressed by close text analyses. Pt. 1: preliminary definitions of the literary epoch; pt. 2: analyses of representative themes, motifs, genres, including philosophical and ideological background material; pt. 3: model interpretations: lyric poetry (Trakl), prose (Kafka), drama (Sternheim), novella (Edschmid). Extensive text passages quoted. The text is well structured and easily accessible. Bibliography of primary and secondary material (761 items), pp. 342-383. This is a solid, well-balanced introduction to Expressionism, which takes some important non-literary aspects of Expressionist art into account. For students it is particularly valuable because of its attention to methodology.

768. Weisstein, Ulrich, ed. *Expressionism as an International Phenomenon. 21 Essays and a Bibliography*. Paris, Budapest: Didier, Akad. Kiado, 1973. 360pp.

Essays by various authors with focus on the non-German aspects of Expressionism, foreign influences on German Expressionism, Expressionism in music and the arts. Extensive bibliography, pp. 329-349. Well organized and easy to use.

769. Willett, John. *Expressionism*. New York: McGraw-Hill, 1970. 256pp. illus.

Focus on literature and painting of the period. Assessment of the 19th-century tradition and the continuation of the movement to the present. Compact and copiously illustrated. Excellent background reading.

d. Weimar Republic (1919-1933)

770. Fähnders, Walter, and Martin Rector. *Linksradikalismus und Literatur. Untersuchungen zur Geschichte der sozialistischen Literatur in der Weimarer Republik.* 2 vols. Reinbek: Rowohlt, 1974. I. 1918-1923. 380pp.; II. 1924-1932. 336pp.

A history of the Communist and leftist parties with but little space allotted to the assessment and interpretation of literature. General remarks with summaries and biographies. Index: II, authors and titles. Bibliography, II, pp. 307-323, mainly primary material.

771. Innes, C.D. *Erwin Piscator's Political Theater. The Development of Modern German Drama.* Cambridge: Cambridge Univ. Pr., 1972. 248pp.

Though focused on the works and contributions of Piscator, the book includes historical analysis of contemporary forms: agitprop, documentary theater, epic theater, total theater. Bibliography. Piscator chronology. A good introduction to one aspect of modern German theater.

772. Klein, Alfred. *Im Auftrag ihrer Klasse. Weg und Leistung der deutschen Arbeiterschriftsteller 1918-1933.* Berlin, Weimar: Aufbau, 1972. 854pp.

An appraisal of the life and work of H. Marchwitza, W. Bredel, A. Scharrer, H. Lorbeer, K. Grünberg, E. Ginkel, W. Tkaczyk. Specimen texts, pp. 625-800. Bibliography. Index: authors and works.

773. Rothe, Wolfgang, ed. *Die deutsche Literatur in der Weimarer Republik.* Stuttgart: Reclam, 1974. 486pp.

A collection of 20 essays covering many facets of the literature, literary life, literary programs, and criticism of the period by well known scholars such as Fügen, Denkler, Koebner, Riha. Notes and bibliography at the end of each chapter. An excellent overview of the period.

774. Williams, Cedric E. *The Broken Eagle. Politics of Austrian Literature from Empire to Anschluss.* London: Paul Elek, 1974. xxii, 281pp.

Range: 1914-1938. Analyzes reactions of major Austrian writers to the politics of the day: Hofmannsthal, Bahr, Schnitzler, Werfel, Roth, S. Zweig, Doderer, Musil, Kraus. Appendix: chronological table, pp. 243-260. Index: author, subject. Bibliography. Work provides good background for period.

e. Third Reich, Inner Emigration, Exile (1933-1945)

775. Berendsohn, Walter A. "Emigrantenliteratur." *Reallexikon* (No. 1288), I, pp. 334-343.

776. Brenner, Hildegard. "Deutsche Literatur im Exil 1933-1947." *Handbuch der deutschen Gegenwartsliteratur* (No. 732), pp. 365-382.

777. Durzak, Manfred, ed. *Die deutsche Exilliteratur 1933-1945.* Stuttgart: Reclam, 1973. 624pp.

A collection of 39 essays in 3 parts: 1. historical data: delineations of the situation of the exile in various countries including Austria, Czechoslovakia, France, Spain, Switzerland, Scandinavia, England, US, USSR, Mexico; 2. analyses of works in the light of the exile experience; authors included: H. Mann, Roth, von Horváth, E. Weiß, Musil, Kaiser, A. Zweig, S. Zweig, Seghers, Wolfskehl, N. Sachs, Becher, Brecht, T. Mann, Döblin, Broch, Feuchtwanger, K. Mann, H. Kesten, Frank, Werfel, Toller, Unruh, Zuckmayer; 3. bio-bibliographical lexicon of authors, brief biographies and primary bibliographies. Index: names. Selected bibliographies at the end of each essay. On the whole quite useful and reliable.

778. Geißler, Rolf. "Dichter und Dichtung des Nationalsozialismus." *Handbuch der deutschen Gegenwartsliteratur* (No. 732), pp. 409-418.

779. Grimm, Reinhold, and Jost Hermand, eds. *Exil und Innere Emigration. Third Wisconsin Workshop.* Frankfurt: Athenäum, 1972. 210pp.

7 essays dealing with the research problems of exile literature, general and specific aspects, including the historical novel, sonnet, etc. Index: names.

780. Hohendahl, Peter Uwe, and Egon Schwarz, eds. *Exil und Innere Emigration II.* Frankfurt: Athenäum, 1973. 170pp.

9 essays on individual aspects and research problems. Index: names.

781. Ketelsen, Uwe-K. *Völkisch-nationale und nationalsozialistische Literatur in Deutschland 1890-1945.* Stuttgart: Metzler, 1976. ix, 116pp.

Resource book: 1. the critical reception of the literature of the Third Reich; 2. definitions; 3. a historical survey 1890-1945. Index: names. Extensive bibliographies in the body of the text.

782. Klieneberger, H.R. *Christian Writers of the Inner Emigration.* Paris, The Hague: Mouton, 1968. 218pp.

An appraisal of the life and work of a heterogeneous group of conservative writers: R.A. Schröder, R. Schneider, Klepper, Bergengruen, Wiechert, von le Fort. Index: names. Bibliography, pp. 201-214, secondary material.

783. Müssener, Helmut. *Exil in Schweden. Politische und kulturelle Emigration nach 1933.* Munich: Hanser, 1974. 603pp.

A detailed historical survey of the major aspects of the German exiles' life and activity in Sweden (discussion not confined to exiled writers). Bibliography. Excellent in its factual approach.

784. Schonauer, Franz. *Deutsche Literatur im Dritten Reich. Versuch einer Darstellung in polemischer didaktischer Absicht.* Olten, Freiburg: Walter, 1961. 196pp.

A solid, detailed introduction.

785. Spalek, John M., and Joseph Strelka, eds. *Deutsche Exilliteratur seit 1933. Band 1. Kalifornien. Teil 1.* Bern, Munich: Francke, 1976. 868pp.

A collection of 51 essays: 1. special problems of the exile in California, including life in Hollywood; Brecht; T. Mann; conditions of work and publication; 2. articles appraising the exile of 27 authors (A-Z); 3. appraisal of 13 script writers (A-Z). Indexes: names, subjects. A valuable examination. For bibliographies see:

786. ———, and Sandra Hawrylchak, eds. *Deutsche Exilliteratur seit 1933. Band 1. Kalifornien. Teil 2.* Bern, Munich: Francke, 1976. 216pp.

1. Author bibliographies of primary and secondary literature, limited to the exile period of the author; 2. archival information, literary remains, documents, pp. 151-216. Comprehensive and reliable.

787. Sternfeld, Wilhelm, and Eva Tiedemann. *Deutsche Exil-Literatur 1933-1945. Eine Bio-Bibliographie.* 2nd rev. and enl. ed. Heidelberg: Lambert Schneider, 1970. 606pp. ([1]1962)

Listing of ca. 1880 authors and scholars, A-Z. Each entry includes biographical dates, travel route in exile, bibliography of books published in exile, prizes, journals contributed to, author bibliography, if any. Appendix: book series, anonymously published books, almanacs, year books, calendars, symposiums, list of publishing houses. Bibliography, pp. 600-605. Reliable.

788. Vondung, Klaus. *Völkisch-nationale und nationalsozialistische Literaturtheorie.* Munich: List, 1973. 247pp.

1. Anthology of original texts, pp. 25-102; 2. survey of research and criticism during the period 1933-1945 and the reevaluation after 1945. Short biographies, pp. 214-225. Index: names. Bibliography, pp. 220-241. An interesting introduction.

789. Walter, Hans-Albert. *Deutsche Exilliteratur 1933-1950.* Darmstadt: Luchterhand, 1972ff. 9 vols. planned.

I. *Bedrohung und Verfolgung bis 1933.* 1972. 318pp. Social and historical background material for 1925-1933. Index: names.

II. *Asylpraxis und Lebensbedingungen in Europa.* 1972. 420pp. The life of the exiles in Europe, their economic, political, and legal situation. Index: names. Notes.

VII. *Exilpresse I.* 1974. 424pp. Analysis of 6 leading exile journals: *Die neue Weltbühne*, *Das neue Tage-Buch*, *Internationale Literatur*, *Die Sammlung*, *Neue deutsche Blätter*, *Das Wort.* Index: names. Notes.

790. Wiesner, Herbert. "'Innere Emigration.' Die innerdeutsche Literatur im Widerstand 1933-1945." *Handbuch der deutschen Gegenwartsliteratur* (No. 732), pp. 383-408.

H. LITERATURE AFTER 1945

1. Forschungsberichte

791. Bilke, Jörg B. "DDR-Literatur. Tradition und Rezeption in Westdeutschland. Ein Literaturbericht." *DU* 21 (1969), 5, Beilage.

792. Seidler, Herbert. "Die österreichische Literatur im wissenschaftlichen Schrifttum des letzten Jahrzehnts." *Wirkendes Wort* 7 (1956/57), 27-40.

793. ———. "Die österreichische Literatur als Problem der Forschung." *Österreich in Geschichte und Literatur* 14 (1970), 354-368.

2. Bibliographies

a. Completed Bibliographies

*** *Bibliographisches Handbuch der deutschen Literaturwissenschaft 1945-1972* (No. 124), II: see section XII, "Deutschsprachige Literatur des 20. Jahrhunderts. B. Die Entwicklung nach 1945." Selected cumulation of (No. 129) to 1972.

794. Cohen, Bertha, comp. "Post-War Publications on German Jewry. A Selected Bibliography of Books and Articles 1973." *Publications of the Leo Baeck Institute Year Book* 19 (1974), 273-367.

795. Glenn, Jerry. *Deutsches Schrifttum der Gegenwart (ab 1945)*. Bern, Munich: Francke, 1971. 128pp.

Pt. 1. Anthologies, handbooks, collections, literary histories, genres, themes, motifs, literary theory; pt. 2. primary and secondary bibliography for 143 authors A-Z. Index: author, subject. A handy, reliable bibliography for quick reference.

796. Hüser, Fritz. *Von der Arbeiterdichtung zur neuen Industriedichtung der Dortmunder Gruppe 61. Abriß und Bibliographie.* Recklinghausen: Paulus, 1967. 36pp.

*** *Internationale Bibliographie zur Geschichte der deutschen Literatur* (No. 122), II, 1: see section "Deutschsprachige Literatur von 1900 bis zur Gegenwart." Selected cumulation to 1969. Marxist-socialist criticism well represented.

797. Kranz, Gisbert. *Christliche Dichtung heute. Bibliographie der Neuerscheinungen von 1960-1975, der Taschenbücher, Schulausgaben und Interpretationen.* Paderborn: Schöningh, 1975. 109pp.

Pt. 1, general literature; pt. 2, anthologies; pt. 3, 225 authors after 1960; pt. 4, editions, monographs, collections of interpretations available in paperback. Not limited to German literature. Written with the teacher in mind.

798. *Schriftsteller der DDR.* Leipzig: Verlag für Buch- und Bibliothekswesen, 1961. Compiled by a collective. 196pp.

Arranged by authors A-Z with a brief biography for each, followed by primary bibliography by genre. List of pseudonyms. Easy to use.

799. Weber, Peter, and Marietta Rost, eds. *Die Literatur der Deutschen Demokratischen Republik seit dem VIII. Parteitag der SED. Eine bibliographische Information aus Anlass des VII. Schriftstellerkongresses.* Leipzig: Deutsche Bücherei, 1973. 96pp.

Bibliography for the years 1971-1973 encompassing publications on literary theory, aesthetics, ideology and literature, primary works by living authors, as well as some reviews. Some annotation. Of very limited value.

800. Wilbert-Collins, Elly. *A Bibliography of Four Contemporary German-Swiss Authors. Friedrich Dürrenmatt, Max Frisch, Robert Walser, Albin Zollinger. The Authors' Publications and the Literary Criticism Relating to Their Works.* Bern: Francke, 1967. 71pp.

b. Current Bibliographies

*** *Bibliographie der deutschen Sprach- und Literaturwissenschaft* (No. 129): see section XIX "20. Jahrhundert. Nach 1945," 1 (1945-1953)-16 (1976)ff. Most reliable and comprehensive current bibliography. Editions and secondary material. Published annually.

*** *Germanistik* (No. 130): see section XXXI, "Vom Naturalismus bis zur Gegenwart," 1 (1960)- 17 (1976)ff. Comprehensive quarterly, up to date. Editions and secondary material. Books are reviewed.

*** *MLA International Bibliography* (No. 125), II: see section "German Literature. VII. Recent Literature," 1921-1975ff. Annual cumulation. Editions and secondary material. Extensive and generally reliable.

*** *Referatendienst zur Literaturgeschichte* (No. 131): see section "Geschichte der Nationalliteraturen. Deutsche Literatur. Literatur der DDR. Literatur der BRD," 1 (1969)-6 (1976)ff. Marxist-socialist quarterly review of books. Limited in scope.

*** *Twentieth Century Literature* 1 (1955)-22 (1976)ff.: see section "Current Bibliography." Quarterly of modern literature. Each issue contains an annotated list of articles (only!), some German material included. Up to date. (No. 1560)

*** *The Year's Work in Modern Language Studies* (No. 127): see section "German Literature, 1880 to the Present Day," 4 (1933)-37 (1975)ff. Covers primary and secondary material for the previous year. Annotated.

3. Literary Histories

a. Contemporary Austrian, Swiss, West German Literature

*** Alker, Ernst. *Profile und Gestalten der deutschen Literatur nach 1914. Mit einem Kapitel über den Expressionismus von Zoran Konstantinović.* Ed. by Eugen Thurnher. Stuttgart: Kröner, 1977. xvi, 880pp. (No. 723)

801. Closs, August. *Twentieth Century German Literature.* New York: Barnes & Noble, 1969. xxiv, 433pp.

Range: 1880's-1960's. Pt. 1: a historical survey of the period, divided according to genre, pp. 1-163; pt. 2: a reference guide for the student: chronological table, important bibliographies, literary journals, interpretations, critical appraisals, anthologies, and author list A-Z with biography and primary bibliography. Appendix: "German Music from the Middle Ages to the 20th century," pp. 409-428. Excellent introduction.

802. Demetz, Peter. *Postwar German Literature. A Critical Introduction.* New York: Pegasus, 1970. xii, 264pp. German ed.: *Die süße Anarchie. Skizzen zur deutschen Literatur seit 1945.* Frankfurt, Berlin, Vienna: Ullstein, 1973. 330pp.

Range: 1945-1960's. This superb introduction focuses on individual authors but also provides cultural background material. Biographical information and interpretive summaries of major works are given for the poets: Sachs, Bobrowski, Bachmann, Celan, Heissenbüttel, Kunert, Enzensberger, Lehmann; playwrights: Hochwälder, Frisch, Weiss, Hacks, Hochhuth, Dürrenmatt; novelists: Koeppen, Gaiser, Andersch, Böll, Walser, Johnson, Grass, Doderer. Bibliography: "Useful further reading," pp. 242-253. Outstanding for beginners.

803. *Deutsche Literatur in unserer Zeit. Mit Beiträgen von W. Kayser, B. v. Wiese, W. Emrich, F. Martini, M. Wehrli, F. Heer.* Göttingen: Vandenhoeck und Ruprecht, 1959. 162pp.

Range: 20th century. A collection of lectures by eminent scholars, dealing with book publication, contemporary poetry, narrative, drama, literature in Switzerland and Austria. Somewhat outdated.

804. Domandi, Agnes K., ed. *Modern German Literature. A Library of Literary Criticism.* 2 vols. New York: Ungar, 1972. I. *A-J.* xvi, 421pp.; II. *K-Z.* x, 413pp.

Arranged by author A-Z; excerpts from articles of criticism from leading US journals. Covers some 200 German authors. Selected bibliography at the end of each section. Quoted material is too brief and too diffuse to be of much use in itself. Index: critics.

805. Durzak, Manfred. *Die deutsche Literatur der Gegenwart. Aspekte und Tendenzen.* Stuttgart: Reclam, 1971. 468pp. (^{3}1976)

24 substantial essays on German literature since 1945 cover the main aspects and genres of West and East German, Austrian, and Swiss literature. Includes chapters on the reception of German literature in France, England, USA, Italy, Scandinavia. Bibliography at the end of each section. A superior introduction.

806. Friedmann, Hermann, and Otto Mann, eds. *Christliche Dichter der Gegenwart. Beiträge zur europäischen Literatur.* Heidelberg: Rothe, 1955. 482pp.

Essays on 28 (13 German) authors of world literature who are deeply concerned with Christian faith today. Arranged by date of author's birth. Bio-bibliographical information at the end of each chapter.

807. ———. *Deutsche Literatur im 20. Jahrhundert. Strukturen und Gestalten.* 2 vols. 4th rev. ed. Heidelberg: Rothe, 1961. 332pp., 382pp. (^{1}1954)

Essays on 26 authors: Benn, Brecht, Broch, Bruckner, Carossa, Döblin, Dürrenmatt, George, Hauptmann, Hesse, Hofmannsthal, Jahnn, E. Jünger, Kafka, Kraus, Langgässer, Lasker-Schüler, T. Mann, Musil, Rilke, Toller, Trakl, R. Walser, Wedekind, Werfel, Zuckmayer. Valuable for the appraisal of contemporary literature.

808. Grenzmann, Wilhelm. *Deutsche Dichtung der Gegenwart.* 2nd ed. Frankfurt: Menck, 1955. 486pp. (^{1}1953)

Intellectual-historical approach: compact discussion and evaluations of single works and artistic development of poets treated. Contains a chapter on Surrealism. For advanced students.

809. ———. *Dichtung und Glaube. Probleme und Gestalten der deutschen Gegenwartsliteratur.* 3rd rev. ed. Bonn: Athenäum, 1957. 397pp. (^{1}1950)

Range: 1900-1950's. A survey of 20th-century authors from a Christian point of view. Essays include a general outline of the writer's thought and an objective appraisal of selected important works. T. Mann, Benn, Kasack, Wiechert, Hesse, Broch, Kafka, E. Jünger, F.G. Jünger, Carossa, Bergengruen,

Langgässer, Andres, Werfel, Schröder, von le Fort, Schaper. Appendix; biographical data, primary works, pp. 387-391.

810. Gsteiger, Manfred, ed. *Kindlers Literaturgeschichte der Gegenwart. Die zeitgenössischen Literaturen der Schweiz. Autoren, Werke, Themen, Tendenzen seit 1945*. Band 4. Zurich, Munich: Kindler, 1974. 752pp.

A substantial, very comprehensive survey of contemporary Swiss literature: general introduction, contemporary German, French, Italian literature and a complete survey of Rhaeto-Romanic literature. Appendix: bio-bibliographical listing of Swiss authors A-Z, pp. 681-724. Index: author and subject. Notes. An excellent introduction.

811. Horst, Karl August. *Kritischer Führer durch die deutsche Literatur der Gegenwart. Roman, Lyrik, Essay*. Munich: Nymphenburger Verlagshandlung, 1962. 525pp. (^{1}1957)

Range: ca. 1900 to post-World War II. Intellectual-historical approach: informal discussion of individual authors and major themes. Pt. 1. "Figuren erzählender und lyrischer Dichtung"; pt. 2: "Figuren des Essays" contains an extensive treatment of 20th-century essayists. A broad acquaintance with the literary works of the period is assumed.

812. ———. "Perspektiven der deutschen Literatur der Nachkriegszeit." *Handbuch der deutschen Gegenwartsliteratur* (No. 732), pp. 419-439.

*** Just, Klaus G. *Von der Gründerzeit bis zur Gegenwart. Geschichte der deutschen Literatur seit 1871*. Bern, Munich: Francke, 1973. 702pp. (No. 730)

*** Kunisch, Hermann, ed. *Handbuch der deutschen Gegenwartsliteratur*. Unter Mitwirkung zahlreicher Fachgelehrter. 2nd rev. ed. 3 vols. Munich: Nymphenburger Verlagshandlung, 1969-1970. (^{1}1965).

813. Kurz, Paul. *On Modern German Literature*. 3 vols. Trans. by Sister Mary McCarthy. Univ. of Alabama Pr., 1970-1972. 249pp., 188pp., 154pp.

I. 9 previously published essays, including chapters on the modern novel, Kafka, Broch, Grass, Heissenbüttel, Sachs. No index or bibliography.

II. 4 essays on T. Mann, Brecht, Frisch, Hans Mayer; some book reviews. Index: author, subject.

III. 5 essays on lyric poetry since 1945, Grass as a lyric poet, current modes of lyric expression, Group 47, the relationship of authors to Christianity. Index: author, subject.

814. Lattmann, Dieter, ed. *Kindlers Literaturgeschichte der Gegenwart. Die Literatur der Bundesrepublik Deutschland*. Munich: Kindler, 1973. 801pp., illus.

A historical survey of literature after 1945. D. Lattmann,

introduction; H. Vormweg, prose (notes, bibl.); K. Krolow, lyric poetry (bibl.); H. Karasek, drama. Index of authors, scholars, and publicists of exile and inner emigration, pp. 703-711. Short biographies of authors included, pp. 712-777. Index: authors, titles, pp. 778-800. Excellent, informative work.

815. Lennartz, Franz. *Deutsche Dichter und Schriftsteller unserer Zeit. Einzeldarstellungen zur schönen Literatur in deutscher Sprache*. 10th rev. ed. Stuttgart: Kröner, 1969. vii, 783pp. ([1]1938)

Range: contemporary authors (1960) plus notable recently deceased authors (T. Mann, Brecht, Traven, Döblin, Feuchtwanger, etc.). A reference work: 328 contemporary authors A-Z with check list and brief description of author's work, including critical reception. Excellent for factual material; particularly good source for information on young authors.

816. Livingstone, Rodney. "German Literature from 1945," *Periods in German Literature* (No. 453), pp. 283-305.

*** Natan, Alex, ed. *German Men of Letters*. IV. *Essays on Contemporary German Literature*. 1969. 280pp. Material on: East German literature, Bachmann, Böll, Celan, Eich, Enzensberger, Gaiser, Grass, Kasack, Lehmann, Nossack. (No. 734)

817. Spiel, Hilde, ed. *Kindlers Literaturgeschichte der Gegenwart. Die zeitgenössische Literatur Österreichs*. Zurich, Munich: Kindler, 1976. 758pp. illus.

Range: 1945-1970. An extensive historical survey. H. Spiel, introduction; P. Kruntorad, prose; K. Klinger, lyric poetry (selected bibl.); G. Böhm, drama; H. Haider-Pregler, radio play; S. Hafner and E. Prunč, literature of ethnic minorities (selected bibl.). Short biographies of authors discussed, pp. 703-731. Indexes: titles, journals and newspapers, authors. Bibliography, pp. 698-702. An excellent, informative volume.

818. Thomas, R. Hinton, and Will van der Will. *The German Novel and the Affluent Society*. Manchester: Manchester Univ. Pr., 1968. xix, 167pp. German edition: *Der deutsche Roman und die Wohlstandsgesellschaft*. Stuttgart: Kohlhammer, 1969. 206pp.

Focuses on the works of Gaiser, Koeppen, Böll, Grass, M. Walser, and Johnson. Literature is examined as a component of contemporary society. A solid study.

819. ———, and Keith Bullivant. *Literature in Upheaval. West German Writers and the Challenge of the 1960's*. New York: Barnes & Noble, 1974. ix, 193pp.

Presentation of various recent literary phenomena including politicized and documentary literature, *Gruppe 61*, *Werkkreis 70*, the sub-culture. A compact introduction with a wealth of detail.

820. Weber, Dietrich. *Deutsche Literatur seit 1945 in Einzeldarstellungen*. Stuttgart: Kröner, 1968. 576pp.

Brief analyses of representative works are followed by a biographical sketch and primary/secondary bibliography. Solid source book for: Aichinger, Andersch, Bachmann, Borchert, Celan, Dürrenmatt, Doderer, Eich, Eisenreich, Enzensberger, Frisch, Frisch, Grass, Heissenbüttel, Hildesheimer, Jens, Johnson, Koeppen, Lenz, Nossack, Sachs, Schmidt, Schnurre, Walser, Weiss.

821. Weiss, Walter, Josef Donnenberg, Adolf Haslinger, Karlheinz Rossbacher, *Gegenswartliteratur. Zugänge zu ihrem Verständnis*. Stuttgart, Berlin, Cologne, Mainz: Kohlhammer, 1973. 195pp.

Twelve compact lectures written as a radio series. Dwells on current forms and topical concerns of modern literature. Good first introduction for the lay reader.

822. Wiese, Benno, ed. *Deutsche Dichter der Gegenwart. Ihr Leben und Werk*. Berlin: Schmidt, 1973. 686pp.

Survey of modern German literature followed by substantial articles on the life and work of 39 writers: Aichinger, Andres, Artmann, Bachmann, Bobrowski, Böll, Canetti, Celan, Doderer, Domin, Dürrenmatt, Eich, Enzensberger, Frisch, Grass, Hacks, Handke, Heissenbüttel, Hermlin, Hildesheimer, Huchel, E. Jünger, F.G. Jünger, Kaschnitz, Koeppen, Krolow, Lavant, Lenz, Nossack, Schmidt, Seghers, Strittmatter, M. Walser, Weiss, Wolf, Zuckmayer.

b. East German Literature

823. Franke, Konrad. *Kindlers Literaturgeschichte der Gegenwart. Die Literatur der Deutschen Demokratischen Republik. Autoren, Werke, Themen. Tendenzen seit 1945. Neubearbeitete Ausgabe mit drei einführenden Essays von Heinrich Vormweg*. Zurich, Munich: Kindler, 1974. 678pp., illus.

Introduction covers various aspects of the relationship between politics and literature in the GDR. Extensive chapters on lyric poetry, prose, and drama with focus on individual authors and their contributions. Index: names and subjects. Bibliography. Short biographies, pp. 633-660. A superb introduction of general interest.

824. Geerdts, Hans Jürgen, ed. *Literatur der DDR. Einzeldarstellungen*. Stuttgart: Kröner, 1974. xxiv, 571pp.

A collection of 27 essays on GDR authors by scholars from the GDR. Each article offers a general appraisal of the work, followed by a short biography, primary bibliography, and selected secondary literature.

825. Haase, Horst, Hans Jürgen Geerdts, Erich Kühne, Walter Pallus. *Geschichte der deutschen Literatur. Elfter Band. Literatur der Deutschen Demokratischen Republik*. Berlin: Volk und Wissen, 1976. 907pp. illus.

Vol. XI of the official Marxist-socialist history of German literature of the GDR. Traces the development of GDR literature in 3 periods: 1945-1949, social, ideological, literary achievements; 1949-1960's, and 1960's to 1970's with emphasis on social and literary aims and achievements. Index: author and title.

826. Hohendahl, Peter Uwe, and Patricia Herminghouse, eds. *Literatur und Literaturtheorie in der DDR.* Frankfurt: Suhrkamp, 1976. 356pp.

Seven of the eight papers presented here were delivered at a symposium in St. Louis, 1974. Emphasis on current literary trends and developments in the GDR; pt. 1: 4 essays on the theoretical and aesthetic developments; pt. 2: 4 essays on the developments in drama, novel, poetry. Presents good insights into current GDR literature, though on the whole in a somewhat cumbersome style.

827. Huebener, Theodore. *The Literature of East Germany.* New York: Ungar, 1970. ix, 134pp.

A succinct, chronological introduction to GDR literature with a brief appraisal of 25 authors. Intended for the general reader in the US. Index: author, subject. Bibliography. Too brief.

828. Jäger, Manfred. *Sozialliteraten. Funktion und Selbstverständnis der Schriftsteller in der DDR.* Düsseldorf: Bertelsmann, 1973. 240pp.

Rather conservative, somewhat denigrating approach to GDR literature with chapters on C. Wolf, Kunze, Braun, Biermann, Harich, Brecht, humor and satire. Notes.

829. Rühle, Jürgen. *Literatur und Revolution. Der Schriftsteller und der Kommunismus.* Cologne: Kiepenheuer & Witsch, 1960. 610pp. English ed.: *Literature and Revolution. A Critical Study of the Writer and Communism in the Twentieth Century.* Trans. by Jean Steinberg. New York, Washington, London: Praeger, 1969. xiv, 520pp.

A study of the oppression of writers in the Communist world from the Revolution to the 1950's. Not limited to the Soviet Union; includes some German writers. Extensive, valuable bibliography in the German edition, pp. 571-599.

830. Sander, Hans-Dietrich. *Geschichte der schönen Literatur in der DDR. Ein Grundriß.* Freiburg: Rombach, 1972. 354pp.

A rather conservative general introduction in three parts: 1. theory, social realism, political premises; 2. survey of the development of Marxist-socialist literature; 3. the question ot a second body of German literature. Relatively little presentation of individual works and authors. Indexes: subject, author.

831. Schmitt, Hans-Jürgen, ed. *Einführung in Theorie, Geschichte und Funktion der DDR-Literatur.* Stuttgart: Metzler, 1975. 340pp.

A collection of 9 essays covering cultural policies, the realism debate of the 1950's, ideology and politics, lyric, drama, prose. A solid, somewhat conservative evaluation. Index: names. Bibliography pp. 329-335.

I. SPECIAL TREATMENTS OF GERMAN LITERATURE: CHRONOLOGIES, OUTLINES, PICTORIAL HISTORIES

832. Albrecht, Günter, Kurt Böttcher, Herbert Greiner-Mai, Paul Günter Krohn, Johannes Mittenzwei. *Deutsche Literaturgeschichte in Bildern. Eine Darstellung von den Anfängen bis zur Gegenwart.* 2 vols. Leipzig: Bibliographisches Institut, 1969, 1971. 370pp., 503pp.

Range: to 1970. Hundreds of well chosen black-and-white photographs with running commentary. Most rewarding for the student. Author-subject index at the end of each volume.

833. Ammon, Hermann. *Deutsche Literaturgeschichte in Frage und Antwort.* 5th rev. and enl. ed. 2 vols. Bonn: Dümmler.

I. *Von den Anfängen bis 1500.* 1958. 104pp.
II. *Von 1500 bis zur Gegenwart.* 1959. 231pp. (Frequent repr.)

Ca. 1700 questions and answers about literary history, interpretation, authors, themes, etc. Positivistic in approach. Index: names. Selected bibliography outdated. Provides a good measure for basic knowledge. Excellent tool for review.

834. Aubert, Joachim. *Handbuch der Grabstätten berühmter Deutscher, Österreicher und Schweizer.* 2nd enl. ed. Munich, Berlin: Deutscher Kunstverlag, 1975. 250pp. illus. (^{1}1973)

A geographical listing of grave sites for over 2800 figures. Index: names.

835. Brett-James, Anthony. *The Triple Stream. Four Centuries of English, French, and German Literature 1531-1930.* Philadelphia: Bowes and Bowes, 1953. x, 178pp.

A chronological table listing year by year the dates of authors and their works. Includes Austrian, Belgian, and Swiss literature. Indexes: authors, works. Facilitates a quick comparison between literatures.

836. Frenzel, Herbert A., and Elisabeth. *Daten deutscher Dichtung. Chronologischer Abriß der deutschen Literaturgeschichte von den Anfängen bis zur Gegenwart.* 3rd rev. ed. Berlin, Cologne: Kiepenheuer & Witsch, 1962. xv, 516pp. (^{1}1953)

Range: 750-1962. Organized by periods. Each section in 3 parts: 1. a historical sketch of the period, a characterization of literary movements including definition, important features such as influences and concepts; 2. a list of major figures with brief biographies; 3. a chronology of important works by date of publication or completion, giving the author, title, description of work and summary of content, stylistic and structural elements, dominant influences, publication history, etc. Extremely reliable; continually being updated in new editions. Indispensable.

837. Könnecke, Gustav. *Deutscher Literaturatlas*. Marburg: Elwert, 1909. xii, 156pp.

Range: 4th century-1908. Reproductions of manuscripts, title pages, woodcuts, etchings, lithographs, portraits of literary figures. For an extended version see: G. Könnecke, *Bilderatlas zur Geschichte der deutschen Nationalliteratur. Eine Ergänzung zu jeder deutschen Literaturgeschichte*. Marburg: Elwert, 1912. xxvi, 426pp.

838. Nadler, Joseph. *Raumzeittafel*. 3rd ed. Regensburg: Habbel, 1931. 51pp.

Range: 800-1914. Chronological table organized by Germanic tribal areas and foreign countries. Provides authors and titles for many minor figures.

839. Oberhauser, Fred and Gabi. *Literarischer Führer durch die Bundesrepublik Deutschland*. Frankfurt: Insel, 1974. xvi, 660pp. illus.

A literary tour guide organized by states, then towns, A-Z, of the FRG. Lists the literary significance of each place, including connections to authors, motifs and themes in literature, literary prizes, archives, organizations, secondary bibliography of places. Indexes: motifs and themes, personal names, places. Bibliography, pp. 607-612. Suggested itineraries, pp. 601-606.

840. Schmitt, Fritz, with Gerhard Fricke. *Deutsche Literaturgeschichte in Tabellen*. 3 vols. Bonn: Athenäum 1949-1952. (^{2}1960)

I. *750-1450*. 1949. xi, 182pp.
II. *1450-1770*. 1950. vi, 231pp.
III. *1770 bis zur Gegenwart*. 1952. vi, 306pp.

Material organized chronologically, divided by literary epochs, and subdivided by movement and genre. Entries provide dates, titles, manuscript information, brief biography, thumbnail description or definition. Movements and periods characterized compactly. Each volume contains helpful special tables on items of particular importance. Indexes in each volume: names, titles.

841. Schmitt, Fritz, and Jörn Göres. *Abriß der deutschen Literatur in Tabellen*. 5th ed. Frankfurt, Bonn: Athenäum, 1965. 344pp. (^{1}1955)

Range: beginnings--1960's. A shortened version of the above. Chronological outline of German literary history. Author and anonyma index. Tables: life and works of Goethe and Schiller;

important dates (works, authors' birth and death). Useful for review; information easily accessible.

842. Spemann, Adolf. *Vergleichende Zeittafel der Weltliteratur vom Mittelalter bis zur Neuzeit (1150-1939)*. Stuttgart: Engelhorn-verlag A. Spemann, 1951. 160pp.

Limited to European literature. Also lists popular literature, memoirs, important histories, philosophical and scientific works. Especially rich for the period 1880-1939. Index of authors has some 11,000 titles.

843. Wilpert, Gero von. *Deutsche Literatur in Bildern*. Stuttgart: Kröner, 1957. vii, 316pp. 861 photographs.

Chronological survey of German literature in pictures with detailed explanatory notes. Photographs carefully selected. Excellent supplementary introduction to German literature.

VIII.

The Genres of German Literature

CONTENTS

A. GENERAL LITERATURE

1. Forschungsbericht

844. Hart-Nibbrig, Christian L. "Literaturtheorie, Methodologie und Gattungspoetik. Forschungsbericht." *Wirkendes Wort* 21 (1971), 187-199 and 23 (1973), 282-293.

2. Bibliographies

845. Hempfer, Klaus W. "Bibliographie zur Gattungspoetik. Allgemeine Gattungstheorie (1890-1971)." *Zeitschrift für französische Sprache und Literatur* 82 (1972), 53-66.

846. Ruttkowski, Wolfgang. *Bibliographie der Gattungspoetik für den Studenten der Literaturwissenschaft. Ein abgekürztes Verzeichnis von über 3000 Büchern, Dissertationen und Zeitungsartikeln in Deutsch, Englisch und Französisch.* Munich: Hueber, 1973. 246pp.

Titles grouped into 140 genres; easily accessible through copious cross references. Individual sections by author A-Z. Very useful for quick reference, particularly for minor genres. Quite reliable.

3. General Criticism and Theory

*** Böckmann, Paul. *Formgeschichte der deutschen Dichtung.* Vol. 1. *Von der Sinnbildsprache zur Ausdruckssprache. Der Wandel der literarischen Formensprache vom Mittelalter zur Neuzeit.* Hamburg: Hoffmann & Campe, 1949. xvi, 700pp. (No. 350)

847. Höffe, Wilhelm. "Die Medien." *Die Literatur* (No. 1281), pp. 146-171.

Includes sections: "Die Sprache," "Gesprochene Sprache," "Die Schrift," and "Folgerungen aus der Entdeckung der Schrift."

848. Jolles, André. *Einfache Formen. Legende, Sage, Mythe, Rätsel, Spruch, Kasus, Memorabile, Märchen, Witz.* 4th ed. Tübingen: Niemeyer, 1968. vi, 272pp. ([1]1930)

Presents thorough analyses of the minor literary genres with definitions, information on origins and development, and discussion of psychological implications. Superbly presented. Indispensable for the advanced student.

849. Kuhn, Hugo. "Gattung." *Handlexikon* (No. 1290), pp. 150-151.

850. Mohr, Wolfgang. "Einfache Formen." *Reallexikon* (No. 1288), I, 321-328.

*** Markwardt, Bruno. *Geschichte der deutschen Poetik*. 5 vols. Berlin: de Gruyter, 1937-1967.

I. *Barock und Frühaufklärung*. 1937 xii, 457pp.
II. *Aufklärung, Rokoko, Sturm und Drang*. 1956 vii, 692pp.
III. *Klassik und Romantik*. 1958 730pp.
IV. *Das neunzehnte Jahrhundert*. 1959 vii, 750pp.
V. *Das zwanzigste Jahrhundert*. 1967 1032pp. (see No. 241)

851. Müller-Dyes, Klaus. "Gattungen." *Die Literatur* (No. 1281), pp. 264-327.

852. Ruttkowski, Wolfgang. *Die literarischen Gattungen. Reflektionen über eine modifizierte Fundamentalpoetik*. Bern, Munich: Francke, 1968. 154pp.

An intensive examination of the 3 traditional genres and a proposal for a 4th genre to include minor forms such as those of aural presentation. Includes a number of useful tables; international bibliography, pp. 137-149. A good introduction to the theory of genre.

853. Schanze, Helmut. *Medienkunde für Literaturwissenschaftler. Einführung und Bibliographie*. Munich: Fink, 1974. 116pp.

A general survey of the performing media and their relation to and use of literature. Definitions, theory and methodology, analyses of the press, of the book trade, of stage, film, radio, and TV. Index: authors. Bibliography, pp. 82-114, arranged to correspond to the text. An informative introduction.

854. Schröder, Walter J. "Form." *Reallexikon* (No. 1288), I, 468-471.

855. Sengle, Friedrich. *Vorschläge zur Reform der literarischen Formenlehre*. 2nd rev. ed. Stuttgart: Metzler, 1969. 52pp. (^{1}1967: *Die literarischen Formenlehre*)

Raises major objections to the traditional system of genres and proposes a new structure of genres to include such forms as the diary, essay, etc. An important contribution to recent poetics.

*** Staiger, Emil. *Grundbegriffe der Poetik*. Zurich, Freiburg: Atlantis, ^{8}1968. 256pp. (^{1}1946) (No. 290)

856. Viëtor, Karl. "Probleme der literarischen Gattungsgeschichte." *DVLG* 9 (1931), 425-447.

4. General Types and Genres

a. Emblematik

857. Henkel, Arthur, and Albrecht Schöne, eds. *Emblemata. Handbuch zur Sinnbildkunst des 16. und 17. Jahrhunderts.* Stuttgart: Metzler, 1967. lxxxi, 2196 cols. illus.

A reprint of 3713 emblems from 47 original sources. Arranged in 8 major subject groupings. Appendix: index to *Physiologus Graecus*, *Hieroglyphica* of Horapollo, *Mundus Symbolicus* of Picinellus. Indexes: mottos, illustrations, subjects. Extensive international bibliography, pp. xxix-xliii. Most comprehensive modern work on emblems. Supplemented by:

858. ———. *Emblemata. Handbuch zur Sinnbildkunst des 16. und 17. Jahrhunderts. Supplement der Erstausgabe.* Stuttgart: Metzler, 1976. 217pp. illus.

Contains an updated and expanded international bibliography with 2335 titles, pp. xxxiii-clxxvi. Includes table of contents for and intended as a supplement to the above.

859. Landwehr, John. *German Emblem Books 1531-1888. A Bibliography.* Utrecht: Dekker & Gumbert, 1972. vii, 184pp.

Lists 661 emblem books in all languages produced in German-speaking countries. Chronological list, pp. 3-15. Entries give author's name, complete title of first edition, collation, etc. Material arranged in 15 different indexes.

860. Rosenfeld, Hellmut. "Emblemliteratur." *Reallexikon* (No. 1288), I, 334-336.

861. Schöne, Albrecht. *Emblematik und Drama im Zeitalter des Barock.* Munich: Beck, 1968. 248pp. illus.

A full treatment of the use of emblems in Baroque drama, including a general discussion of emblems, emblematic themes and motifs, and the emblematic structure of drama. Bibliography, pp. 234-247, lists emblem books and secondary material.

862. Selig, Karl-Ludwig. "Emblem Literature. Directions in Recent Scholarship." *Yearbook of Comparative and General Literature* 12 (1963), 36-41.

b. Das Groteske

863. Kayser, Wolfgang. *Das Groteske. Seine Gestaltung in Malerei und Dichtung.* Oldenburg, Hamburg: Stalling, 1957. 228pp. illus. English ed.: *The Grotesque in Art and Literature.* Trans. by Ulrich Weisstein. Bloomington: Indiana Univ. Pr., 1963. 224pp.

864. Petsch, Robert. "Das Groteske." In: R.P., *Deutsche Literaturwissenschaft. Aufsätze zur Begründung der Methode.* Berlin: Ebering, 1940, pp. 214-229.

c. Humor

865. Preisendanz, Wolfgang. *Humor als dichterische Einbildungskraft.* Munich: Eidos, 1963. 347pp.

Discussion limited to the 19th century: F. Schlegel, Solger, E.T.A. Hoffmann, Hegel, Keller, Fontane, Raabe. Bibliography, pp. 342-347.

866. ———. *Über den Witz.* Konstanz: Universitätsverlag, 1970. 36pp. Inaugural lecture, 1968.

d. Kitsch

867. Ueding, Gert. *Glanzvolles Elend. Versuch über Kitsch und Kolportage.* Frankfurt: Suhrkamp, 1973. 206pp.

Range: 19th-20th century. A sociological study: conditions and causes of Kitsch; close analysis of novels of Karl May; appraisal of Ernst Bloch's theories. Index: author. Not an introduction to the subject.

e. Lehrhafte Dichtung

868. Richter, Werner. "Lehrhafte Dichtung." *Reallexikon* (No. 1288), II, 31-39.

869. Siegrist, Christoph. *Das Lehrgedicht der Aufklärung.* Stuttgart: Metzler, 1974. x, 323pp.

Detailed assessment of the genre, including definitions, poetics, elements of composition, major themes and motifs. Primary and secondary bibliography, pp. 295-316. Index: names. Excellent general survey.

870. Sowinski, Bernhard. *Lehrhafte Dichtung des Mittelalters.* Stuttgart: Metzler, 1971. x, 134pp.

Range: 8th to 15th century. Definitions, historical survey of development of didactic literature, survey of research. Bibliography at the end of each section. Indexes: author, subject, secondary literature. Excellent resource book.

f. Manierismus

871. Hocke, Gustav René. *Manierismus in der Literatur. Sprachalchemie und esoterische Kombinationskunst.* Hamburg: Rowohlt, 1959. 339pp.

The standard history of mannerism in European literature. Focus is on the 16th and 17th centuries. Index: authors, subjects. Bibliography, pp. 309-320. Appendix: a small anthology of text specimens. Excellent; quite demanding.

g. Parodie

872. Liede, Alfred. "Parodie." *Reallexikon* (No. 1288), III, 12-72.

873. Rotermund, Erwin. *Die Parodie in der modernen deutschen Lyrik.* Munich: Eidos, 1963. 189pp.

Definitions, followed by chapters on Gumppenberg, Morgenstern, Holz, the Dadaists, Mehring, Brecht. Bibliography, pp. 181-189.

h. Satire

874. Brummack, Jürgen. "Zu Begriff und Theorie der Satire." *DVLG* (1971), Sonderheft, 275-377.

875. ———. "Satire." *Reallexikon* (No. 1288), III, 601-614.

876. Ebeling, Friedrich Wilhelm. *Geschichte der komischen Literatur in Deutschland seit der Mitte des 18. Jahrhunderts. I. Geschichte der komischen Literatur in Deutschland während der 2. Hälfte des 18. Jahrhunderts.* 3 vols. Leipzig: Haynel, 1865-1869. 572pp., 560pp., 778pp. (Repr. 1971)

A history of satire and humorous literature with a wealth of names and titles. Primary material extensively reprinted with little analysis. I and II contain major Catholic authors, literary satires, the epigram, major themes. III covers special forms of satire in poetry, the comic novel, and drama. Somewhat encyclopedic. Index: names.

i. Schlüsselliteratur

877. Kanzog, Klaus. "Schlüsselliteratur." *Reallexikon* (No. 1288), III, 646-665.

878. Schneider, George. *Die Schlüsselliteratur.* 3 vols. Stuttgart: Hiersemann, 1951-1953.

I. *Das literarische Gesamtbild.* 1951. xvi, 214pp. A general survey of the history and extent of the use of historical characters and events in works of fiction. Examination of the external and psychological factors which influence an author to portray his time in fiction.
II. *Entschlüsselung deutscher Romane und Dramen*, 1952. vii, 212pp. Articles listed by author A-Z.
III. *Entschlüsselung ausländischer Romane und Dramen.* 1953. x, 189pp. Articles listed by author A-Z.

B. THE DRAMATIC GENRES

1. Forschungsberichte

879. Michael, Wolfgang F. "Das deutsche Drama und Theater vor der Reformation." *DVLG* 31 (1957), 106-153. Repr. *DVLG* 47 (1973), Sonderheft, 1-47.

880. Tarot, Rolf. "Literatur zum deutschen Drama und Theater des 16. und 17. Jahrhunderts. Ein Forschungsbericht. 1945-1962." *Euphorion* 57 (1963), 411-453.

881. Wittkowski, Wolfgang. "Zur Ästhetik und Interpretation des Dramas. Ein Literaturbericht." *DU* 15 (1963), 6, Beilage.

882. Carpenter, Charles A. "The New Bibliography of Modern Drama Studies." *Modern Drama* 12 (1969/70), 49-56.

883. Hart-Nibbrig, Christian L. "Zum neueren Drama. Forschungsbericht." *Wirkendes Wort* 23 (1973), 212-217.

884. Thomke, Hellmut. "Das deutsche Drama der letzten fünfzig Jahre. Forschungsbericht." *Wirkendes Wort* 24 (1974), 415-525.

2. Bibliographies

a. Completed Bibliographies

*** *Bibliographisches Handbuch der deutschen Literaturwissenschaft 1945-1969*. (No. 123, No. 124). I: see section IV. "Deutsche Literaturgeschichte. D. Formen und Gattungen (Theorie und Geschichte). Drama (Schauspiel/Tragödie)," and V. "Mittelalter," VI. "Renaissance, Humanismus, Reformation," VII. "Zeitalter des Barock," VIII. "18 Jahrhundert," IX. "Zeitalter der Klassik und Romantik." Selected cumulation of (No. 129) to 1969.

II. see section X. "Neunzehntes Jahrhundert: 1830-1880."
XI. "19. Jahrhundert. Ende und Übergang zum 20. (1880-1914)."
XII. "Deutschsprachige Literatur des 20. Jahrhunderts." Selected cumulation of (No. 129) to 1972.

885. Gabel, Gernot Uwe. *Drama und Theater des deutschen Barock. Eine Handbibliographie der Sekundärliteratur*. Hamburg: Selbstverlag, 1974. xv, 182pp.

Range: 1580-1700. Bibliographical material from 19th century to 1970's. Ca. 2400 listings limited to drama and theater, and divided into 5 categories: general literature, German literary history, German literature of the Baroque, history of the theater, 28 authors. Indexes: author, subject. Information not always reliable.

886. Gebhard, Helga. "Bibliographie zur Gattungspoetik. Theorie des Komischen, der Komödie und der Tragödie (1900-1972)." *Zeitschrift für französische Sprache und Literatur* 84 (1974), 236-248.

887. Hill, Claude, and Ralph Ley. *The Drama of German Expressionism. A German-English Bibliography.* Chapel Hill: Univ. of N. Carolina Pr., 1960. xi, 211pp.

A comprehensive bibliography to 1958. Pt. 1: German drama and Expressionism in general (pp. 6-38); pt. 2: 16 authors--Barlach, Brecht, Bronnen, Goering, Hasenclever, Jahnn, Johst, Kaiser, Kokoschka, Kornfeld, Rubiner, Sorge, Sternheim, Toller, F. v. Unruh, Werfel (pp. 39-191)--primary and secondary material. In each section German and English entries are listed separately. American sources are emphasized. Indexes: author, title. Information is easily accessible. An excellent bibliography for the beginner.

*** *Internationale Bibliographie zur Geschichte der deutschen Literatur* (No. 122), I: see section "Geschichte und Theorie der literarischen Gattungen. Dramatik" and "Deutsche Literatur von den Anfängen bis 1050," "... von 1050 bis 1160," "... von 1160 bis 1230," "... von 1230 bis 1480," "... von 1480 bis 1680," "Deutschsprachige Literatur von 1680 bis 1789." Selected cumulation to 1967. II, 1: see section "Deutschsprachige Literatur von 1789 bis 1830." "Deutschsprachige Literatur von 1830 bis 1900," and "Deutschsprachige Literatur von 1900 bis zur Gegenwart. Theorie und Geschichte der Gattungen und Genres." Selected cumulation to 1969. Marxist-socialist criticism well represented.

888. Pfister, Manfred. "Bibliographie zur Gattungspoetik. Theorie des Komischen, der Komödie und der Tragikomödie (1943-1972)," *Zeitschrift für französische Sprache und Literatur* 83 (1973), 240-254.

*** Ruttkowski, Wolfgang. *Bibliographie der Gattungspoetik für den Studenten der Literaturwissenschaft. Ein abgekürztes Verzeichnis von über 3000 Büchern, Dissertationen und Zeitungsartikeln in Deutsch, Englisch und Französisch.* Munich: Hueber, 1973. 246pp. (No. 846)

889. Schindler, Otto G. *Theaterliteratur. Ein bibliographischer Behelf für das Studium der Theaterwissenschaft. Mit einem Anhang. Bibliographie zur österreichischen Theatergeschichte zusammengestellt von Fritz Fuhrich.* 4th ed. Vienna: Wiener Gesellschaft für Theaterforschung, 1975. vi, 161pp.

A handbook for students; includes primary and secondary sources: bibliographies, histories, journals, and the bibliography in the appendix. Contains 1805 items with emphasis on Austrian material. International in scope. A useful tool.

890. Stratman, Carl J. *Bibliography of Medieval Drama.* 2nd rev. and enl. ed. 2 vols. New York: Ungar, 1972. ([1]1954) I. xv, 670pp.; II. ix, pp. 671-1035.

International bibliography with 9,200 items. Covers liturgical Latin, English, Byzantine, French, German, Italian, Low Countries, and Spanish drama. Section VII. "German Drama" (II, 779-861) contains 831 items on bibliography, general studies, religious drama, special genres, and Hrosvitha von Gandersheim. Research of the 19th and early 20th century well represented.

b. Current Bibliographies

*** *Bibliographie der deutschen Sprach- und Literaturwissenschaft* (No. 129): see section VIII. "Deutsche Literaturgeschichte. Formen und Gattungen (Theorie und Geschichte). Drama (Schauspiel/Tragödie)," and IX--XIX. "(Einzelne) Gattungen," 1 (1945)--15 (1975)ff. Most reliable and comprehensive current bibliography available. Editions and secondary material listed. Publ. annually.

*** *Germanistik* (No. 130): see section XVII. "Allgemeines zur Literaturwissenschaft. Poetik: Gattungen und Arten" and XXII. --XXXI. "Drama," 1 (1960)-17 (1976)ff. Comprehensive quarterly, up to date. Lists editions and secondary material. Reviews of books.

891. *Maske und Kothurn.* "Bibliographie des in den Jahren ... angezeigten theaterwissenschaftlichen Schrifttums," ed. Franz Hadamowsky. 1 (1955), 195-199; 2 (1956), 377-384; 3 (1957), 185-192, 368-380; 4 (1958), 271-288; 5 (1959), 359-380; 6 (1960), 366-388; 8 (1962), 354-380; 9 (1963), 339-380; 10 (1964), 78-96, 187-192; 11 (1965), 272-288; 12 (1966), 92-104; 13 (1967), 213-232; 14 (1968), 363-380; 15 (1969), 271-288; 17 (1971), 256-272; 18 (1972), 177-196, 253-271; 19 (1973), 260-279; 21 (1975), 216-233; 22 (1976), 361-382. International in scope; includes drama, spoken records.

*** *MLA International Bibliography* (No. 125), II: see section "German Literature. II. Themes, Types, Special Topics" and "German Literature. III.--German Literature VII. Drama and Theater," 1921-1975ff. Annual cumulation. Lists editions and secondary material. Extensive and reliable.

892. *Modern Drama.* "A Selective Bibliography of Works Published in English" for 1959: 3 (1960/61), 143-161; for 1960 and 1961: 5 (1962/63), 223-244; for 1962: 6 (1963/64), 204-217; for 1963 and 1964: 8 (1965/66), 204-226; for 1965: 9 (1966/67), 210-226; for 1966: 10 (1967/68), 202-215; for 1967: 11 (1968/69), 195-213; publication lapsed for five years.
"Modern Drama. An Annual Bibliography," ed. Charles A. Carpenter, 17 (1964), 67-120; 18 (1975), 61-116; 19 (1976), 177-220. International listing of articles and books, divided according to national literature. To be continued.

*** *Referatendienst zur Literaturwissenschaft* (No. 131): see section "Gattungen. Allgemein. Drama," 1 (1969)-6 (1975)ff. Marxist-socialist quarterly review of books. Limited in scope.

3. Drama Theory

893. Ermatinger, Emil. *Die Kunstform des Dramas.* 2nd ed. Leipzig: Quelle & Meyer, 1931. 42pp. ([1]1925)

Extremely compact introduction to the elements of drama.

894. Flemming, Willi. *Epik und Dramatik. Versuch ihrer Wesensdeutung.* 2nd ed. Bern: Francke, 1955. 143pp. ([1]1925)

Attempts to define the "timeless" principles of epic and dramatic form. Sections cover the linguistic and structural elements of each, as well as the differences in characterization, plot, and theme. A succinct introduction.

895. Grimm, Reinhold, ed. *Deutsche Dramentheorien. Beiträge zu einer historischen Poetik des Dramas in Deutschland.* 2 vols. Frankfurt: Athenäum, 1971. I. xxviii, 292pp.; II. pp. 293-591.

A collection of 17 essays: H.-J. Schings, Baroque; K. Wölfel, 18th century; F. Martini, Storm and Stress; J. Müller, Goethe; K.L. Berghahn, Schiller; P. Schmidt, Romanticism; W. Wittkowski, Kleist; U. Fülleborn, Grillparzer; H.-J. Anders, Hebbel; H. Denkler, 1830-1848; H. Schanze, Realism; G. Schulz, Naturalism; J. Hermand, 1890's to early 20th century; D. Kimpel, Hofmannsthal; V. Žmegač, Expressionism; U. Weisstein, Piscator; W.H. Sokel, Brecht. Index: names. Work of high quality throughout.

896. Klotz, Volker. *Offene und geschlossene Form im Drama.* 2nd ed. Munich: Hanser, 1962. 275pp. ([1]1960)

An intensive examination of two structural types of drama and the consequences for other elements of the drama. Most important for the study of drama. Bibliography.

897. Petsch, Robert. *Wesen und Formen des Dramas. Allgemeine Dramaturgie.* Halle: Niemeyer, 1945. xv, 478pp.

An extensive treatment of the genre including definitions, structural and stylistic elements, language, etc. Indexes: names, subjects.

4. History and Interpretation

a. General Histories

898. Arnold, Robert Franz, ed. *Das deutsche Drama.* Munich: Beck, 1925. x, 868pp. (Repr. 1972)

Range: 10th century-1925. An excellent factual survey, still useful for its discussion of "contemporary" drama and theater, i.e. Naturalism, Expressionism. Indexes: names, dramas. Chronological table: drama 900-1925, pp. 833-841. Bibl.

899. Borcherdt, Hans Heinrich. "Geschichte des deutschen Theaters." *Dt. Phil. im Aufriß* (No. 1283), III, 1099-1244.

Range: Middle Ages-mid 20th century. A chronological history of the theater in German-speaking countries. Individual epochs are analyzed. "Bibliographie zur deutschen Theatergeschichte" by K. Braun; cols. 1238-1243.

900. Dietrich, Margret. *Das moderne Drama. Strömungen, Gestalten, Motive.* 3rd rev. ed. Stuttgart: Kröner, 1974. 936pp. ([1]1961)

An extensive survey of European and American drama from the turn of the century to the 1970's. Contains numerous interpretations of individual works, synchronic and diachronic analyses, examinations of major themes and motifs. Indexes: authors, titles. Bibl. pp. 885-905. Well structured; may be used as a handbook. Superb presentation.

901. Fechter, Paul. *Das europäische Drama. Geist und Kultur im Spiegel des Theaters.* 3 vols. Mannheim: Bibliographisches Institut, 1956-1958.

I. *Vom Barock zum Naturalismus.* 1956. 511pp.
II. *Vom Naturalismus zum Expressionismus.* 1957. 558pp.
III. *Vom Expressionismus zur Gegenwart.* 1958. 543pp.

Range: 17th century-1950's. Periods treated by national literatures; work of representative playwrights analyzed. Very broad, often summary intellectual-historical treatment. Manuscript for III published as it was at Fechter's death.

902. Kehrein, Joseph. *Die dramatische Poesie der Deutschen. Versuch einer Entwicklung derselben von der ältesten Zeit bis zur Gegenwart. Beitrag zur Geschichte der deutschen Nationalliteratur.* 2 vols. in 1. Leipzig: Hinrichs, 1840.

Range: 17th century-1830's. Thorough history of tragedy, comedy, music drama and their special genres. Contains a large number of minor figures. Still useful for its factual information. Bibliography, pp. 39-46. Indexes: authors, pseudonyms.

903. Kindermann, Heinz. *Theatergeschichte Europas.* 10 vols. Salzburg: Müller.

I. *Das Theater der Antike und des Mittelalters.* 1957. 542pp.
II. *Das Theater der Renaissance.* 1959. 496pp.
III. *Das Theater der Barockzeit.* 1959. 756pp.
IV. *Von der Aufklärung zur Romantik (1. Teil).* 1961. 846pp.
V. *Von der Aufklärung zur Romantik (2. Teil).* 1962. 879pp.
VI. *Romantik.* 1964. 464pp.
VII. *Realismus.* 1965. 521pp.
VIII. *Naturalismus und Impressionismus. 1. Teil. Deutschland, Österreich, Schweiz.* 1968. 892pp.
IX. *Naturalismus und Impressionismus. 2. Teil. Frankreich, Rußland, England, Skandinavien.* 1970. 800pp.
X. *Naturalismus und Impressionismus. 3. Teil. Holland, Belgien, Lettland, Litauen, Estland, Polen, Tschechoslo-*

wakei, Jugoslawien, Bulgarien, Ungarn, Rumänien, Italien, Spanien, Portugal, Türkei, Griechenland. 1974. 763pp. A collection of 18 essays by various specialists.

A standard chronological history with focus on the stage, stagecraft, and dramatic production, including opera. All volumes contain a chronological table, notes, and an extensive bibliography. Indexes: places, names and titles, subjects. Numerous illustrations. An excellent supplement to literary studies.

904. Knudsen, Hans. *Deutsche Theatergeschichte.* 2nd ed. Stuttgart: Kröner, 1970. xii, 455pp. (^{1}1959)

Range: 9th-20th century. A survey of the development of German theater emphasizing architecture, stage, staging, and acting. Comprehensive bibliography, pp. 365-383. Index: subject.

905. Mann, Otto. *Geschichte des deutschen Dramas.* 3rd rev. ed. Stuttgart: Kröner, 1969. viii, 651pp. (^{1}1960)

Range: 1600-1965. Detailed chronological history with synopses of major dramas. Evaluation of individual authors conservative with strong Christian orientation. Introduction: outline of drama history from Classical antiquity to 1600. Text, part 1: development of drama in Germany modeled after Classical antiquity, 1600-1800; part 2: drama in an age of secularization. Includes Austrian and Swiss drama. Excellent introduction to the genre.

*** Schillemeit, Jost, ed. *Interpretationen, II: Deutsche Dramen von Gryphius bis Brecht.* Frankfurt: Fischer, 1965. 341pp. (No. 1258)

*** Wiese, Benno von, ed. *Das deutsche Drama vom Barock bis zur Gegenwart. Interpretationen.* 2 vols. Düsseldorf: Bagel, 1960. (No. 1259)

b. Middle Ages and Renaissance

906. Borcherdt, Hans Heinrich. *Das europäische Theater im Mittelalter und in der Renaissance.* Leipzig: Weber, 1935. 209pp. illus.

A compact history of German, French, Italian, Dutch theater. Emphasis is on stagecraft and dramatic production. A solid general study.

907. Hartl, Eduard, and Friederike Weber. "Das Drama des Mittelalters." *Dt. Phil. im Aufriß* (No. 1283), II, 1949-1996.

Range: 10th century-15th century. A brief discussion of drama origins, stage, audience, actors, costumes, relationship between life style and art in the Middle Ages. Extensive bibliography appended. Excellent introduction.

908. Michael, Wolfgang F. *Das deutsche Drama des Mittelalters.* Berlin, New York: de Gruyter, 1971. xi, 304pp.

Range: 10th-16th century. Chronological history by genre: liturgical drama, secular drama, humanist drama. Focus on individual works, geographical centers, or authors. Index: authors and subjects. Bibliography, pp. 277-298, also includes older titles. An excellent, detailed analysis.

909. Roloff, Hans-Gert. "Neulateinisches Drama," *Reallexikon* (No. 1288), II, 645-678.

910. Van Abbé, Derek. *Drama in Renaissance Germany and Switzerland.* Melbourne: Melbourne Univ. Pr., 1961. xvi, 164pp.

Range: 16th century. A compact study of religious drama, low comedy. Biblical dramas, and Humanist theater. A good introduction. Extensive bibliography, pp. 139-157. Appendix: plays performed 1500-1540.

c. Eighteenth and Nineteenth Centuries

911. Bruford, Horace Walter. *Theatre, Drama and Audience in Goethe's Germany.* London: Routledge & Kegan Paul, 1950. xi, 388pp.

A social history of drama in the 18th century with emphasis on Gottsched, Lessing, Storm and Stress, Schiller, and Goethe. Appendix: the Weimar repertoire in the opening months of 1803. Bibliography, pp. 367-375. Indexes: plays, names and subjects. A superb introduction to the century.

912. Denkler, Horst. *Restauration und Revolution. Politische Tendenzen im Drama zwischen Wiener Kongreß und Märzrevolution.* Munich: Fink, 1973. 384pp.

Range: 1815 to 1850's. A chronological examination of the political and social content of *Vormärz* dramas. Covers a vast number of plays, including many by unknown and minor poets. Somewhat encyclopedic in approach. Index: authors.

913. Hoefert, Sigfrid. *Das Drama des Naturalismus.* Stuttgart: Metzler, 1968. xii, 106pp.

A compact survey: 1. historical, philosophical, and scientific developments preceding the period; 2. the work of individual authors, with primary and secondary bibliographies, including some authors of prose fiction; 3. limited *Forschungsbericht.* Index: author. Bibliography at the end of each section.

914. Kaufmann, Friedrich Wilhelm. *German Dramatists of the 19th Century.* Los Angeles: Lymanhouse, 1940. vi, 215pp. (Repr. 1970)

Chronological history with focus on individual authors: Kleist, Grillparzer, Grabbe, Büchner, Hebbel, Ludwig, Wagner, Ibsen. Positivistic approach with little analysis of works. Somewhat outdated.

915. Kistler, Mark O. *Drama of the Storm and Stress.* New York: Twayne, 1969. 170pp.

A basic, rather limited examination of dramas between 1771-1776 by Lenz, Wagner, Maler Müller, Klinger, Leisewitz. Analyses include detailed summaries.

916. Osborne, John. *The Naturalist Drama in Germany*. Manchester: Manchester Univ. Pr., 1971. viii, 185pp.

A general introduction focusing chiefly on Hauptmann. Pt. 1: theory and background; Naturalism and theater; pt. 2: detailed analyses with summaries of Hauptmann's plays. Bibliography. A solid introduction to the subject.

917. Stockmeyer, Clara. *Soziale Probleme im Drama des Sturmes und Dranges. Eine literaturhistorische Studie*. Frankfurt: Diesterweg, 1922. v, 244pp. (Repr. 1974)

An encyclopedic compilation of materials on the theme of social problems in (pt. 1) the family, (pt. 2) social classes, (pt. 3) the political power structure. Bibliography. Useful for its attention to detail.

d. Twentieth Century

918. Bab, Julius. *Die Chronik des deutschen Dramas*. 5 vols. Berlin: Osterheld, 1921-1926. (Repr. 1972)

I. *1900-1906*. 1922. 191pp.
II. *1907-1910*. 1921. 164pp.
III. *1911-1913*. 1922. 188pp.
IV. *1914-1918*. 1922. 168pp.
V. *1919-1926*. 1926. 375pp.

Essays, personal observations about the early 20th-century theater scene, its authors and their dramas, often in the style of a review. Indexes: IV, authors and titles for I-IV; V, authors and titles. Valuable for its first-hand information on German theater, major and minor authors.

*** Brauneck, Manfred, ed. *Das deutsche Drama vom Expressionismus bis zur Gegenwart. Interpretationen*. Bamberg: Buchner, 1970. 293pp. (No. 1257)

919. Daiber, Hans. *Deutsches Theater seit 1945*. Stuttgart: Reclam, 1976. 428pp., illus.

A history of the stage after 1945 covering FRG, Austria, GDR, and Switzerland. Contains sections on drama, opera, musicals, dance. Good background information on the dramatic arts. Index: names. Bibliography, pp. 407-409.

920. Denkler, Horst. *Drama des Expressionismus. Programm. Spieltext. Theater*. Munich: Fink, 1967. 260pp.

Author attempts to work out a typology of Expressionist drama on the basis of form, structure, content. On the basis of an examination of some 50 dramas, with particular attention to change and development of the central character, he offers some conclusions which are valuable as an introduction to Expressionist drama. Index: names. Bibliography.

921. Dosenheimer, Elise. *Das deutsche soziale Drama von Lessing bis Sternheim.* Constance: Südverlag, 1949. 351pp.

Short evaluations and summaries of major plot components for some 80 plays by 18 authors. Index: authors, titles. Compact analyses helpful for the beginner.

922. Garten, H.F. *Modern German Drama.* 2nd ed. London: Methuen, 1964. 296pp. (^{1}1959)

Range: 1800's-1950's. A historical survey: Naturalism, Neo-Romanticism, Expressionism, New Realism, National Socialism, post-1945. Excellent introduction to the development of drama in the 20th century. Extensive bibliography includes list of English translations.

923. Hayman, Ronald, ed. *The German Theater. A Symposium.* London: Wolff, 1975. 287pp.

Range: 18th to 20th century. A collection of 13 papers on the development of German drama from Lessing to the present. Includes Austrian, Swiss, GDR, FRG literature and information on German stage, directors, and theater management. Bibliography.

924. Hinck, Walter. *Das moderne Drama in Deutschland. Vom expressionistischen zum dokumentarischen Theater.* Göttingen: Vandenhoeck & Ruprecht, 1973. 241pp.

Range: 1910 to 1970's. A survey of 20th-century dramas centered around major themes and developments. A solid study containing many analyses of individual plays. Index: author and subject.

925. Kesting, Marianne. *Das epische Theater. Zur Struktur des modernen Dramas.* 2nd ed. Stuttgart: Kohlhammer, 1969. 160pp. (^{1}1959)

Contemporary theater defined in terms of epic theater. 1: poetics; 2: the epic theater of Brecht, Claudel, Wilder, Williams, Lorca, Schehade, Beckett, Adamov, Ionesco. Useful for its comparative analyses.

926. Kienzle, Siegfried. *Modernes Welttheater. Ein Führer durch das internationale Schauspiel der Nachkriegszeit in 755 Einzelinterpretationen.* Stuttgart: Kröner, 1966. viii, 598pp.

Range: 1945-1960's. Listed by author A-Z. Reliable summaries of plays and bibliographies. Index: plays.

927. English ed.: *Modern World Theater. A Guide to Productions in Europe and the United States since 1945.* Trans. by Alexander and Elizabeth Henderson. New York: Ungar, 1970. v, 509pp.

Includes 563 plays of the above plus 15 additional plays. Listed by author A-Z with titles in English. Index: titles.

928. ———. *Schauspielführer der Gegenwart. 714 Einzelinterpretationen zum Schauspiel seit 1945.* 2nd rev. ed. Stuttgart: Kröner. 1973. 591pp. Range: 1945-1973.

929. Kohlschmidt, Werner. "Drama (Neuzeit)." *Reallexikon* (No. 1288), I, 289-310.

930. Mennemeier, Franz Norbert. *Modernes deutsches Drama. Kritiken und Charakteristiken.* 2 vols. Munich: Fink, 1973, 1975. I. 375pp.; II. 410pp.

Range: 1910 to 1970's. An extensive survey combining work analyses and literary history. Thematic division with focus on major writers: I: Sorge, Rubiner, Brust, Stramm, F.v. Unruh, Hasenclever, Bronnen, Kornfeld, Goering, Sternheim, Lasker-Schüler, Kaiser, Goll, Toller, Jung, Lask, A. Herzog, Wittfogel, Mühsam, F. Wolf, early Brecht; II: Horváth, Brecht, drama of the Third Reich, Borchert, Frisch, Dürrenmatt, Grass, Weiss, Le Fort, Hochhuth, Handke, M. Walser, Kroetz, Bernhard, Baver, Braun, Stolper, Baierl, Hacks. Index: authors. Bibliography, I. pp. 360-370, II. pp. 370-406. Excellent, detailed analyses; superb for the student.

931. Ritchie, James M. *German Expressionist Drama.* Boston: Twayne, 1976. 198pp.

A broad survey concentrating on major themes and trends of the period. Much interpretation of and commentary on the literature. Index: names, titles, subjects. Selected annotated bibliography. An excellent survey for the non-German-speaking student.

932. Rühle, Günther. *Theater für die Republik 1917-1933 im Spiegel der Kritik.* Frankfurt: Fischer, 1967. ii, 1264pp.

Compendium of contemporary criticism of German theater performances (emphasis on Berlin). Each play introduced by a short paragraph followed by press reviews. Includes a detailed account of the German stage during the Weimar Republic. Extensive indexes make reference hunting easy.

933. Samuel, Richard, and R. Hinton Thomas. *Expressionism in German Life, Literature and the Theatre (1910-1924).* Cambridge: Heffer, 1939. viii, 203pp.

Though the emphasis is on plays and analysis of single plays, some attention is given to poetry as social expression; other art forms are largely omitted from consideration. A somewhat outdated but still useful introduction.

934. Spalter, Max. *Brecht's Tradition.* Baltimore: Johns Hopkins Univ. Pr., 1967. xii, 271pp.

Range: 18th to 20th centuries. Contains analyses of intrinsic and extrinsic factors in dramas by Lenz, Grabbe, Büchner, Wedekind, Kraus viewed as forerunners of Brecht. Reliable summaries of works interpreted. Appendix: scenes (in translation) from Lenz's *The Tutor*, Grabbe's *Napoleon or the Hundred Days*, and Kraus' *The Last Days of Mankind*. A significant contribution.

935. Szondi, Peter. *Theorie des modernen Dramas.* Frankfurt: Suhrkamp, 1959. 144pp.

Range: 1860's (Ibsen) to 1950's (A. Miller). Broad theoretical examination of Western drama from its earlier crisis (antithesis of form and content) to later attempts at resolution. Analyzes numerous works by major dramatists. Difficult for the beginner. A standard work.

936. Viviani, Annalisa. *Das Drama des Expressionismus. Kommentar zu einer Epoche*. Munich: Winkler, 1970. 190pp.

A history of the period with chronological table 1906-1925. Brief analyses of dramas by Wedekind, Sternheim, Kokoschka, Sorge, Hasenclever, Kaiser (3), Kornfeld, Johst, Goering, Unruh, Barlach, Toller, Werfel. Primary and secondary bibliography, pp. 149-184. Index: names. A good introduction.

937. Vogelsang, Hans. *Österreichische Dramatik des 20. Jahrhunderts*. Stuttgart, Vienna: Braumüller, 1963. 223pp.

A collection of 7 essays detailing the contribution of ca. 40 major and numerous minor authors to the Austrian theater from the 1890's to the 1960's. Little analysis: often too brief. Some secondary bibliography.

938. Wächter, Hans-Christof. *Theater im Exil. Sozialgeschichte des deutschen Exiltheaters 1933-1945. Mit einem Beitrag von Louis Naef, Theater der deutschen Schweiz*. Munich: Hanser, 1973. 298pp.

Focuses on political, economic, and social conditions with particular emphasis on Brecht, Bruckner, Toller, Werfel, and Wolf. Covers performances in Czechoslovakia, France, Britain, Denmark, Sweden, Soviet Union, USA, Latin America, Shanghai, Switzerland. Indexes: names, plays listed by author A-Z, performances, dramas not performed before 1945. Bibliography pp. 282-292: primary and secondary material.

939. Ziegler, Klaus. "Das deutsche Drama der Neuzeit." *Dt. Phil. im Aufriß* (No. 1283), II, 1997-2350.

Range: 15th century to 1920. Extensive compact outline history with emphasis on the social and intellectual setting which determined form and content. Brief general bibliography.

5. Tragedy (Trauerspiel, Tragödie)

940. Benjamin, Walter. *Ursprung des deutschen Trauerspiels*. Frankfurt: Suhrkamp, 1963. 272pp. ([1]1928)

Range: 17th century. A superb and extensive theoretical discussion of German Baroque tragedy. No wide-ranging analyses of individual works; focuses on philosophical and historical aspects of Baroque tragedy. Still one of the standard works on the subject; has been highly influential on the development of recent social and socialist directions in criticism.

*** Daunicht, Richard. *Die Entstehung des bürgerlichen Trauerspiels in Deutschland*. 2nd rev. ed. Berlin: de Gruyter, 1965. 326pp. ([1]1962) (No. 959)

941. Heitner, Robert R. *German Tragedy in the Age of Enlightenment. A Study in the Development of Original Tragedies, 1724-1768*. Berkeley, Los Angeles: Univ. of Calif. Pr., 1963. xviii, 467pp.

A chronological in-depth examination of tragedy and its various forms. Much information on the development of the Enlightenment, philosophical as well as literary. Appendices: plays published 1729-1768, commentary on plays not discussed in main text. Excellent resource book on the period.

942. Mann, Otto. *Poetik der Tragödie*. Bern: Francke, 1958. 344pp.

A comprehensive discussion of the nature of tragedy, its elements, effectiveness, and philosophical implications.

943. Sander, Volkmar, ed. *Tragik und Tragödie*. Darmstadt: Wissenschaftliche Buchsgesellschaft, 1971. xii, 481pp.

A collection of 19 previously published, one original essay by eminent scholars including Jaspers, Szondi, J. Müller, Peacock, Steiner. Provides an excellent overview of important research done from 1947-1970.

944. Szondi, Peter. *Versuch über des Tragische*. 2nd ed. Frankfurt: Insel, 1964. 117pp. ([1]1961)

1. Brief discussion of the concept of tragedy by 12 leading thinkers including Schelling, Hölderlin, Hegel, Goethe, Schopenhauer, Kierkegaard, Hebbel, Nietzsche. 2. 8 brilliant analyses of plays by Sophocles, Calderon, Shakespeare, Gryphius, Racine, Schiller, Kleist, Büchner. Superb and demanding reading.

945. Wiese, Benno von. *Die deutsche Tragödie von Lessing bis Hebbel. Erster Teil: Tragödie und Theodizee. Zweiter Teil: Tragödie und Nihilismus*. 7th ed. Hamburg: Hoffmann & Campe, 1967. xviii, 712pp.

Range: 1750-1865. Chronological account with concentration on: pt. 1: Lessing, Goethe, Schiller; pt. 2: Kleist, Hölderlin, Grillparzer, Grabbe, Büchner, Hebbel. Comprehensive interpretation of individual works which are seen as symptomatic for epochs covered. Sees secularization in period from Lessing to Hebbel as dominant force in the conception of the tragic. Conservative in view; demanding reading.

6. Tragicomedy (Tragikomödie)

946. Guthke, Karl S. *Geschichte und Poetik der deutschen Tragikomödie*. Göttingen: Vandenhoeck & Ruprecht, 1961. 450pp.

Range: 18th to 20th century. Postulates the tragi-comic view of existence. Scrutinizes individual plays in great detail, relating them to literary epochs. Highpoints in the development of the genre seen in Lessing, Romanticism, 20th century. Presentation of individual authors and epochs valuable beyond the discussions of the genre.

947. ———. *Modern Tragicomedy. An Investigation into the Nature of the Genre.* New York: Random House, 1966. xv, 205pp. German ed.: *Die moderne Tragikömodie. Theorie und Gestalt.* Trans. by Gerhard Raabe. Göttingen: Vandenhoeck & Ruprecht, 1968. 191pp.

Range: 17th to 20th century. A superb introduction to the genre, including definitions, theory, significance, and model analysis (Ch. 3) of Ibsen's *Wild Duck.* Indexes: authors, plays. Bibliography, notes, pp. 185-188.

7. Comedy (Lustspiel, Komödie)

948. Catholy, Eckehard. *Das deutsche Lustspiel. Vom Mittelalter bis zum Ende der Barockzeit.* Stuttgart, Berlin, Cologne, Mainz: Kohlhammer, 1969. 220pp.

Chronological history in 2 parts: 1. early period of German comedy; 2. 17th century, Italian and English influence, Gryphius, Hollenius, Weise, Reuter. Indexes: author, title. Bibliography, pp. 211-215, contains primary and secondary material. Somewhat demanding.

949. Ebeling, Friedrich Wilhelm. *Geschichte der komischen Literatur in Deutschland seit der Mitte des 18. Jahrhunderts. I. Geschichte der komischen Literatur in Deutschland während der 2. Hälfte des 18. Jahrhunderts.* 3 vols. Leipzig: Haynel, 1865-1869. 572pp., 560pp., 778pp.

See especially III, section 5, which covers comedy, farce, the comic *Singspiel* and opera. A large number of authors and titles recorded for the period.

950. Grimm, Reinhold, and Klaus L. Berghahn, eds. *Wesen und Formen des Komischen im Drama.* Darmstadt: Wissenschaftliche Buchgesellschaft, 1975. xxx, 469pp.

A collection of 15 essays published 1943-1971 by some of the finest scholars in the field, including O. Rommel, Kindermann, Frye, R. Grimm, Martini, Catholy, Arntzen. Index: names. Introduction contains a brief appraisal of research. Excellent overview of research on comedy.

951. Hinck, Walter, ed. *Die deutsche Komödie. Vom Mittelalter bis zur Gegenwart.* Düsseldorf: Bagel, 1977. 411pp.

An introductory essay on the concept of comedy, a survey of comedy from the Middle Ages to Lessing, interpretations of plays by Lessing, Lenz, Kleist, Tieck, Grabbe, Büchner, Raimund,

Kotzebue, Nestroy, G. Hauptmann, Sternheim, Hofmannsthal, Horváth, Zuckmayer, Brecht, Frisch, Dürrenmatt, Hacks. Notes include bibliography. Solid interpretations.

952. Holl, Karl. *Geschichte des deutschen Lustspiels*. Leipzig: Weber, 1923. xv, 439pp.

Range: 1300-1920 (Middle Ages to Expressionism). Detailed chronological account of German comedy from its inception with an emphasis on the intellectual-historical features. Many minor authors included. Richly illustrated. Discussion assumes familiarity with plays treated.

953. Martini, Fritz. *Lustspiele--und das Lustspiel*. Stuttgart: Klett, 1974. 276pp.

Range: 18th to 20th century. Seven previously published essays on the poetics of comedy and interpretations of works by J.E. Schlegel, Lessing, Goethe, Kleist, Grillparzer, Hauptmann, Brecht. Analyses are superb; a solid look at comedy.

954. Paulsen, Wolfgang, ed. *Die deutsche Komödie im zwanzigsten Jahrhundert. Sechstes Amherster Kolloquium zur modernen deutschen Literatur 1972*. Heidelberg: Stiehm, 1976. 233pp.

A collection of 8 papers read by Catholy, W. Marsch, K. Mommsen, Paulsen, R. Grimm, Weisstein, F. Trommler, J. Zipes. A good overview.

955. Prang, Helmut. *Geschichte des Lustspiels. Von der Antike bis zur Gegenwart*. Stuttgart: Kröner, 1968. ix, 390pp.

Range: 5th century B.C.-1960's. A strictly diachronic history of European comedy, with emphasis on the developments in Germany; includes brief summaries of major works and appraisals of major authors. Index: names. Quite satisfactory as a history.

956. Steffen, Hans, ed. *Das deutsche Lustspiel*. 2 vols. Göttingen: Vandenhoeck & Ruprecht, 1968-1969. I, 242pp., II, 217pp.

Range: 18th to 20th century. This anthology of 20 essays by eminent scholars includes surveys of periods (18th century, Romanticism) and interpretations of major works by Lessing, Lenz, Goethe, Raimund, Grillparzer, H.v. Kleist, Grabbe, Büchner, Nestroy, G. Hauptmann, Schnitzler, Wedekind, Sternheim, Hofmannsthal, Musil, Brecht, Frisch, and Dürrenmatt. Not a history of comedy. As a whole, essays are excellent.

957. Steinmetz, Horst. *Die Komödie der Aufklärung*. 2nd ed. Stuttgart: Metzler, 1971. viii, 80pp. ([1]1966)

A concise historical survey with bibliography at the end of each section.

8. Other Forms of the Drama

a. *Bürgerliches Drama*

958. Gauwerky, Ursula. "Bürgerliches Drama." *Reallexikon* (No. 1288), I, 199-203.

b. *Bürgerliches Trauerspiel*

959. Daunicht, Richard. *Die Entstehung des bürgerlichen Trauerspiels in Deutschland.* 2nd rev. ed. Berlin: de Gruyter, 1965. 326pp. ([1]1962)

Range: 17th to 18th century. Examination of the development of middle-class tragedy in Europe and its reception and influence in Germany. Detailed analysis of Lessing's *Miss Sara Sampson.* Excellent comparative introduction, valuable for references to British and French drama.

960. Guthke, Karl S. *Das bürgerliche Trauerspiel.* Stuttgart: Metzler, 1972. 108pp.

Outstanding resource book with historical survey of genre, definitions, and critical appraisal of research. Bibliography at the end of each section.

c. *Einakter*

961. Schnetz, Diemut. *Der moderne Einakter.* Eine poetologische Untersuchung. Bern, Munich: Francke, 1967. 244pp.

Range: 20th century. Includes definitions, a brief historical survey, elements of form: plot, characters, time, place, language. Focuses on the parabolic nature of the genre. Little work analysis or interpretation. Indexes: names, German one-act plays, pp. 212-224, one-act plays in foreign languages, pp. 225-237. Bibliography, pp. 204-211, primary and secondary material. Of uneven quality.

d. *Fastnachtspiel*

962. Catholy, Eckehard. *Fastnachtspiel.* Stuttgart: Metzler, 1966. xvi, 88pp.

Range: 14th to 16th century. History of *Fastnachtspiel*: typology, forms, themes; geographical centers of activity in the 15th and 16th centuries; literary-historical significance. Each section accompanied by extensive bibliography. Basic to the study of *Fastnachtspiel*.

e. *Film*

963. Eisner, Lotte. *The Haunted Screen. Expressionism in the German Cinema and the Influence of Max Reinhardt.* Berkeley: Univ. of Calif. Pr., 1969. 360pp. illus.

Range: beginnings to Nazi era. Definition of Expressionism in film and analyses of all major German films with many stills. Bibliogr., pp. 346-347. A useful filmography (1913-1933) gives German and English titles, film company, director, and other information. Very informative.

964. Kracauer, Siegfried. *From Caligari to Hitler. A Psychological History of German Film.* Princeton: Princeton Univ. Pr., 1947. xii, 361pp. illus.

Comprehensive and informative introduction. Somewhat tendentious but is still a standard work in English on the German film. Bibliography, pp. 333-346.

965. Stepun, Fedor. "Der Film." *Dt. Phil. im Aufriß* (No. 1283), III, 1383-1398.

f. Historisches Drama

966. Sengle, Friedrich. *Das historische Drama.* 2nd rev. ed. Stuttgart: Metzler, 1969. 279pp. ([1]1952: *Das deutsche Geschichtsdrama*)

Range: 1700-1900. Chronological history with special emphasis on the poet's reevaluation of his historical *sujet*.

g. Hörspiel

967. Fischer, Eugen Kurt. *Das Hörspiel. Form und Funktion.* Stuttgart: Kröner, 1964. 327pp.

Traces changes in the form and function of the radio play. Extensive discussion of the mass medium, its conception and production. Little interpretation of individual plays. Emphasis on formal and technical aspects of the genre. Table: radio plays 1924-1962. Extensive bibl.

968. Klose, Werner. "Neues vom Hörspiel." *Wirkendes Wort* 9 (1959), 176-181.

969. Rosenbaum, Uwe. *Das Hörspiel. Eine Bibliographie. Texte, Tondokumente, Literatur.* Hamburg: Verlag Hans-Bredow-Institut, 1974. xv, 459pp.

Primary and secondary material 1923-1974: pt. 1: anthologies, primary works by individual authors, A-Z; pt. 2: records and audio documents 1927-1944; pt. 3: literary criticism, anthologies (listed by author examined), reviews; pt. 4: critical analyses of the medium, bibliographies, the radio play in foreign countries, aesthetic aspects, related media, production, popular reception; pt. 5: appendix, unpubl. essays, prizes awarded, important German addresses, listing of journals and trade publications. Indexes: titles, authors of secondary literature. A comprehensive volume.

970. Schwitzke, Heinz. *Das Hörspiel. Dramaturgie und Geschichte.* Cologne, Berlin: Kiepenheuer & Witsch, 1963. 488pp.

Range: 1923-1960. Chronological history of the German radio-play. Pt. 1: 1923-1945; pt. 2: theory and medium; pt. 3: contemporary scene. Includes synopses with interpretations and evaluations of important authors. Table: chronology of radio plays. A comprehensive introduction to the genre.

971. Seeberger, Kurt. "Der Rundfunk--Entwicklung und Eigenart." *Dt. Phil. im Aufriß* (No. 1283), III, 1353-1382.

h. Schwank

972. Strassner, Erich. *Schwank*. Stuttgart: Metzler, 1968. xii, 108pp.

A resource book: definitions and differentiation from other genres, historical survey, discussion of primary sources. Index: author, subject. Bibliography at end of each section.

i. Singspiel

973. Koch, Hans-Albrecht. *Das deutsche Singspiel*. Stuttgart: Metzler, 1974. 108pp.

A survey of the genre, including foreign influences, the 18th century, Goethe, and Romanticism. Covers the major aspects of research. Valuable bibliographies at the end of each section. Index: authors.

974. Kunze, Stefan. "Singspiel." *Reallexikon* (No. 1288), III, 830-841.

C. THE PROSE GENRES

1. Forschungsberichte

975. Stammler, Wolfgang. "Von mittelalterlicher Prosa. Rechenschaft und Aufgabe." *JEGP* 48 (1949), 15-44.

976. Martini, Fritz. "Deutsche Prosadichtung im 19. Jahrhundert. Ein kritischer Literaturbericht." *DU* 5 (1953), 1, 112-128.

977. Pabst, Walter. "Literatur zur Theorie des Romans." *DVLG* 34 (1960), 264-289.

978. Lockemann, Wolfgang. "Zur Lage der Erzählforschung." *GRM* NF 15 (1965), 63-84.

979. Martini, Fritz. "Geschichte und Poetik des Romans. Ein Literaturbericht." *DU* 3 (1965), 3, 86-99.

980. Knapp, Gerhard P. "Der deutsche Roman seit 1925. Forschungsbericht." *Wirkendes Wort* 22 (1972), 347-362 and 25 (1975), 400-424.

2. Bibliographies

a. Completed Bibliographies

*** *Bibliographisches Handbuch der deutschen Literaturwissenschaft 1945-1969.* (No. 123), I: see section IV. "Deutsche Literaturgeschichte. D. Formen und Gattungen (Theorie und Geschichte). Epik (Erzählkunst/Roman)," and V. "Mittelalter," VI. "Renaissance, Humanismus, Reformation," VII. "Zeitalter des Barock," VIII. "18. Jahrhundert," IX. "Zeitalter der Klassik und Romantik." Selected cumulation of (No. 129) to 1969.
II: see section X. "Neunzehntes Jahrhundert: 1830-1880," XI. "19 Jahrhundert. Ende und Übergang zum 20. (1880-1914)," XII. "Deutschsprachige Literatur des 20. Jahrhunderts." Selected cumulation of (No. 129) to 1972.

981. Handschin, Charles H. "Bibliographie zur Technik des neueren deutschen Romans." *Modern Language Notes* 24 (1909), 230-234 and 25 (1910), 5-8. Titles mainly from 1890's to 1900's.

Continued by:

982. Frey, John R. "Bibliographie zur Theorie und Technik des deutschen Romans." For the years 1910-1938 in: *Modern Language Notes* 54 (1939), 557-567. For the years 1939-1953 in: *Modern Language Notes* 69 (1954), 77-88.

983. Haubrichs, Wolfgang, "Auswahlbibliographie zur Erzählforschung." *Erzählforschung* 1 (1976), 257-331.

*** *Internationale Bibliographie zur Geschichte der deutschen Literatur* (No. 122), I: see sections "Geschichte und Theorie der literarischen Gattungen. Epik/Künstlerische Prosa," "Deutsche Literatur von den Anfängen bis 1050," "... von 1050 bis 1160," "... von 1160 bis 1230," "... von 1230 bis 1480," "... von 1480 bis 1680," and "Deutschsprachige Literatur von 1680 bis 1789." Selected cumulation to 1967. (No. 122), II, 1: see sections "Deutschsprachige Literatur von 1789 bis 1830," "Deutschsprachige Literatur von 1830 bis 1900," and "Deutschsprachige Literatur von 1900 bis zur Gegenwart. Theorie und Geschichte der Gattungen und Genres." Selected cumulation to 1969. Marxist-socialist criticism well represented.

*** Ruttkowski, Wolfgang. *Bibliographie der Gattungspoetik für den Studenten der Literaturwissenschaft. Ein abgekürztes Verzeichnis von über 3000 Büchern, Dissertationen und Zeitungsartikeln in Deutsch, Englisch und Französisch.* Munich: Hueber, 1973. 246pp. (No. 846)

b. Current Bibliographies

*** *Bibliographie der deutschen Sprach- und Literaturwissenschaft* (No. 129): see section VIII. "Deutsche Literaturgeschichte. Formen und Gattungen (Theorie und Geschichte). Epik (Erzählkunst/Roman)" and IX.-XIX. "(Einzelne) Gattungen," 1 (1945)-15 (1975)ff. Most reliable and comprehensive current bibliography available. Editions and secondary material. Publ. annually.

*** *Germanistik* (No. 130): see section XVII. "Allgemeines zur Literaturwissenschaft. Poetik: Gattungen und Arten" and XXII.-XXXI. "Epik," 1 (1960)-17 (1976)ff. Comprehensive quarterly, up to date. Lists editions and secondary material. Books are reviewed.

*** *MLA International Bibliography* (No. 125), II: see section "German Literature. II. Themes, Types, Special Topics" and "German Literature. III.-German literature. VII. Prose Fiction," 1921-1975ff. Annual cumulation. Editions and secondary material. Extensive and reliable.

*** *Referatendienst zur Literaturwissenschaft* (No. 131): see section "Gattungen. Allgemein. Epik," 1 (1969)-6 (1975)ff. Marxist-socialist quarterly review of books. Limited in scope.

3. Prose Fiction Theory

984. Behrmann, Alfred. *Einführung in die Analyse von Prosatexten*. 3rd ed. Stuttgart: Metzler, 1971. x, 91pp. ([1]1967)

An exacting introduction to the rhetoric of prose fiction: rhythm, syntax, language, etc. Mechanics of analysis demonstrated on specimen texts. Highly technical and very compact; presumes some knowledge of literary technique. Indexes: author, subject; definitions of terminology.

985. Lämmert, Eberhard. *Bauformen des Erzählens*. 4th ed. Stuttgart: Metzler, 1970. 301pp. ([1]1955)

Intrinsic analysis of the narrative structure of prose fiction. Contents: 1. "Der sukzessive Aufbau des Erzählwerks"; 2. "Die sphärische Geschlossenheit des Erzählwerks"; 3. "Die Dimension der Rede im Erzählvorgang." Examples not limited to German literature. Bibliography. Author index. A standard work on the subject.

986. Petsch, Robert. *Wesen und Formen der Erzählkunst*. 2nd rev. and enl. ed. Halle: Niemeyer, 1942. viii, 582pp. ([1]1934)

Extensive survey of the genre in 6 chapters. Discusses earliest traces and forms, definitions, structural elements, stylistic elements, verse and prose, forms (*Heldenlied*, *Ballade*, *Anekdote*, *Schwank*, *Novelle*, *Epos*, *Roman*). Author and subject index.

987. Vogt, Jochen. *Aspekte erzählender Prosa.* Düsseldorf: Bertelsmann, 1972. 95pp.

Designed as an introduction for students to the major aspects of prose narration, such as narrator, time, structure. Relies on established critics such as K. Hamburger, Kayser, Lämmert, Stanzel. Often too simplified and brief. Contains helpful hints for further study at the end of each section. Bibliography, pp. 94-95; notes.

988. Zobel, Klaus. "Erzählformen." *Die Literatur* (No. 1281), pp. 171-217.

4. Novel

a. Novel Theory

989. Grimm, Reinhold, ed. *Deutsche Romantheorien. Beiträge zu einer historischen Poetik des Romans in Deutschland.* 2nd ed. Frankfurt: Athenäum, 1968. 420pp.

A collection of 17 previously published and original articles on the theory of the novel from the 17th to the 20th century. Essays on epochs include the Baroque, 1830-1850, Realism, 20th century. Essays on individual authors include F.v. Blankenburg, F. Schlegel, Novalis, Jean Paul, Spielhagen, Raabe, Fontane, Rilke, T. Mann, Döblin, Kafka, Broch, Musil. Index: author. Notes. Valuable anthology.

990. Hillebrand, Bruno. *Theorie des Romans.* 2 vols. Munich: Winkler, 1972. I. *Von Heliodor bis Jean Paul.* 234pp. II. *Von Hegel bis Handke.* 296pp.

A substantial historical survey of the theory of the novel with its focus on developments in Germany. Major portion of the work deals with 20th-century literature, particularly with T. Mann, H. Mann, Kafka, Broch, Musil, Döblin, and changes in the genre after 1945. Index: author, I, II; bibliography, II, 279-292.

991. Kayser, Wolfgang. "Die Anfänge des modernen Romans im 18. Jahrhundert und seine heutige Krise." *DVLG* 28 (1954), 417-446.

992. ———. *Entstehung und Krise des modernen Romans.* Stuttgart: Metzler, 1955. 35pp.

Survey of the novel from the 17th century to the 20th with focus on the mutations of the modern novel; the concerns expressed are now somewhat outdated.

993. Klotz, Volker, ed. *Zur Poetik des Romans.* Darmstadt: Wissenschaftliche Buchgesellschaft, 1965. xvi, 406pp.

A collection of 14 essays published from 1883-1966 by eminent scholars and authors, including Spielhagen, Vossler, Kayser,

G. Müller, Stanzel, Lukács, Döblin, Schirokauer, O. Ludwig, H. Meyer.

994. Lukács, Georg. *Die Theorie des Romans. Ein geschichtsphilosophischer Versuch über die Formen der großen Epik.* 3rd ed. Neuwied: Luchterhand, 1965. 169pp. ([1]1920)

An important, influential work.

995. Migner, Karl. *Theorie des modernen Romans. Eine Einführung.* Stuttgart: Kröner, 1970. 180pp.

Range: 17th century to 1960's. Sketches the history of the novel, focusing on the narrator, character and character development, structure, realism. Rather conservative in its approach to modern literature. Index: author and subject; notes.

996. Stanzel, Franz K. *Typische Formen des Romans.* 5th ed. Göttingen: Vandenhoeck & Ruprecht, 1970. 77pp. ([1]1964)

Typology of the novel: the different roles and functions of the narrator in Western fiction. A standard work on the subject.

997. Steinecke, Hartmut. *Romantheorie und Romankritik in Deutschland. Die Entwicklung des Gattungsverständnisses von der Scott-Rezeption bis zum programmatischen Realismus.* 2 vols. Stuttgart: Metzler. I. 1975. xii, 340pp.; II. *Quellen.* 1976. xii, 324pp.

Range: 1815-1850's. I: An extensive history of novel theory, focusing on major aesthetic, critical, and artistic contributions; II: The major article and text sources for I. Discussion is not limited to developments in Germany.

b. History and Interpretation

i. General Histories

998. Emmel, Hildegard. *Geschichte des deutschen Romans.* 2 vols. Bern, Munich: Francke. I. 1972. 372pp.; II. 1975. 354pp.

Range: 16th-20th centuries. A strictly chronological history from a positivistic point of view with little analysis beyond summaries of plot and major theme. Useful only as a first introduction. Index: names.

999. ———. "Roman." *Reallexikon* (No. 1288), III, 490-519.

1000. Majut, Rudolf. "Der deutsche Roman von Biedermeier bis zur Gegenwart." *Dt. Phil. im Aufriß* (No. 1283), II, 1357-1794.

Range: 1815-1957. Excellent and very extensive summary of the development of the novel. Organized by periods and novel types within period. Brief general bibliography follows each section.

1001. Pascal, Roy. *The German Novel. Studies.* Toronto: Univ. of Toronto Pr., 1956. ix, 344pp.

Range: 1785-1950's. A survey of the German novel in 2 parts. Pt. 1: the *Bildungsroman*: analyses of individual novels by Goethe, Keller, Stifter, Mann. Pt. 2: novelists: Gotthelf, Raabe, Fontane, Kafka, Mann, survey of major works and contribution. Excellent introduction.

1002. Rehm, Walter. *Geschichte des deutschen Romans. Auf Grund der Milkeschen Darstellung.* 2 vols. Berlin: de Gruyter, 1927. I. *Vom Mittelalter bis zum Realismus.* 175pp.; II. *Vom Naturalismus bis zur Gegenwart.* 104pp.

Little more than a compact outline survey. Somewhat outdated.

1003. Spiero, Heinrich. *Geschichte des deutschen Romans.* Berlin: de Gruyter, 1950. viii, 591pp.

A survey of the novel from Classicism to Naturalism and Neo-Romanticism. Individual works summarized and evaluated without interpretation. Treatment of major authors too summary; valuable for inclusion of many minor writers. Indexes: persons and circles, periodicals.

**** Schillemeit, Jost, ed. *Interpretationen. III: Deutsche Romane von Grimmelshausen bis Musil.* Frankfurt: Fischer, 1966. 320pp. (No. 1269)

**** ———. *Interpretationen. IV: Deutsche Erzählungen von Wieland bis Kafka.* Frankfurt: Fischer, 1966. 341pp. (No. 1270)

1004. Weydt, Günther. "Der deutsche Roman von der Renaissance bis zu Goethes Tod," *Dt. Phil. im Aufriß* (No. 1283), II, 1217-1356.

Range: 1400-1832. Concise chronological account, clearly organized by periods. Includes a full account of Romanticism. Ample bibliography at the end of each section. Excellent introduction. Excellent survey of criticism from beginnings to the present.

1005. Wiese, Benno von, ed. *Der deutsche Roman vom Barock bis zur Gegenwart. Struktur und Geschichte.* 2 vols. Düsseldorf: Bagel, 1963. 442pp.; 454pp. Often reprinted.

Range: 1669-1943. Each chapter interprets a representative novel by a major author: I. Grimmelshausen, Wieland, Moritz, Goethe, Jean Paul, Novalis, Hoffmann, Tieck, Immermann. II. Gotthelf, Stifter, Keller, Raabe, Fontane, T. Mann, Kafka, Döblin, Broch, Musil. Interpretations solid and reliable. Excellent for beginners.

ii. Beginnings to 1700

1006. Bobertag, Felix. *Geschichte des Romans und der ihm verwandten Dichtungsgattungen in Deutschland. 1. Abteilung. Bis zum Anfang des XVIII. Jahrhunderts.* 2 vols. in 3 parts. Berlin: Simion, 1881-1884.

Mainly of historical interest; includes extensive material from original sources.

1007. Borcherdt, Hans Heinrich. *Geschichte des Romans und der Novelle in Deutschland. Erster Teil. Vom frühen Mittelalter bis zu Wieland.* Leipzig: Weber, 1926. 331pp.

Intellectual-historical approach with emphasis on structure and content of German novel in European context. I: novel of the Middle Ages; II: novella of the Renaissance; III: novel of the Baroque; IV: novel of German Idealism. Reader should be familiar with works discussed since interpretation is relatively sparse.

1008. Meid, Volker. *Der deutsche Barockroman.* Stuttgart: Metzler, 1974. viii, 104pp.

A resource book: definitions, foreign influences, theories of the novel, various related genres. Index: names and subjects. Most valuable for bibliographical information contained at the end of each section.

1009. Rötzer, Hans Gerd. *Der Roman des Barock, 1600-1700. Kommentar zu einer Epoche.* Munich: Winkler, 1972. 190pp.

A compact survey of pre-Baroque developments, foreign influences, the Baroque from the standpoint of genre, Grimmelshausen's achievement. An encyclopedic enumeration with little depth. Indexes: authors, works. Chronological table, pp. 135-155. Bibliography, pp. 156-178.

1010. Stammler, Wolfgang. "Mittelalterliche Prosa in deutscher Sprache." *Dt. Phil. im Aufriß* (No. 1283), II, 749-1102. Extensive bibliography.

1011. Wagener, Hans. *The German Baroque Novel.* New York: Twayne, 1973. 183pp.

A superb, basic introduction to the pastoral, picaresque, and the courtly-historical novel. Good interpretations. Annotated bibliography, pp. 173-177. Index: authors, titles.

iii. Eighteenth and Nineteenth Centuries

**** Borcherdt, Hans Heinrich. *Geschichte des Romans und der Novelle in Deutschland. Erster Teil. Vom frühen Mittelalter bis zu Wieland.* Leipzig: Weber, 1926. 331pp. (No. 1007)

1012. ———. *Der Roman der Goethezeit.* Urach, Stuttgart: Port, 1949. 600pp.

Range: 1770-1829. Intellectual-historical approach with emphasis on concise interpretation of individual novels. Examination of structure and content for lesser novels included. Good introduction.

1013. Jacobs, Jürgen. *Prosa der Aufklärung. Moralische Wochenschriften, Autobiographie, Satire, Roman. Kommentar zu einer Epoche.* Munich: Winkler, 1976. 266pp .

1. background material for the study of the 18th century and a survey of the prose genres; chronology, pp. 71-76. 2. commentaries on individual works: 4 autobiographies, 4 satires, 12 novels. Commentary centers on social and ideological content; summaries of the text are not given. Indexes: names, titles. Bibliography, pp. 243-253. A valuable book.

1014. Kimpel, Dieter. *Der Roman der Aufklärung.* Stuttgart: Metzler, 1967. xii, 123pp.

Mainly a history of the theory of the novel in the 18th century and German contributions to the genre. Does not formally appraise current and past research. Uneven and encyclopedic. Useful bibliographies at the end of each section.

1015. Rausse, Hubert. *Geschichte des deutschen Romans bis 1800.* Kempten, Munich: Kösel, 1914. vii, 172pp.

A brief historical outline: from the medieval French prose novel and the German courtly epic to *Wilhelm Meister* and *Wahlverwandtschaften*. No interpretation of individual works. Bibliography. Index: names.

1016. Sammons, Jeffrey L. *Six Essays on the Young German Novel.* Chapel Hill: Univ. of North Carolina Pr., 1972. xi, 184pp.

A general introduction to the fiction of the Young German movement, with individual authors and works seen as characteristic of the whole. Chapters on: evaluation of fiction of the period, Gutzkow, Mundt, Kühne, Laube, Immermann. Index: proper names. Bibliography.

1017. Singer, Herbert. *Der deutsche Roman zwischen Barock und Rokoko.* Cologne, Graz: Böhlau, 1963. viii, 210pp.

Range: ca. 1690-1740. Traces development of courtly novel from Ziegler to Gellert with emphasis on Hunold's contribution. Excellent introduction with extensive interpretations. Bibliography of editions and library locations.

iv. *Twentieth Century*

1018. Arnold, Armin. *Prosa des Expressionismus. Herkunft, Analyse, Inventar.* Stuttgart, Berlin, Cologne, Mainz: Kohlhammer, 1972. 210pp.

Chronological survey of largely unknown Expressionist novels with focus on the works of Franz Jung, Edschmid, Flake, Corrinth. Index: names. Bibliography. Table of Expressionist prose by year of publication, pp. 167-188.

1019. Arnold, Heinz Ludwig, and Theo Buck, ed. *Positionen im deutschen Roman der sechziger Jahre.* Munich: Text und Kritiker, 1974. 172pp.

A collection of eight lectures. Introductory survey of the modern German novel followed by appraisals of the work of Grass, M. Walser, U. Johnson, C. Wolf, and others. Informative, strictly introductory examination.

1020. Boa, Elisabeth, and J.R. Reid. *Critical Strategies. German Fiction in the Twentieth Century.* London: Arnold, 1972. viii, 206pp.

Intrinsic study of the techniques of modern fiction: structure (point of view, time, space); textures (tone, imagery, dialogue, narrative); themes (character, man and society, man and nature, politics, history, Utopia); modes (realism, symbolism, essayism, irony). Analyses proceed from text specimens. Indexes: author and subject. Bibliography. Well done.

1021. Durzak, Manfred. *Der deutsche Roman der Gegenwart.* 2nd enl. ed. Stuttgart, Berlin, Cologne, Mainz: Kohlhammer, 1973. 422pp.

Range: 1945-1970's. A standard work analyzing major novels by Böll, Grass, Johnson, Wolf, Jens, Härtling, Handke, Wiener. Index: names; notes.

1022. Hatfield, Henry. *Crisis and Continuity in Modern German Fiction. Ten Essays.* Ithaca: Cornell Univ. Pr., 1969. xviii, 201pp.

Each essay treats a major theme and its expression in one major novel by Fontane, Musil, Kafka, Hesse, T. Mann, Doderer, Broch, Grass, Johnson. Not a history of the modern novel. Of limited usefulness. Bibliography. Index: author, subject.

1023. Heitner, Robert R., ed. *The Contemporary Novel in German. A Symposium.* Austin, London: Univ. of Texas Pr., 1967. 141pp.

Five symposium papers (1965): Sokel on Böll, Politzer on Doderer, Gaiser on the modern novelist, Hoffmann on Frisch, Hatfield on Grass.

**** Martini, Fritz. *Das Wagnis der Sprache. Interpretationen deutscher Prosa von Nietzsche bis Benn.* Stuttgart: Klett, 1964. 529pp. (No. 1268)

1024. Töpelmann, Sigrid. *Autoren--Figuren--Entwicklungen. Zur erzählenden Literatur in der DDR.* Berlin, Weimar: Aufbau, 1975. 362pp.

Range: 1945-1960's. Traces major developments of GDR prose through Seghers, Becher, Fühmann, Thürk, Noll, de Bruyn, M.W. Schulz. Strong reliance on Soviet literary critics. Some critique of developments in the FRG. Index: names and subject; notes.

1025. Waidson, H.M. *The Modern German Novel 1945-1965.* 2nd ed. London, New York, Toronto: Oxford Univ. Pr., 1971. vii, 168pp. (^{1}1959)

Short portraits of some sixty authors from Austria, GDR and FRG. List of translations into English, pp. 163-165. Bibliography, pp. 147-162, mainly English titles.

1026. Welzig, Werner. *Die deutsche Roman im 20. Jahrhundert.* Stuttgart: Kröner, 1967. viii, 406pp.

Range: 1900-1965. Approximately 130 novels are examined by themes with extensive interpretation of individual novels. Excellent introduction to the modern novel with comprehensive bibliography.

**** Zimmermann, Werner. *Deutsche Prosadichtungen unseres Jahrhunderts. Interpretationen für Lehrende und Lernende.* 2 vols. Düsseldorf: Schwann, 1966, 1969. (No. 1272)

1027. Ziolkowski, Theodore. *Dimensions of the Modern Novel. German Texts and European Contexts.* Princeton: Princeton Univ. Pr., 1969. xi, 378pp.

1: Interpretations of novels by Rilke, Kafka, T. Mann, Döblin, Broch. 2: themes and motifs of the German novels viewed in terms of European literary tradition. Outstanding contributions to the German novel prior to WW II. Imaginative and clear presentation: excellent study.

c. Special Forms of the Novel

i. Bauernroman

1028. Greiner, Martin. "Bauernroman." *Reallexikon* (No. 1288), I, 139-141.

1029. Zimmermann, Peter. *Der Bauernroman. Antifeudalismus, Konservatismus--Faschismus.* Stuttgart: Metzler, 1975. vii, 277pp.

Range: 1830-1970. 1. Analysis of major ideological and structural tendencies (1830-1945). 2. Genre history and a typology based on the work of 300 authors. No interpretations. Appendix: chronology of authors and novels, pp. 198-232. Notes. Bibliography, pp. 262-270. Index: names.

ii. Bildungsroman, Erziehungsroman

1030. Borcherdt, Hans Heinrich. "Bildungsroman." *Reallexikon* (No. 1288), I, 175-178.

1031. Jacobs, Jürgen. *Wilhelm Meister und seine Brüder. Untersuchungen zum deutschen Bildungsroman.* Munich: Fink, 1972. 232pp.

The first German literary history of the *Bildungsroman.* History of the genre, definitions, forerunners, analyses of ca. 40 novels. Takes European developments into account. Index: author, subject. Notes.

1032. Köhn, Lothar. *Entwicklungs- und Bildungsroman. Ein Forschungsbericht--Mit einem Nachtrag.* Stuttgart: Metzler, 1969. viii, 115pp.

A review of research to 1969, presenting definitions, a history of the genre, discussion of individual authors, novels, and themes. An expanded version of Köhn's report in *DVLG* 42 (1968), 3, 427-473 and 4, 590-632.

iii. Galanter Roman

1033. Flemming, Willi. "Heroisch-galanter Roman." *Reallexikon* (No. 1288), I, 647-650.

1034. Singer, Herbert. *Der galante Roman.* Stuttgart: Metzler, 1961. 64pp.

An excellent introduction to the study of *Trivialliteratur.* The origins and history of the 18th-century courtly novel in Germany. Extensive bibliography somewhat outdated.

iv. Historischer Roman

1035. Lukács, Georg. *Der historische Roman.* Berlin: Aufbau, 1955. 393pp. English ed.: *The Historical Novel.* Trans. by Hannah and Stanley Mitchell. London: Merlin, 1962. 363pp.

Focus is on the 19th and 20th centuries. An important work.

1036. Nussberger, Max, and Werner Kohlschmidt. "Historischer Roman." *Reallexikon* (No. 1288), I, 658-666.

v. Utopischer Roman

1037. Biesterfeld, Wolfgang. *Die literarische Utopie.* Stuttgart: Metzler, 1974. xiii, 94pp.

Resource book: definitions and historical survey of Utopian literature from Plato to the 20th century, including material on imagery, themes, and science fiction. International in scope. Author index. Bibliography at the end of each section.

1038. Reichert, Karl. "Utopie und Staatsroman." *DVLG* 39 (1965). 259-287.

5. Novelle

a. *Novelle Theory*

1039. Burger, Heinz Otto. "Theorie und Wissenschaft von der deutschen Novelle." *DU* 3 (1951), 2, 82-98.

1040. Kunz, Josef, ed. *Novelle.* 2nd enl. ed. Darmstadt: Wissenschaftliche Buchgesellschaft, 1973. 519pp. (^{1}1968)

A collection of 44 previously published essays in three parts: 1. early studies from Wieland to Lukács; 2. the first phase of scholarly criticism, including Walzel, Jolles, Pongs, Petsch, Klein, Hankammer; 3. new directions in criticism, including Pabst, Burger, Lockemann, Martini, J. Müller. Bibliography in chronological order from 1915, pp. 501-516 (234 items). Index: authors listed in bibliography.

1041. Malmede, Hans Hermann. *Wege zur Novelle. Theorie und Interpretation der Gattung Novelle in der deutschen Literatur-*

wissenschaft. Stuttgart, Berlin, Cologne, Mainz: Kohlhammer: 1966. 204pp.

A critical appraisal of the *Novelle* theory of 12 scholars: Pabst, V. Grolmann, v. Arx, Lockemann, Bruch, Kunz, Hirsch, Walzel, Klein, Petsch, Pongs, v. Wiese. Somewhat polemical in tone but solid.

1042. Pabst, Walter. "Die Theorie der Novelle in Deutschland (1920-1940)," *Romanistisches Jahrbuch* 2 (1949), 81-124.

1043. Polheim, Karl K. "Novellentheorie und Novellenforschung. 1945-1963," *DVLG* 38 (1964), Sonderheft 208-316.

1044. ———. *Novellentheorie und Novellenforschung. Ein Forschungsbericht 1945-1964*. Stuttgart: Metzler, 1965. 122pp.

Reprint in enlarged form of report in *DVLG* 38 (1964) Sonderheft. Index: names; notes.

1045. Wiese, Benno von. *Novelle*. Stuttgart: Metzler, 1963. vi, 89pp.

Range: origins-20th century. 1: genre (definition, theory, research); 2. history (origins, Goethe, Romanticism, Realism, 20th century and short story). Each section cites most important research. Excellent introduction.

b. History and Interpretation

1046. Bennett, E.K., revised and continued by H.M. Waidson. *A History of the German Novelle*. Cambridge: Cambridge Univ. Pr., 1965. xiv, 315pp. (^{1}1934)

Range: 1795 to 20th century. Extensive positivistic history of the *Novelle*, preceded by a brief discussion of the genre. Important *Novellen* interpreted. See especially: chapters on Poetic Realism and Keller. Many minor *Novellen* mentioned without commentary; definition of genre not consistently applied throughout. Basic introduction written with beginner in mind.

1047. Ellis, John M. *Narration in the German Novelle. Theory and Interpretation*. Cambridge: Cambridge Univ. Pr., 1974. vii, 219pp.

An analysis of the narrator's function in 8 *Novellen*: Kleist, Tieck, E.T.A. Hoffmann, Grillparzer, Keller, Storm, G. Hauptmann, Kafka. Bibliography, pp. 213-219. On the whole a valuable study which opens new aspects of interpretation.

1048. Himmel, Helmuth. *Geschichte der deutschen Novelle*. Bern, Munich: Francke, 1963. 547pp.

Range: 1795 to 20th century. Chronological history with stress on varying forms of the genre and their development. Excellent, readable introduction.

1049. Klein, Johannes. *Geschichte der deutschen Novelle von Goethe bis zur Gegenwart*. 4th rev. ed. Wiesbaden: Steiner, 1960. xx, 674pp. ([1]1954)

Range: 1795-1958. Introduction discusses definitions, history, and contrasts *Novelle* with other genres. Text chronological by author; chapters in two parts: 1. summary of the author's work, 2. representative *Novellen* comprehensively analyzed. Excellent source for discussion of individual *Novellen*.

1050. Kunz, Josef. *Die Deutsche Novelle. Zwischen Klassik und Romantik*. Berlin: Schmidt, 1966. 164pp.

Range: 1790's to 1840's. Historical survey centered about the theme of chaos versus order as the primary feature of the genre. Includes Goethe, Wackenroder, Tieck, Brentano, E.T.A. Hoffman, Arnim, Eichendorff, Kleist. Detailed summary and analysis of major works. Bibliography at the end of each chapter.

1051. ———. *Die deutsche Novelle. Im 19. Jahrhundert*. Berlin: Schmidt, 1970. 178pp.

Range: 1820's to 1880's. Continues historical survey begun by Kunze (above) with a similar approach: 1. late Romanticism/ Realism: Tieck, Hauff, Laube, Mörike, Grillparzer, Büchner, Droste-Hülshoff; 2. mid-19th century: Stifter, Gotthelf, Keller, Meyer, Heyse, Ludwig, Storm; 3. transition to the 20th century: Raabe, Fontane. Index: author and subject; bibliography at the end of each section.

1052. ———. "Geschichte der deutschen Novelle vom 18. Jahrhundert bis auf die Gegenwart," *Dt. Phil. im Aufriß* (No. 1283), II, 1795-1896.

Range: 1795-1940. Comprehensive historical summary. Good bibliography appended.

1053. Lockemann, Fritz. *Gestalt und Wandel der deutschen Novelle. Geschichte einer literarischen Gattung im 19. und 20. Jahrhundert*. Munich: Hueber, 1957. 391pp.

Chronological history of the German *Novelle*. Analyses (some little more than summaries) are with reference to a defined prototype. Index of *Novellen*. Bibliography. Somewhat too obscure to serve as an introduction.

1054. Silz, Walter. *Realism and Reality. Studies in the German Novelle of Poetic Realism*. Chapel Hill: The Univ. of N. Carolina Pr., 1962. x, 168pp. ([1]1954)

Range: 1838-1892. Concentrated examinations of *Novellen* by Brentano, von Arnim, Droste-Hülshoff, Stifter, Grillparzer, Keller, Meyer, Storm, Hauptmann. While the term "realism" is not always applied uniformly, the interpretations are solid. Very helpful for the beginner.

**** Wiese, Benno von, ed. *Die deutsche Novelle von Goethe bis Kafka. Interpretationen*. 2 vols. Düsseldorf: Bagel, 1957, 1962. (No. 1271)

6. Other Narrative and Prose Forms

a. Anekdote

1055. Grenzmann, Wilhelm. "Anekdote." *Reallexikon* (No. 1288), I, 63-66.

1056. Grothe, Heinz. *Anekdote*. Stuttgart: Metzler, 1971. 102pp.

A resource book: definitions, written and oral forms, historical survey, typology. International in scope. Index: names. Bibliography at end of each section.

1057. Pongs, Hermann. "Die Anekdote als Kunstform zwischen Kalendergeschichte und Kurzgeschichte." *DU* 9 (1957), 5-20.

b. Aphorismus

1058. Grenzmann, Wilhelm. "Aphorismus." *Reallexikon* (No. 1288), I, 94-97.

1059. ———. "Probleme des Aphorismus." *Jahrbuch für Aesthetik und allgemeine Kunstwissenschaft* 1 (1951), 122-144.

1060. Neumann, Gerhard, ed. *Der Aphorismus. Zur Geschichte, zu den Formen und Möglichkeiten einer literarischen Gattung.* Darmstadt: Wissenschaftliche Buchgesellschaft, 1976. 509pp.

A collection of 16 previously published and 3 original essays on the definition, the history, ideological background, linguistic analysis, and themes of the genre. Affords a good review of major research 1933-1973. Index: names. Bibliography (163 items). European in scope. An excellent introduction.

c. Arbeiterliteratur

1061. Stieg, Gerald, and Bernd Witte. *Abriß einer Geschichte der deutschen Arbeiterliteratur*. Stuttgart: Klett, 1973. 201pp.

Range: 19th to 20th century. A historical survey from the beginnings to the present (FRG and GDR). Includes some analyses. Focus is on the political and sociological manifestations. Introduction is meant for students. Questions, pp. 180-189. Index: names.

d. Autobiographie

1062. Aichinger, Ingrid. "Selbstbiographie." *Reallexikon* (No. 1288), III, 801-819.

1063. Bode, Ingrid. *Die Autobiographien zur deutschen Literatur, Kunst und Musik 1900-1965. Bibliographie und Nachweis der persönlichen Begegnungen und Charakteristiken.* Stuttgart: Metzler, 1966. x, 308pp.

Pt. 1. autobiography title list (ca. 500) A-Z, brief biographical information about author, table of contents; pt. 2. proper names of persons mentioned in the autobiographies A-Z; pt. 3. index classified by subject and including foreign authors, the arts, music, theater, etc. Excellent resource book for eyewitness accounts of leading 20th-century figures.

1064. Pascal, Roy. *Design and Truth in Autobiography*. Cambridge: Harvard Univ. Pr., 1960. 202pp. German ed.: *Die Autobiographie. Gehalt und Gestalt*. Trans. by M. Schaible. Stuttgart, Berlin, Cologne, Mainz: Kohlhammer, 1965. 244pp.

Provides a definition, an historical account of European developments, major themes and other constituent elements. Bibliography, pp. 235-240, of primary and secondary material. Index: names.

e. Comics

1065. Kemkes, Wolfgang. *Bibliographie der internationalen Literatur über Comics. International Bibliography of Comics Literature*. 2nd rev. ed. Munich-Pullach: Dokumentation, 1974. 293pp. illus.

Range: 1950's-1972. Material organized under 8 headings: the history of comics, structure, commercial aspects, readership, effects of comics, comics and education, use of comics, comics and the law. Index: authors. A reliable bibliography.

f. Dorfgeschichte

1066. Greiner, Martin. "Dorfgeschichte." *Reallexikon* (No. 1288), I, 274-279.

1067. Hein, Jürgen. *Dorfgeschichte*. Stuttgart: Metzler, 1976. ix, 151pp.

Range: 1672-1976. Resource book: definitions, historical survey, special research problems. Chronology of works and authors, pp. 8-19. Indexes: names, subjects. Bibliographies at the end of each section.

g. Epos

1068. Halbach, Kurt Herbert. "Epik des Mittelalters." *Dt. Phil. im Aufriß* (No. 1283), II, 397-684.

Range: 750-1450. Substantial examination, based on most recent scholarship, of the courtly epic and its decline. Each subsection followed by an extensive selected bibliography.

1069. Maiworm, Heinrich. "Epos der Neuzeit." *Dt. Phil. im Aufriß* (No. 1283), II, 685-748.

Range: 16th century to 1945. Excellent introduction to the verse epic after its decline in the late Middle Ages; summarizes research problems, indicating work to be done. Bibliography limited to several titles on theory and history of the epic.

1070. ———. *Neue deutsche Epik*. Berlin: Schmidt, 1968. 186pp.

Range: 1450-1930. Comprehensive history of the verse epic on the basis of the most recent scholarship. 1. Aesthetics, 2. thematic typology, 3. diachronic history. Excellent introduction.

1071. Ruh, Kurt. *Höfische Epik des deutschen Mittelalters. Erster Teil. Von den Anfängen bis zu Hartmann von Aue*. Berlin: Schmidt, 1967. 165pp.

Introduction to the genre. Analyses of major examples include literary assessment, interpretation, plot summary. Index: names, titles. Bibliography included in each section. Excellent for the student.

1072. Rupp, Heinz. "Neue Literatur zur höfischen Epik." *DU* 6 (1954), 5, 108-113.

1073. Schneider, Hermann, and Wolfgang Mohr. "Höfisches Epos." *Reallexikon* (No. 1288), I, 669-683.

1074. Schröder, Walter Johannes. "Epos (Theorie)." *Reallexikon* (No. 1288), I, 381-388.

1075. ———. *Das deutsche Versepos*. Darmstadt: Wissenschaftliche Buchgesellschaft, 1969. ix, 435pp.

A collection of 15 essays published 1814-1942 which examines the verse epic from the Middle Ages to the 20th century and affords an excellent overview of the research done on the genre.

1076. Wiegand, Julius. "Epos, Neuhochdeutsches." *Reallexikon* (No. 1288), I, 388-393.

1077. ———. "Komisches Epos." *Reallexikon* (No. 1288), I, 876-879.

h. Essay

1078. Berger, Bruno. *Der Essay. Form und Geschichte*. Bern, Munich: Francke, 1964. 283pp.

Range: 16th to 20th century. Extensive discussion of the genre (themes and forms) with a brief history and a discussion of major essayists. Definition of essay somewhat inconclusive. Treatment haphazard.

1079. Bleckwenn, Helga. "Essay." *Handlexikon* (No. 1290), pp. 121-127.

1080. Haas, Gerhard. *Essay*. Stuttgart: Metzler, 1969. 88pp.

Range: 16th to 20th century. Comprehensive introduction to

the genre. Form and themes, relation to other genres, and problems of scholarship. Excellent introduction with valuable bibliographical references.

1081. Just, Klaus Günther. "Essay." *Dt. Phil. im Aufriß* (No. 1283), II, 1897-1948.

Range: 16th to 20th century. Outline history of the development and flowering of the genre, state of scholarship, definition and typology, history. Selected bibliography.

1082. Martini, Fritz. "Essay." *Reallexikon* (No. 1288), I, 408-410.

i. Fabel

1083. Dithmar, Reinhard. *Die Fabel. Geschichte, Struktur, Didaktik.* Paderborn: Schöningh, 1971. 216pp.

Pt. 1: historical survey from Greek literature to the 20th century; pt. 2: systematic examination of structural features; pt. 3: the genre and its use in the classroom. Volume designed for teachers, not literature students. Index: texts used for teaching. Bibliography, pp. 205-216.

1084. Markschies, Hans L. "Fabel." *Reallexikon* (No. 1288), I, 433-441.

1085. Leibfried, Erwin. *Fabel.* 2nd rev. ed. Stuttgart: Metzler, 1973. viii, 114pp. ([1]1967)

Resource book: definitions, survey of research, themes, genres, stylistic elements, structural typology, historical survey, use of fable in schools, future research directions. Indexes: author, subject. Bibliography at the end of each section.

1086. Lindner, Hermann. "Theorie und Geschichte der Fabel." *Zeitschrift für französische Sprache und Literatur* 85 (1975), 247-259.

j. Fachprosa

1087. Assion, Peter. *Altdeutsche Fachliteratur.* Berlin: Schmidt, 1973. 235pp.

Pt. 1: introduction to the discipline and survey of research; pt. 2: extensive examination of available material; pt. 3: comprehensive bibliography, pp. 178-219. Indexes: proper names and titles of anonymous works to 1800, modern scholars in the field.

1088. Eis, Gerhard. *Mittelalterliche Fachliteratur.* Stuttgart: Metzler, 1962. 88pp.

Resource book: survey of research, editions, and history of important non-belletristic writing of the Middle Ages. For the specialist. Extensive bibliography.

1089. ———. "Mittelalterliche Fachprosa der Artes." *Dt. Phil. im Aufriß* (No. 1283), II, 1103-1216.

k. Heldendichtung

1090. Betz, Werner. "Die deutsche Heldendichtung." *Dt. Phil. im Aufriß* (No. 1283), III, 1871-1970.

1091. Beyschlag, Siegfried. "Heldendichtung." *Handlexikon* (No. 1290), pp. 169-175.

1092. Gillespie, George T. *A Catalog of Persons Named in the German Heroic Literature (700-1600). Including Named Animals and Objects and Ethnic Names.* Oxford: Oxford Univ. Pr., 1973. xxxvii, 166pp.

A concordance to primary literature A-Z. Entries give account of activity or function of persons in the work(s) in which they appear. Extensive cross references include Scandinavian and English sources. Bibliography, pp. 28-37. A valuable reference work for study of the period.

1093. Hauck, Karl, ed. *Zur germanisch-deutschen Heldensage. 16 Aufsätze zum neuen Forschungsstand.* Darmstadt: Wissenschaftliche Buchgesellschaft, 1961. xv, 449pp.

An anthology of essays by the outstanding scholars in the field covering research 1925-1961. Focus is on the *Nibelungenlied.*

1094. Hoffmann, Werner. *Mittelhochdeutsche Heldendichtung.* Berlin: Schmidt, 1974. 229pp.

Pt. 1: definition and theoretical introduction; pt. 2: individual epics: Nibelungen, Walther and Hildegund, Kudrun, Ortnit, Wolfdietrich, Dietrich. Bibliography at the end of each section. Index: author, subject. A good, basic, up-to-date introduction.

1095. Schneider, Hermann. *Deutsche Heldensage.* 2nd ed. Berlin: de Gruyter, 1962. viii, 556pp. (^{1}1928)

Range: 4th to 13th centuries. History of the origin and evolution of the genre. Presents a close analysis of the major saga cycles. Extensive bibliography, pp. 458-541. Still the standard work in the field.

1096. ——— and Wolfgang Mohr. "Heldendichtung." *Reallexikon* (No. 1288), I, 631-646.

1097. See, Klaus von. "Heldensage. Ein Forschungsbericht." *Göttinger Gelehrte Anzeigen* 218 (1966), 52-98.

1098. ———. *Germanische Heldensage. Stoffe, Probleme, Methoden. Eine Einführung.* Frankfurt: Athenäum, 1971. 178pp., illus.

Not a history, but analyses of major sagas, their relation to fairy tales, myth, history, and their survival in other genres.

Includes evaluation of research. Indexes: author, subject. Excellent introduction for the beginner.

1099. Uecker, Heiko. *Germanische Heldensage*. Stuttgart: Metzler, 1972. ix, 143pp.

Resource book: definitions, individual sagas and saga cycles, appraisal of research. Index: sources, characters, historical personages, secondary literature. Bibliography at the end of each section. Often too compact.

1100. Wisniewski, Roswitha. "Bibliographie zur deutschen Heldensage 1928-1960." In: H. Schneider, Germanische Heldensage. 2nd ed. Berlin: de Gruyter, 1962. I, 458-541.

l. Idylle

1101. Böschenstein-Schäfer, Renate. *Idylle*. Stuttgart: Metzler, 1967. x, 125pp.

Range: beginnings to 20th century. Resource book: definitions, historical survey, appraisal of research. Bibliography at the end of each section. Index: names.

1102. Merker, Erna. "Idylle." *Reallexikon* (No. 1288), I, 742-749.

m. Industrieliteratur

1103. Dithmar, Reinhard. *Industrieliteratur*. Munich: Deutscher Taschenbuch Verlag, 1973. 234pp.

Pt. 1: a historical survey: 19th-century beginnings to the developments in the 1920's, the GDR, and Group 61. Pt. 2: important literary and theoretical specimen texts. Extensive bibliography, pp. 149-152. Marxist-socialist approach.

n. Kurzgeschichte

1104. Doderer, Klaus. *Die Kurzgeschichte in Deutschland. Ihre Form und ihre Entwicklung*. Mit einer Vorbemerkung und bibliographischen Ergänzungen. 2nd ed. Darmstadt: Wissenschaftliche Buchgesellschaft, 1969. xvi, 103pp. ([1]1953)

A brief historical survey precedes a typological approach with emphasis on defining *Kurzgeschichte*. A good general introduction. Bibliography somewhat outdated.

1105. Klein, Johannes. "Kurzgeschichte." *Reallexikon* (No. 1288), I, 912-915.

1106. Kilchermann, Ruth J. *Die Kurzgeschichte. Formen und Entwicklung*. Stuttgart: Kohlhammer, 1967. 218pp.

Range: 1800-1960. Origins and development of the short story in the US and Europe with particular emphasis on the German short story. Theoretical portions differentiate the short story from the *Novelle*. Short story seen as expressive of 20th-century attitudes. Not always convincing.

1107. Rohner, Ludwig. *Theorie der Kurzgeschichte*. Frankfurt: Athena. xii, 283pp.

Discussion of various elements of the genre, definitions, theory of reception of the short story, differentiation from related genres. Tone occasionally polemic. Excellent survey of research, pp. 37-107, includes list of anthologies and bibliography of interpretations.

1108. Stahl, August. "Kurzgeschichte." *Handlexikon* (No. 1290), pp. 236-240.

o. Legende

1109. Jolles, André. "Legende." In: A.J., *Einfache Formen* (No. 848), pp. 23-61.

1110. Rosenfeld, Hellmut. "Legende." *Reallexikon* (No. 1288), II, 13-31.

1111. ———. *Legende*. 2nd ed. Stuttgart: Metzler, 1964. 87pp. ([1]1961)

An excellent source book on legend as literary form, containing sections of definition, history, and a survey of research. Extensive bibliography at the end of each section.

p. Märchen

1112. Jolles, André. "Märchen." In: A.J., *Einfache Formen* (No. 848), pp. 218-246.

1113. Karlinger, Felix, ed. *Wege der Märchenforschung*. Darmstadt: Wissenschaftliche Buchgesellschaft, 1973. xvi, 489pp.

An anthology of 1 original, 23 previously published (1903-1970) essays, many of them the most important papers in the field. Index: names, subjects. Chronological bibliography (197 items), pp. 467-475, not intended for quick reference.

1114. Lobeck, Helmut. "Kunstmärchen." *Reallexikon* (No. 1288), I, 909-912.

1115. Lüthi, Max. *Das europäische Volksmärchen. Form und Wesen*. Bern, Munich: Francke, 1947. 127pp.

A lucid introduction to the fairy tale, its form, techniques of presentation and narration, themes and motifs, and features which distinguish it from other genres. Still a classic in its field.

1116. ———. *Märchen*. 4th rev. ed. Stuttgart: Metzler, 1971. xii, 121pp. ([1]1962)

Resource book: definitions, differentiation from related genres, typology, elements of the European and non-European fairy tale, historical survey, appraisal of research. Index: author, subject. Bibliography at the end of each section.

1117. ———. *Das Volksmärchen als Dichtung. Ästhetik und Anthropologie.* Düsseldorf, Cologne: Diederichs, 1975, 224pp.

An examination of the fairy tale as a European phenomenon, its style and composition, motifs and themes, the image of human beings presented. Emphasizes the idea of beauty in all its varied forms in the fairy tale. Index: author, subject. Glossary of terms and abbreviations. Notes.

1118. Peuckert, Will-Erich. "Märchen." *Dt. Phil. im Aufriß* (No. 1283), III, 2677-2726.

1119. Ranke, Kurt, ed. *Enzyklopädie des Märchens. Handwörterbuch zur historischen und vergleichenden Erzählforschung.* Berlin, New York: de Gruyter, 1975ff. Fasc. 1ff. 12 vols. planned.

Promises to be the standard reference work for the field.

1120. Röhrich, Lutz. "Märchen." *Handlexikon* (No. 1290), pp. 299-306.

1121. ———. "Neue Wege der Märchenforschung." *DU* 8 (1956), 6, 92-116.

**** ———. *Sage und Märchen. Erzählforschung heute.* Freiburg, Basel, Vienna, 1976. 348pp. (No. 1131)

1122. Wagner, Kurt. "Märchen." *Reallexikon* (No. 1288), II, 262-271.

q. Predigt

1123. Morvay, Karin, and Dagmar Grube. *Bibliographie der deutschen Predigt des Mittelalters. Veröffentlichte Predigten.* Munich: Beck, 1974. xvi, 363pp.

Range: 8th to 15th century. Provides sample texts of the published medieval sermons as well as sources of printed texts and location of manuscripts. Specialized indexes make the volume readily accessible.

1124. Wolf, Herbert. "Predigt." *Reallexikon* (No. 1288), III, 223-257.

r. Rätsel

1125. Jolles, André. "Rätsel." In: A.J., *Einfache Formen* (No. 848), pp. 126-149.

1126. Hain, Mathilde. "Sprichwort und Rätsel." *Dt. Phil im Aufriß* (No. 1283), III, 2727-2754.

1127. ———. *Rätsel.* Stuttgart: Metzler, 1966. 62pp.

An historical survey of the genre with some appraisal of research, little on theory. Contains a chapter on collections of riddles. Index: names and subjects. Bibliography at the end of each section.

1128. Wagner, Kurt. "Rätsel." *Reallexikon* (No. 1288), III, 3316-3321.

s. Sage

1129. Jolles, André. "Sage." In: A.J., *Einfache Formen* (No. 848), pp. 62-90.

1130. Peuckert, Will-Erich. "Sage." *Dt. Phil im Aufriß* (No. 1283), III, 2641-2676.

1131. Röhrich, Lutz. *Sage und Märchen. Erzählforschung heute.* Freiburg, Basel, Vienna: Herder, 1976. 348pp.

A collection of 17 previously published essays and lectures which presents an overview of some recent major research areas. Includes general material and definitions, important collections of materials and essays on specific aspects of the genres. Index: author, subject. Notes.

t. Science Fiction

1132. Klein, Klaus-Peter. *Zukunft zwischen Trauma und Mythos: Science Fiction. Zur Wirkungsästhetik Sozialpsychologie und Didaktik eines literarischen Massenphänomens.* Stuttgart: Klett, 1976. 248pp.

1133. Nagl, Manfred. *Science-fiction in Deutschland. Untersuchungen zur Genese, Soziologie und Ideologie der phantastischen Massenliteratur.* Tübingen: Tübinger Vereinigung für Volkskunde, 1972. 279pp.

u. Spielmannsepik

1134. Curschmann, Michael. *Spielmannsepik. Wege und Ergebnisse der Forschung von 1907-1965. Mit Ergänzung und Nachtrag bis 1967.* Stuttgart: Metzler, 1968. viii, 131pp.

1135. Schröder, Walter Johannes. *Spielmannsepik.* Stuttgart: Metzler, 1962. viii, 81pp.

Pt. 1: critical appraisal of research on 12th-century minstrel epics; pt. 2: editions, summaries, themes, and structure of the surviving epics. Each section is followed by an exhaustive bibliography.

v. Tagebuch

1136. Boerner, Peter. *Tagebuch.* Stuttgart: Metzler, 1969. vi, 90pp.

Range: beginnings to the present. A survey of research on the diary as a literary form. Brief history of the genre. Includes chapter on the diary in modern literature. Each section followed by an exhaustive bibliography. Contains index of writers of diaries. Excellent resource book.

w. Trivialliteratur

1137. Domagalski, Peter. "Trivialliteratur." *Die Literatur* (No. 1281), pp. 66-85.

1138. Klein, Albert. "Trivialliteratur." *Handlexikon* (No. 1290), pp. 487-493.

1139. Kreuzer, Helmut. "Trivialliteratur als Forschungsproblem. Zur Kritik des deutschen Trivialromans seit der Aufklärung." *DVLG* 41 (1967), 173-191.

1140. Sichelschmidt, Gustav. *Liebe, Mord und Abenteuer. Eine Geschichte der deutschen Unterhaltungsliteratur.* Berlin: Haude & Spenersche Verlagsbuchhandlung, 1969. 259pp.

A typological survey focusing on the novel. Covers an immense amount of material. Index: authors.

x. Volkserzählung

1141. Brückner, Wolfgang, ed. *Volkserzählung und Reformation. Ein Handbuch zur Tradition und Funktion von Erzählstoffen und Erzählliteratur.* Berlin: Schmidt, 1974. 904pp. illus.

Range: 16th and 17th centuries. A detailed survey and appraisal of research plus essays on K. Goltwurm, H. Reuscher, J. Fincel, the figure of Luther in sagas, tales of the devil. Index: authors, motifs. Bibliography, pp. 758-822. Comprehensive coverage.

1142. Hain, Mathilde. "Die Volkserzählung. Ein Forschungsbericht über die letzten Jahrzehnte (etwa 1945-1970)." *DVLG* 45 (1971), Sonderheft, 243-274.

D. THE LYRICAL GENRES

1. Forschungsberichte

1143. Hollerer, Walter. "Deutsche Lyrik 1900 bis 1950. Versuch einer Überschau und Forschungsbericht." *DU* 5 (1953), 4, 72-104.

1144. Thomas, Helmuth. "Minnesang in neuer Gestalt." *Wirkendes Wort* 4 (1953/54), 164-177.

1145. Maurer, Friedrich. "Neue Literatur zum Minnesang." *DU* 5 (1953), 2, 94-98 and 6 (1954), 5, 113-114.

1146. Rasch, Wolfdietrich. "Probleme der Lyrik-Interpretation." *GRM* 35, *NF* 4 (1954), 282-289.

1147. Schröder, Franz R. "Neuere Minnesangarbeiten." *GRM* 35, *NF* 4 (1954), 69-74 and 37, *NF* 6 (1956), 404-410.

1148. Thomas, Helmuth. "Die jüngere deutsche Minnesangforschung." *Wirkendes Wort* 7 (1956/57), 269-286.

1149. Jungbluth, Günther. "Neue Forschungen zur mittelhochdeutschen Lyrik." *Euphorion*, *F.* 3, 51 (1957), 192-221.

1150. Trost, Pavel. "Neue Forschungen zum Minnesang." *Philologica Pragensia* 6 (1963), 298-300.

1151. Curschmann, Michael. "Oral Poetry in Medieval English, French, and German Literature. Some Notes on Recent Research." *Speculum* 42 (1967), 36-52.

1152. Gorceix, Bernhard. "Aspects du lyrisme allemand en 1972." *Revue d'Allemagne* 5 (1973), 926-937.

2. Bibliographies

a. Completed Bibliographies

**** *Bibliographisches Handbuch der deutschen Literaturwissenschaft 1945-1969* (No. 123, No. 124), I: see section IV. "Deutsche Literaturgeschichte. D. Formen und Gattungen (Theorie und Geschichte). Lyrik," and V. "Mittelalter," VI. "Renaissance, Humanismus, Reformation," VII. "Zeitalter des Barock," VIII. "18. Jahrhundert," IX. "Zeitalter der Klassik und Romantik." Selected cumulation of (No. 129) to 1969.
II: see section X. "Neunzehntes Jahrhundert: 1830-1880," XI. "19. Jahrhundert. Ende und Übergang zum 20. (1880-1914)," XII. "Deutschsprachige Literatur des 20. Jahrhunderts." Selected cumulation of (No. 129) to 1972.

1153. Glasmeier, Michael C. "Auswahl-Bibliographie zur Theorie der phonetischen Poesie." *Sprache im technischen Zeitalter* (1975), 286-290.

1154. Hirschenauer, Rupert, and Albrecht Weber, eds. *Wege zum Gedicht*. Munich, Zurich: Schnell und Steiner, 1956. "Bibliographie zur Interpretation von Lyrik," pp. 405-455 (covers lit. from the 1930's to 1956). This bibliography updated to Jan. 1, 1961 by Richard Jüngst in the 2nd ed., 1965, pp. 403-470 and to July 1, 1967 by Carsten Schlingmann in the 7th ed., 1968, pp. 447-549.

**** *Internationale Bibliographie zur Geschichte der deutschen Literatur* (No. 122), I: see section "Geschichte und Theorie der literarischen Gattungen. Lyrik," and "Deutsche Literatur von den Anfängen bis 1050," "... von 1050 bis 1160," "von 1160 bis 1230," "... von 1230 bis 1480," "... von 1480 bis 1680," "Deutschsprachige Literatur von 1680 bis 1789." Selected cumulation to 1967.

II, 1: see section "Deutschsprachige Literatur von 1789 bis 1830," "Deutschsprachige Literatur von 1830 bis 1900," and "Deutschsprachige Literatur von 1900 bis zur Gegenwart. Theorie und Geschichte der Gattungen und Genres." Selected cumulation to 1969. Marxist-socialist criticism well represented.

1155. Linker, Robert W. *Music of the Minnesinger and Early Meistersinger. A Bibliography.* Chapel Hill: Univ. of N. Carolina Pr., 1962. xvi, 79pp.

Manuscript list provides locations and bibliography. Bibliography of *Minnesinger* and *Meistersinger* arranged by composer A-Z with song titles for each A-Z. For each song manuscript sources are given. Lacks index.

1156. Paulus, Rolf, and Ursula Steuler. *Bibliographie zur deutschen Lyrik nach 1945.* Frankfurt: Athenaion, 1974. xi, 157pp.

Does not include Benn, Brecht, and "traditional" lyricists. 1334 numbered items under the headings: 1. general research material, 2. poetics, 3. author bibliographies for Bachmann, Bobrowski, Celan, Eich, Enzensberger, Heissenbüttel, Kaschnitz, Krolow, Piontek: primary and secondary bibliographies to 1971, including interpretations of individual poems, 4. anthologies. Index: authors.

1157. Rössler, Martin. *Bibliographie der deutschen Liedpredigt.* Nieuwkoop: de Graaf, 1976. 306pp.

Contains a chronological listing (1526-1766) of *Liedpredigt* by title A-Z, a list of undated works by author A-Z, and a chronological list of hymnological works by author A-Z. Entries include a complete transcription of title, bibliographical description, reference to other bibliographies, and locations of copies of the work. Indexes: songs, authors, publishers.

**** Ruttkowski, Wolfgang. *Bibliographie der Gattungspoetik für den Studenten der Literaturwissenschaft. Ein abgekürztes Verzeichnis von über 3000 Büchern, Dissertationen und Zeitungsartikeln in Deutsch, Englisch und Französisch.* Munich: Hueber, 1973. 246pp. (No. 846)

1158. Schlütter, Hans-Jürgen, and Anneliese, eds. *Lyrik, 25 Jahre. Bibliographie der deutschsprachigen Lyrikpublikationen 1945-1970.* New York: Olms, 1974. 499pp.

Lists 9,767 publications of German authors, A-Z, who lived after 1945; also lists revised editions, spoken recordings, and posthumous publications of exiles. Does not include reprints. A second volume is planned. Useful for its inclusion of primary publications.

1159. Tervooren, Helmut. *Bibliographie zum Minnesang aus "Des Minnesangs Frühling." Mit einem Geleitwort von Hugo Moser.* Berlin: Schmidt, 1969. 91pp.

A select bibliography for students, listing 714 items in 2 parts: 1. general works, in chronological order, 2. authors A-Z. Reliable and easily accessible.

b. Current Bibliographies

**** *Bibliographie der deutschen Sprach- und Literaturwissenschaft* (No. 129): see section VIII. "Deutsche Literaturgeschichte. Formen und Gattungen (Theorie und Geschichte). Lyrik," and IX.-XIX. "(Einzelne) Gattungen," 1 (1945)-15 (1975)ff. Most reliable and comprehensive current bibliography available. Editions and secondary material.

**** *Germanistik* (No. 130): see section XVII. "Allgemeines zur Literaturwissenschaft. Poetik: Gattungen und Arten" and XXII.-XXXI. "Lyrik," 1 (1960)-17 (1976)ff. Comprehensive quarterly, up to date. Lists editions and secondary material. Books are reviewed.

**** *MLA International Bibliography* (No. 125), II: see section "German Literature. II. Themes, Types, Special Topics," and "German Literature. III.-German Literature. VII. Poetry," 1921-1975ff. Annual cumulation. Editions and secondary material. Extensive and reliable.

**** *Referatendienst zur Literaturwissenschaft* (No. 131): see section "Gattungen. Allgemein. Lyrik," 1 (1969)-6 (1975)ff. Marxist-socialist quarterly review of books. Limited in scope.

3. Poetry Theory

1160. Grimm, Reinhold, ed. *Zur Lyrik-Diskussion*. Darmstadt: Wissenschaftliche Buchgesellschaft, 1966. x, 469pp.

A collection of one original and 16 previously published essays on modern poetry, particularly informative for the development of the 50's and 60's. Eminent contributors, including Staiger, Böckmann, Höllerer, H. Friedrich, Burger, Grimm, Jauß, Conrady, Killy. Affords a good overview of modern poetry criticism.

1161. Kommerell, Max. *Gedanken über Gedichte*. 2nd ed. Frankfurt: Klostermann, 1956. 503pp. ([1]1943)

Almost exclusively on Goethe's poetry.

1162. Lockemann, Fritz. *Das Gedicht und seine Klanggestalt*. Emsdetten/Westfalen: Lechte, 1952. xii, 232pp.

A thorough, technical approach to sound structure with many illustrative examples. Appendix: "Klangtafel" (range of sound and rhythm and their designations) and 4 sample analyses. Index: names.

1163. Markwardt, Bruno. "Lyrik (Theorie)." *Reallexikon* (No. 1288), II, 240-252.

1164. Petsch, Robert. *Die lyrische Dichtkunst. Ihr Wesen und ihre Formen.* Halle: Niemeyer, 1939. 154pp.

A definition of the lyric genre. Bibliography.

1165. Pfeiffer, Johannes. *Das lyrische Gedicht als ästhetisches Gebilde. Ein phänomenischer Versuch.* Halle: Niemeyer, 1931. 113pp.

An attempt to apply the views of Husserl and Heidegger to poetry. Also reviews similar attempts by others.

1166. Wiegand, Julius. *Abriß der lyrischen Technik.* Fulda: Parzeller, 1950. 160pp.

Compact catalog of structural elements and their definitions; good for the beginner. Subject index.

4. Prosody

1167. Arndt, Erwin. *Deutsche Verslehre. Ein Abriß.* Berlin: Volk und Wissen, 1968. 259pp. ([1]1958)

A carefully systematized survey of German prosody (9th to 20th century) in 4 parts: A. introduction: prosody, form and function of verse, B. bases of German prosody, C. metric forms, D. historical development of metrical forms. Definitions are clear and well illustrated; previous research taken into account. Brief, sometimes annotated bibliography, pp. 251-253; subject index facilitates use as a reference work. The historical orientation is very useful for the beginner. This is a much more ambitious and thorough introduction than Kayser (No. 1178). Excellent.

1168. Asmuth, Bernhard. *Aspekte der Lyrik. Mit einer Einführung in die Verslehre.* Düsseldorf: Bertelsmann, 1972. 155pp.

Pt. 1: introduction, including accent, meter, rhyme, etc.; pt. 2: 10 modes of lyric poetry, including *Dinggedicht*, concrete poetry, absolute poetry, etc. Indexes: author, subject; bibliography; notes. Contains study questions. Presentation often very brief and compact.

1169. Atkins, Henry Gibson. *A History of German Versification. Ten Centuries of Metrical Evolution.* London: Methuen, 1923. xvi, 282pp.

Divided into 4 "books": "The Principles," "History of German Versification," "The Chief Modern German Lines," "Modern Strophes." An excellent, thorough introduction, particularly valuable for material on OHG, MHG, and late medieval verse. Bibliogr. notes outdated. Index: names, subject.

1170. Behrmann, Alfred. *Einführung in die Analyse von Verstexten.* Stuttgart: Metzler, 1970. ix, 115pp.

A general introduction to the rhetoric of verse: meter, stanza, poem, figures of speech, etc. Analyses proceed from text specimens. An excellent but demanding introduction to poetry analysis. Indexes: author, subject; definitions of terminology.

1171. Bennett, W. *German Verse in Classical Metres.* The Hague: Mouton, 1963. 315pp.

Organized by classical forms commonly used. In each case the history of major examples of usage is detailed. Glossary of terminology, pp. 146-147. Appendices: meters and their poets; poets and their meters; undated poets. Bibliography. Excellent for quick orientation; valuable for the beginner.

1172. Closs, August. *Die freien Rhythmen in der deutschen Lyrik. Versuch einer übersichtlichen Zusammenfassung ihrer entwicklungsgeschichtlichen Eigengesetzlichkeit.* Bern: Francke, 1947. 198pp.

Definitions, historical survey from the 18th century to Expressionism. Bibliography, pp. 194-198.

1173. Habermann, Paul. "Antike Versmaße und Strophen-(Oden-)formen." *Reallexikon* (No. 1288), I, 70-84.

1174. Heusler, Andreas. *Deutsche Versgeschichte mit Einschluß des altenglischen und altnordischen Stabreimverses.* 3 vols. Berlin, Leipzig: de Gruyter, 1925-1929.

I, pts. 1, 2. *Einführendes. Grundbegriffe der Verslehre. Der altgermanische Vers.* 1925, iii, 314pp. Range: to the 9th century.
II, pt. 3. *Der altdeutsche Vers.* 1927. vii, 341pp. Range: 9th to 14th century.
III, pts. 4, 5. *Der frühneudeutsche Vers. Der neudeutsche Vers.* 1929. v, 427pp. Range: 14th to 20th century. Index to I-III.

Standard work on German prosody.

1175. Hoffmann, Werner. *Altdeutsche Metrik.* Stuttgart: Metzler, 1967. ix, 105pp.

Resource book: survey of research, definitions, outline history of OHG Stabreim, early Middle High German verse forms, MHG epic and lyric forms. Complex and thorough. Bibliography at end of each section.

1176. Jünger, Friedrich Georg. *Rhythmus und Sprache im deutschen Gedicht.* 2nd ed. Stuttgart: Klett, 1966. ([1]1952)

A discussion of rhythm, scansion, verse, stanza, free rhythms which seeks to dispel some traditional erroneous notions. Systematic discussion but not intended as an introductory prosody. No bibliography, no index.

1177. Kauffmann, Friedrich. *Deutsche Metrik nach ihrer geschichtlichen Entwicklung. Neue Bearbeitung der aus dem Nachlaß Dr. A.F.C. Vilmars von Dr. C.W.M. Grein herausgegebenen Deutschen Verskunst.* 2nd ed. Marburg: Elwert, 1907. viii, 254pp.

Of historical interest.

1178. Kayser, Wolfgang. *Kleine deutsche Versschule.* Bern, Munich: Francke, 1946. 123pp. (frequent reprintings)

A justly popular introduction to German prosody (17th to 20th century) with chapters on verse, line, stanza, poem forms, appropriateness of word choice, rhyme, and rhythm. Systematic coverage, clear definitions with ample illustrations, in an engagingly informal style. Index of names and concepts facilitates use as a reference work. Excellent for beginners interested in a simplified but reliable approach.

1179. Lehmann, Winfried. *The Development of Germanic Verse Form.* Austin, Texas: Univ. of Texas Pr., 1956. xix, 217pp.

Delineates changes in poetic rhythm for Proto-Germanic, Old Norse, Old English, Old Saxon, and Old High German. The foreword includes a survey of sources. Specimen texts are translated.

1180. Mohr, Wolfgang. "Romanische Versmaße und Strophenformen (im Deutschen)." *Reallexikon* (No. 1288), III, 557-578.

1181. Neumann, Friedrich. "Deutsche Literatur bis 1500: Versgeschichte (Metrik)." *Kurzer Grundriß der germanischen Philologie bis 1500*, II, pp. 608-655. (No. 483)

A compact outline of German metrics from the Old High German period to Klopstock. Introduces the historical survey by presenting the most important terminology with illustrations. Excellent for beginners.

1182. Newton, Robert P. *Form in the Menschheitsdämmerung. A Study of Prosodic Elements and Style in German Expressionistic Poetry.* The Hague: Mouton, 1971. 270pp.

Careful technical analysis of the poetry of the famous anthology tries to define the features of Expressionistic poetry and its debt to tradition. Includes guidelines to the interpretation of Expressionistic poetry. To be used in conjunction with *Menschheitsdämmerung.* Bibliography.

1183. Paul, Otto, and Ingeborg Glier. *Deutsche Metrik.* 5th ed. Munich: Hueber, 1964. 191pp. ([1]1930)

A detailed but compact, carefully organized presentation of German metrics (8th-20th century). 1. basic concepts, 2. *Stabreimvers*, 3. medieval verse, 4, New High German rhymed verse, 5. New High German unrhymed verse, 6. outline history of New High German versification. Bibliography; subject index. An outstanding treatment. NOTE: particularly valuable for material not presented in most introductions to prosody: older German verse, medieval verse and *Meistersang*, the church song of the 16th century.

1184. Pretzel, Ulrich. "Deutsche Verskunst. Mit einem Beitrag über altdeutsche Strophik von H. Thomas." *Dt. Phil. im Aufriß* (No. 1283), III, 2357-2546.

1185. Saran, Franz. *Deutsche Verskunst. Ein Handbuch für Schule, Sprechsaal, Bühne.* Albert Riemann, ed., with the collaboration of Paul Habermann. Berlin: Junker & Dünnhaupt, 1934. xiii, 425pp.

A detailed manual which employs an intricate system of signs and symbols to instruct the student in the art of reading a poem aloud. Examples from the entire range of German poetry beginning with OHG verse. Indexes: terminology and names, poems discussed.

1186. Schlawe, Fritz. *Die deutschen Strophenformen. Systematisches-chronologisches Register zur deutschen Lyrik 1600-1950.* Stuttgart: Metzler, 1972. xviii, 578pp.

Contains the analysis of some 25,000 stanzaic forms, including the complete lyrics of some major poets, representative works by lesser known poets, and *Des Knaben Wunderhorn*. CAUTION: uses a somewhat complex system of symbols which is explained in the introduction. Two listings: 1) author A-Z: stanzaic scheme, year, poem title, no. of stanzas, rhyme scheme; 2) stanzaic scheme: same information as author listing. Index: titles. Excellent for quick reference.

1187. Storz, Gerhard. *Der Vers in der neueren deutschen Dichtung.* Stuttgart: Reclam, 1970. 239pp.

A compact, but comprehensive presentation of German metrics (17th-20th century), including stanza forms. A final chapter offers a brief survey of the history of New High German verse. Bibliography pp. 232-234. Subject index. A handy pocket guide. Organization less clear than in most prosodies.

1188. Stummer, Josef Viktor. *Vers, Reim, Strophe, Gedicht. Ein Lehr- und Lesebuch über das Handwerkliche der deutschen Dichtkunst. Mit ausführlichem Schlagwörterverzeichnis.* Thun, Munich: Ott, 1968. 219pp.

A comprehensive and systematic presentation of German metrics (16th-20th century): 1. metric feet, 2. verses, 3. rhymes, 4. stanzas, 5. poem forms. Thorough coverage includes many minor, seldom encountered aspects. Examples often taken from minor poets or fashioned by the author where he did not find examples. Subject index. Bibliography. No historical information.

1189. Touber, Anthonius Hendrikus. *Deutsche Strophenformen des Mittelalters.* Stuttgart: Metzler, 1975. xii, 164pp.

Computer analysis of the versification of all major medieval collections of poetry. Handy resource book.

5. History and Interpretation

a. General Histories

1190. Browning, Robert M. *German Poetry. A Critical Anthology.* New York: Appleton-Century-Crofts, 1962. xxii, 404pp.

Range: Luther to Langgässer. Not a literary history but a work-study book for the student. Individual poets and their literary significance briefly stated. Each selection accompanied by questions. Excellent for textbook use.

**** Burger, Heinz Otto, ed. *Gedicht und Gedanke. Auslegungen deutscher Gedichte.* Halle: Niemeyer, 1942. 434pp. (No. 1261)

1191. Closs, August. "Die neuere deutsche Lyrik vom Barock bis zur Gegenwart." *Dt. Phil. im Aufriß* (No. 1283), II, 133-348.

Excellent historical survey to 1950, though for Expressionism, a more recent survey should be consulted.

1192. ———. *The Genius of the German Lyric. An Historical Survey of Its Formal and Metaphysical Values.* 2nd rev. ed. Philadelphia: Dufour, 1962. xxiii, 387pp. (^{1}1938)

Range: 1150-1956, Minnesang to Gottfried Benn. Chronological history of lyric poetry. Examples of poetry in the text are not extensively interpreted but serve to illustrate characteristics of their period. A good informative introduction. Index: author and subject.

1193. Ermatinger, Emil. *Die deutsche Lyrik seit Herder.* 2nd ed. 3 vols. Leipzig, Berlin: Teubner, 1925. (^{1}1921)

I. *Von Herder zu Goethe.* xi, 310pp.
II. *Die Romantik.* 286pp.
III. *Vom Realismus bis zur Gegenwart.* 320pp.

Individual chapters centered about major figures.

1194. Haller, Rudolf. *Geschichte der deutschen Lyrik vom Ausgang des Mittelalters bis zu Goethes Tod.* Bern, Munich: Francke, 1967. 487pp.

Chronological presentation with emphasis on formal and stylistic aspects shown in brief analyses. 1: Baroque; 2: Enlightenment; 3: Storm and Stress, Classicism. A fine, compact presentation which avoids subjective judgments and biographical digressions.

1195. Hienger, Jörg, and Rudolf Knauf, eds. *Deutsche Gedichte von Andreas Gryphius bis Ingeborg Bachmann.* Göttingen: Vandenhoeck & Ruprecht, 1969. 216pp.

Designed specifically to introduce the foreign student to German poetry. Covers 28 authors. Each entry assesses the work of the poet, provides a text specimen and a compact interpretation. Sometimes too brief. Adequate only as a first introduction. Glossary, pp. 210-213.

**** Hirschenauer, Rupert, and Albert Weber, eds. *Wege zum Gedicht.* 2 vols. Munich, Zürich: Schnell und Steiner, 1965, 1964 (No. 1264)

1196. Klein, Johannes. *Geschichte der deutschen Lyrik von Luther bis zum Ausgang des zweiten Weltkriegs.* 2nd rev. ed. Wiesbaden: Steiner, 1960. xvi, 906pp. ([1]1957)

Comprehensive historical survey; each part is divided into an intellectual-historical description of the epoch, followed by a discussion of individual authors, a summary of their lyrical oeuvre and a brief analysis of characteristic poems. Period from 1920-1950 somewhat cursorily treated. Excellent introduction.

**** Prawer, Siegbert Salomon. *German Lyric Poetry. A Critical Analysis of Selected Poems from Klopstock to Rilke.* New York: Barnes & Noble, 1965. x, 264pp. (No. 1265)

**** Schillemeit, Jost, ed. *Interpretationen. I: Deutsche Lyrik von Weckherlin bis Benn.* Frankfurt: Fischer, 1965. 338pp. (No. 1266)

**** Wiese, Benno von, ed. *Die deutsche Lyrik. Form und Geschichte.* 2 vols. Düsseldorf: Bagel, 1956. (No. 1267)

1197. Witkop, Philipp. *Die deutschen Lyriker von Luther bis Nietzsche.* 2nd ed. 2 vols. Leipzig: Teubner, 1921. I. *Von Luther bis Hölderlin.* 271pp.; II. *Von Novalis bis Nietzsche.* 302pp.

b. Middle Ages

1198. Dronke, Peter. *The Medieval Lyric.* London: Hutchinson Univ. Library, 1968. 266pp.

A superb survey of the European lyric from the 8th to the 13th century, including chapters on performance, religious poetry, the love lyric, the Alba, dance songs, and "lyrics of realism." Presentation based on excellent interpretations with copious bilingual examples. Much information on German literature and its place in the European tradition. Written in a lively style. Melody specimens, pp. 231-240. Selected bibliography of primary and secondary literature, pp. 241-256. Index: names, subjects.

1199. Fromm, Hans, ed. *Der deutsche Minnesang. Aufsätze zu seiner Erforschung.* Bad Homburg: Gentner, 1961. x, 456pp.

Minnesang research 1914-1957 reflected in a collection of 9 previously published essays by eminent scholars in the field. Indexes: poets, beginnings of first lines.

1200. Jungbluth, Günther, ed. *Interpretationen mittelhochdeutscher Lyrik.* Bad Homburg, Berlin, Zurich: Gehlen, 1969. 291pp.

13 articles by specialists, each containing a critical rendition of the text, a translation, and an interpretation. Index: authors, titles. Quite demanding; for the specialist.

1201. Kienast, Richard. "Die deutschsprachige Lyrik des Mittelalters." *Dt. Phil. im Aufriß* (No. 1283), II, 1-132.

Range: beginnings to 1520. Excellent compact but comprehensive diachronic presentation starting with the oldest Germanic verse but concentrating on medieval poetry. Incorporates significant scholarship and provides bibliographical references.

1202. Neumann, Friedrich. "Minnesang." *Reallexikon* (No. 1288), II, 303-314.

1203. Richey, M.F. *Essays on Medieval German Poetry. With Translations in English Verse.* 2nd expanded ed. New York: Barnes & Noble, 1969. vii, 179pp. ([1]1943)

Range: 12th and 13th centuries. Discusses the history and form of Minnesang. 9 representative poets treated in detail. Appendices on Wolfram von Eschenbach, Hartmann von Aue. Copious translations make it an excellent introduction for those who do not read Middle High German.

1204. Werbow, Stanley N., ed. *Formal Aspects of Medieval German Poetry. A Symposium.* Austin: Univ. of Texas Pr., 1969. 129pp.

5 essays: performance, music, prosody, numerical composition, late medieval poetry. Bibliography on numerical composition, pp. 113-119. Index: author, subject. Of varying quality.

c. Seventeenth Century

**** Bircher, Martin, and Alois M. Haas. *Deutsche Barocklyrik. Gedichtinterpretationen von Spee bis Haller.* Bern, Munich: Francke, 1973. 361pp. (No. 1260)

1205. Browning, Robert M. *German Baroque Poetry 1618-1723.* University Park, London: Pennsylvania State Univ. Pr., 1971. x, 292pp.

Thorough analyses of the works of major Baroque poets and their contribution to the movement. An outstanding combination of literary history and insightful interpretation. Invaluable for the beginner.

1206. Cysarz, Herbert. *Deutsches Barock in der Lyrik.* Leipzig: Reclam, 1936. 135pp.

Somewhat outdated but still useful as a compact survey of the period.

**** De Capua, Angelo G. *German Baroque Poetry. Interpretive Readings.* Albany: State Univ. of New York Pr., 1973. vii, 213pp. (No. 1262)

1207. Gillespie, Gerald. *German Baroque Poetry.* New York: Twayne, 1971. 221pp.

Traces the development of Baroque poetry from its Renaissance roots to Weckherlin, Opitz, Fleming, regional centers, religious poetry, Hofmannswaldau. Note: little material on Gryphius. Index: author and subject; bibliography pp. 199-213. Competent general introduction within its limits.

d. Nineteenth and Twentieth Centuries

1208. Büttner, Ludwig. *Von Benn zu Enzensberger. Eine Einführung in die zeitgenössische Lyrik 1945-1970.* Nuremberg: Carl, 1971. 228pp.

Brief appraisal of some 90 poets with text specimens; too encyclopedic and brief to be of much use. Bibliography, pp. 214-228.

1209. Flores, John. *Poetry in East Germany. Adjustments, Visions, and Provocations 1945-1970.* New Haven, London: Yale Univ. Pr., 1971. xiv, 354pp.

Traces the development of four major poets: Hermlin, Fühmann, Huchel, Bobrowski, and appraises the work of Kunert, Braun, Mickel, and Biermann. Contains much solid interpretation. Appendix: wartime poems by Fühmann, Bobrowsky, pp. 317-327; bibliography, pp. 328-344; index: author, subject.

1210. Friedrich, Hugo. *Die Struktur der modernen Lyrik. Von der Mitte des 19. bis zur Mitte des 20. Jahrhunderts.* Hamburg: Rowohlt, ^{11}1970. 216pp. (^{1}1956) English ed. *The Structure of Modern Poetry. From the Mid-Nineteenth to the Twentieth Century.* Trans. by Joachim Neugroschel. Evanston: Northwestern Univ. Pr., 1974. xvii, 181pp.

Traces the development of modernism in European lyric poetry from the French forerunners; discussion proceeds on the basis of style and structure rather than chronology. Appendix: modern poetry with translations, chronological table. A standard work on the development of poetry.

1211. Hartung, Harald. *Experimentelle Literatur und konkrete Poesie.* Göttingen: Vandenhoeck & Ruprecht, 1975. 115pp.

Range: 1880's to 1970's. Succinct historical survey of experimental literature from Naturalism, Expressionism, Dada, to post-1945 pluralism. Excellent introduction. Select bibliography, pp. 104-107.

1212. Heselhaus, Clemens. *Deutsche Lyrik der Moderne von Nietzsche bis Ivan Goll. Die Rückkehr zur Bildlichkeit der Sprache.* Düsseldorf: Bagel, 1961. 480pp.

Range: 1888-1948. A typology of modern poetry based on thorough analyses of representative poems by some 40 poets. Analyses concentrate on imagery. Although chronologically arranged, this is not a history. Exemplary interpretations.

1213. Killy, Walther. *Wandlungen des lyrischen Bildes.* 4th ed. Göttingen: Vandenhoeck & Ruprecht, 1964. 141pp. (^{1}1956)

Range: 18th to 20th century. Discusses the evolution of imagery in German poetry. Intrinsic analysis of poems by Goethe, Hölderlin, C. Brentano, Mörike, Heine, Geibel, Trakl, Benn. A superb but demanding introduction to one aspect of poetry.

1214. Knörrich, Otto. *Die deutsche Lyrik der Gegenwart 1945-1970.* Stuttgart: Kröner, 1971. 394pp.

A solid introduction to the major lyricists of the German language since 1945: a historical survey, discussion of the traditionalists, nature poets, Dada and Surrealism, and the political lyric. Bibliography pp. 384-390.

1215. Liptzin, Solomon. *Lyric Pioneers of Modern Germany. Studies in German Social Poetry.* New York: Columbia Univ. Pr., 1928. 187pp.

Range: 1830's to 1920's. One of the earliest surveys of its kind. Provides extensive information on specific poems.

1216. Prawer, Siegbert, ed. *17 Modern German Poets.* London: Oxford Univ. Pr., 1971. 203pp.

Range: 20th century. An introduction designed for students: brief survey, pp. 13-40, German text, notes, pp. 143-198, include translation aids, hints on interpretation, etc. Index: first lines. Bibliography.

1217. Schutte, Jürgen. *Lyrik des Naturalismus (1885-1893).* Stuttgart: Metzler, 1976. vii, 94pp.

Resource book: historical survey and critical appraisal of research. Bibliography at the end of each section. General bibliography, pp. 81-90; chronological table; index: names and titles.

6. Other Lyrical Forms

a. Ballade

1218. Hirschenauer, Rupert, and Albert Weber, eds. *Wege zum Gedicht. II. Interpretationen von Balladen.* Munich, Zurich: Schnell und Steiner, 1964. 547pp. (No. 1264) "Bibliographie zur Interpretation von Balladen," pp. 586-603.

1219. Kretschmann, Wilhelm. "Ballade." *Handlexikon* (No. 1290), pp. 56-62.

1220. Pflüger-Bouillon, Elisabeth, ed. *Probleme der Balladenforschung.* Darmstadt: Wissenschaftliche Buchgesellschaft, 1975. vi, 443pp.

11 essays published from 1892-1964 covering definitions, history of the genre, problems of oral transmission and ballad research. International bibliography presented by country, pp. 433-443. Excellent point of departure for the study of the ballad.

1221. Wildbolz, Rudolf. "Kunstballade." *Reallexikon* (No. 1288), I, 902-909.

b. Bänkelsang

1222. Petzoldt, Leander. *Bänkelsang. Vom historischen Bänkelsang zum literarischen Chanson.* Stuttgart: Metzler, 1974. ix, 141pp.

Range: 18th to 20th century. Includes definitions, sources, structures, themes, and a historical survey. The most important research is appraised within each chapter, followed by bibliography. Index: proper names. A good resource book.

c. Bildgedicht

1223. Kranz, Gisbert. *Das Bildgedicht in Europa. Zur Theorie und Geschichte einer literarischen Gattung.* Paderborn: Schöningh, 1973. 235pp.

A brief introduction with definitions and a historical survey of the genre. A somewhat encyclopedic formulation. Valuable for its international bibliography of poems, by author A-Z, pp. 121-200, and list of poets, A-Z, whose works are discussed. Index: authors.

1224. Rosenfeld, Hellmut. *Das deutsche Bildgedicht. Seine antiken Vorbilder und seine Entwicklung bis zur Gegenwart.* Leipzig: Mayer & Müller, 1935. viii, 272pp. (Repr. 1967)

Survey in 2 pts.: 1. chronological survey from Greek literature to the 18th century, 2. changes in form and function during the 19th and early 20th century due to ideological and historical developments. Indexes: authors, subjects. Notes. Still of some value.

d. Briefgedicht

1225. Grenzmann, Wilhelm. "Briefgedicht." *Reallexikon* (No. 1288), I, 193-195.

1226. Motsch, Markus. *Die poetische Epistel. Ein Beitrag zur Geschichte der deutschen Literatur und Literaturkritik des 18. Jahrhunderts.* Bern, Frankfurt: Lang, 1974. 217pp.

Pt. 1: historical survey of genre from antiquity to the 18th century; pt. 2: survey of the 18th century; pt. 3: literary criticism. Appendix: definitions and theoretical considerations. Indexes: author, subject. Bibliography.

e. Elegie

1227. Beißner, Friedrich. *Geschichte der deutschen Elegie.* Berlin: de Gruyter, 1941. xiii, 246pp. (Repr. 1965)

Defines elegy in terms of content and form, and traces the genre from Classical Antiquity through German Classicism. Includes a brief sketch of influence of Classical elegy on 19th-century poets. Exemplary in its portrayal and analysis of the elegy.

1228. Weissenberger, Klaus. *Formen der Elegie von Goethe bis Celan.* Bern, Munich: Francke, 1969. 163pp.

A morphological history and reappraisal of the genre, especially in the 20th-century idiom. Includes numerous analyses. Bibliography, pp. 159-161. A good, compact survey of the genre.

1229. Wiegand, Julius. "Elegie." *Reallexikon* (No. 1288), I, 332-334.

f. Epigramm

1230. Angress, Ruth K. *The Early German Epigram. A Study in Baroque Poetry.* Lexington: Univ. of Kentucky Pr., 1971. 134pp.

A definition and survey of function and themes of the epigram during the 16th and 17th centuries. Bibliography.

1231. Wiegand, Julius. "Epigramm." *Reallexikon* (No. 1288), I, 374-379.

g. Lied

1232. Brody, Elaine, and Robert A. Fowkes. *The German Lied and Its Poetry.* New York: New York Univ. Pr., 1971. viii, 316pp.

A chronological history, focusing on major figures of the 19th century and intended as an introduction.

1233. Klein, Ulrich. "Lied." *Handlexikon* (No. 1290), pp. 241-247.

1234. Müller, Günther. "Lied (literaturgeschichtlich)." *Reallexikon* (No. 1288), II, 42-56.

1235. ———. *Geschichte des deutschen Liedes vom Zeitalter des Barock bis zur Gegenwart.* Munich: Drei Masken, 1925. x, 335pp. Appendix: 48pp.

Thorough presentation of the history (1570-late 19th century) as well as form and content of the German art song from its inception to the turn of the century. Expressionism scantily treated. Appendix: specimen scores.

1236. Reichert, Georg. "Lied (musikalisch)." *Reallexikon* (No. 1288), II, 56-62.

1237. Stein, Jack M. *Poem and Music in the German Lied from Gluck to Hugo Wolf.* Cambridge: Harvard Univ. Pr., 1971. 238pp.

Includes a chapter on the problems of combining poem and music, individual sections devoted to authors and composers. Major songs are analyzed from a musical point of view with copious musical and textual examples. A lively survey for the interested non-specialist. Indexes: titles and first lines, general index. Bibliography, pp. 206-213.

1238. Taylor, Ronald J. *Die Melodien der weltlichen Lieder des Mittelalters. Darstellungsband.* Stuttgart: Metzler, 1964. viii, 72pp.

A brief survey of music history from the beginnings to the 13th century with copious references to further readings.

h. Meistersang

1239. Nagel, Bert. *Der deutsche Meistersang. Poetische Technik, musikalische Form und Sprachgestaltung der Meistersinger.* Heidelberg: Kerle, 1952. 228pp.

An extensive examination of the genre, including its poetics, versification, and style. Primary and secondary bibliography. For the specialist.

1240. ———. *Der deutsche Meistersang.* 2nd ed. Stuttgart: Metzler, 1971. viii, 108pp. ([1]1961)

Resource book: definitions, report on research, chronological and geographical survey of the genre. Bibliography at the end of each section.

1241. Taylor, Archer. *The Literary History of Meistersang.* New York: Modern Language Association, 1937. x, 134pp. (Repr. 1966)

A compact survey of the historical, formal, and literary aspects of *Meistersang* (not including *Fastnachtspiel*), somewhat outdated but still useful. Indexes: author, subject.

1242. Stammler, Wolfgang. "Meistergesang." *Reallexikon* (No. 1288). II, 292-301.

i. Ode

1243. Viëtor, Karl. *Geschichte der deutschen Ode.* Munich: Drei Masken, 1923. vii, 198pp.

Range: Middle Ages through 20th century. The first attempt in German criticism to write a history of a genre. Introduction contains valuable discussion of methodological principles. Inductive approach, chronological treatment. Excellent. Somewhat ponderous.

1244. Wiegand, Julius, and Werner Kohlschmidt. "Ode." *Reallexikon* (No. 1288), II, 709-717.

j. Sonett

1245. Mönch, Walter. *Das Sonett. Gestalt und Geschichte.* Heidelberg: Kerle, 1955. 341pp.

A comparative history of the sonnet in European literature (13th to 20th century): 1. structure, 2. early Renaissance to Baroque: Italy, Spain, Portugal, France, England, Germany; the sonnet, 19th and 20th century. Comprehensive presentation with little interpretation of individual authors or poems. Good selected international bibliography. Excellent introduction.

k. Volkslied

1246. Brednich, Rolf Wilhelm, Lutz Röhrich, and Wolfgang Suppan, eds. *Handbuch des Volksliedes. I. Die Gattungen des Volksliedes.* Munich: Fink, 1973-1975. One vol. in 2 parts: pt. 1: 967pp., 41 illus.; pt. 2: 826pp.

A superior encyclopedia. Articles on the various genres are written by a number of different contributors. Items are clearly subdivided into definitions, historical development, appraisal of most recent research. Abundant examples. Indexes for both parts in pt. 2: proper names, first lines, subjects.

1247. Röhrich, Lutz. "Volkslied." *Handlexikon* (No. 1290), pp. 512-519.

1248. Seemann, Erich, and Walter Wiora. "Volkslied." *Dt. Phil. im Aufriß* (No. 1283), II, 349-396.

A brief but comprehensive sketch of the history of folksong collecting: the nature, origin, development of folksongs; the history of folksong from the beginning to the present. Bibliography extensive and well organized.

1249. Suppan, Wolfgang. *Volkslied. Seine Sammlung und Erforschung.* Stuttgart: Metzler, 1966. ix, 59pp.

l. Volkspoesie

1250. Bausinger, Hermann. *Formen der Volkspoesie.* Berlin: Schmidt, 1968. 291pp.

A compact typology of genres with an historical survey and critical appraisal of research. Includes formula, idiom, proverb, saying, inscription, riddle, joke, *Schwank*, fairy tale, saga, legend, drama, song. Selected bibliography at the end of each section.

IX.

Collections of Interpretations, Critical Summaries, Digests and Plot Outlines

CONTENTS

A. COLLECTIONS OF INTERPRETATIONS AND CRITICAL SUMMARIES

1. Bibliographies

1251. Blume, Bernhard, and Adolf E. Schroeder. "Interpretations of German Poetry (1939-1956). A Bibliography." *Monatshefte* 49 (1957), 241-263.

1252. Jungbauer, Fritz. *Kleine Kunde der Interpretationen und Deutungen von Werken der deutschen Literatur.* Vienna: Hollinek, 1966. 142pp.

A compilation of 100 titles of collected interpretations, publishers' series, etc. for Austrian, German, and Swiss literature. Indexes: interpreters, publishers, poets and their works. Easy to use.

1253. Schlepper, Reinhard. *Was ist wo interpretiert? Eine bibliographische Handreichung für den Deutschunterricht.* 3rd enl. ed. Paderborn: Schöningh, 1970. 311pp.

Range: 1945-1969. An extensive reference guide covering novels, *Novellen*, short stories, dramas, radio plays, poems. Listed by author A-Z. Also covers foreign authors taught at the German secondary-school level.

2. Literary Periods

1254. *Erläuterungen zur deutschen Literatur: Aufklärung.* Ed. by the Kollektiv für Literaturgeschichte dir. by Kurt Böttcher. 3rd ed. Berlin: Volk und Wissen, 1971. 770pp. ([1]1958)

Range: ca. 1680 to 1770. A detailed survey of the Enlightenment from a Marxist point of view. Organized around the major figures with biographical information, summaries and close readings of representative works. Enlightenment regarded as the initial phase of modern German literature. The ideological orientation should be borne in mind.

1255. *Erläuterungen zur deutschen Literatur: Klassik.* Ed. by the Kollektiv für Literaturgeschichte dir. by Kurt Böttcher. 4th ed. Berlin: Volk und Wissen, 1974. 508pp. ([1]1957)

Range: Goethe and Schiller. A survey from the Marxist point of view. The major works of Goethe and Schiller are summarized and analyzed in detail with emphasis on the reflection of social and economic conditions in their work. Exemplary Marxist methodology.

1256. *Erläuterungen zur deutschen Literatur: Romantik.* Ed. by the Kollektiv für Literaturgeschichte dir. by Kurt Böttcher. Berlin: Volk und Wissen, 1973. 668pp. ([1]1967)

Centered around leading figures in their historical and cultural setting. Major works are summarized and analyzed in subsections. Includes section on Romanticism in Austria. Excellent general introduction; methodology should be borne in mind.

3. Drama

1257. Brauneck, Manfred, ed. *Das deutsche Drama vom Expressionismus bis zur Gegenwart. Interpretationen.* Bamberg: Buchner, 1970. 293pp.

Analyses (some previously published) of works by Kaiser, Toller, Sternheim, Goll, Zuckmayer, Borchert, Brecht (5), Dürrenmatt (2), Frisch, Hildesheimer, Hochhuth, Kipphardt, Weiss (2), Sperr, Handke. Essays often too brief and summary.

1258. Schillemeit, Jost. ed. *Interpretationen. II. Deutsche Dramen von Gryphius bis Brecht.* Frankfurt: Fischer, 1965. 341pp.

Range: 17th to 20th century. 16 essays by leading scholars analyzing single plays or aspects of plays by: Gryphius, Lessing (2), Goethe (3), Schiller (2), Kleist, Grillparzer, Büchner, Hebbel, Hauptmann, Hofmannsthal, Brecht. Somewhat demanding.

1259. Wiese, Benno von, ed. *Das deutsche Drama vom Barock bis zur Gegenwart. Interpretationen.* 2 vols. Düsseldorf: Bagel, 1960.

I. *Vom Barock bis zur klassisch-romantischen Zeit.* 500pp.
II. *Vom Realismus bis zur Gegenwart.* 464pp.

Detailed analyses of 44 plays. Authors represented: I. Bidermann, Gryphius, Gottsched, Lessing (3), Lenz, Goethe (4), Schiller (4), Kleist (3), Grillparzer (3); II: Raimund, Nestroy, Grabbe, Büchner (2), Hebbel (3), Hauptmann (3), Wedekind, Hofmannsthal (3), Sternheim, Kaiser (2), Barlach, Kraus, Brecht (2), Dürrenmatt. Index: author and title. On the whole quite reliable. Excellent interpretations by specialists.

4. Poetry

1260. Bircher, Martin, and Alois M. Haas. *Deutsche Barocklyrik. Gedichtinterpretationen von Spee bis Haller.* Bern, Munich: Francke, 1973. 361pp.

Range: 17th to 18th century. 14 analyses of poems or poem cycles by Spee, Rollenhagen, Balde, Silesius, Stieler, Grimmelshausen (2), Gryphius, Greiffenberg, Kuhlmann, Hofmannswaldau, Wiedemann, Sancta Clara, Haller. Discussions generally quite illuminating. Indexes: proper names, subject; notes.

1261. Burger, Heinz Otto. *Gedicht und Gedanke. Auslegungen deutscher Gedichte.* Halle: Niemeyer, 1942. 434pp.

Range: 12th to 20th century. Interpretations of individual poems. This is an early attempt to break the hegemony of the intellectual-historical approach to literature and, though somewhat influenced by the time in which it was written, it contains interpretations which are still useful.

1262. De Capua, Angelo G. *German Baroque Poetry. Interpretive Readings.* Albany: State Univ. of New York Pr., 1973. vii, 213pp.

Range: 1575-1725. A chronological history of poetry based on dominant morphological and thematic features illustrated in the analysis of texts by 14 major and minor figures. Analyses somewhat superficial. Index: author and subject. Bibliography. Glossary: notes on cited text samples, pp. 194-200.

1263. Domin, Hilde, ed. *Doppelinterpretationen. Das zeitgenössische Gedicht zwischen Autor und Leser.* Frankfurt, Bonn: Athenäum, 1966. 365pp.

A collection of 31 poems which are simultaneously interpreted by their authors and a literary critic. An introduction on interpreting poetry. List of poems, pp. 50-84. Interpretations somewhat uneven.

**** Hienger, Jörg, and Rudolf Knauf, eds. *Deutsche Gedichte von Andreas Gryphius bis Ingeborg Bachmann.* Göttingen: Vandenhoeck & Ruprecht, 1969. 216pp. (No. 1195)

1264. Hirschenauer, Rupert, and Albert Weber, eds. *Wege zum Gedicht.* 2nd ed. 2 vols. Munich, Zurich: Schnell und Steiner, 1965, 1964. 471pp., 574pp. (^{1}1956, ^{1}1963)

Range: beginnings to the 20th century.

I. Introductory essays on interpretation followed by analyses of 58 poems by major authors from Hartmann von Aue to Ingeborg Bachmann. The contributions are by various scholars. Extensive bibliography to 1961, pp. 403-470.

II. Subtitle: Interpretationen von Balladen. Introductory essays include the history of the ballad. 45 analyses of the entire range, from folk ballad to Brecht. Extensive bibliography, pp. 551-572. Both volumes outstanding.

**** Jungbluth, Günther, ed. *Interpretationen mittelhochdeutscher Lyrik*. Bad Homburg, Berlin, Zurich: Gehlen, 1969. 291pp. (No. 1200)

1265. Prawer, Siegbert Salomon. *German Lyric Poetry. A Critical Analysis of Selected Poems from Klopstock to Rilke*. New York: Barnes & Noble, 1965. x, 264pp. ([1]1952)

Range: 18th to 20th century. A survey of German poetry highlighted by close analysis of well known poems by Gellert, Hagedorn, Klopstock, Hölty, Claudius, Goethe (6), Schiller, Hölderlin (2), Novalis, Brentano, Eichendorff (2), Heine (3), Platen, Droste-Hülshoff, Mörike, Keller, Storm, Heyse, Meyer, George (2), Hofmannsthal (2), Rilke (3). Notes, pp. 231-245. Selected bibliography including section on translations. Indexes: subject and author, first lines. Well suited for the English reader.

1266. Schillemeit, Jost, ed. *Interpretationen. I. Deutsche Lyrik von Weckherlin bis Benn*. Frankfurt: Fischer, 1965. 338pp.

Range: 17th to 20th century. A representative collection of 21 essays (for the most part reprints) by eminent scholars on individual poems: Benn, Brentano, Droste-Hülshoff, Eichendorff, George, Goethe, Gryphius, Hölderlin, Meyer, Mörike, Rilke, Schiller, Trakl, Weckherlin. Somewhat demanding; for the advanced student.

1267. Wiese, Benno von, ed. *Die deutsche Lyrik. Form und Geschichte*. 2 vols. Düsseldorf: Bagel, 1956. I. *Interpretationen. Vom Mittelalter bis zur Frühromantik*. 447pp.; II. *Interpretationen. Von der Spätromantik bis zur Gegenwart*. 512pp.

Range: 12th to 20th century. 52 interpretations by leading scholars. Each essay provides references to the origin and historical or literary significance of the poem but concentrates on a close interpretation of the text. Poets represented: I. D.v. Eist, F.v. Hausen, H. Morungen, R.v. Hagenau, W.v.d. Vogelweide (4), W.v. Eschenbach, N.v. Reuental, folksong "Ich hört ein sichelin rauschen," M. Opitz (3), P. Fleming, A Gryphius (3), J. Günther, Gellert, Klopstock, Claudius, v. Salis-Seewis, Goethe (7), Schiller (3), Hölderlin (5), Novalis. II. Brentano (3), Eichendorff (3), Mörike (4), Uhland, Meyer (3), Rückert, Platen, Heine (3), Lenau, Droste-Hülshoff (3), Hebbel, Storm, Keller, Nietzsche (2), George (3), Hofmannsthal (2), Rilke (5), Borchardt, R.A. Schröder, Miegel, Stadler, Trakl (3), Heym, Benn, Weinheber, Britting (2), Brecht.

5. Prose

1268. Martini, Fritz. *Das Wagnis der Sprache. Interpretationen deutscher Prosa von Nietzsche bis Benn.* Stuttgart: Klett, 1964. 529pp. (^{1}1954)

Range: 1891-1949. Superb intrinsic interpretations of individual prose works by Benn, Broch, Carossa, Döblin, Hauptmann, Hofmannsthal, Holz, T. Mann, Nietzsche, and Rilke. Each essay begins with a text specimen. Excellent, demanding.

1269. Schillemeit, Jost, ed. *Interpretationen. III. Deutsche Romane von Grimmelshausen bis Musil.* Frankfurt: Fischer, 1966. 320pp.

Range: 17th to 20th century. A collection of 15 interpretations of important German novels by established scholars. Brief analyses of single novels by: Grimmelshausen, Goethe (2), Jean Paul, Novalis, Eichendorff, Arnim, Mörike, Keller, Stifter, Raabe, Fontane, T. Mann, Kafka, Musil. Somewhat demanding reading.

1270. ———. *Interpretationen. IV. Deutsche Erzählungen von Wieland bis Kafka.* Frankfurt: Fischer, 1966. 341pp.

Range: 18th to 20th century. A collection of 15 detailed interpretations by renowned scholars of narrative prose: Wieland, Goethe (2), Jean Paul, Kleist, Brentano, Arnim, E.T.A. Hoffmann, Eichendorff, Stifter, Keller, Meyer, Hofmannsthal, T. Mann, Kafka. Somewhat demanding reading.

1271. Wiese, Benno von. *Die deutsche Novelle von Goethe bis Kafka. Interpretationen.* 2 vols. Düsseldorf: Bagel, 1957, 1962. 350pp., 356pp. (Frequent repr.)

Range: 1785-1924. Outstanding analyses of representative German *Novellen.*

I. *Wesen und Geschichte der deutschen Novelle seit Goethe.* Introduction, with emphasis on historical survey of the genre; Schiller, Kleist, Brentano, Eichendorff, Chamisso, Tieck, Grillparzer, Gotthelf, Stifter, Mörike, Keller, Meyer, Hauptmann, Hofmannsthal, T. Mann, Kafka.

II. *Vom Spielraum des novellistischen Erzählens.* Introduction: role of the narrator in the *Novelle*; Goethe, Kleist, Arnim, Hoffmann, Büchner, Stifter, Keller, Meyer, Raabe, Storm, Fontane, Schnitzler, Keyserling, Musil, Kafka. Selected bibliographies at the end of each volume. Indispensable for the student.

1272. Zimmermann, Werner. *Deutsche Prosadichtungen unseres Jahrhunderts. Interpretationen für Lehrende und Lernende.* 2 vols. Düsseldorf: Pädagogischer Verlag Schwann, 1966, 1969. 397pp., 368pp.

Range: 1887-1965.

I. 21 interpretations of short stories and *Novellen* from 1887-1940.

II. 24 interpretations of short stories and novels, 1945-1965. Intended as an aid to teachers and students: analyses pedagogically sound; study questions provided. Each volume introduced by a brief outline of relevant literary history. Bibliographies.

B. DIGESTS AND PLOT OUTLINES

1273. Beer, Johannes, with Wilhelm Schuster. *Reclams Romanführer.* 2 vols. Stuttgart: Reclam, 1962-1963.

I. *Deutsche Romane von Grimmelshausen bis Thomas Mann.* 707pp.
II. *Deutsche Romane der Gegenwart (nach 1918).* 706pp.

Divided according to major epochs. Each section has introduction. For each author a brief biography, then summaries of representative novels or, in some cases, shorter prose pieces.

1274. Böttcher, Kurt, and Günter Albrecht, eds. *Romanführer A-Z.* 2 pts. in 3 vols. Berlin: Volk und Wissen, 1972-1974.

I. *Der deutsche, österreichische und schweizerische Roman. Von den Anfängen bis Ende des 19. Jahrhunderts.* 1972. 423pp. 107 authors.
II. 1. *20. Jahrhundert. Der deutsche Roman bis 1949. Romane der DDR. A-K.* 1974. 455pp. 87 authors.
II. 2. *20. Jahrhundert. Der deutsche Roman bis 1949. Romane der DDR. L-Z.* 1974. 525pp. 81 authors.

Each entry includes author and dates, summary, bibliography of additional novels. No major West German, Austrian, or Swiss authors after 1945 included. Chronological table in I.

1275. *Der Schauspielführer.* Originated by Joseph Gregor, continued by Margaret Dietrich. Vols 1-10ff. Stuttgart: Hiersemann, 1953-1976ff.

Plays by author, A-Z; plot summaries scene by scene. For German see: I, II, VI-IX.

I. *Das deutsche Schauspiel vom Mittelalter bis zum Expressionismus.*
II. *Das deutsche Schauspiel der Gegenwart; Das Schauspiel der romanischen Völker, Teil 1* (Italian, Spanish, Portuguese, French)
III. *Das Schauspiel der romanischen Völker, Teil 2* (Italian, Spanish, French, Belgian, Rumanian); *Das niederländische Schauspiel; Das englische Schauspiel, Teil 1, 2.*
IV. *Das englische Schauspiel, Teil 3. Nordamerika; Das Schauspiel der nordischen Völker* (Denmark, Norway, Sweden, Finland); *Das Schauspiel der slawischen Völker* (Russia, Ukraine).
V. *Das Schauspiel der slawischen Völker* (Poland, Czechoslovakia, Croatia, Dalmatia, Slovenia, Bulgaria, Serbia);

Das Schauspiel Ungarns and Griechenlands, des Nahen und Fernen Ostens (Hungary, Greece, Turkey, Israel, China, Japan); *Die antiken dramatischen Kulturen* (Greece, Rome, India, Peru).

VI. *Nachträge zu Band I-IV* (titles A-Z). *Vergleichender Abriß der dramatischen Weltliteratur. Gesamtregister zu Band I-IV* (indexes: author, title).

VII. *Ergänzungen zu Band I-IV. Das Schauspiel bis 1956.* (All countries by authors)

VIII. *Das Schauspiel der Gegenwart von 1956-1965.* (All countries by authors.)

IX. *Das Schauspiel der Gegenwart von 1966 bis 1970. Der Inhalt der wichtigsten zeitgenössischen Theaterstücke aus aller Welt.* (All countries by authors.)

X. *Das Schauspiel der Gegenwart von 1971 bis 1973. Der Inhalt der wichtigsten zeitgenössischen Theaterstücke aus aller Welt.* (All countries by authors.)

1276. *Kindlers Literatur-Lexikon.* Ed. by Wolfgang von Einsiedel. 8 vols. Zurich: Kindler, 1965-1972, 1974.

I. *Werke, A-Cn.* 1965. xxxii, 2710 cols.
II. *Werke, Co-Fk.* 1966. xxviii, 2974 cols.
III. *Werke, Fl-Jh.* 1967. xxviii, 2894 cols.
IV. *Werke, Ji-Mt.* 1968. xxxi, 1994 cols.
V. *Werke, Mu-Ra.* 1969. xxxi, 3092 cols.
VI. *Werke, Rb-Tz.* 1971. xxxi, 3246 cols.
VII. *Werke, U-Z. Essays. Register.* 1972. xxxv, 1526 cols., and 1098pp.
Ergänzungsband. Werke A-Z. 1974. xxxviii, 1376 cols.

Based on the *Dizionario delle opere di tutti i tempe e di tutte le letterature*, ed. Valentino Bompiani. 20,000 works included. CAUTION: titles listed (A-Z) are those of the first printed edition in the original language. Each entry includes a summary, an appraisal, and a bibliography (editions, translations, selected secondary bibliography, information on adaptations for films, music, drama). All foreign titles are either translated or the established German title is provided. Entries for: literature which has appeared in book form, important humanistic and scientific works, popular literature, complete books of poetry (no individual poems), a selection of correspondences and diaries. *Features* of VII: approximately 100 essays surveying 130 national literatures with general bibliography at the end of each section. Selected bibliography of lexica and compendia of world literature, pp. 701-702. Indexes: authors A-Z, pp. 705-919; anonymous works, works by more than one author, pp. 921-955; German translations, short titles, title variants, pp. 957-1067; proper names, subjects in essays of VII, pp. 1069-1092; illustrations, pp. 1093-1098. This work is excellent; at the present time it is the best of all collections of summaries.

1277. Kluge, Manfred, and Rudolf Radler, eds. *Hauptwerke der deutschen Literatur.* Munich: Kindler, 1974. 626pp.

A reprint of major articles on German literature from *Kindlers Literatur-Lexikon* (above). Organized chronologically in 7 chapters, each subsection by author A-Z, anonyma at the end of each chapter. Index: authors and titles; abbreviations. Work appraisals and summaries are excellent; bibliographies are well selected. There are similar reprints for English, American, and Classical literature.

1278. Olbrich, Wilhelm, and Johannes Beer. *Der Romanführer. Der Inhalt der Romane und Novellen der Weltliteratur.* 15 vols. Stuttgart: Hiersemann, 1950-1971.

Range: 14th to 20th century. All summaries by author A-Z. CAUTION: details not always reliable.

Novels and Novellen written in German:
I, II. Baroque to Naturalism
III, V. 20th century
XIII. 1954-1963 + supplement to I-V; index: German authors

Foreign Authors: Novels and *Novellen* from the beginnings to the 20th century. By author A-Z in each country.

VI. French, Italian, Spanish, Portuguese
VII. English, North American, Flemish, Dutch
VIII. Scandinavian, Slavic, Hungarian, Rumanian

Foreign Authors. 20th century (for most recent works, see XIV):

IX. French, Italian, Spanish, Portuguese
X. English, Flemish, Dutch
XI. North American
XII. Scandinavian, Russian, Polish, Czech, Hungarian, Southeast European
XIV. Foreign novels and *Novellen* between 1956-1965; language areas by author A-Z
XV. Index volume: author indexes: A-Z, language; title indexes: German title A-Z, original title A-Z; index by kind of novel.

1279. Schwitzke, Heinz. *Reclams Hörspielführer.* Stuttgart: Reclam, 1969. 671pp.

Arranged by author A-Z with brief biographies and plot summaries. Includes information on initial broadcast and printed sources. Glossary of terms. Indexes: major primary publications in the field, literary prizes and awards for radio plays, names, titles. Reliable and quite useful.

X.

General and Comparative Literature

CONTENTS

A. DICTIONARIES AND ENCYCLOPEDIAS

1. Glossary

1280. Ruttkowski, Wolfgang V., and R.E. Blake. *Literaturwörterbuch - Glossary of Literary Terms - Glossaire de termes littéraires. In English, German, French with Greek and Latin Derivations of Terms for the Student of General and Comparative Literature.* (Subtitle also in German and French.) Bern, Munich: Francke, 1969. 68pp.

Glossary in German, English, and French. Divided into 5 subject areas with cross references; antonyms, synonyms often cited. No definitions are given. Terms are not always precise equivalents in translation. Excellent for basic items.

2. Encyclopedias

1281. Böing, Günther, ed. *Die Literatur. Wege zum Verständnis der Literatur. Autor, Gattungen, Sprache, Schrift, Buch, Theater.* 2nd ed. Freiburg, Basel, Vienna: Herder, 1973. 711pp. illus.

A lexicon of literature with 10 informative essays on the nature of literature: 1. definitions, 2. kinds of literature (belles-lettres, popular fiction, non-fiction), 3. the author (social history of authors, academies, organizations, prizes), 4. means of expression (media, structural elements, style), 5. genres, 6. themes and motifs, 7. interpreting literature, 8. translation, 9. survey of literature from a comparative point of view, 10. historical descriptions of literary epochs (A-Z). Numerous summaries in table form. A superb presentation.

1282. Best, Otto F. *Handbuch literarischer Fachbegriffe. Definitionen und Beispiele.* Frankfurt: Fischer Taschenbuch, 1972. 318pp.

Definitions for ca. 1,000 technical terms in the areas of stylistics, prosody, grammar, literary history, and genres; each definition is amply illustrated with examples from German literature. Definitions somewhat uneven, but the handbook is excellent for the student of literature.

1283. *Deutsche Philologie im Aufriß*. 2nd rev. ed. Ed. by Wolfgang Stammler. 3 vols. and an index. Berlin: Schmidt, 1957-1962. (^{1}1952-1957)

I. 1957. xvi, 2000 cols.
II. 1960. xii, 2624 cols.
III. 1962. xvi, 3050 cols.
Register zu Band I bis III. Maria-Lioba Lechner, Lydia Tschakert, Theresia Zimmer, eds. 1969. viii, 228pp.

A collection of 86 extensive articles on various aspects of German studies. Most of the essays are of superb quality and represent the most recent scholarship. The compendium is divided into 5 parts: 1. methodology, 2. the history of the German language and its dialects, 3. German literary history by genre, German literary relations, German literature and the other arts, contributions by German authors, 4. cultural history and the history of religion, 5. folklore. Each of the articles is clearly divided into compact, smaller subdivisions to facilitate its use as a reference work. Sections contain comprehensive selected bibliographies. Index volume lists names and anonyma A-Z. This is one of the most authoritative and useful encyclopedias of German studies.

1284. Fleischmann, Wolfgang Bernard. *Encyclopedia of World Literature in the 20th Century in Three Volumes. An Enlarged and Updated Edition of the Herder Lexikon der Weltliteratur im 20. Jahrhundert*. New York: Ungar, 1967-1971.

I. *A-F*. xxiv, 425pp.
II. *G-N*. xxiv, 469pp.
III. *O-Z*. xxvii, 591pp.
IV. *Supplement and Index*. Frederick Ungar, Lina Mainiero, eds. 1975. xvii, 462pp.

Range: 1900-1970's. Listing A-Z of authors, subjects such as national literatures, literary genres, movements, schools of criticism, literary terminology, etc. Author listings include biographical data, primary and secondary bibliographies. Articles on German literature are not translations from Herder but written by eminent scholars in the US. Information succinct and reliable. IV includes additional authors and new subject categories, e.g. science fiction. Contains index for I-IV.

1285. Friedrich, Wolf-Hartmut, and Walter Killy, eds. *Literatur 1. Das Fischer Lexikon*. Frankfurt: Fischer Bücherei, 1964. 341pp.

Range: Antiquity to the 20th century. 22 chronological sketches of national and regional literatures, including Greek, Roman, Medieval Latin literature. Important works and authors mentioned. Entries very brief. Index; bibliography, pp. 310-321. Integrated with:

1286. ———, *Literatur 2. Das Fischer Lexikon*. 2 vols. Frankfurt: Fischer Bücherei, 1965. 718pp.

47 extensive articles on literary terminology: styles, epochs, genres, methodology, aesthetics, etc. Sections include definitions and a historical survey. International in scope. Designed for use with *Literatur 1. Das Fischer Lexikon.* Index for I and II. Bibliography, pp. 640-670.

1287. Garland, Henry and Mary. *The Oxford Companion to German Literature.* Oxford: Clarendon Pr., 1976. vii, 977pp.

Range: 800 to the 1970's. A lexicon containing a wide variety of entries: authors (including some minor authors), genres, forms, techniques, first lines, titles, characters, historical personages, historical events, etc. Copious cross-references provided. A handy reference aid of excellent quality for both the general reader and the beginning student of German literature and history.

1288. Kohlschmidt, Werner, and Wolfgang Mohr, eds. *Reallexikon der deutschen Literaturgeschichte.* 2nd rev. ed. Berlin, New York: de Gruyter, 1958ff.

I. *A-K.* 1958. xvi, 915pp.
II. *L-O.* 1965. 874pp.
III. *P-Sk.* 1977. 873pp.
IV. 1977ff. (fascicles being published)

Differences from the 1st ed. (No. 1292): material has been completely reworked and updated; the number of articles on theater and stagecraft and of small entries has been reduced. Best available encyclopedia on German literature, with coverage of terminology, forms, techniques, types, genres, epochs, national literatures, etc. Each entry is well structured with definitions, historical survey, and well chosen primary and secondary bibliography. Indispensable to both beginner and specialist.

1289. Krahl, Siegfried, and Josef Kurz. *Kleines Wörterbuch der Stilkunde.* 2nd ed. Leipzig: Bibliographisches Institut, 1973. 141pp. (^{1}1970)

Lexicon of stylistics A-Z. Items presented in a clear and simple manner. The large number of cross references is somewhat cumbersome.

1290. Krywalski, Diether, ed. *Handlexikon zur Literaturwissenschaft.* Munich: Ehrenwirt, 1974. 544pp.

Articles on major terminology, literary history, genres. Literature of the Third Reich and contemporary literature largely neglected. Index: authors. Short bibliographies at the end of each article. General quality very high, definitions reliable.

1291. *Lexikon der Weltliteratur im 20. Jahrhundert.* 3rd ed. 2 vols. Freiburg, Basel, Vienna: Herder, 1965-1966. I, A-J. 1096 cols.; II, K-Z. 1326 cols. + 24pp. indexes.

Range: 1900-1960. Approximately 1900 articles on authors, literary concepts, articles on national literatures A-Z. Individual entries contain primary/secondary bibliography;

for major authors critical appraisals are included. Indexes: names, contributors, subjects, national literatures. A reliable reference work.

1292. Merker, Paul, and Wolfgang Stammler, eds. *Reallexikon der deutschen Literaturgeschichte*. 4 vols. Berlin: de Gruyter, 1926-1931.

I. *Abenteuerroman-Hyperbel*. 1926. xii, 593pp.
II. *Jambus-Quatrain*. 1928. 754pp.
III. *Rahmenerzählung-Zwischenakt*. 1929. 225pp.
IV. *Nachträge. Auslanddeutsches Schrifttum-Trunkenheitsliteratur. Register*. 1931. 216pp.

I-III contain some 800 articles, IV: indexes: personal names and titles of anonyma; subject; author. Work is methodologically outdated; factually, however, still one of the best reference works where it is not superseded by the 2nd ed. (No. 1288)

1293. *Meyers Handbuch über die Literatur*. Fachredaktion des Bibliographischen Instituts, ed. Mannheim: Bibliographisches Institut, 1964. 959pp. + 17pp. illus. (^{2}1970)

Range: world literature B.C. to the 1960's. Material divided into 3 pts.: 1. specialized terminology, national literatures, etc., pp. 13-130; 2. authors A-Z, biography and select bibliography, pp. 131-885; 3. outlines and tables: national literatures, Nobel prizes, well known novels about artists, historical novels, German libraries, publishing statistics, etc. Intended for the interested layman.

1294. Müller, Udo, ed. *Herder-Lexikon der Literatur. Sachwörterbuch*. 3rd ed. Freiburg, Basel, Vienna: Herder, 1976. 237pp. (^{1}1974)

Lists ca. 2300 items, A-Z, including genres, structural elements, styles, periods. Definitions often too brief. No secondary literature cited. Many tables and text samples in addition to material presented in the margins. A handy volume but too rudimentary to be of lasting value.

1295. Pongs, Hermann. *Das kleine Lexikon der Weltliteratur*. 6th enl. ed. Stuttgart: Union, 1967. 1986 cols. (^{1}1954)

Range: B.C. to 1950's. Listing, A-Z, of authors, titles, characters, literary epochs; entries provide summaries, biographies, brief interpretations, bibliographical information. Of limited usefulness.

1296. Rüdiger, Horst, and Erwin Koppen, eds. *Kleines literarisches Lexikon*. 4th rev. ed. 3 vols. in 4 pts. Bern, Munich: Francke, 1966 (III), 1969 (I, II) (^{1}1947 ed. Wolfgang Kayser)

I. *Autoren. Von den Anfängen bis zum 19. Jahrhundert*. 840pp. Includes authors born before 1863.
II. *Autoren II. 20. Jahrhundert. Erster Teil: A-K*. 449pp. *Autoren II. 20. Jahrhundert. Zweiter Teil: L-Z*. 550pp. Includes authors born 1864ff. I-II list authors, A-Z,

from world literature and provide biographical data, editions, and translations into German. Appendix: author list by national literature; anthologies of foreign literatures in German for I, II, pp. 463-550.

III. *Sachbegriffe.* 458pp. A lexicon of literary terminology for world literature, including brief references to secondary literature. Quite useful.

1297. Wilpert, Gero von. *Sachwörterbuch der Literatur.* 5th rev. and enl. ed. Stuttgart: Kröner, 1969. viii, 865pp. ([1]1955)

Lists some 4,200 items, A-Z, including genres, structural elements, styles, periods, terms from prosody and rhetoric. For each entry as appropriate: etymology, definition, historical sketch, brief examples, cross references, brief bibliography. Information extremely reliable, takes recent research into account. Easy to use; an indispensable tool for quick reference or orientation.

B. COMPARATIVE LITERATURE

1. Bibliographies

a. Completed Bibliographies

1298. Baldensperger, Fernand, and Werner P. Friedrich. *Bibliography of Comparative Literature.* Chapel Hill: Univ. of N. Carolina Pr., 1950. xxiv, 701pp. ([2]1966)

Ca. 33,000 books and articles listed in 4 sections: 1. "Generalities, Intermediaries, Thematology, Literary Genres"; 2. "The Orient, Antiquity (Greece and Rome), Judaism, Early Christianity, Mohammedanism and Their Contributions"; 3. "Aspects of Western Culture: Modern Christianity, Literary Currents, International Literary Relations, Collective Influences upon Continents, Nations, and Individuals"; 4. "The Modern World." Chapters differ in organization; easiest access is through table of contents. Includes themes and motifs, pp. 70-177. This bibliography continued by:

**** *Yearbook of Comparative and General Literature* (No. 1614): see section "Bibliography of Comparative Literature" 1 (1952)-9 (1960), then "Annual Bibliography" 10 (1961)-19 (1970). Continued by No. 125.

**** *Bibliographisches Handbuch der deutschen Literaturwissenschaft 1945-1969.* (No. 123) I: see section III. "Allgemeine Literaturgeschichte. D. Vergleichende Literaturgeschichte."

b. Current Bibliographies

**** *Bibliographie der deutschen Sprach- und Literaturwissenschaft* (No. 129): see section III. "Allgemeine Literaturgeschichte (Weltliteratur/Vergleichende Literaturgeschichte)." 1 (1945-1953)-16 (1976)ff. Most reliable and comprehensive current bibliography available. Editions and secondary literature. Publ. annually.

**** *Germanistik* (No. 130): see section XVIII. "Vergleichende Literaturwissenschaft," 2 (1961)-17 (1976)ff. Comprehensive quarterly, generally up to date. Lists editions and secondary material. Books are reviewed.

**** *MLA International Bibliography* (No. 125) I: see section "General Literature and Related Topics. 3. Literature, General and Comparative." 1953ff.

**** *Referatendienst zur Literaturgeschichte* (No. 131): see section "Allgemeine und vergleichende Literaturgeschichte. Perioden, Autoren." 1 (1969)-6 (1976)ff. Marxist-socialist quarterly review of books. Limited in scope.

2. Introduction, Theory, and Methodology

1299. Eppelsheimer, Hanns W. *Handbuch der Weltliteratur von den Anfängen bis zur Gegenwart*. 3rd rev. ed. Frankfurt: Klostermann, 1960. xiv, 808pp. ([1]1937)

Range: beginnings to World War I. Compact chapters on world literature including Oriental, Indian, Ancient, Eastern, Islamic, with an emphasis on the literature of Classical Antiquity and the West. Intellectual-historical orientation. Entries on individual authors contain brief biographical sketch and analysis of contributions to world literature with primary and secondary bibliography. German section especially useful for its extensive bibliography on material from 1910-1930. Appendix 1: bibliography of literary history of individual nations. Appendix 2: synchronic bibliography of forms, genres, themes, and motifs.

1300. Fügen, Hans Norbert, ed. *Vergleichende Literaturwissenschaft*. Düsseldorf, Vienna, Econ, 1973. 272pp.

A collection of previously published essays assessing the state of comparative literature studies: 3 essays on the history of comparative literature study, 3 essays each on French and US comp. lit. studies, 4 on Marxist comp. lit. studies, 2 on structuralism, 2 on psychological and sociological aspects. Index: names. Affords a good overview.

1301. McCormick, John O., ed. *A Syllabus of Comparative Literature*. Compiled by the Faculty of Comparative Literature, Rutgers Univ. Metuchen, N.J.: Scarecrow, [2]1972. xiii, 220pp. ([1]1964)

Range: Antiquity to ca. 1928. A basic reading list for students of comparative literature, organized by epochs: Antiquity, Medieval literature, Renaissance, etc. listing primary works with some secondary and background material at end of each section. Appendix A: Introduction to Indian, Japanese, Chinese Literature; Appendix B: Primitive and Archaic Literatures.

1302. Rüdiger, Horst, ed. *Komparatistik. Aufgaben und Methoden.* Stuttgart, Berlin, Cologne, Mainz: Kohlhammer, 1973. 165pp.

A collection of 9 previously published essays on the theory, methodology, and problems of comparative literature by some of the outstanding specialists past and present, including Remak, Baldensperger, Croce, Wellek, Rüdiger, Weisstein. Critical, annotated bibliography, pp. 32-54, excellent and very useful.

1303. Stallknecht, Newton P., and Horst Frenz. *Comparative Literature. Method and Perspective.* Carbondale, Ill.: Southern Illinois Univ. Pr., 1961. xii, 317pp.

12 essays by eminent scholars on the nature and methodology of comparative literature. Many chapters contain helpful selected bibliography. Survey chapters provide an excellent introduction.

1304. Wais, Kurt, ed. *Forschungsprobleme der vergleichenden Literaturgeschichte. Internationale Beiträge zur Tübinger Literaturhistoriker-Tagung September 1950.* Tübingen: Niemeyer, 1951. 188pp. *2. Folge.* 1958; 199pp.

Essays on the problem of literary relationships. Surveys of research in Great Britain and the US, general methodology. *2. Folge* updates research.

1305. Weisstein, Ulrich. *Einführung in die vergleichende Literaturwissenschaft.* Stuttgart: Kohlhammer, 1968. viii, 256pp. English ed.: *Comparative and Literary Theory. Survey and Introduction.* Trans. by William Riggan. Bloomington, Ind., London: Indiana Univ. Pr., 1973. xii, 339pp.

An excellent straightforward introduction to comparative literature covering a wide range of basic questions and problems: definition, influence and imitation, reception and survival, epoch, period, generation and literary movement, genre, thematology, interrelationship of the arts, bibliographical problems.

1306. Wilpert, Gero von, and Ivar Ivask, eds. *Moderne Weltliteratur. Die Gegenwartsliteraturen Europas und Amerikas.* Stuttgart: Kröner, 1972. xvi, 902pp.

Range: post-1945. Succinct surveys of 29 national literatures: French, Spanish, Catalan, Portuguese, Latin American, Italian, Rumanian, British, US, Canadian, Icelandic, Norwegian, Swedish, Danish, German, Dutch, Russian, Ukranian, Polish, Czechoslovakian, Yugoslavian, Bulgarian, Finnish, Hungarian, Estonian,

Lettish, Lithuanian, Yiddish, Modern Greek. Short bibliography with each section. Index: authors. Good overview.

C. THEMES, MOTIFS, TOPOI

1. Bibliographies

a. Completed Bibliographies

i. General

**** Baldensperger, Ferdinand, and Werner P. Friedrich. *Bibliography of Comparative Literature* (No. 1298), Chapter 6, pp. 70-177.

**** *Bibliographisches Handbuch der deutschen Literaturwissenschaft 1945-1969* (No. 123), I: see section IV. "Deutsche Literaturgeschichte. Allgemein. E. Stoffe, Motive, Themen, Gestalten, Topoi." A selected cumulation of (No. 129) to 1969.

1307. Thompson, Stith, ed. *Motif-Index to Folk Literature. A Classification of Narrative Elements in Folktales, Ballads, Myths, Fables, Medieval Romances, Examples, Fabliaux, Jest-Books, and Local Legends*. 6 vols. 2nd ed. Bloomington: Indiana Univ. Pr., 1955-1958. ([1]1932-1936)

I. *A-C*. 1955. 554pp.
II. *D-E*. 1956. 517pp.
III. *F-H*. 1956. 519pp.
IV. *I-K*. 1957. 499pp.
V. *L-Z*. 1957. 567pp.
VI. *Index*. 1958. 892pp.

Standard motif index for folklore studies, culled from ca. 600 sources. Organized according to subject categories. For easiest access start with index volume. Copious cross references.

**** *Yearbook of Comparative and General Literature* (No. 1614): see section "Bibliography of Comparative Literature. VI. Literary Themes"; 1960-1970, see: "Annual Bibliography. III. Themes, Motifs, and Topoi." Continued by No. 125.

ii. German Literature

1308. Bauernhorst, Kurt. *Bibliographie der Stoff-und Motivgeschichte der deutschen Literatur*. Berlin, Leipzig: de Gruyter, 1932. xvi, 118pp.

Range: antiquity to 1930's. Organized by broad subjects such as history, church history, intellectual history, myth and legend, saga, fairy tale, fable, the supernatural, human life, world literature, miscellaneous. Difficult to use but has excellent author and subject indexes.

1309. Luther, Arthur. *Deutsches Land in deutscher Erzählung. Ein literarisches Ortslexikon*. Leipzig: Hiersemann, 1936. 892 cols.

Range: ca. 1800-1930's. Bibliography of German, Austrian, Swiss place names appearing in regional prose literature. Region, town, etc. A-Z. Systematic geographical and author indexes facilitate access.

1310. ———. *Deutsche Geschichte in deutscher Erzählung. Ein literarisches Lexikon*. 2nd rev. ed. Leipzig: Hiersemann, 1943. xi, 494 cols.

Range: Beginnings to ca. 1900. Bibliography divided according to historical epochs: "Alte Zeit," "Mittelalter," "Zeit der Glaubenskämpfe," "Barock und Rokoko," "Neuzeit," "Gesammelte Erzählungen," "Familien- und Sippengeschichte." Lists historical personages and events in prose literature. Indexes: author, subject.

1311. ——— and Heinz Friesenhalm. *Land und Leute in deutscher Erzählung. Ein bibliographisches Literaturlexikon*. 3rd completely rev. ed. of No. 1309 and No. 1310. Stuttgart: Hiersemann, 1954. v, 556 cols.

Supplements No. 1309 with titles after 1937 and No. 1310 with titles after 1943. Pt. II: cols. 1-364, place names A-Z. Approximately 430 places and 8000 titles. All references in No. 1309 to places with population less than 20,000 omitted. Pt. II: cols. 365-498, 2,700 historical personages, approximately 2,200 titles of biographical novels and tales A-Z. Memoirs, autobiographies, etc. not included. Historical events listed in No. 1310 omitted. Bibliography very reliable.

1312. Schmitt, Franz Anselm. *Beruf und Arbeit in deutscher Erzählung. Ein literarisches Lexikon*. Stuttgart: Hiersemann, 1952. xvi, 668 cols.

A-Z listing by occupation. Particularly thorough for 18th and 19th century. Anti-social occupations not included. Composers listed but sparse mention of poets. Indexes: author, occupations.

1313. ———. *Stoff- und Motivgeschichte der deutschen Literatur. Eine Bibliographie begründet von Kurt Bauernhorst*. 2nd completely rev. ed. Berlin: de Gruyter, 1965. xi, 332pp. (^{1}1958)

Includes 4,982 titles and 1,242 themes and motifs in alphabetical order. Organization by subject. Does not include themes and motifs of folklore, nor themes and motifs of a single author. Includes themes and motifs in the work of more than two poets or of a literary epoch. Indexes: author, subject; appendix, pp. 313-332.

1314. ———. *Stoff- und Motivgeschichte der deutschen Literatur. Eine Bibliographie*. 3rd rev. ed. Berlin, New York: de Gruyter, 1976. xiv, 437pp.

Supplements earlier editions with publications 1964-1975. Lists 8,044 titles in 1,544 subject categories A-Z. Indexes: subject categories, authors. Bibliography and sources, pp. 1-4. Lists only secondary material. Excellent and reliable resource book.

b. Current Bibliographies

**** *Bibliographie der deutschen Sprach- und Literaturwissenschaft* (No. 129): see section VIII, "Deutsche Literaturgeschichte. Stoff- und Motivgeschichte/Themen." 1 (1945-1953)-15 (1975)ff. Most reliable and comprehensive bibliography available. Editions and secondary literature. Publ. annually.

**** *Germanistik* (No. 130): see section XVII, "Allgemeines zur Literaturwissenschaft. Bilder und Figuren. Stoffe und Motive." 1 (1960)-17 (1976)ff. Comprehensive quarterly, generally up to date. Lists editions and secondary material. Books are reviewed.

**** *MLA International Bibliography* (No. 125). I: see section "General Literature and Related Topics. 4. Themes and Types." 1957ff. II: see section "German Literature. 2. Themes, Types, and Special Topics." 1969ff.

2. Introduction, Theory, and Methodology

1315. Baeumer, Max, ed. *Toposforschung.* Darmstadt: Wissenschaftliche Buchgesellschaft, 1973. xvii, 365pp.

8 articles published 1938-1972 on theory, methodology, and interpretation. Index: authors. Bibliography, pp. 349-353. Articles which are shortened in Peter Jehn (No. 1320) appear here in their entirety.

1316. Daemmrich, Horst and Ingrid. *Wiederholte Spiegelungen. Themen und Motive in der Literatur.* Bern, Munich: Francke, 1978. 253pp.

An incisive survey of research on motif study, definitions of theme, motif, image, etc. Examination of the theme "journey of life" in European literature. An excellent introduction to the study of themes and motifs.

1317. Frenzel, Elisabeth. *Stoffe der Weltliteratur. Ein Lexikon dichtungsgeschichtlicher Längsschnitte.* 3rd rev. ed. Stuttgart: Kröner, 1970. xvi, 785pp. ([1]1962)

Range: to 1969. Ca. 300 themes and motifs A-Z; literary treatment listed with select secondary bibliography. Material from sagas and fairy tales not included. Useful source book.

1318. ———. *Stoff-, Motiv- und Symbolforschung.* 2nd rev. ed. Stuttgart: Metzler, 1966. vii, 115pp. ([1]1963)

Resource book: critical examination of research, definitions, directions for future research. Index: names and subjects. Bibliography at the end of each section. Quite handy and useful.

1319. ———. *Stoff- und Motivgeschichte.* Berlin: Schmidt, 1966. 172pp.

A basic introduction to methods and research in the field; includes definitions, historical, critical survey of research. Notes, pp. 159-172. A compact study.

1320. Jehn, Peter. *Toposforschung. Eine Dokumentation.* Frankfurt: Athenäum, 1972. lxiv, 348pp.

A collection of 17 articles, published 1938-1971, on theory and methodology, and interpretations, published 1952-1972. Extensive international bibliography to 1969, pp. 320-348. Caution: some of the articles have been shortened.

1321. Petersen, Julius. "Das Motiv in der Dichtung." *Dichtung und Volkstum* 38 (1937), 44-65.

1322. Petsch, Robert. "Motiv, Formel und Stoff." In: R.P., *Deutsche Literaturwissenschaft. Aufsätze zur Begründung der Methode.* Berlin: Ebering, 1940, pp. 129-150.

1323. Veit, Walter. "Toposforschung. Ein Forschungsbericht." *DVLG* 37 (1963), 120-163.

D. METAPHOR AND SYMBOL

1. Forschungsbericht

1324. Pausch, Holger A. "Forschungsbericht. Die Metapher." *Wirkendes Wort* 24 (1974), 56-69.

2. Bibliographies

1325. Lurker, Manfred, ed. *Bibliographie zur Symbolik, Ikonographie und Mythologie.* Baden-Baden: Koerner, 1974. 198pp.

Brief introduction by August Closs on the use of the term symbol in literary criticism. Review of 562 books, articles, manuals, dissertations, reprints, handbooks from 1960 to the present. Little material specifically on German literature. Useful for the comparatist. Indexes: proper names, subject.

1326. Shibles, Warren A. *Metaphor. An Annotated Bibliography and History.* Whitewater, Wisc.: The Language Pr., 1971. xvi, 414pp.

Extensive listings for 19th and 20th centuries by author A-Z with thorough analysis of major works. Includes articles, books, dissertations, chapters in books. 1. Extensive works on metaphor, pp. 319-320; 2. general terms and names, pp. 321-369; 3. key-word index, pp. 371-414. Good reference tool for comparative literature; copious German references. Organization somewhat diffuse--easiest access is through the key-word index, which thoroughly analyses the material.

XI.
Literature in Translation and Literary Relations

CONTENTS

A. LITERATURE IN TRANSLATION

1. Bibliographies

a. General Bibliographies

1327. Holtermann, Horst. "Die künstlerische Übersetzung." *Die Literatur* (No. 1281), pp. 445-460.

1328. Olmstead, Hugh M. *Translations and Translating. A Selected Bibliography of Bibliographies, Indexes, and Guides. Preliminary version.* Binghamton: State Univ. of New York, Center for Translation, 1975. 54pp.

1329. Van Hoof, Henry. *Internationale Bibliographie der Übersetzungen. International Bibliography of Translation.* Munich-Pullach: Dokumentation, 1973. xvi, 591pp.

A listing of ca. 4,600 items (1950-1971), designed for the professional translator or student interested in written translation. Pt. 1: bibliographies of translation, theory of translation, translator training (manuals, methodology, institutes), the profession (organizations, conventions, prizes), typology of translation. Pt. 2: organizations, study and research centers. Pt. 3: publications, journals, bibliographies, etc. Listings by author A-Z where appropriate. Index: periodicals, pp. 573-591; authors, pp. 544-572.

b. Translations from German to English

i. Completed Bibliographies

1330. Mönnig, Richard, ed. *Translations from the German. English 1948-1964.* 2nd rev. ed. Göttingen: Vandenhoeck & Ruprecht, 1968. v, 509pp. ([1]1957 for the years 1948-1955)

This bibliography embraces a wide field of knowledge (including sciences), listing 8,304 English translations, 3,513 books on Germany written in English, 114 journals. Author index. Complete bibliographical listings for literature and language, textbooks, grammars, dictionaries, prose and fiction, foreign fiction in Germany. Easy to use.

1331. Morgan, Bayard Quincy. *A Critical Bibliography of German Literature in English Translation, 1481-1927.* 2nd rev. ed. New York, London: Scarecrow, 1965. 690pp. ([1]1922, 2nd rev. ed. 1938 with *Supplement Embracing the Years 1928-1935*)

Alphabetical list by author of German humane letters (literature, travelogues, history, etc.) in English translation: 10,797 titles. Lists of anonymous items and anthologized works included; index of translators. Very readily accessible; for explanation of symbols designating evaluation, see foreword.

**** *Yearbook of Comparative and General Literature* 24 (1975), 108-111. "Bibliography of Translations in Periodicals and Magazines." List of translations, excluding poetry, which appeared up to and including 1970 in 31 journals. Much German material cited.

1332. Morgan, Bayard Quincy. *A Critical Bibliography of German Literature in Translation: Supplement Embracing the Years 1928-1955.* New York, London: Scarecrow, 1965. vii, 601pp.

List by author A-Z of German belles-lettres and popular scientific material (ca. 9000 titles) in translation. List of anonymous items, anthologized works (including hymns and songs). No index of translators, no evaluations. Very readily accessible.

1333. Smith, Murray F. *A Selected Bibliography of German Literature in English Translation, 1956-1960: A Second Supplement to Bayard Quincy Morgan's A Critical Bibliography of German Literature in English Translation.* Metuchen, N.J: Scarecrow, 1972. v, 398pp.

Titles, listed by author A-Z, include anonyma, collections, societies, and institutions. Covers arts and sciences. Readily accessible.

ii. Current Bibliographies

1334. *Babel*: see section "Bibliographie internationale de la traduction," 1 (1955)-16 (1970), continued as "International Bibliography on Translation and Applied Linguistics," 17 (1971)-20 (1974); scope limited to contain only a bibliography of translation with lexicographical information: 21 (1975)ff.

**** *Books in Print. An Author-Title-Series Index to the Publishers' Trade List Annual, 1948ff.* New York: Bowker, 1948ff. Annual publ. Since 1966 author and title indexes in different vols. (No. 71)

**** *Subject Guide to Books in Print. An Index to the Publishers' Trade List Annual, 1957ff.* New York: Bowker, 1957ff. Annual publ. (No. 73)

As a companion to the above:

**** *Forthcoming Books, Now Including New Books in Print. A Forecast of Books to Come, 1966ff.* New York: Bowker, 1966ff. vol. 1ff. publ. bimonthly (No. 74).

**** *Subject Guide to Forthcoming Books, 1967ff.* New York: Bowker, 1967ff. vol. 1ff. publ. bimonthly (No. 75).

1335. *Chartotheca alphabetica translationum. International Bibliography of Translations.* Hans Willi Bentz, ed. Frankfurt, Bad Homburg: Bentz, 1962ff.

Titles by author A-Z, anthologies, organizations, etc. Titles of translations from foreign language into German and German into selected foreign languages. Entries not consistently reliable. Listings more selective but more current (monthly card service) than:

1336. *Index Translationum. Repertoire internationale des traductions.* Paris: International Institute of Intellectual Cooperation, 1932-1940, nos. 1-31. NS. Paris: UNESCO, 1949ff. Vol. 1ff. 1931-1939 publ. quarterly; 1948ff. publ. annually.

Entries arranged by country and subdivided by subject. Individual listings by author A-Z. Indexes: author, publisher, translator; statistics on translations. Section 8: Literature includes secondary material and children's literature. Use author index for locating individual publications.

**** *Paperbound Books in Print.* New York: Bowker, 1955ff. Semi-annual; contains separate title, author, subject indexes (No. 72).

**** *Yearbook of Comparative and General Literature*: see section "List of Translations: 1960ff." 10 (1961)ff.

Comprehensive, up-to-date bibliographies of translations published in the US. Primarily belles-lettres and important critical works. Organized by country.

2. General Studies of German Literature in English Translation

See also Section B.
German-American and German-English Literary Relations.

1337. Bauland, Peter. *The Hooded Eagle. Modern German Drama on the New York Stage.* Syracuse, New York: Syracuse Univ. Pr., 1968. ix, 299pp.

Critical history of German drama in translation or adapted for the New York stage. Contains important insights into the reception of German plays in the US. Appendix: German plays on the New York stage between 1894-1965. Index: author, subject. Bibliography.

1338. Davis, Edward Ziegler. *Translations of German Poetry in American Magazines 1714-1810. Together with Translations of Other Teutonic Poetry and Original Poems Referring to the*

German Countries. Philadelphia: Americana Germanica, 1905. viii, 229pp. (Repr. 1966)

Listed chronologically: Ch. 1: German poetry (translation included for most entries); Ch. 2: Dutch, Danish, Norwegian, Icelandic (also with translations). Poems and authors are best located through index.

1339. Davis, Garold N. *German Thought and Culture in England 1700-1770. A Preliminary Survey. Including a Chronological Bibliography of German Literature in English Translation.* Chapel Hill: North Carolina Univ. Pr., 1969. 143pp.

A compact survey. Primary bibliography, pp. 115-133; secondary bibliography, pp. 134-139.

1340. Goodnight, Scott Holland. *German Literature in American Magazines Prior to 1846*. Madison: Univ. of Wisconsin Pr., 1907. i, 264pp.

Comprehensive description of German authors and their reception in the US, influence, translations, etc. Appendix A: chronological list of translations (esp. 1800-1846) including reviews of translations. Appendix B: list of German authors from all periods mentioned in magazines. Table: German titles in translation in the US.

1341. Hathaway, Lillie V. *German Literature of the Mid-Nineteenth Century in England and America as Reflected in the Journals 1840-1914*. Boston: Chapman & Grimes. 1935. 341pp.

Discussion of the reception of German poetry, prose, drama in the US and England, based on reviews and journal articles. Appendix A (England) and B (America): chronological list of translations and reviews; Appendix C: index of German authors. Individual titles of translations difficult to locate.

1342. Kopp, La Marr W. *German Literature in the United States 1945-1960*. Chapel Hill: Univ. of N. Carolina Pr., 1967. 230pp.

A comprehensive discussion of the reception of German literature in the US by period: Middle High German period to the beginnings of the Classical period; Goethe, Schiller, the 19th century, the 20th century. Contains "Title List of German Literature in English Translation in the United States 1945-1960." A-Z. Selected bibliography for the reception of German literature in the US.

1343. Morgan, Bayard Quincy, and A.R. Hohlfeld (eds.). *German Literature in British Magazines 1750-1860*; by Walter Roloff for 1750-1810, Morton E. Mix for 1811-1835, and Martha Nicolai for 1836-1860. Madison: Univ. of Wisconsin Pr., 1949. v, 364pp.

An extensive historical introduction surveying Anglo-German literary relationships as reflected in 164 English magazines. Chronological list of references (translations, reviews, etc.) and author index.

1344. Stockley, Violet. *German Literature as Known in England 1750-1830*. London: Rutledge, 1929. xiv, 339pp.

Comprehensive description of the reception of German works in England listed according to author and genre with data about translators. Appendix A: alphabetical list of works; Appendix B: chronological list of translations; Appendix C: bibliography of literary relationships.

3. Anthologies of German Literature in English Translation

a. *Reviews of Recent Translations*

1345. "Reviews of Recent Translations." *Yearbook of Comparative and General Literature* 1 (1952)ff.

1346. Weisstein, Ulrich. "Recent Translations of 20th Century German Poetry and Drama. A Collective Review." *German Quarterly* 37 (1964), 516-526. Covers 1945-1964.

1347. Krumpelmann, John T. "Classical German Drama in Recent English Translation. A Collective Review." *German Quarterly* 39 (1966), 77-91. 40 drama translations reviewed.

b. *General*

1348. Francke, Kuno, ed. *The German Classics of the Nineteenth and Twentieth Centuries. Masterpieces of German Literature. Trans. into English.* 20 vols. New York: The German Publication Society, 1913-1914. The most extensive collection of German prose, poetry, and drama in translation available.

c. *Drama*

1349. Benedikt, Michael, and George Wellwarth, eds. and trans. *Postwar German Theater. An Anthology of Plays.* New York: Dutton, 1967. xxvii, 348pp.

Range: 1943-1962. Introductory essay followed by avantgarde plays by Kaiser, Sylvanus, Dürrenmatt, Frisch, Dorst, Laszlo (2), Grass, Hildesheimer, Weiss, Borchert.

1350. Corrigan, Robert, ed. *Masterpieces of the Modern German Theater.* New York: Macmillan, 1967. 416pp.

Plays by Büchner, Hebbel, Hauptmann, Wedekind, Brecht. Short introduction and explicatory excerpts from other writings or commentary by the authors. Bibliography.

1351. Esslin, Martin. *The Genius of German Theater.* New York: New American Library, 1968. 640pp.

Pt. 1: 7 plays, each preceded by an incisive introduction:

Lessing, Goethe, Schiller, Kleist, Büchner, Wedekind, Brecht; pt. 2: essays on drama by Lessing, Schiller, Goethe, Hebbel, and Esslin (on Brecht). Bibliography.

1352. Ritchie, J.M., and H.F. Garten, trans. *Seven Expressionist Plays: Kokoschka to Barlach*. London: Calder and Boyars, 1968. 201pp.

Introduction, pp. 7-22; plays by Kokoschka, Stramm, Kafka, Kaiser, Goll, Brust, Barlach. Does not duplicate No. 1356 (*German Drama between the Wars*).

1353. ——— and J.D. Stowell, trans. *Vision and Aftermath. Four Expressionist War Plays*. London: Calder and Boyars, 1969. 208pp.

Introduction, pp. 7-20. Plays by C. Hauptmann, Goering, Hasenclever, Toller.

1354. Roloff, Michael, ed. *Contemporary German Theater*. New York: Avon, 1972. 379pp.

Brief introduction. 5 plays: Frisch, Walser, Weiss, Sperr, Handke.

1355. Sokel, Walter H., ed. *Anthology of German Expressionist Drama. A Prelude to the Absurd*. Garden City, N.Y.: Doubleday, 1963. xxxii, 368pp.

Excellent general introduction followed by pt. 1: important essays by writers of the period, pt. 2: plays by Kokoschka (2), Sorge, Sternheim, Hasenclever, Kaiser, Goll, Lauckner, Brecht.

1356. Wellwarth, George, ed. *German Drama between the Wars. An Anthology of Plays*. New York: Dutton, 1972. xvii, 366pp.

Range: 1917-1936. Plays by Kokoschka, Broch, Tucholsky, Hasenclever, Zuckmayer, Toller, and Kraus (excerpt). The plays included are not commonly available in English translation.

d. Poetry

1357. Bridgewater, Patrick, ed. *Twentieth-Century German Verse. With Plain Prose Translations of Each Poem*. Baltimore: Penguin, 1963. lxxiii, 336pp. A bilingual anthology of 66 poets.

1358. Deutsch, Babette, and Avrahm Yarmolinsky, trans. *Contemporary German Poetry*. New York: Harcourt, Brace and Co., 1923. xxvii, 201pp. An anthology of 32 poets from the early 1900's. Still useful.

1359. Flores, Angel, ed. *An Anthology of German Poetry from Hölderlin to Rilke in English Translation*. Gloucester, Mass.: Smith, 1960. xxii, 458pp.

A presentation of 14 poets with original poems and verse translations. Includes brief introduction to the poets. Bibliography.

1360. Forster, Leonard, ed. *The Penguin Book of German Verse. With Plain Prose Translations of Each Poem.* Harmondsworth: Penguin, 1957. xlii, 466pp.

Range: 800 A.D.-20th century. Most extensive anthology of German poems with English translations available; the translations are intended as an aid to understanding the German text. Index: titles and first lines.

1361. Gode, Alexander, and Frederick Ungar, eds. *Anthology of German Poetry through the 19th Century. In English Translations with German Originals.* 2nd enl. ed. New York: Ungar, 1972. xvi, 270pp. (^{1}1964)

Presents 35 representative poets, 12th to 19th century. Indexes: translators, titles and first lines.

1362. Hamburger, Michael, and Christopher Middleton. *Modern German Poetry 1910-1960. An Anthology with Verse Translations.* London: MacGibbon and Kee, 1962. xliv, 419pp.

An outstanding anthology of 56 German poets. Index: authors.

1363. ———. *East German Poetry. An Anthology.* New York: Dutton, 1973. xxii, 213pp.

Introductory essay on GDR poetry followed by poetry, German originals with English translation: Brecht, Huchel, Bobrowski, Kunert, Kahlau, Kunze, Mickel, Biermann, Bartsch, Braun, Jentzsch, Kirsch.

1364. ———. *German Poetry 1910-1975.* New York: Urizen, 1976. xxxiii, 559pp. Bilingual presentation of 75 poets in verse translations.

Replaces No. 1362 (*Modern German Poetry 1910-1960*). Best anthology of modern German poetry available.

1365. Kaufmann, Walter. *Twenty-five German Poets. A Bilingual Collection.* New York: Norton, 1975. xx, 325pp. (^{1}1962: *Twenty German Poets*)

Introductions to the poets, ranging from the 17th to the 20th century. Verse translations.

1366. Mathieu, Gustave, and Guy Stern, eds. *German Poetry. A Selection from Walther von der Vogelweide to Bertolt Brecht in German with English Translation.* 2nd ed. New York: Dover, 1970. 169pp.

A sampler of 34 poets, represented for the most part with a single poem each. Translations in verse.

1367. Münsterberg, Margarete, trans. *A Harvest of German Verse.* New York, London: Appleton & Co., 1916. xvi, 242pp.

Range: Minnesang-20th century. A selection of poetry in verse translation. Very conservative, includes some obscure poets not readily found elsewhere.

1368. Plotz, Helen, ed. *Poems from the German*. New York: Crowell, 1967. vii, 182pp.

An anthology of representative poems by 34 poets from the late 12th to the 20th century. Verse translations of excellent quality. Designed for younger audience.

1369. Roberts, Helen Kurz, ed., et al. *A Treasury of German Ballads. Bilingual Edition*. New York: Ungar, 1964. 293pp.

German originals with English verse translations: 14 poets from the 18th and 19th centuries.

1370. Rothenburg, Jerome, ed. and trans. *New Young Poets*. San Francisco: City Lights Book, 1959. 63pp.

An anthology of 10 poets from the 1950's.

1371. Salinger, Herman, trans. *Twentieth-Century German Verse*. Princeton: Princeton Univ. Pr., 1952. xxiii, 93pp.

Bilingual anthology: 22 poets.

1372. Sayce, Olive, ed. *Poets of the Minnesang*. Oxford: Oxford Univ. Pr., 1967. xxxv, 318pp.

Range: 1150-1400. An anthology of 26 poets, represented by 169 poems of the period. German text only but accompanied by copious notes in English, including an explanation of metrical forms for each poem, and a glossary for translation. Index: first lines. Bibliography. Designed as a textbook for English-speaking students.

1373. Schoolfield, George C. *The German Lyric of the Baroque in English Translation*. New York: AMS Press, 1961. 380pp.

Introductory survey of 17th-century poetry followed by poems in German and English by some 60 poets (A-Z). Indexes: short biography of poets; poems and sources by author, A-Z. Most comprehensive anthology of Baroque poetry in translation.

1374. Schwebell, Gertrude Clorius. *Contemporary German Poetry. An Anthology. With an Introduction by Victor Lange*. Norfolk, Conn.: New Directions, 1962. xxxix, 186pp.

A bilingual presentation of 39 major and lesser 20th-century poets. Notes.

1375. Thomas, John W. *German Verse from the 12th to the 20th Century in English Translation*. Chapel Hill: Univ. of North Carolina Pr., 1963. 160pp.

1376. ———. *Medieval German Lyric Verse in English Translation*. Chapel Hill: Univ. of N. Carolina Pr., 1968. 251pp.

Range: 12th to 15th centuries. Some 20 poets represented.

Brief surveys of the epoch and its authors are interspersed among the translations. Indexes: authors, first lines.

1377. Watts, Harriett, trans. *Three Painter-Poets. Arp, Schwitters, Klee. Selected Poems.* Baltimore: Penguin, 1974. 160pp.

A brief introduction. 30 poems by Arp, 34 by Schwitters, 39 by Klee. English text only.

e. Prose

1378. Cerf, Bennett A., ed. *Great German Short Novels and Stories.* New York: The Modern Library, 1933. ix, 475pp.

15 pieces by Goethe, Schiller, Hoffmann, J. Grimm, W. Grimm, Heine, Storm, Keller, Sudermann, Schnitzler, G. Hauptmann, Wasserman, T. Mann, S. Zweig, A. Zweig. By various translators; anthology still very valuable.

1379. Engel, Eva J., ed. *German Narrative Prose.* Vol. 1. London: Wolff, 1965. 352pp. Kleist, Arnim, Tieck, Stifter, Grillparzer, Keller, Storm, Holz and Schlaf.

1380. Flores, Angel, ed. *Nineteenth Century German Tales.* New York: Ungar, 1966. vi, 390pp. Jean Paul, Kleist, E.T.A. Hoffmann, Gotthelf, Stifter, Keller, Mörike.

1381. Lamport, Francis John, ed. *The Penguin Book of German Stories.* Baltimore: Penguin, 1974. xi, 347pp.

Anthology of 13 stories by Goethe, Hoffmann, Kleist, Büchner, Storm, Keller, Heyse, G. Hauptmann, Schnitzler, T. Mann, Kafka, Gaiser, Böll.

1382. Middleton, Christopher, compiler. *German Writing Today.* Baltimore: Penguin, 1967. 238pp.

An anthology of short prose and poetry from the years 1950-1965.

1383. Rehfeld, Werner, ed. *German Narrative Prose.* Vol. 3. London: Wolff, 1968. 224pp.

E. Jünger, Johnson, Lenz, Aichinger, Bachmann, Dürrenmatt, Jens, Grass, Böll, Heckmann, Frisch, Richter, M. Walser, Weiss. Includes biographical notes and selected primary bibliography.

1384. Scher, Helene, trans. *Four Romantic Tales from 19th-Century German.* New York: 1975. xxi, 114pp. Tieck, Brentano, Arnim, E.T.A. Hoffmann.

1385. Steinhauer, Harry, trans. *Ten German Novellas.* Garden City, N.Y.: Doubleday, 1969. xxv, 570pp.

Anthology of Wieland, Kleist, Chamisso, Storm, Keller, Meyer, T. Mann, G. Hauptmann, Schnitzler, Bergengruen.

B. GERMAN-AMERICAN AND GERMAN-ENGLISH LITERARY RELATIONS

1. Bibliographies

a. Completed Bibliographies

1386. Galinsky, Hans. *Amerikanisch-deutsche Sprach- und Literaturbeziehungen. Systematische Übersicht und Forschungsbericht 1945-1970.* Frankfurt: Athenäum, 1972. 253pp.

Pt. 1: Anglo-American influences on the development of the German language since 1945, including vocabulary, morphology, syntax; pt. 2: German-American literary relations. Good resource book; clearly organized.

1387. Pochmann, Henry A., Lawrence M. Price, John R. Frey, et al., eds. "Anglo-German Bibliography." *JEGP* 34 (1935)-40 (1941), 45 (1946)-70 (1971).

1388. ———, compiler, and Arthur R. Schultz, ed. *Bibliography of German Culture in America to 1940.* Madison: Wisconsin Univ. Pr., 1953. xxxii, 483pp.

Range: 15th century to 1940. 12,000 listings of German-Americana.

1389. Tolzmann, Don Heinrich. *German-Americans. A Bibliography.* Metuchen, N.J.: Scarecrow, 1975. xi, 348pp.

Range: emphasis on 1941-1973. Lists 5,307 items, including books, pamphlets, records, photograph albums, dissertations, government documents, newspapers and periodical articles. Material grouped according to: immigration, settlement, ethnicity, state histories, politics, language and literature, book trade, religious life, education, customs, folklore, intellectual history, music and theater, business and industry, political radicalism, and biography. Index: authors. Detailed table of contents. Bibliography is also excellent for current activities of German-American communities, with directories of current and recent German-American organizations and a list of German bookstores in the US and German-American schools.

For historical and cultural material:

**** *Bibliographisches Handbuch der deutschen Literaturwissenschaft 1945-1969* (No. 123): see section III. "Allgemeine Literaturgeschichte. D. Vergleichende Literaturgeschichte."

1390. Rosenberg, Ralph P. "American Doctoral Studies in Germanic Cultures. A Study in German-American Relations." *Yearbook of Comparative and General Literature* 4 (1955), 30-44.

**** *Yearbook of Comparative and General Literature* (No. 1614): see sections D. VIII. "English Contributions. Influences upon Individual Countries," D. X. "German Contributions," and XI.

"American Contributions. Influences upon Individual Countries." 1 (1952)-10 (1960). Discontinued in this format.

1391. Zucker, A.E., Dieter Cunz, Felix Reichmann, Arthur R. Schultz, et al., eds. "Bibliography Americana-Germanica." *American German Review* 9 (1942)-33 (1966). Continued by:

1392. Schultz, Arthur R. "Bibliography Americana-Germanica." *German Quarterly* 41 (1968)-44 (1971). Continued by the *MLA International Bibliography* (No. 125).

b. Current Bibliographies

**** *Bibliographie der deutschen Sprach- und Literaturwissenschaft* (No. 129): see section III. "Allgemeine Literaturgeschichte (Weltliteratur/Vergleichende Literaturgeschichte). Einzelne Völkergruppen in literarischen Beziehungen zu Deutschland. Einzelne Völker in literarischer Beziehung zu Deutschland. Fremde Dichter und Schriftsteller in ihren Beziehungen zu Deutschland." 1 (1945-1953)-16 (1976)ff. Most reliable and comprehensive current bibliography available. Editions and secondary literature. Publ. annually.

**** *Germanistik* (No. 130): see section XVIII. "Vergleichende Literaturwissenschaft. Deutsche Literatur und: angelsächsische Literatur." 1 (1960)-17 (1976)ff. Comprehensive quarterly, generally up to date. Lists editions and secondary material. Books are reviewed.

**** *MLA International Bibliography* (No. 125), II: see section "German Literature. 8. Americana Germanica." 1959ff. Continues earlier American bibliographies (No. 1391, No. 1392).

2. General Studies of Literary Relations

1393. Arndt, Karl J.R., amd May E. Olson. *German-American Newspapers and Periodicals 1732-1955. History and Bibliography.* 2nd rev. ed. New York: Johnson Reprint Co., 1965. 811pp. (^{1}1961)

Listing arranged by states with a historical introd. for each state followed by a detailed bibliographical description of each item. Title index, list of libraries and collections, selected bibliography of sources. Addendum: POW newspapers.

1394. Arndt, Karl J., and May E. Olson. *The German-Language Press of the Americas, 1732-1968. History and Bibliography.* Munich-Pullach: Dokumentation, 1973. 709pp. illus.

II: Argentina, Bolivia, Brazil, Canada, Chile, Colombia, Costa Rica, Cuba, Dominican Republic, Ecuador, Guatemala, Guiana, Mexico, Paraguay, Peru, USA (addenda), Uruguay, Venezuela. Format same as 1961 vol. (above) for US. Addenda to I, pp. 337-602, bring extensive updating of material on US.

Bibliography, pp. 613-688; list of libraries and collections, pp. 690-708.

1395. Jantz, Harold. "Amerika im deutschen Dichten und Denken." *Dt. Phil. im Aufriß* (No. 1283), III, 309-372.

1396. Mielke, Gerda, and Horst Oppel. "Englische Literatur (Einfluß auf die deutsche)." *Reallexikon* (No. 1288), I, pp. 353-372.

1397. Oppel, Horst. "Amerikanische Literatur." *Reallexikon* (No. 1288), II, pp. 47-60.

1398. ———. "Der Einfluß der englischen Literatur auf die deutsche." *Dt. Phil. im Aufriß* (No. 1283), III, 201-308.

1399. ———. *Englisch-deutsche Literaturbeziehungen.* 2 vols. Berlin: Schmidt, 1971.

I. *Von den Anfängen bis zum Ausgang des 18. Jahrhunderts.* 142pp.
II. *Von der Romantik bis zur Gegenwart.* 160pp.

Range: 5th century to the 1960's. A chronological survey of the reception of German literature in England and the reception of English literature in Germany. Critical bibliography at the end of each section. Index: author, in each vol. Excellent, compact summary.

1400. Pochmann, Henry A. *German Culture in America. Philosophical and Literary Influences 1600-1900.* Madison: Wisconsin Univ. Pr., 1957. xv, 865pp.

For literary relations see: "Book Two. German Literary Influence," pp. 327-492. Focus is on the 19th century and its major figures including Irving, Hawthorne, Poe, Longfellow, Thoreau, Melville, Whitman. Indexes: author, title, subject. Excellent introduction.

1401. Price, Lawrence Marsden. *The Reception of English Literature in Germany.* Berkeley, Calif.: Univ. of Calif. Pr., 1932. vii, 596pp. (^{1}1919)

Range: 17th to 20th century. Chronological survey, including American literature. Major authors and their impact upon German literature are analyzed in detail. Index: authors. Extensive bibliography: pp. 447-566. Despite age, still useful.

1402. ———. *Die Aufnahme englischer Literatur in Deutschland, 1500-1960.* Trans. by Maxwell E. Knight. Bern: Francke, 1961. 496pp.

Chronological survey covering the Reformation, Renaissance, 18th century, Shakespeare in Germany, the 19th and 20th centuries. Particularly valuable for its rich bibliography (to the 1950's), pp. 379-464.

1403. ———. *The Reception of United States Literature in Germany.* Chapel Hill: The Univ. of N. Carolina Pr., 1966. 245pp.

Range: 1775-1965. Traces the image of the US in German literature and the evaluation of US literature in Germany. Focus on the 19th century. Of particular value as a first introduction; material presented in summary fashion. Extensive bibliographical references in text; valuable bibliography, pp. 189-231. Indexes: authors and critics, contributors.

1404. Thierfelder, Franz. *Die deutsche Sprache im Ausland.* 2 vols. Hamburg, Berlin, Bonn: R.v. Deckers Verlag, G. Schenk.

I. *Der Völkerverkehr als sprachliche Aufgabe.* 1956. 196pp.
II. *Die Verbreitung der deutschen Sprache in der Welt.* 1957. xi, 402pp.

Analyzes the geographical distribution of German and discusses German as a global language; II analyzes (with tables) the situation of the German language in individual countries. Somewhat outdated.

1405. ———. "Deutsche Sprache im Ausland." *Dt. Phil. im Aufriß* (No. 1283), I, 1397-1480.

1406. Wellek, René. *Confrontations. Studies in the Intellectual and Literary Relations between Germany, England, and the United States during the 19th Century.* Princeton: Princeton Univ. Pr., 1965. vi, 221pp.

6 essays published between 1929-1963 on: German and English Romanticism, the relation of German literature to Carlyle, De Quincey, Emerson, and others. Indexes: author, subject. A good overview for the comparatist.

3. Other Literatures and German Literature

General surveys of the influence of foreign literatures on German literature may be found in *Dt. Phil. im Aufriß* (No. 1283) (ancient Greek and Roman, Czech, Dutch, Finnish, French, Hungarian, Indian, Italian, Oriental, Polish, Russian, Scandinavian incl. Old Norse, South Slavic, Spanish) and in *Reallexikon* (No. 1288) (Dutch, Romance literatures, Oriental, Scandinavian).

XII.

Literary Newspapers, Journals, Periodicals, Yearbooks

CONTENTS

A. GENERAL DISCUSSION AND DEFINITION

1407. d'Ester, Karl. "Zeitung und Zeitschrift." *Dt. Phil. im Aufriß* (No. 1283), III, 1245-1352.

1408. Meyer, Reinhart. "Literarische Zeitschriften." *Handlexikon* (No. 1290), pp. 519-524.

1409. Rosenfeld, Hellmut. "Familienblatt." *Reallexikon* (No. 1288), I, 450-456.

1410. Schmolke, Michael. "Zeitung." *Handlexikon* (No. 1290), pp. 525-530.

1411. Wiegand, Julius, and Werner Kohlschmidt. "Moralische Wochenschriften." *Reallexikon* (No. 1288), II, 421-427.

B. BIBLIOGRAPHIES

1. Completed Bibliographies

1412. Bogel, Else, and Elger Blühm. *Die deutschen Zeitungen des 17. Jahrhunderts. Ein Bestandsverzeichnis mit historischen und bibliographischen Angaben.* 2 vols. Bremen: Schünemann, 1971. I: *Text.* xxxi, 308pp.; II: *Abbildungen.* 321pp.

I contains complete bibliographical information, publication history, locations of holdings, secondary bibliography. Indexes: names, places of printing, titles. II contains reproductions of title pages with cross references to the text volume.

1413. Diesch, Carl. *Bibliographie der germanistischen Zeitschriften.* Leipzig: Hiersemann, 1927. xv, 441pp. (Repr. 1970)

Range: 18th to 20th century. Lists approximately 5,000 titles of scholarly and popular journals concerned with German arts and letters, including foreign titles. Divided into 5 groupings, beginning with 18th century; grouping 4: Theaterzeitschriften. Supplementary material, pp. 339-368. Provides bibliographical information, names of holding institutions, plus frequent annotations. Indexes: publishers, titles.

1414. Fischer, Heinz-Dietrich, ed. *Deutsche Zeitschriften des 17. bis 20. Jahrhunderts.* Munich-Pullach: Dokumentation, 1973. 445pp.

Outlines the publication history of 29 major journals 1682-1971; includes full bibliographical information, editorial policy, appraisal of contribution.

1415. ———, ed. *Deutsche Zeitungen des 17. bis 20. Jahrhunderts.* Munich-Pullach: Dokumentation, 1972. 415pp.

A short publication history of 25 important German newspapers published from 1617-1945. Index: names. Notes.

1416. Hagelweide, Gert. *Deutsche Zeitungsbestände in Bibliotheken und Archiven. German Newspapers in Libraries and Archives.* Düsseldorf: Droste, 1974. 372pp.

Lists the locations and holdings of 2,006 newspapers in 530 East and West German libraries. Organized by location (A-Z), each entry provides title, title variants, holdings of library. Introduction in German and English.

1417. Halfmann, Horst, ed. *Zeitschriften und Zeitungen des Exils 1933-1945. Bestandsverzeichnis der Deutschen Bücherei.* 2nd enl. and rev. ed. Leipzig: Deutsche Bücherei, 1975. xvii, 106pp.

Lists ca. 400 titles of serial publications published in German by exiled writers; includes editors, place of publication. Dates of publication not given. Holdings of the Deutsche Bücherei are identified. Index: names, country of publication.

1418. Hocks, Peter, and Peter Schmidt. *Literarische und politische Zeitschriften 1789-1805.* Stuttgart: Metzler, 1975. 138pp.

Analyses 41 journals with complete bibliographical information, compact and informative history and appraisal. Index of journals, names. Names of figures associated with each journal and secondary bibliography provided at the end of each section. A second volume is planned for the period 1806-1830.

1419. King, Janet K. *Literarische Zeitschriften 1945-1970.* Stuttgart: Metzler, 1974. viii, 105pp.

Contains analyses of 65 journals of East and West Germany, Austria, and Switzerland. Summarizes publication history, editorial policy, contributors. Secondary bibliography at the end of each section. Chronological table. Indexes: titles, publishers and editors.

1420. Kirchner, Joachim. *Die Zeitschriften des deutschen Sprachgebietes von den Anfängen bis 1900.* 4 vols. Stuttgart: Hiersemann, 1969ff.

I. *Die Zeitschriften des deutschen Sprachgebietes von den Anfängen bis 1830.* 1969. xv, 489pp.
II. *1831-1870.* J. Kirchner, ed. 1977. xi, 400pp.

III. *1871-1900*. Hans Jessen, ed. 1977. 730pp.
IV. *Gesamtregister zu Band I-III*. Edith Chorherr, ed. Fasc. 1ff. 1978ff.

Contains complete bibliographical information and current location of periodical holdings. Lists title, title history, editors, dates, publishers, place, size, etc. 24,450 items. Organized by field. Particularly pertinent sections: "Philologische Zeitschriften," "Literarische und literaturwissenschaftliche Zeitschriften." An important research tool.

1421. Laakmann, Dagmar, and Reinhard Tgahrt. *Literarische Zeitschriften und Jahrbücher 1880-1970. Verzeichnis der im Deutschen Literaturarchiv erschlossenen Periodica*. Marbach: Deutsches Literaturarchiv, 1972. 227pp.

Title list A-Z of 492 journals and yearbooks, owned by the Archiv, with detailed bibliographical information, including editors, special issues. Includes periodicals for art and culture as well as literary reviews and journals publishing chiefly belles-lettres and critiques. Index: author. Chronological list of periodicals.

1422. Raabe, Paul. "Die Zeitschriften des literarischen Expressionismus 1910-1921. Eine Bibliographie." *Imprimatur* 3 (1961/62), 126-177.

1423. ———. *Die Zeitschriften und Sammlungen des literarischen Expressionismus. Repertorium der Zeitschriften, Jahrbücher, Anthologien, Sammelwerke, Schriftenreihen und Almanache, 1910-1921*. Stuttgart: Metzler, 1964. xiv, 263pp.

Lists and analyzes journals 1914-1921, yearbooks, anthologies, book series, and literary almanacs. Each entry includes complete bibliographical information, description of content and editorial policy, selected secondary bibliography. Indexes: names, publishing houses, artists, contributors, publishers and editors, titles. An introductory essay describes literary life of the era. An excellent resource book.

1424. Schlawe, Fritz. *Literarische Zeitschriften 1885-1910*. 2nd ed. Stuttgart: Metzler, 1965. ix, 110pp. (^{1}1961) 71 items.

1425. ———. *Literarische Zeitschriften 1910-1933. (Teil II)*. 2nd ed. Stuttgart: Metzler, 1973. xii, 113pp. (^{1}1962) 72 items.

Journals grouped by type (progressive, neutral, review, theater, etc.). Bibliographical information includes publishing history, description, editors, secondary bibliography, and locations of holdings. Annotations give history, editorial policy, important features, important contributors, status, etc. Compact but full of information. Use as reference work facilitated by a chronological list of journals and by indexes: I: publishers and independent editors, authors; II: journals, publishers and independent editors, contributors. Note: II does not repeat material in I but gives cross references where I treats the same journal. For complete information on journals spanning both periods, both volumes should be consulted.

**** Walter, Hans-Albert. *Deutsche Exilliteratur 1933-1950* (No. 789) *VII. Exilpresse I.* Darmstadt: Luchterhand, 1974. 424pp.

2. Current Bibliographies

1426. *Internationale Bibliographie der Zeitschriftenliteratur aus allen Gebieten des Wissens.* Begun by Felix Dietrich, continued by Reinhard Dietrich. Leipzig: Dietrich, 1897ff.; Osnabrück: Dietrich, 1948ff.

The most extensive of all periodical indexes; known as "IBZ" or "Dietrich." Appeared until 1964 in 3 parts:

A. *Bibliographie der deutschen Zeitschriftenliteratur mit Einschluß von Sammelwerken.* Leipzig, Osnabrück: Dietrich, 1897-1964. Ceased publication with vol. 128. Repr. 1961-1962. Includes 7 vols. of author and subject indexes, 20 supplemental vols. for the years 1861-1896 (not in chronological order!), 31 vols. covering articles in German newspapers 1900-1944; NOTE: vols. 95 and 96 (July-Dec. 1944-1946) were never published.
B. *Bibliographie der fremdsprachigen Zeitschriftenliteratur. Repertoire bibliographique international des revues. International Index to Periodicals.* Leipzig, Osnabrück: Dietrich, 1911-1919, 1925-1964. Vols. 19, 20 cover the years 1914-1920, vol. 21 covers 1920-1924, vol. 22 covers 1921-1925. Neue Folge: vol. 1 (1925-1926)-51 (1962-1964). Appeared semi-annually. 1943-1944 to 1948-1949 not covered. Since 1934 limited to English, French, Italian, and Dutch. 77 vols.
C. *Bibliographie der Rezensionen und Referate.* Leipzig: Dietrich, 1901-1944. Ceased publication during WW II. Indexes reviews of German books 1900-1944; non-German books are indexed beginning 1925. CAUTION: the volumes covering 1900-1911 index only German reviews; the vols. 1912-1943 appear in two series, numbered alternately, one for German journals, one for foreign journals. Ca. 6,000 journals cited in A and B are covered. No indexes. For a continuation of review bibliography, see No. 1433.

1427. *Internationale Bibliographie der Zeitschriftenliteratur aus allen Gebieten des Wissens. International Bibliography of Periodical Literature Covering All Fields of Knowledge.* Ed. Otto Zeller. Vol. 1ff. 1963/64ff. Osnabrück: Dietrich, 1965ff. Appears semi-annually.

Combines A and B of *Internationale Bibliographie der Zeitschriftenliteratur* (see above). Lists ca. 300,000 articles from a master list of about 8,500 German and foreign periodicals. Divided into 3 parts: A. periodicals consulted; B. German classified subject index (with English equivalents);

C. index of authors. For journal title abbreviations see *Sigelverzeichnis*.

1428. *Index of Key Words 1896-1974 A-Z*. 2 vols. 1975. A cumulative classified subject index for the period. Cross references are limited to the period 1965-1974 and are designated by a "K" plus numerals indicating the volume and part.

1429. *Reader's Guide to Periodical Literature. An Author and Subject Index, 1900ff.* New York: Wilson, 1905ff. Vol. 1ff. Semimonthly (July, August monthly) cumulated yearly and in biennial volumes.

Indexes a master list of some 130 American popular magazines and "journals of general interest." Entries under author, subject, and title A-Z (with cross references). Of limited usefulness to the Germanist.

1430. *The Subject Index to Periodicals*. 1915ff. London: The Library Association, 1919ff. Annual. 1954-1961 quarterly with yearly cumulations. Ceased publication. New title:

1431. *British Humanities Index*. 1962ff. London: The Library Association, 1963ff. Quarterly with yearly cumulation.

Indexes some 350 British journals by subject and author. Cross referenced. Covers the arts and politics but does *not* cover creative writing.

3. Bibliographies of Reviews

1432. Fetzer, John. "Bibliography of Book Reviews for German Literature." *Acta Germanica* 4 (1969), 197-240; 5 (1970), 245-300; 6 (1971), 177-222; 7 (1972), 151-213. Easily accessible listings. No longer published.

1433. *Internationale Bibliographie der Rezensionen wissenschaftlicher Literatur. International Bibliography of Book Reviews of Scholarly Literature*. Ed. by Otto Zeller. Vol. 1ff. Osnabrück: Dietrich, 1971ff.

Biyearly cumulation of 2 vols. in 3 pts. each. Each volume is divided into 4 pts.: A. Periodica: index of periodicals consulted; B. Index rerum: classified subject index of book reviews; C. Index autorum: index of book reviews by authors of book reviews; D. Index recensorum: index of book reviews by reviewers. Periodical titles cited by number, see pt. A. Coverage for German literature is uneven and incomplete.

C. JOURNALS AND YEARBOOKS

Note: language(s) in which articles are published are indicated by capital letters in parentheses. "3/yr." indicates 3 issues yearly.

1. Book Publishing, Book Reviews, Library Science

1434. *Biblos. Österreichische Zeitschrift für Buch- und Bibliothekswesen, Dokumentation, Bibliographie und Bibliophilie.* 1 (1952)ff. 4/yr.

Organ of the Vereinigung österreichischer Bibliothekare and Österreichisches Institut fur Bibliotheksforschung, Dokumentations- und Informationswesen. Articles on library history, library science theory and training in Austria, bibliography, news and reviews. Brief international notes on manuscript and autograph finds, exhibitions, edition publication, etc.

1435. *Buch und Bibliothek.* 1 (1948/49)ff. 12/yr.

Organ of the Verein der Bibliothekare an öffentlichen Büchereien. Former title: *Bücherei und Bildung* 1 (1948/49)-22 (1970). *Bücherei und Bildung* contained mostly reviews; *Buch und Bibliothek* contains articles (G) on criteria for book selection. Annotated bibliography: current books with recommendation for or against purchase. Notes: professional activities. Reviews.

1436. *Bücherschiff. Die deutsche Bücherzeitung.* 1 (1950)ff. 4/yr.

Descriptive reviews (G) of new publications, primary and secondary, in Germany, particularly in the area of culture and the arts.

1437. *Critique. Revue génêrale des publications françaises et étrangères.* 1 (1944)ff. 12/yr.

Reviews (F) in all humanistic subject areas, usually several books on the same subject reviewed; commentary on articles.

1438. *Deutsche Bücher.* 1 (1971)ff. 4/yr.

20 to 40 new publications in German belles-lettres and literary criticism are reviewed in each issue. Interviews with prominent writers a regular feature.

1439. *Deutsche Literaturzeitung für Kritik der internationalen Wissenschaft.* 1 (1880)ff. 12/yr.

Publ. for the Akademien der Wissenschaften zu Berlin, Göttingen, Heidelberg, Leipzig, München, Wien. Since 1972: publ. for the Akademie der Wissenschaften der DDR. Contains reviews of editions and secondary works, including bibliographies.

1440. *Erasmus. Speculum Scientarum. International Bulletin of Contemporary Scholarship.* 1 (1947)ff. 24/yr.

Book reviews (G, E, F) of works on religion, social sciences, philology, literature, archaeology, history, antiquity, etc.

**** *Germanistik. Internationales Referatenorgan mit bibliographischen Hinweisen.* 1960ff. 4/yr. (No. 130)

1441. *Göttingsche Gelehrte Anzeigen.* 1 (1739)ff. 2/yr.

Extensive review articles (G) on works published in all disciplines, including German literature. Emphasis on antiquity and history. Excellent intensive studies.

1442. *Literature. Music. Fine Arts. A Review of German-Language Research Contributions on Literature, Music, and Fine Arts. German Studies III.* 1 (1968)ff. 2/yr.

Each issue divided into 3 sections; first section, "Literature," contains 35-40 reviews in English by scholars of German literature. Nearly all works are on German literature or German literary theory. A good selection and a useful source of reviews.

1443. *Philobiblon. Eine Vierteljahresschrift für Bücher- und Graphiksammler.* 1 (1957)ff. 4/yr.

Publ. for the Maximilian-Gesellschaft, Hamburg. Articles (G, E) on manuscripts, painters; checklists of authors, literary histories, editions, etc. Notes: new books, auctions, exhibits, catalogues, reprints.

**** *Referatendienst zur Literaturwissenschaft.* 1 (1969)ff. 4/yr. (No. 131)

1444. *Scriptorium. Revue internationale des études aux manuscrits. International Review of Manuscript Studies.* 1 (1946/47)ff. 2/yr.

Extensive lists (F, G, E) of bibliographies and codicils. Primary material: manuscript excerpts.

1445. *Wolfenbütteler Beiträge. Aus den Schätzen der Herzog August Bibliothek.* 1 (1972)ff. 1/yr.

Notes, articles (G) with data on manuscripts, history of the Wolfenbüttel Library. Primary Texts.

1446. *Zentralblatt für Bibliothekswesen.* 1 (1884)ff. 12/yr.

GDR journal for librarians. Bibliography: articles on libraries, bibliography, etc. Reviews. Notes: professional news.

1447. *Zeitschrift für Bibliothekswesen und Bibliographie.* 1 (1954)ff. 6/yr.

Organ of the Verein Deutscher Bibliothekare and of the Verein der Diplombibliothekare an wissenschaftlichen Bibliotheken. Articles (G) on the development and problems of libraries. Reviews. "Neue Bücher" a good source of information about new current bibliographies. News: professional activities.

2. Literary and Cultural Reviews

1448. *Akzente. Zeitschrift für Literatur.* 1 (1954)ff. 6/yr.

Literary criticism. Modern but mostly contemporary German poetry, prose, etc., some material translated from other literatures.

1449. *Alternative. Zeitschrift für Literatur und Diskussion.* 1958ff. 6/yr.

Thematic issues take critical (leftist) stance toward the FRG. Early issues brought poetry, prose; emphasis now on essays and theoretical discussions. Reports on literary conferences in socialist countries, translations of political poetry, etc.

1450. *Das Argument. Zeitschrift für Philosophie und Sozialwissenschaften.* 1959ff. 4/yr.

Thematic issues bring essays, interviews, and reportage in left-oriented critique of the establishment. Poetry.

1451. *Ästhetik und Kommunikation. Beiträge zur politischen Erziehung.* 1970ff. 4/yr.

Essays and discussions (leftist) on current cultural and political problems, with particular reference to education and the school system. Book reviews.

1452. *Basis. Jahrbuch für deutsche Gegenwartsliteratur.* 1 (1970)ff. 1/yr.

Articles (G) chiefly on post-1945 literature. Extensive reviews of primary and secondary material. Excellent for students of contemporary literature.

1453. *Die Bühne.* 1 (1958)ff. 12/yr.

An Austrian review of theater, opera, and ballet. Abundant photographs. Articles (G) on productions, profiles of directors, actors, etc. Viennese repertoire listed. Notes: new books, records.

1454. *Castrum Peregrini.* 1 (1951)ff. 5/yr.

Continues the tradition of S. George's *Blätter für die Kunst:* articles (G) on culture, literature, and the fine arts. Much material on George and his circle.

1455. *Dimension. Contemporary German Arts and Letters.* 1 (1968)ff. 3/yr.

Provides a "forum for poets and poetwatchers on the contemporary scene in Germany." Special issues on individual writers. Presents contemporary German prose, lyric, drama with original text and English translation. Excellent for lesser known writers. "Letter from Germany" reports on current developments.

1456. *Ensemble*. 1969ff. 1/yr.

Prose, poetry, essays (G). International in scope and deliberately apolitical.

1457. *Eröffnungen. Magazin für Literatur und bildende Kunst*. 1961ff. appears irreg.

Publishes Austrian contemporary writers and artists; foreign writers in translation. Translations of poetry. Book reviews.

1458. *Filmkunst. Zeitschrift für Filmkultur und Filmwissenschaft*. 1 (1949) 4/yr.

Publ. by the Österreichische Gesellschaft für Filmwissenschaft, Kommunikations- und Medienforschung. Reviews Austrian films (many photographs); articles (G) on film research, aesthetics. Occasional filmography.

1459. *Frankfurter Hefte. Zeitschrift für Kultur und Politik*. 1 (1946)ff. 12/yr.

Notes, articles (G) of conservative bent on cultural life. Essays on contemporary literature, religion, the church, social sciences, philosophy, education, art, etc. Book reviews; reviews of movies, drama, TV, radio plays.

1460. *Die Horen. Zeitschrift für Grafik, Literatur und Kritik. Monatsschrift des jungen Literaturkreises*. 1955ff. 4/yr.

Began as a neutral, humanist organ (G) for young engaged writers; now leftist. Thematic issues.

1461. *Jahresring. Literatur und Kunst der Gegenwart*. 1954ff. 1/yr.

Publ. by the Kulturkreis im Bundesverband der deutschen Industrie. Excellent reproductions of art; literary pieces; excellent articles (G) on the arts. "Chronik": cultural events. A good source of information on literature and the arts in West Germany.

1462. *Kürbiskern. Zeitschrift für Literatur und Kritik*. 1965ff. 4/yr.

Leftist review with thematic issues on current cultural and political problems. Takes a lively interest in current events. Essays (G) and book reviews.

1463. *Kursbuch*. 1965ff. 4/yr.

"Organ of the New Left in Germany, but not bound to any political organization" (H.M. Enzensberger, ed.). International perspective; foreign contributors. No literary texts in recent years; essays (G) on cultural, literary, political questions.

1464. *Der Literat. Zeitschrift für Literatur und Kunst*. 1 (1959)ff. 12/yr.

Articles (G) bringing international reports on the status of the writer, news of writers, writers' societies, prizes, exhibits, etc. Reviews. Poetry, short prose.

1465. *Literatur und Kritik. Österreichische Monatsschrift.* 1 (1955)ff. 10/yr.

Former title: *Wort in der Zeit* 1 (1955)-12 (1966). Publ. poetry, prose; essays (G), appreciations, portraits, interpretation, biographical material. Reviews.

1466. *Manuskripte. Zeitschrift für Literatur, Kunst und Kritik.* 1960ff. 3/yr.

Publ. Austrian contemporary writers, particularly experimental literature: poetry, prose, drama.

1467. *Merkur. Deutsche Zeitschrift für europäisches Denken.* 1 (1947)ff. 12/yr.

A cultural periodical of excellent quality with emphasis on the fine arts. Poetry, short prose, articles (G) on literature, notes. Reviews of primary literature.

1468. *Neue deutsche Hefte.* 1 (1954)ff. 4/yr.

Essays (G) on cultural questions, literature, profiles of prominent figures; occasional *Forschungsberichte*. Notes: cultural and literary news. Reviews. Conservative, international stance. Poetry.

1469. *Neue deutsche Literatur. Monatsschrift für schöne Literatur und Kritik.* 1 (1953)ff. 12/yr.

Publ. by the Deutscher Schriftstellerverband. Novel excerpts, poetry, drama; articles (G) on criticism, aesthetics; essays on current topics by prominent literary figures; reviews. Excellent orientation on social realism, Marxist criticism, current literary activity in the GDR.

1470. *Die neue Rundschau.* 1 (1890)ff. 4/yr.

Original title: *Freie Bühne für modernes Leben*, then: *Freie Bühne für den Entwicklungskampf der Zeit* 3 (1892)ff., then: *Neue deutsche Rundschau* 5 (1894)ff., present title 15 (1904)ff. Focuses on current issues; excellent essays (G) on 20th-century literature; poems, short stories, novel excerpts. Notes: discussion and replies. Bibliography: "Bücher-Rundschau" lists new titles (mostly literature) for the year. Extensive reviews of primary German and foreign literature.

1471. *New German Critique. An Interdisciplinary Journal of German Studies.* 1 (1974)ff. 3/yr.

Articles (G, E) on all aspects of GDR culture. *Forschungsberichte*. Reviews.

1472. *Protokolle. Wiener Halbjahresschrift für Literatur, bildende Kunst und Musik.* 1966ff. 2/yr.

Publishes prose, poetry, art of contemporary and avantgarde Austrian writers and artists.

1473. *Schweizer Monatshefte für Politik, Wirtschaft, Kultur.* 1 (1921)ff. 12/yr.

Articles (G) on Swiss economic, political, cultural affairs; occasional articles on literature and writers. Reviews. News of cultural events.

1474. *Sinn und Form. Beiträge zur Literatur.* 1 (1949)ff. 6/yr.+ supplements.

Publ. by the Deutsche Akademie der Künste zu Berlin. Substantial articles (G) on authors, works, problems of criticism. Marxist-socialist orientation. Primary material: interviews with writers, documents, some prose, drama, poetry. Bibliographies.

1475. *Spielplatz. Jahrbuch für Theater.* 1 (1971/72)ff. 1/yr.

Each volume publishes 4-6 full-length plays by German-language dramatists. Reports, documents, biographical material. Bibliography: all plays in German published as a book or stage script during the preceding year.

1476. *Sprache im technischen Zeitalter.* 1954ff. 4/yr.

Articles (G) on literature, popular literature, aesthetics, pedagogy from the viewpoint of contemporary language. Discussion of problems of modern communication, the mass media. Some thematic issues.

1477. *Stimmen der Zeit.* 1 (1869)ff. 12/yr.

Originally a Catholic review. Articles (G) on all aspects of modern German culture from theology to psychology, history, economics, education, the media. Reviews.

1478. *Text + Kritik. Zeitschrift für Literatur.* 1 (1963)/64)ff. 4/yr.

Each issue devoted to one (usually German) author: primary texts, selected bibliography on author, photograph of author. Excellent for contemporary literature.

1479. *Theater der Zeit.* 1 (1946)ff. 12/yr. + supplements.

Organ of the Verband der Theaterschaffenden der DDR. Articles (G) on current theater activities, playwrights, theater figures, notes regarding performances. Copious illustrations. A complete play or an excerpt in each issue. Supplements: season repertoires.

1480. *Theater heute. Die deutsche Theaterzeitschrift.* 1 (1960)ff. 12/yr.

Copiously illustrated articles (G) on theater performances, theater figures, etc. in the FRG. Notes: professional news; discussions with directors, authors, actors; theater repertoires. One complete play or excerpt in each issue.

1481. *Tintenfisch.* 1968ff. 1/yr.

Publishes contemporary German writers as well as many reprints of texts published in other reviews. Current bibliography: "Bücher deutscher Autoren" (at end of each volume).

1482. *Universitas. Zeitschrift für Wissenschaft, Kunst und Literatur.* 1 (1946)ff. 12/yr.

Articles (G) on intellectual, cultural trends, social, legal, and political problems. Reviews. News of cultural events.

1483. *Universitas. A German Review of the Arts and Sciences. Quarterly English Language Edition.* 1 (1946)ff. 4/yr.

Publishes a selection of articles from the above in English translation.

1484. *Welt der Bücher. Literarische Beihefte zur Herder-Korrespondenz Orbis librorum.* 1954ff. 2/yr.

Supplement to *Herder Korrespondenz (Orbis catholicus).* A Catholic review containing brief articles (G) on cultural and literary subjects. Reviews many books, both scholarly and literary. Includes material from the GDR. *Forschungsberichte.*

1485. *Welt und Wort. Literarische Monatsschrift.* 1 (1946)ff. 12/yr.

Brief articles (G) on current subjects: culture, fine arts, especially literature; excerpts of coming works. Substantial review section: popular and serious literature, the arts, television, intellectual history. "Literarische Umschau": biographical information on authors.

1486. *World Literature Today. An International Quarterly.* 1 (1927)ff. 4/yr.

Formerly: *Books Abroad* 1 (1927)-50 (1976). Articles (E) on contemporary writers, literary movements in foreign countries; frequent thematic issues. Reviews: literary criticism and primary material.

1487. *Zeitwende. Die neue Furche.* 1 (1919)ff. 6/yr.

A Protestant review with articles (G) on theological and Christian problems, cultural and sociological topics, essays on literature. Poetry.

3. Theory of Literary Criticism and Literary History

1488. *Journal of Aesthetics and Art Criticism.* 1 (1941/42)ff. 4/yr.

Publ. by the American Society for Aesthetics. Articles (E) on aesthetic theory; some literary analysis. Reviews.

1489. *Poetica. Zeitschrift für Sprach- und Literaturwissenschaft.* 1 (1967)ff. 4/yr.

Substantial articles (G) on broad topics in poetics, literary epochs (world literature), linguistics. Individual works seldom treated. Reviews. Notes: discussions by several authors on same broad topic. Provides excellent orientation on broad topics.

1490. *Poetics. International Review for the Theory of Literature.* 1 (1971)ff. Publ. irregularly.

Technical articles (E, G, F) on the theory of literature, methodology of scholarship, theory of linguistics in relation to literature. Reviews. Announcements of symposia, etc.

1491. *Poétique.* 1 (1970)ff. 4/yr.

Articles (F) on literary theory; texts discussed are usually from French literature, sometimes English or American. Bibliographies.

1492. *New Literary History. A Journal of Theory and Interpretation.* 1 (1969/70)ff. 3/yr.

Editors hope to fill the need for a periodical concentrating on historical problems of literature study: periodization, reasons for literary change, evolution of styles, interconnection between national literary histories, etc. Articles (E) focus on English and American literature but others are not excluded.

1493. *Zeitschrift für Ästhetik und allgemeine Kunstwissenschaft.* 1 (1951)ff. 1-2/yr.

Recent articles (G, F, E) are on the whole not highly technical; emphasis is on art and literature. Some theory. Occasional thematic issues. Reviews.

4. German Literary History and Criticism

a. *General*

1494. *Acta Germanica. Jahrbuch des Südafrikanischen Germanistenverbandes.* 1 (1966)ff. 1/yr.

Articles (G, E) on literature of all periods: interpretation, analysis, literary history. Reports on German studies in South Africa. A few reviews.

1495. *Akademie der Wissenschaften und der Literatur in Mainz. Abhandlungen der Klasse der Literatur.* 1-3 (1950)ff. 4-6/yr.

Substantial articles (G) on literary aesthetics and critical studies.

1496. *Annali. Sezione Germanica.* 1 (1958)ff. 1/yr.

Publ. by the Istituto universario orientale, Napoli. Articles (I, E, G) on Germanic (including Scandinavian) literature. Reviews.

1497. *AUMLA. Journal of the Australasian Language and Literature Association. A Journal of Literary Criticism, Philology and Linguistics.* 1 (1953)ff. 2/yr.

Articles (E and others) on Classical and European literature and linguistics from the beginnings to the present. Substantial review section.

1498. *Colloquia Germanica. Internationale Zeitschrift für germanische Sprach- und Literaturwissenschaft.* 1 (1967)ff. 4/yr.

Articles (G, E, F), notes on literature, often comparative. Reports on German studies in various countries. Articles on linguistics. Reviews.

1499. *Deutsche Akademie der Wissenschaften zu Berlin. Veröffentlichungen der Sprachwissenschaftlichen Kommission.* 1958ff. Publ. irregularly.

Book-length monographs (G).

1500. *Deutsche Vierteljahresschrift für Literaturwissenschaft und Geistesgeschichte.* 1 (1923)ff. 4/yr.

Articles (G, E) on literature with emphasis on later literature (17th to 20th century), criticism, methodology, aesthetics. Major *Forschungsberichte* reprinted as separate volumes.

1501. *Doitsu Bungaku.* 1 (1953)ff. 2/yr.

Publ. for the Japanische Gesellschaft für Germanistik. Articles (in Japanese) on linguistics and literature. Most articles accompanied by summary in German.

1502. *Etudes germaniques. Revue trimestrielle de la Société des Etudes Germaniques.* 1 (1946)ff. 4/yr.

Articles (F, G) of high quality on literature, language, linguistics. Thematic issues; reviews; notes: discussion of articles by readers; bibliography, "Revue des Revues," lists journal articles for preceding year.

1503. *Euphorion. Zeitschrift für Literaturgeschichte.* 1 (1894)-34 (1933); 45 (1950)ff. 4/yr.

During the Third Reich publ. under the title *Dichtung und Volkstum* (1933-1944). Articles (G, E) primarily on German literature since the Middle Ages but some space given in nearly every issue to older literature. Notes; discussion; bibliographies; *Forschungsberichte;* motif studies of comparatist scope.

1504. *Forum for Modern Language Studies.* 1 (1965)ff. 4/yr.

Articles (E) on literature, few on language or pedagogy. Good, critical reviews.

1505. *German Life and Letters. A Quarterly Review.* 1 (1936/37)ff. 1 NS (1947/48)ff. 4/yr.

Some cultural studies; chiefly articles (E) on literature. Notes. Reviews (discontinued 1978).

1506. *The German Quarterly.* 1 (1925)ff. 4/yr.

Publ. by the American Association of Teachers of German. Articles (E, G) on literature; substantial section of reviews; notes: news items.

1507. *The Germanic Review.* 1 (1926)ff. 4/yr.

Once oriented toward philology, now articles (E, G) on literature, particularly interpretations. Reviews.

1508. *Germanisch-Romanische Monatsschrift.* 1 (1909)-31 (1943); NS 1 (1950)ff. 4/yr.

Articles (G) and notes on literature; excellent introductions to works and motifs. Reviews. Occasional *Forschungsberichte*.

1509. *Jahrbuch für Internationale Germanistik.* 1 (1969)ff. 2/yr.

Publ. in association with the Internationale Vereinigung für Germanische Sprach- und Literaturwissenschaft for the purpose of disseminating information on current research, reports on editions, international personalia for Dutch, German, and Scandinavian language and literature. *Forschungsberichte* regularly. Dissertations in progress (see No. 156, No. 157).

1510. *Journal of English and Germanic Philology.* 1 (1897)ff. 4/yr.

High quality articles (E, G) on German and English literature and philology; substantial reviews. Anglo-American bibliography to 1970.

1511. *MLN.* 1 (1886)ff. 4/yr.

Title until 77 (1962): *Modern Language Notes.* Originally a vehicle for publishing notes only; now brings lengthier articles (E, G, F, S, I). April issue is devoted to German literature. *Forschungsberichte.*

1512. *Modern Language Quarterly.* 1 (1940)ff. 4/yr.

Interpretive articles (E) on European literature chiefly by British and American scholars. Reviews.

1513. *Modern Language Review.* 1 (1905)ff. 4/yr.

Publ. by the Modern Humanities Research Association. Articles (E) on English and foreign literatures, medieval through contemporary. Reviews.

1514. *Modern Philology.* 1 (1903)ff. 2/yr. (2 yrs. = 1 vol.)

Articles (E) on literature from Beowulf to 19th century, with emphasis on earlier phases, especially Elizabethan. Little on German literature. Notes and documents. Reviews: many works of criticism on German literature.

1515. *Moderna Språk.* 1 (1907)ff. 4/yr.

Publ. for the Modern Language Teachers' Association of Sweden. Articles (Swedish, G, E, F, S, I) on literature and language (pedagogy). Reviews.

1516. *Monatshefte. A Journal Devoted to the Study of German Language and Literature.* 1 (1899)ff. 4/yr.

Articles (G, E) on all aspects of German literature; an occasional article on language. Reviews. Fall issue brings "Personalia": a list of faculty in major German departments in the US and Canada, promotions, visitors from abroad, doctoral degrees granted including dissertation title and supervisor.

1517. *Neophilologus. An International Journal Devoted to the Study of Modern and Medieval Language and Literature Including General Linguistics, Literary Theory and Comparative Literature.* 1 (1916)ff. 4/yr.

Articles (E, F, G, I, S) as described in subtitle. Reviews and review articles.

1518. *New German Studies.* 1 (1973)ff. 3/yr.

Short articles (E) and notes: interpretation, comparative studies. Occasional bibliography.

1519. *Österreich in Geschichte und Literatur mit Geographie.* 1 (1957)ff. 1/yr.

Articles (G) on Austrian history and literature. Reports of conferences. Reviews.

1520. *Orbis litterarum. International Review of Literary Studies.* 1 (1943)-8 (1950); 9 (1954)ff. 4/yr.

Aesthetics, comparative literature, European and American literature. Articles (G, E, F) of high quality treat individual works and motifs. Occasional bibliographies.

1521. *Papers on Language and Literature.* 1 (1965)ff. 4/yr. + occasional supplements.

Articles (E) primarily on English and American literature but also on other literatures, particularly on specific works.

1522. *Philologica Pragensia. Časopis pro moderní filologii.* 1 (1958)ff. 4/yr.

Journal of the Prague Philological Society. *Časopis pro moderní filologii* included 1972ff. Articles and notes (E,

G, F, S) on literature and linguistics, the Prague Circle, Marxist criticism. Reviews.

1523. *Philological Quarterly. A Journal Devoted to Scholarly Investigation in the Classical and Modern Languages and Literatures.* 1 (1922)ff. 4/yr.

Articles and notes (E, G, S) mainly on English and American literature, individual works, authors, motifs, etc. Bibliographies on authors and movements. Reviews (irreg.) "The Romantic Movement: A Selective and Critical Bibliography" (No. 627) appeared 29 (1950)-43 (1964).

1524. *PMLA. Publications of the Modern Language Association of America.* 1 (1884/85)ff. 6/yr.

Articles (E, G, F, S, I) on all aspects of English, American, and modern Romance and Germanic literatures. Annual bibliography for English, American, and other modern literatures, folklore, and linguistics (see No. 125). Notes: MLA news, discussion. Articles on German literature less frequent in recent years.

1525. *Recherches germaniques.* 1 (1971)ff. 1/yr.

Articles (F, G) on 18th-20th-century literature. Primary material: unpublished fragments.

1526. *Revue germanique. Allemagne, Autriche, Pays-bas, Scandinavie.* 1 (1950)ff. 4/yr.

High quality articles (F) on all aspects of German literary history with occasional focus on French-German literary relationships. Bibliographies: selective title lists. "Revues annuelles": survey of developments in contemporary novel, theater, poetry. Notes.

1527. *Revue des langues vivantes. Tijdschrift voor levende talen.* 1 (1935)ff. 6/yr.

Publ. for l'Association des professeurs des langues vivantes de Belgique. Articles (E, F, G) on literature and general linguistic topics. Frequent articles on German literature. Reviews.

1528. *Seminar. A Journal of Germanic Studies.* 1 (1965)ff. 3/yr.

Publ. by the Canadian Association of University Teachers of German and the German Section of the Australasian Universities Language and Literature Association. Articles (E, G) on individual literary works, authors, poetics and aesthetics, interdisciplinary studies, Canadian-German literary relationships. Reviews. Occasional *Forschungsberichte.* Notes: comments and criticism by writers and readers.

1529. *Sprachkunst. Beiträge zur Literaturwissenschaft.* 1 (1970)ff. 4/yr.

Publ. by the Österreichische Akademie der Wissenschaften. Excellent articles (G, E, F, R) on aesthetics, poetics, authors, individual works. International and comparative in scope but mostly concerned with German literature and literary history. Reviews. "Verzeichnis der literaturwissenschaftlichen Dissertationen an österreichischen Hochschulen" (annual listing).

1530. *Studia Germanica Gandensia*. 1 (1959)ff. Appears irreg.

"Devoted to the study of Germanic languages and literatures." Articles (Dutch, E, G) mostly on Dutch language and literature but does publish some very significant articles on German literature.

1531. *Studia Neophilologica. A Journal of Germanic and Romance Philology*. 1 (1928)ff. 2/yr.

Articles (E, G, F, S, I) and notes on linguistics and literature. Articles on German literature not numerous but of excellent quality: history, interpretations. Reviews.

1532. *Studier i modern Språkvetenskap*. 1 (1898)-19 (1956/59); NS 1 (1960)ff. Publ. irreg.

Publ. by Nyfilologiska Sällskapet i Stockholm. Contains occasional articles (Swedish, E, G, F) on German literature. Bibliographies covering 4-5 yr. period in each issue: "Bibliography of Swedish Works on Romance, English and German Philology."

1533. *Studies in Philology*. 1 (1906)ff. 5/yr.

Articles (E) on all European literatures, chiefly English and US, little linguistics. Little on German literature. Bibliographies.

1534. *Symposium. A Quarterly Journal in Modern Foreign Literatures*. 1 (1946/47)ff. 4/yr.

Articles (E, F, G) "pertinent to the modern *foreign* languages and literatures." Some thematic issues, which are helpful to the comparatist.

1535. *Weimarer Beiträge. Zeitschrift für Literaturwissenschaft. Ästhetik und Kulturtheorie*. 1 (1955)ff. 12/yr.

Articles (G) on literature and linguistics, theory of literature, interpretation, particularly of GDR literature. Reports. Reviews. Substantial bibliographies.

1536. *Zeitschrift für deutsche Philologie*. 1 (1868)ff. 4/yr.

High quality articles (G) on all aspects of German literature and linguistics. Thematic issues (*Sonderhefte*). Reviews. Frequent *Forschungsberichte*.

b. Older Literature

1537. *Arkiv för nordisk Filologi.* 1 (1883)ff. 1/yr.

Articles (Scandinavian, G, E, F) on Scandinavian historical linguistics and older literature. Reviews.

1538. *Beiträge zur Geschichte der deutschen Sprache und Literatur.* 1 (1874)ff. 3/yr.

Articles (G) on older dialects and literature. Reviews.

1539. *Leuvense Bijdragen. Tijdskrift voor Germaanse Filologie.* 1 (1896)ff. 1/yr.

Articles (F, G, E, Dutch) on linguistics and literature. Good, critical reviews.

1540. *Neuphilologische Mitteilungen. Bulletin of the Modern Language Society (Helsinki).* 1 (1899)ff. 4/yr.

Articles (E, F, G) on literature and linguistics. "Finnish Theses and Dissertations in Modern Languages and Literature; Work in Progress." Reviews.

1541. *Niederdeutsche Mitteilungen.* 1 (1945)ff. 1/yr.

Articles (G) on Low German linguistics and older literature. Reviews.

c. Middle Ages and Baroque

1542. *Classica et Mediaevalia. Revue Danoise de philologie et d'histoire.* 1 (1938)ff. 1/yr.

Publ. by the Societas Danica Indagationis Antiquitatis et Mediaevi. Articles (E, G, F) often of general appeal on classical and medieval subjects. Little philology.

1543. *Daphnis. Zeitschrift für Mittlere Deutsche Literatur.* 1 (1972)ff. 4/yr.

Notes and articles (G, E) on late medieval and Baroque literature by international scholars. Reviews.

1544. *Deutsches Archiv für Erforschung des Mittelalters.* 1 (1937)ff. 2/yr.

Publ. for Monumenta Germaniae Historica. Scholarly articles (G) on medieval history and critiques of scholarly literature on the Middle Ages. Bibliographies. *Forschungsberichte.* Notes.

1545. *Medium Aevum.* 1 (1932)ff. 3/yr.

Publ. for the Society for the Study of Medieval Languages and Literature. Articles (E) on all aspects of medieval language and literature, but little on specifically German material. Reviews.

1546. *Österreichische Akademie der Wissenschaften. Wien. Philosophisch-historische Klasse. Sitzungsberichte.* 1 (1848)ff. Number of monographs varies.

A monograph series with some shorter articles (G): covers older dialects, medieval studies. Grillparzer studies: 275, 280.

1547. *Renaissance Quarterly.* 1 (1948)ff. 4/yr.

Published by the Renaissance Society of America. Articles (E) on all aspects of the Renaissance. Very little on the German Renaissance. Bibliography: "Renaissance Books." Reviews. Notes: news of the Society, new editions, conferences, etc.

1548. *Revue Belge de Philologie et d'histoire.* 1 (1972)ff. 4/yr.

Publ. by the Société pour le progrès des études philosophiques et historiques. Articles (F, E, G, Flemish) on antiquity, Middle Ages: literature, linguistics, history. Reviews. "Chronique": summary of new books. Bibliography: chiefly Belgian literature and history.

1549. *Speculum. A Journal for Medieval Studies.* 1 (1926)ff. 4/yr.

Publ. by the Mediaeval Academy of America. Articles (E) on medieval literature and culture in Europe. "Bibliography of American Periodical Literature." Reviews. "Notes and Documents."

1550. *Studies in the Renaissance.* 1 (1954)ff. 1/yr.

Publ. by the Renaissance Society of America. Articles (E) on all aspects of the Renaissance.

1551. *Wolfenbütteler Barock Nachrichten.* 1 (1974)ff. 4/yr.

Substantial bibliographical information including regular "Addenda" to standard bibliographies. New book announcements, literary historical notes (G), personal news, professional announcements.

1552. *Zeitschrift für deutsches Altertum und deutsche Literatur.* 1 (1841)ff. 4/yr.

Articles (G) on medieval and older literature and languages. Primary material: texts. Substantial reviews in section: *Anzeiger für deutsches Altertum und deutsche Literatur.* 1 (1876)ff.

d. Eighteenth Century

1553. *Wolfenbütteler Studien zur Aufklärung.* 1 (1974)ff. 1/yr.

Publ. for the Lessing-Akademie. Excellent studies (G) in 18th-century literature and culture in Germany and Europe.

e. Nineteenth and Twentieth Centuries

1554. *Contemporary Literature.* 1 (1960)ff. 4/yr.

Some thematic issues; some comparative essays. Items on German literature infrequent. Reviews.

1555. *Critique. Studies in Modern Fiction.* 1 (1956)ff. 3/yr.

Essays (E) on contemporary fiction, particularly English and American. Primary bibliography: checklists for individual authors.

1556. *Diacritics. A Review of Contemporary Criticism.* 1 (1971)ff. 4/yr.

Extended reviews (E) of criticism (almost *Forschungsberichte*). Each issue contains an interview with an artist. Little on German literature but good background reading.

1557. *Literatur in Wissenschaft und Unterricht. LWU.* 1 (1968)ff. 4/yr.

Articles (G) on German, French, American, and English literature with emphasis on the 20th century; also comparative articles. Reviews. Despite title, articles are not pedagogically oriented.

1558. *Studies in Romanticism.* 1 (1961)ff. 4/yr.

Articles (E) on all aspects of Romanticism, some interdisciplinary and comparative. Frequent articles on German Romanticism. Reviews. Contains excellent materials for orientation in Romanticism.

1559. *The Twentieth Century.* 1 (1877)ff. 4/yr.

A journal of 20th-century culture: articles (E) on current political events, important figures in art, politics, literature; after 1960 less emphasis on politics, more on economic, religious, social, class problems. Poetry. Reviews.

1560. *Twentieth Century Literature. A Scholarly and Critical Journal.* 1 (1955)ff. 4/yr.

Articles (E) mainly on English and American literature. Bibliographies; useful annotated selected bibliography on world literature and current bibliography of the arts in other periodicals.

5. Genres

a. Drama and Theater

1561. *Comparative Drama.* 1 (1967/68)ff. 4/yr.

Articles (E) on specific dramas, motifs, etc., of good quality though not "international in spirit and interdisciplinary in scope." German subjects sparse.

1562. *The Drama Review.* 1 (1955)ff. 4/yr.

Thematic issues mainly on 20th-century world theater. Provides good orientation on current trends. German theater well represented (especially Brecht).

1563. *Educational Theater Journal.* 1 (1949)ff. 4/yr.

Articles (E) of non-professional quality. Reviews of stage productions. Book reviews. News.

1564. *Jahrbuch der Gesellschaft für Wiener Theaterforschung.* 1 (1944)ff. 1/yr.

Documents and history of Viennese theater, stage productions, etc. Valuable source of information.

1565. *Maske und Kothurn. Internationale Beiträge zur Theaterwissenschaft.* 1 (1955)ff. 4/yr.

Publ. by the Institut für Theaterwissenschaft an der Univ. Wien. Articles (G) of high quality on the performing arts and especially on drama. Thematic issues. Portraits of theater greats. Reviews. "Bibliographie des theaterwissenschaftlichen Schrifttums und der Sprechplatten." 1955ff.; "Wiener theaterwissenschaftliche Dissertationen." 16 (1970)ff.

1566. *Modern Drama.* 1 (1958)ff. 4/yr.

Articles (E) on 20th-century drama, emphasis on contemporary plays. Interpretation, structure analysis, motifs, etc. Much on German theater in English translation. Reviews: books on theater. Bibliographical notes.

1567. *Theatre Documentation.* 1 (1968)ff. 2/yr.

Publ. by The Theatre Library Association. Brings bibliographies and articles (E, F) on theater practice and education, news of international theater scholarship. Thus far no material on German theater.

1568. *Theatre Research International.* 1 (1958)-13 (1974) under title: *Theatre Research*; 1 (1975)ff. 3/yr.

Publ. by the International Federation for Theatre Research. Articles (F, E) on directors, actors, and theater; well illustrated. Reviews. Non-scholarly but useful for background.

1569. *World Theatre.* 1 (1951)ff. 6/yr.

Publ. for the International Theater Institute, subsidized by UNESCO. Good material (bilingual: E, F) on theater, staging, productions; illustrations abundant. Emphasis is on more recent theater; some thematic issues. In each issue premieres in all countries are summarized with an excerpt from a press review.

b. Fiction

1570. *Modern Fiction Studies.* 1 (1955)ff. 4/yr.

Articles (E) and notes "devoted to criticism, scholarship, and bibliography of American, English, and European fiction since about 1880"; some thematic issues. Bibliographies. German literature scantily represented.

1571. *Novel. A Forum on Fiction.* 1 (1967)ff. 3/yr.

Articles (E) of high quality on the novel, poetics of the novel, especially English and American; does publish on the German novel. Reviews, often extensive. Notes: readers' response to articles.

1572. *Studies in the Novel.* 1 (1969)ff. 4/yr.

Some thematic issues. Articles (E) on British and American novels and novelists; some material on European novel but not on the German novel. Reviews. Checklists of criticism.

1573. *Studies in Short Fiction.* 1 (1963/64)ff. 4/yr.

Articles (E) and notes on short fiction, short stories. Reviews. Frequent bibliographies: translations, new publications, etc. Occasional articles on German fiction.

6. Literary Society Publications and Institute Yearbooks

The following selection includes the most important serial publications of literary societies within Germany and Austria and German literary societies outside of Germany. For detailed information concerning the German and Austrian literary societies, see: "Deutsche Dichtergesellschaften." *Jahrbuch für Internationale Germanistik* 6 (1974), 2, 143-166 and 8 (1976), 1, 132-179.

1574. *Aurora. Jahrbuch der Eichendorff-Gesellschaft (Würzburg).* 1 (1929)ff. 1/yr.

Articles (G) usually on Eichendorff or figures of his period: biographical, interpretive, comparative essays. Eichendorff bibliography (current). News. Reviews. Final page gives a succinct summary in English of all articles.

1575. *Blätter der Rilke-Gesellschaft.* H. 1 (1972)ff. 1/yr.

Publ. by the Rilke-Gesellschaft (Saas-Fee). Brings papers read at the annual meetings of the society: biography, interpretation and studies. Notes. Reports.

1576. *Blätter der Thomas-Mann-Gesellschaft.* 1 (1958)ff. Appears irreg.

Publ. by the Thomas-Mann-Gesellschaft and the Thomas-Mann-Archiv (Zurich). Publishes documents, letters, etc.; news and reports of the society, membership list.

1577. *Brecht-Jahrbuch. Jahrbuch der Internationalen Brecht-Gesellschaft.* 1 (1971)ff. 1/yr.

Former title: *Brecht-heute--Brecht Today.* 1971-1973. Articles (G, E, F) of high quality on Brecht. Reports on performances. Reviews.

1578. *Faust-Blätter. Archiv-Nachrichten. Halbjahresschrift der Faust-Gesellschaft (Knittlingen).* H. 1, 2 (1967)ff. 2/yr.

Archive reports (G), *Forschungsberichte*, personal and Society news, reviews of performances, bibliography. Some interpretation and criticism of *Faust.*

1579. *Fontane-Blätter.* 1 (1965)ff. Appears irreg.: 3 (1976)

Publ. by the Theodor Fontane Archiv der Deutschen Staatsbibliothek (Potsdam). Brings letters and documents, criticism, analyses, biography. Reviews. Bibliographical notes.

1580. *Goethe-Jahrbuch.* 1 (1885)ff. 1/yr.

Publ. for the Goethe-Gesellschaft (Weimar). Papers read at meetings of the Society: biography, sources, interpretation, philosophy. *Forschungsberichte.* News of the Society.

1581. *Grillparzer Forum Forchtenstein. Vorträge, Forschungen, Berichte.* 1965ff. 1/yr.

Organ of the Grillparzer-Forum Forchtenstein, which holds annual symposia at Forchtenstein (1962)ff. Publishes news of G.-Forum affairs, speeches. International Grillparzer bibliography in each issue. Frequent Grillparzer *Forschungsberichte.*

1582. *Gustav-Freytag-Blätter. Mitteilungen der Deutschen Gustav-Freytag-Gesellschaft* (Wiesbaden). 1 (1954)ff. (irreg.)

Publ. letters, biographical information, notes on reception of Freytag's works, *Forschungsberichte*, personal news.

1583. *Hebbel-Jahrbuch.* 1 (1939)ff. 1/yr.

Publ. by the Hebbel-Gesellschaft (Wesselburen). Articles (G) on Hebbel: biography, documents, interpretation, reports on drama productions. *Forschungsbericht*: "Literaturbericht" for the publications of the year preceding. Notes and news for members.

1584. *Heine-Jahrbuch.* 1 (1962)ff. 1/yr.

Publ. by the Heinrich Heine-Institut (Heinrich Heine-Archiv) and the Heinrich Heine-Gesellschaft (Düsseldorf). Articles (G, E, F) on Heine and his works. Some documentary material. Reports of interest to Heine scholars. Bibliography: "Heine-Literatur" for the year preceding.

1585. *Hofmannsthal-Blätter.* H. 1 (1968)ff. 2/yr.

Publ. by the Hugo von Hofmannsthal-Gesellschaft (Frankfurt). Publishes documents, manuscripts, letters. Notes (G) on sources, influences, reception, performances. Hofmannsthal bibliography (current).

1586. *Hölderlin-Jahrbuch*. 1 (1947)ff. 1/yr.

Publ. for the Hölderlin-Gesellschaft (Tübingen). Brings articles (G) on Hölderlin: archive holdings, biography, documents, interpretation, analysis of symbolism, etc. Hölderlin bibliography (current) includes reports on theater performances and conferences.

1587. *Jahrbuch der Deutschen Schiller-Gesellschaft*. 1 (1957)ff. 1/yr.

Publ. for the Deutsche Schiller-Gesellschaft, the Schiller Nationalmuseum. Deutsches Literaturarchiv Marbach. Articles (G) on 17th to 20th-century literature: genre, structure, interpretation, archive holdings. Occasional bibliography. Unpublished letters, documents.

1588. *Jahrbuch der Droste-Gesellschaft*. 1 (1929)ff. Appears irreg.

Publ. by the Droste-Gesellschaft (Münster). Publishes (G) letters, and documents, biographical information, interpretations, motif studies, etc.

1589. *Jahrbuch der Grillparzer-Gesellschaft*. 1890-1937; 1941-1944; 1953ff. 1/yr.

Publ. by the Grillparzer-Gesellschaft (Vienna). Publishes (G) papers on Grillparzer read at meetings of the Society.

1590. *Jahrbuch der Jean-Paul-Gesellschaft*. 1966ff. 1/yr.

Publ. by the Jean-Paul-Gesellschaft (Bayreuth). Articles (G) usually about or concerned with Jean-Paul. Substantial reviews. Jean-Paul bibliography: 1966 (for 1963-1965), 1970 (for 1966-1969).

1591. *Jahrbuch der Karl-May-Gesellschaft*. 1970ff. 1/yr.

Publ. by the Karl-May-Gesellschaft (Hamburg). Publishes documents, biography, interpretations, genre studies, *Forschungsberichte*, news of the Society.

1592. *Jahrbuch der Raabe-Gesellschaft*. 1 (1960)ff. 1/yr.

Publ. by the Raabe-Gesellschaft (Braunschweig) whose *Mitteilungen der Raabe-Gesellschaft* began with 45 (1958) to include bibliography and studies. The *Mitteilungen* were then supplanted by the *Jahrbuch* but continue in their function of publishing reports and news of the Society. The *Jahrbuch* publishes studies on motif, theme, structure, influence, interpretations, and a continuing Raabe bibliography. Reviews. Reports. "Literaturbericht": reviews of pertinent books and articles.

1593. *Jahrbuch des Freien Deutschen Hochstifts*. 1902ff. 1/yr.

Publ. by Das Freie Deutsche Hochstift (Frankfurt). Articles (G) on literature, emphasis on Goethezeit. Interpretation, documents, biographical material. *Jahresbericht* on proceedings of the Hochstift.

1594. *Jahrbuch des Wiener Goethe-Vereins.* 1 (1886)ff. 1/yr.

Publ. by the Wiener Goethe Verein (Vienna), 1 (1886)-63 (1959) under the title *Chronik des Wiener Goethe-Vereins.* Publishes critical articles (G) on Goethe and other authors.

1595. *Jahresgabe. Josef-Weinheber-Gesellschaft Wien.* 1 (1957)ff. 1/yr.

Biography, documents, personal and professional news, reports on the Weinheber edition, tributes. Poetry by Weinheber's friends.

1596. *Jahresgabe. Klaus-Groth-Gesellschaft.* 1959ff. 1/yr.

Publ. by the Klaus-Groth-Gesellschaft (Heide in Holstein). Biographical material, letters and documents, studies (G).

1597. *Lenau-Forum. Vierteljahresschrift für vergleichende Literaturforschung.* 1 (1969)ff. 4/yr.

Publ. for the Internationale Lenau-Gesellschaft (Vienna). Articles (G) emphasize Austrian and Hungarian literature (Donau-, Sudeten- und Karpathenraum). Of little use to the comparatist: emphasis is on Hungarian, Czech, Polish writers and reception of literature.

1598. *Lessing Yearbook.* 1 (1969)ff. 1/yr.

Publ. for the American Lessing Society. Articles (G, E) on German literature and thought of the 18th century, occasional documents. Substantial reviews. Occasional bibliography.

1599. *Literaturwissenschaftliches Jahrbuch.* 1 (1926)-9 (1939); *NF* 1 (1960)ff. 1/yr.

Publ. by the Görres Gesellschaft zur Pflege der Wissenschaft im Katholischen Deutschland (Bonn). Substantial articles (G, E) on the German Middle Ages, modern and comparative literature. Christian orientation, conservative. Reviews; archive reports.

1600. *Mitteilungen der E.T.A. Hoffmann-Gesellschaft.* 1 (1938)ff. 1/yr.

Publ. by the E.T.A. Hoffmann-Gesellschaft (Bamberg). Articles (G) on Hoffmann: biography, interpretation, letters and documents, news of the Society. Reviews. Hoffmann bibliography (not current).

1601. *Modern Austrian Literature. Journal of the International Arthur Schnitzler Research Association* (Binghamton, N.Y.) 1 (1968)ff. 4/yr.

Articles (E, G) on all aspects of Austrian literature and culture of the Schnitzler period. Reviews. Occasional bibliographies.

1602. *Das Musil-Forum.* 1, 2 (1975)ff. 2/yr.

Publ. by the Internationale Robert-Musil-Gesellschaft (Saarbrücken). Publishes letters and documents, biographical information, reception. Reviews.

1603. *Publications of the English Goethe Society* (London). 1 (1886)-14 (1912); NS 1 (1924)ff. 1/yr.

Publishes papers (E, G) read before the Society, usually on Goethe or the Goethe period. News of the Society.

1604. *Schriften der Theodor-Storm-Gesellschaft.* 1 (1952)ff. 1/yr.

Publ. by the Theodor-Storm-Gesellschaft (Husum). Notes and articles (G) on Theodor Storm: biography, documents; theme and motif studies, poetry interpretation. *Forschungsberichte.* Storm bibliography in each volume. Society news.

1605. *Vierteljahresschrift. Adalbert Stifter-Institut des Landes Oberösterreich.* 1 (1952)ff. 4/yr.

Publ. by the Adalbert Stifter-Institut des Landes Oberösterreich (Linz). Articles (G) on Stifter's works: themes, interpretation, evaluation. Some documents.

1606. *Wilhelm-Busch-Jahrbuch.* 15 (1949)ff. 1/yr.

Began as *Zwanglose Mitteilungen*, 1932-1949, published irregularly. Publ. by the Wilhelm-Busch-Gesellschaft (Hannover). Articles (G) on Busch; news of Society.

1607. *Yearbook. Publications of the Leo Baeck Institute.* 1 (1956)ff. 1/yr.

Publ. by the Leo Baeck Institute (Jerusalem, London, New York). Articles (E, G) and reports on German Jewry; bibliography, 1956ff. "Postwar Publications on German Jewry"; notes: research, communications of interest to Jews. Important for articles on Jews in exile.

7. Comparative Arts and Literature

1608. *Arcadia. Zeitschrift für vergleichende Literaturwissenschaft.* 1 (1966)ff. 3/yr.

Articles, notes (G, E) on comparative literature topics. Reviews. Publishes current list of members of the Deutsche Gesellschaft für allgemeine und vergleichende Literaturwissenschaft.

1609. *Comparative Literature (cl).* 1 (1949)ff. 4/yr.

An official journal of the American Comp. Lit. Association. Substantial articles (E) on all aspects of literary interrelations and problems of literary criticism. Lengthy critical book reviews.

1610. *Comparative Literature Studies.* 1 (1964)ff. 4/yr.

Articles (E, S, F, I, G) with comparatist perspective on literary history, intellectual history. Interdisciplinary and international in scope though not much material on German literature. Reviews (often extensive). Excellent background reading.

1611. *Mosaic. A Journal for the Comparative Study of Literature and Ideas.* 1 (1967/68)ff. 4/yr.

Articles (E) with comparative approach; thematic issues. Reviews.

1612. *Revue de littérature comparée.* 1 (1921)ff. 4/yr.

Notes and articles (F, E) usually of comparative nature. Some thematic issues. Little material directly relative to German literature. Reviews.

1613. *Studium Generale. Zeitschrift für interdisziplinäre Studien. Journal for Interdisciplinary Studies.* 1 (1947/48)ff. 12/yr.

Articles (E, G) aim to show the unity of sciences in their development of concepts and methodology. Occasional articles on literature. Reviews. Bibliographies.

1614. *Yearbook of Comparative and General Literature.* 1 (1952)ff. 1/yr.

Publ. for: Comparative Literature Committee of the National Council of Teachers of English, American Comparative Literature Association, Comparative Literature Section of MLA. Excellent articles (E) on comparative literature topics. Bibliography: 1952-1970 contains a selected comp. lit. bibliography with reference to the MLA bibliography; 1961ff., list of translations of foreign language literature into English. News and notes.

8. Related Disciplines

1615. *The American Imago. A Psychoanalytic Journal for Culture, Science, and the Arts.* 1 (1939/40)ff. 4/yr.

Publ. for the Assoc. for Applied Psychoanalysis, Inc. Articles on psychology, psychoanalysis applied to literature; little specifically on German literature. Reviews.

1616. *Archiv für Kulturgeschichte.* 1 (1903)ff. 2/yr.

Historically oriented articles (G) about general cultural subjects, not limited to Germany. Reviews. Good background reading.

1617. *Fabula. Zeitschrift für Erzählforschung. Journal of Folk Tale Studies. Revue des Études sur le conte populaire.* 1 (1958)ff. 3/yr.

Articles (G, E, F, R) on folktale motifs (international); reviews; works in progress (irreg.); *Forschungsberichte*.

1618. *Jahrbuch für ostdeutsche Volkskunde*. 1 (1958)ff. 1/yr.

Articles (G) on all aspects of folklore, including folk literature, in eastern Germany. Biographical profiles of folklorists.

1619. *Jahrbuch für Volkskunde und Kulturgeschichte*. 1 (1955)-16 *NF* 1 (1974)ff. 1/yr.

Articles (G) on German cultural history from the GDR Marxist-socialist perspective; less space given to German folklore. Bibliographies. Substantial review section.

1620. *Jahrbuch für Volksliedforschung*. 1 (1956)ff. 1/yr.

Articles (G, E) by international scholars. Reports on professional activities. Reviews of books and records; selected abstracts of books and articles.

1621. *Journal of European Studies. Literature and Ideas from the Renaissance to the Present*. 1 (1971)ff. 4/yr.

Articles (E) on literary and cultural history of Europe. Reviews. A good source of cultural background studies.

1622. *Journal of the History of Ideas. A Quarterly Devoted to Cultural and Intellectual History*. 1 (1940)ff. 4/yr.

Articles (E) and notes treating the influence of classical thought upon modern thought, European thought upon American, the influence of philosophy, science, etc. Reviews. Little reference to German literature.

1623. *Lili. Zeitschrift für Literaturwissenschaft und Linguistik*. 1 (1971)ff. 4/yr.

Articles (G) on linguistics applied to literature, aesthetics, methodology. Not confined to German literature.

1624. *Linguistische Berichte*. 1-6 (1969)ff. 6/yr.

Articles (G, E) on linguistics research; occasional articles on linguistics applied to criticism. Reviews.

1625. *Literature and Psychology*. 1 (1951)ff. 4/yr.

Articles (E) analysing world literature in terms of depth psychology. Annual selected bibliography of journal articles. Substantial reviews. Replies to articles.

1626. *Muttersprache. Zeitschrift zur Pflege und Erforschung der deutschen Sprache*. 1 (1886)ff. 6/yr.

Publ. by the Gesellschaft für deutsche Sprache. Articles (G) on linguistic problems of German; some application of linguistics to literature. Reviews, notes, discussion.

1627. *Niederdeutsches Jahrbuch. Jahrbuch des Vereins für Niederdeutsche Sprachforschung.* 1 (1875)ff. 1/yr.

Articles (G) on Low German dialects and culture. Reviews.

1628. *Philologus. Zeitschrift für das klassische Altertum.* 1 (1846)ff. 4/yr.

Publ. for the Zentralinstitut für Alte Geschichte und Archäologie der Deutschen Akademie der Wissenschaften zu Berlin. Articles (G, E) on classical antiquity: literature, philosophy, archaeology, history, mythology, linguistics. Primary material: manuscripts.

1629. *Zeitschrift für Volkskunde.* 1 (1891)ff. 2/yr.

Publ. for the Deutsche Gesellschaft für Volkskunde. Articles (G) on folklore. Personal news. Reviews.

9. German Relations to the US and Other Countries

1630. *American German Review (AGR).* 1 (1934/35)-37 (1970/71). 6/yr.

Was publ. by the National Carl Schurz Association. Articles (E) on art, pop culture, literature, politics. Notes: cultural news. Occasional short stories, poetry in English translation. Reviews. Bibliography Americana Germanica for year preceding publication. Excellent for teachers.

1631. *German-American Studies. A Journal Devoted to the Literature, History, and Cultural Achievements of the German-Speaking Element in the United States.* 1 (1969)ff. Appears irreg.

Publ. by The Society for German-American Studies. Short articles (E, G) of interest to students of German relationships in the US.

1632. *Germano-Slavica. A Canadian Journal of Germanic and Slavic Comparative Studies.* 1 (1976)ff. 2/yr.

Articles (E, G, F) on German-Slavic relations in language and literature. Reviews.

1633. *Jahrbuch für Amerikastudien.* 1 (1956)ff. 1/yr.

Publ. by the Gesellschaft für Amerikastudien. Articles (G, E) and notes mostly by Germans: US history, culture, politics, sociology; later issues focus mainly on literature. Reviews. Bibliography: "Deutsche amerikakundliche Veröffentlichungen" 1956ff.; US literature; emigration.

1634. *Zeitschrift für Kulturaustausch.* 1 (1951)ff. 4/yr.

Publ. by the Institut für Auslandsbeziehungen (Stuttgart). Copiously illustrated. Cultural news (G), particularly of Germans in foreign countries; occasional significant items on German literature and the reception of German writers abroad. Occasional bibliographies. Reviews. Personal news.

10. Translation and Literature in Translation

1635. *Babel. International Journal of Translation. Quarterly Journal Devoted to Information and Research in the Field of Translation.* 1 (1955)ff. 4/yr.

Organ of the International Federation of Translators. Articles (F, E, G) on all aspects of translations, notes. Reviews. Current bibliographies: lexicography (important source for hidden glossaries); "International Bibliography on Translation and Applied Linguistics."

1636. *Contemporary Literature in Translation.* 1968ff. 3/yr.

Presents literature from all languages, chiefly poetry and short prose. German literature generously represented.

**** *Dimension. Contemporary German Arts and Letters.* 1 (1968)ff. 3/yr. (No. 1455)

1637. *Lebende Sprachen. Zeitschrift für fremde Sprachen in Wissenschaft und Praxis.* 1 (1956)ff. 4/yr.

Organ of the Bundesverband der Dolmetscher und Übersetzer. Articles (G, F, S, E) on problems of translation, new word meanings, neologisms, borrowings, special vocabularies for recent technical developments, foreign languages in relation to German. Bibliography. Reviews. Professional news. Excellent for hard-to-find contemporary vocabulary English to German.

1638. *Modern Poetry in Translation.* 1 (1965)ff. 4/yr.

Presents poetry of all nations with emphasis on the 20th century.

1639. *Poet-Lore. A National Quarterly of World Poetry.* 1 (1889)ff. 4/yr.

Originally a "monthly magazine devoted to Shakespeare and Browning and to a comparative study of literature," much German poetry was published in translation. Recent issues carry little. 2 index vols. provide handy access to early years: Frank Holmes, *A Complete Index. Vols. 1-25 of Poet-Lore. A Magazine of Letters.* Boston: Gotham Pr., 1916; Alice Very, *A Comprehensive Index of Poet Lore. Vols. 1-58: 1889-1963.* Boston: Branden Publ., 1966.

11. Pedagogy

1640. *The Canadian Modern Language Review.* 1 (1944/45)ff. 4/yr.

Publ. by the Ontario Modern Language Teachers' Association. Articles (E, G, F), notes on language pedagogy. Reviews.

1641. *Deutschunterricht.* 1 (1948)ff. 12/yr.

A pedagogical journal for the GDR teacher. Lesson plans for individual literary works; articles (G) on literature, literary currents, teaching. Reports. Reviews.

1642. *Der Deutschunterricht. Beiträge zu seiner Praxis und wissenschaftlicher Grundlegung.* 1 (1949)ff. 6/yr.

Articles (G) on all aspects of teaching language and literature; thematic issues for areas of major concern. Supplements: *Forschungsberichte.* Articles excellent for the beginner.

1643. *Deutschunterricht für Ausländer. Zeitschrift für Unterrichtsmethodik und angewandte Sprachwissenschaft.* 1 (1951/52)ff. 6/yr.

Publ. under the auspices of the Goethe Institut (Munich). Articles (G) on problems of teaching and learning German, problems of grammar, usage. Excellent quality. Reviews.

1644. *IRAL. International Review of Applied Linguistics in Language Teaching.* 1 (1963)ff. 4/yr.

Theoretical articles (E, F, G) not confined to a particular language. Reviews. Notes and discussion.

1645. *Jahrbuch Deutsch als Fremdsprache.* 1 (1975)ff. 1/yr.

Articles on theoretical aspects of teaching and learning German as a foreign language and on the practical aspects of teaching German to foreigners in Germany. Reports: news of similar experiments, problems, etc. in other countries. Reviews.

1646. *Journal of Verbal Learning and Verbal Behavior.* 1 (1962/63)ff. 6/yr.

Technical articles (E) and notes on the psychology of language learning. Little of direct relevance to German studies.

1647. *Language Learning. A Journal of Applied Linguistics.* 1 (1948)ff. 2/yr.

Publ. by the Research Club in Language Learning. Articles (E) on theoretical or practical aspects of language learning, and pedagogy of second language. Professional announcements.

1648. *Language Teaching Abstracts.* 1 (1968)ff. 4/yr.

Publ. by the English-Teaching Information Centre and the Centre for Information on Language Teaching. Abstracts, articles (E); brief notes on new books; checklist of language-teaching periodicals used for compiling abstracts; works abstracted indexed by author and subject, not by title.

1649. *Linguistik und Didaktik.* 1 (1970)ff. 4/yr.

Articles (G) concerning the teaching of German and foreign languages, linguistics-based analyses of current German. Capsule reviews. In each issue: "Kleines Lexikon für Linguistik" (terminology). Good for teachers and students of modern German.

1650. *Modern Language Journal.* 1 (1916)ff. 8/yr.

Publ. by the National Federation of Modern Language Teachers' Associations. Articles (E) "devoted primarily to methods, pedagogical research and topics of professional interest to all language teachers." Conference news. Reviews.

1651. *Modern Languages. Journal of the Modern Language Association.* 1 (1919/20)ff. 4/yr.

Articles (E) primarily on pedagogy, some on literature. Notes. Reviews.

1652. *Neue Sammlung. Göttinger Zeitschrift für Erziehung und Gesellschaft.* 1 (1961)ff. 6/yr.

Based on H. Nohl's *Sammlung* (1945-1961). Articles (G) on pedagogy, school reform, philosophy of education, teaching hints, occasional articles on literature. Concerned chiefly with the German school system.

1653. *Die neueren Sprachen. Zeitschrift für Forschung, Unterricht und Kontaktstudium auf dem Gebiet der modernen Fremdsprachen.* 1 (1894)-50 (1951); *NF* 1 (1952)ff. 12/yr. + supplements.

Combined 1952ff. with *Die lebenden Fremdsprachen* and *Neuphilologische Zeitschrift.* Articles (G, earlier issues also E, F) on pedagogy and literature for use in foreign language classes. Reviews. Professional news.

1654. *Der Sprachdienst.* 1 (1957)ff. 12/yr.

Publ. by the Gesellschaft für deutsche Sprache. Articles (G) on questions of grammar, vocabulary choice, semantics, contemporary German usage. Reviews.

1655. *Sprachflege. Zeitschrift für gutes Deutsch.* 1 (1952)ff. 12/yr.

Articles (G) on proper usage, orthography, use of articles, etc. A non-technical journal, very useful for the teacher of German.

1656. *Sprachpraxis. Arbeitsmaterial für den Deutschlernenden Ausländer.* 1 (1973)ff. 6/yr.

Supplement to *Deutsch als Fremdsprache.* Brings news of the teaching profession in the GDR, cultural news, teaching material for beginners (exercises, jokes, idioms) and for advanced students.

1657. *Die Unterrichtspraxis. For the Teaching of German.* 1 (1968)ff. 2/yr.

Publ. by the American Association of Teachers of German. Articles (E, G) on the teaching of German and German literature, grammar problems, culture. Reports. Indispensable for the teacher.

1658. *Wirkendes Wort. Deutsche Sprache in Forschung und Lehre.* 1 (1950)ff. 6/yr.

Articles (G) addressed to German Gymnasium and university professors: problems of teaching literature, applied linguistics, interpretation, and methodology. *Forschungsberichte* regularly. Reviews. Notes: personal news, conferences.

1659. *Zeitschrift für deutsche Sprache.* 20 (1964)ff. 3/yr.

A continuation of: *Zeitschrift für deutsche Wortforschung.* Articles (G) on the history of the German language, etymology, dialectology, contemporary German. Reviews.

1660. *Zielsprache Deutsch. Zeitschrift für Unterrichtsmethodik und angewandte Sprachwissenschaft.* 1 (1970)ff. 4/yr.

Continues *Deutschunterricht für Ausländer* which ended with H. 5/6, 1968. Articles (G, E) addressed to the teacher of German in Germany, on methodology, teaching devices. Reviews.

XIII.

Related Fields

Checklist of Information on German Art, Music, Philosophy, History, Geography, Folklore, Philology, Language Teaching

CONTENTS

A. HANDBOOKS AND BIBLIOGRAPHIES FOR GERMAN STUDIES

1661. Bithell, Jethro, ed. *Germany. A Companion to German Studies.* 5th rev. and enl. ed. London: Methuen, 1955. xii, 578pp. ([1]1932)

1662. Hersch, Gisela. *A Bibliography of German Studies 1945-1971.* Bloomington, London: Indiana Univ. Pr., 1972. xvi, 603pp.

1663. Pasley, Malcolm, ed. *Germany. A Companion to German Studies.* London: Methuen, 1972. viii, 678pp.

B. GENERAL ENCYCLOPEDIAS

1664. *Allgemeine Encyklopädie der Wissenschaften und Künste.* Ed. by Johann Samuel Ersch and Johann Gottfried Gruber. 167 vols. Leipzig: Gleditsch, 1818-1889. (Repr. 1969) Completed only for A-G, H-Ligatur, O-Phyxius.

1665. *Brockhaus Enzyklopädie in 20 Bänden.* 17th rev. ed. of *Der Große Brockhaus.* Wiesbaden: Brockhaus, 1966-1974. ([1]1796-1810)

1666. *Der Große Brockhaus.* 16th rev. ed. 14 vols. Wiesbaden: Brockhaus, 1952-1964.

1667. *Der Große Herder.* 5th rev. ed. of *Herders Konversations-lexikon.* 10 vols. Freiburg: Herder, 1952-1958. ([1]1854-1857)

1668. *Meyers Enzyklopädisches Lexikon in 25 Bänden.* 9th completely rev. ed. Mannheim, Vienna, Zurich: Bibliographisches Institut, 1973. ([1]1840-1855)

1669. *Meyers Neues Lexikon in 18 Bänden.* Ed. by the Lexikonredaktion des VEB Bibliographischen Instituts. Leipzig: Bibliographisches Institut, 1971.

1670. *Österreich-Lexikon.* Ed. by Richard Bamberger and Franz Maier-Bruck. 2 vols. Vienna, Österreichischer Bundesverlag, 1966.

1671. *Schweizer Lexikon*. 7 vols. Zurich: Encyclios-Verlag, 1945-1948.

1672. Zedler, Johann Heinrich. *Großes vollständiges Universal-Lexicon aller Wissenschaften und Künste*. 68 vols. Halle, Leipzig: Zedler, 1732-1754. (Repr. 1961-1964)

C. ART AND ARCHITECTURE

1673. Andrews, Keith. *The Nazarenes. A Brotherhood of German Painters in Rome*. Oxford: Clarendon Pr., 1964. xiii, 148pp.

1674. Argan. Giulio Carlo. *Die Kunst des 20. Jahrhunderts, 1880-1940*. Berlin: Propyläen, 1977. 420pp. illus.

1675. Beckwith, John. *Early Medieval Art*. New York: Praeger, 1964. 270pp. illus.

1676. Benesch, Otto. *The Art of the Renaissance in Northern Europe. Its Relation to the Contemporary Spiritual and Intellectual Movements*. New York: Phaidon, 1965. ix, 195pp. illus.

1677. ———. *German Painting from Dürer to Holbein*. Cleveland: World, 1966. 197pp. illus.

1678. Benz, Richard, and Arthur von Schneider. *Die Kunst der deutschen Romantik*. Munich: Piper, 1939. 227pp. illus.

1679. Bialostocki, Jan. *Spätmittelalter und beginnende Neuzeit*. Berlin: Propyläen, 1972. 474pp. illus.

1680. Bock, Elfried. *Geschichte der graphischen Kunst von ihren Anfängen bis zur Gegenwart*. Berlin: Propyläen, 1930. 716pp. illus.

1681. Brenner, Hildegard. *Die Kunstpolitik des Nationalsozialismus*. Reinbek: Rowholt, 1963. 287pp. illus.

1682. Brinckmann, Albert Erich. *Die Kunst des Rokoko*. Berlin: Propyläen, 1940. 670pp. illus.

1683. Buchheim, Lothar-Günther. *Der blaue Reiter und die "Neue Künstlervereinigung München."* Feldafing: Buchheim, 1959. 344pp.

1684. Burger, Fritz, Hermann Schmitz, and Ignaz Beth. *Die deutsche Malerei vom ausgehenden Mittelalter bis zum Ende der Renaissance*. 3 vols. Berlin-Neubabelsberg: Athenaion, 1913-1922.

1685. Conant, Kenneth John. *Carolingian and Romanesque Architecture, 800 to 1200*. Baltimore: Penguin, 1959. 343pp. illus.

1686. Dehio, Georg Gottfried. *Handbuch der deutschen Kunstdenkmäler.* 7 vols. Munich, Berlin: Deutscher Kunstverlag, 1965-1972.

1687. *Deutsche Kunstdenkmäler. Ein Bildhandbuch.* Ed. by Reinhard Hootz. Vol. 1ff. Munich, Berlin: Deutscher Kunstverlag, 1958ff.

1688. Dube, Wolf-Dieter. *Expressionism.* New York, Washington: Praeger, 1973. 215pp. illus.

1689. Einstein, Carl. *Die Kunst des 20. Jahrhunderts.* Berlin: Propyläen, 1926. 575pp. illus.

1690. Feulner, Adolf, and Theodor Müller. *Geschichte der deutschen Plastik.* Munich: Bruckmann, 1953. 665pp. illus.

1691. Fillitz, Hermann. *Das Mittelalter.* 2 vols. Berlin: Propyläen, 1969-1972.

1692. Fischer, Otto. *Geschichte der deutschen Malerei.* 3rd ed. Munich: Bruckmann, 1956. 494pp. illus.

1693. Gantner, Joseph. *Kunstgeschichte der Schweiz von den Anfängen bis zum Beginn des 20. Jahrhunderts.* 4 vols. Frauenfeld: Huber, 1947-1968.

1694. Glück, Gustav. *Die Kunst der Renaissance in Deutschland, den Niederlanden, Frankreich, etc.* Berlin: Propyläen, 1928. 658pp. illus.

1695. Haftmann, Werner. *Painting in the Twentieth Century.* 2 vols. New York: Praeger, 1965.

1696. Hamann, Richard. *Die deutsche Malerei im 19. Jahrhundert.* 2 vols. Leipzig: Teubner, 1914.

1697. ———. *Die deutsche Malerei vom 18. bis zum Beginn des 20. Jahrhunderts.* Leipzig, Berlin: Teubner, 1925. viii, 472pp. illus.

1698. Hamilton, George Read. *Painting and Sculpture in Europe, 1800 to 1940.* Baltimore: Penguin, 1967. xxiv, 443pp. illus.

1699. Hauttmann, Max. *Die Kunst des frühen Mittelalters.* Berlin: Propyläen, 1929. 756pp. illus.

1700. Hempel, Eberhard. *Geschichte der deutschen Baukunst.* 2nd rev. ed. Munich: Bruckmann, 1956. 596pp. illus.

1701. ———. *Baroque Art and Architecture in Central Europe. Germany, Austria, Switzerland, Hungary, Czechoslovakia, Poland. Painting and Sculpture: Seventeenth and Eighteenth Centuries. Architecture: Sixteenth to Eighteenth Centuries.* Harmondsworth: Penguin, 1965. xxiii, 370pp. illus.

1702. Hildebrandt, Hans. *Die Kunst des 19. und 20. Jahrhunderts. Handbuch der Kunstwissenschaft.* Wildpark-Potsdam: Athenaion, 1924. 458pp. illus.

1703. Hinks, Roger P. *Carolingian Art. A Study of Early Medieval Painting and Sculpture in Western Europe.* Ann Arbor: Univ. of Michigan Pr., 1962. 226pp. illus. ([1]1935)

1704. Hitchcock, Henry Russell. *Architecture. Nineteenth and Twentieth Centuries.* 2nd ed. Baltimore: Penguin, 1963. xxix, 510pp. illus.

1705. Hofmann, Werner. *Das irdische Paradies. Kunst im 19. Jahrhundert.* Munich: Prestel, 1960. 411pp. illus. English version: *The Earthly Paradise. Art in the Nineteenth Century.* Trans. Brian Battershaw. New York: Braziller, 1961. 430pp. illus.

1706. ———. *Modern Painting in Austria.* Vienna: Kunstverlag Wolfrum, 1965. 209pp. illus.

1707. Hubala, Erich. *Die Kunst des 17. Jahrhunderts.* Berlin: Propyläen, 1970. 387pp. illus.

1708. Hütt, Wolfgang. *Deutsche Malerei und Graphik der frühbürgerlichen Revolution.* Leipzig: Seemann, 1973. 592pp. illus.

1709. ———. *Deutsche Malerei und Graphik im 20. Jahrhundert.* Berlin: Henschelverlag, 1969. 602pp. illus.

1710. Karlinger, Hans. *Die Kunst der Gotik.* Berlin: Propyläen, 1927. 678pp. illus.

1711. Kauffmann, Georg. *Die Kunst des 16. Jahrhunderts.* Berlin: Propyläen, 1970. 468pp. illus.

1712. Keller, Harold. *Die Kunst des 18. Jahrhunderts.* Berlin: Propyläen, 1971. 479pp. illus.

1713. *Kindlers Malerei Lexikon.* Ed. by Germain Bazin et al. 6 vols. Zurich, Munich: Kindler, 1964-1971.

1714. Keopf, Hans. *Deutsche Baukunst von der Römerzeit bis zur Gegenwart.* Stuttgart: Deutsche Fachzeitschriften- und Fachbuch-Verlag, 1956. x, 625pp.

1715. Kohlhaussen, Heinrich. *Geschichte des deutschen Kunsthandwerks.* Munich: Bruckmann, 1955. 591pp. illus.

1716. Landsberger, Franz. *Die Kunst der Goethezeit. Kunst und Kunstanschauung von 1750 bis 1830.* Leipzig: Insel, 1931. 319pp.

1717. Lankheit, Klaus. *Revolution und Restauration.* Baden-Baden: Holle, 1965. 285pp. illus.

1718. Lasko, Peter. *Ars Sacra, 800 to 1200.* Baltimore: Penguin, 1972. xxix, 338pp. illus.

1719. Lindemann, Gottfried. *History of German Art. Painting, Sculpture, Architecture.* New York: Praeger, 1971. 228pp. illus.

1720. Müller, Theodor. *Sculpture in the Netherlands, Germany, France and Spain, 1400 to 1500.* Harmondsworth: Penguin, 1966. xxiv, 262pp. illus.

1721. Müller-Mehlis, Reinhard. *Die Kunst im Dritten Reich.* Munich: Heyne, 1976. 230pp. illus.

1722. Müseler, Wilhelm. *Deutsche Kunst im Wandel der Zeiten.* Berlin: Safari, 1959. 189pp. illus.

1723. Myers, Bernard S. *The German Expressionists. A Generation in Revolt.* New York: McGraw-Hill, 1963. 348pp. illus.

1724. ——— and Shirley D. Myers. *Dictionary of 20th Century Art.* New York: McGraw-Hill, 1974. 440pp. illus.

1725. Novotny, Fritz. *Painting and Sculpture in Europe, 1780-1880.* Baltimore: Penguin, 1960. xxii, 288pp. illus.

1726. Osborn, Max. *Die Kunst des Rokoko.* Berlin: Propyläen, 1929. 658pp. illus.

1727. Osten, Gert von der, and Horst Vey. *Painting and Sculpture in Germany and the Netherlands, 1500 to 1600.* Baltimore: Penguin, 1969. xxii, 403pp. illus.

1728. *The Oxford Companion to Art.* Ed. by Harold Osborne. Oxford: Clarendon Pr., 1970. xii, 1277pp.

1729. Pauli, Gustav. *Die Kunst des Klassizismus und der Romantik.* 2nd ed. Berlin: Propyläen, 1925. xiv, 526pp. illus.

1730. Platz, Gustav Adolf. *Die Baukunst der neuesten Zeit.* Berlin: Propyläen, 1927. 607pp. illus.

1731. *Reallexikon zur deutschen Kunstgeschichte.* Ed. by Otto Schmitt. Vols. 1-6ff. Munich: Druckenmüller, 1973ff.

1732. Roh, Franz. *"Entartete" Kunst. Kunstbarbare im Dritten Reich.* Hannover: Fackelträger, 1962. 330pp. illus.

1733. ———. *Geschichte der deutschen Kunst von 1900 bis zur Gegenwart.* Munich: Bruckmann, 1958. 478pp. illus.

1734. ——— and Juliane Roh. *German Art in the 20th Century.* New York: Graphic Society, 1968. 516pp. illus.

1735. Roh, Juliane. *Deutsche Kunst der 60er Jahre. Malerei, Collage, Op-Art, Graphik.* Munich: Bruckmann, 1971. 284pp.

1736. Selz, Peter. *German Expressionist Painting.* Berkeley, Los Angeles: Univ. of Calif. Pr., 1957. xx, 379pp. illus.

1737. Thieme, Ulrich, and Felix Becker, eds. *Allgemeines Lexikon der bildenden Künstler von der Antike bis zur Gegenwart.* 37 vols. Leipzig: Engelmann, 1907-1950. Supplemented and continued by:

1738. Vollmer, Hans, ed. *Allgemeines Lexikon der bildenden Künstler des XX. Jahrhunderts.* 6 vols. Leipzig: Seemann, 1953-1962.

1739. Vogt, Paul. *Geschichte der deutschen Malerei im 20. Jahrhundert.* Cologne: M. Du Mont Schauberg, 1972. 528pp. illus.

1740. Waldmann, Emil. *Die Kunst des Realismus und Impressionismus im 19. Jahrhundert.* Berlin: Propyläen, 1927. 652pp. illus.

1741. Weigert, Hans. *Geschichte der deutschen Kunst von der Vorzeit bis zur Gegenwart.* Berlin: Propyläen, 1942. viii, 1010pp. illus.

1742. Weisbach, Werner. *Die Kunst des Barock in Italien, Frankreich, Deutschland und Spanien.* Berlin: Propyläen, 1924. 535pp. illus.

1743. Zeitler, Rudolf W. *Die Kunst des 19. Jahrhunderts.* Berlin: Propyläen, 1966. 411pp. illus.

D. MUSIC

1744. Baker, Theodore. *Biographical Dictionary of Musicians.* Ed. by Nicolas Slonimsky. 5th ed. New York: Schirmer, 1958. xv, 1855pp.

1745. Besseler, Heinrich, and Max Schneider, eds. *Musikgeschichte in Bildern.* Vol. 1ff. Leipzig: Deutscher Verlag für Musik, 1961ff.

1746. Einstein, Alfred. *Music in the Romantic Era.* New York: Norton, 1947. xii, 371pp.

1747. ———. *A Short History of Music.* 4th rev. ed. New York: Vintage, 1954. 205, viii pp. ([1]1938)

1748. *Grove's Dictionary of Music and Musicians.* Ed. by Eric Blom. 5th ed. 10 vols. New York: St. Martin's Pr., 1966.

1749. Herzfeld, Friedrich. *Ullstein Musiklexikon. Mit 4500 Stichwörtern. 600 Notenbeispielen, 1000 Abbildungen und 32 Tafelseiten.* Berlin, Frankfurt, Vienna: Ullstein, 1965. 631pp.

1750. Knepler, Georg. *Musikgeschichte des 19. Jahrhunderts.* 2 vols. Berlin: Henschelverlag, 1961.

1751. Lang, Paul Henry. *Music in Western Civilization.* New York: Norton, 1941. xvi, 1107pp.

1752. Moser, Hans Joachim. *Das deutsche Lied seit Mozart.* 2nd rev. ed. Tutzing: Schneider, 1968. 440pp.

1753. ———. *Geschichte der deutschen Musik.* Rev. and enl. ed. 3 vols. Hildesheim: Olms, 1968.

1754. ———. *Die Musik der deutschen Stämme.* Vienna: Wancura, 1957. 1087pp.

1755. ———. *Musiklexikon.* 2 vols. 4th ed. Hamburg: Sikorski, 1955. ([1]1935)

1756. *Die Musik in Geschichte und Gegenwart. Allgemeine Enzyklopädie der Musik.* Ed. by Friedrich Blume. 15 vols. Kassel, Basel: 1943-1973.

1757. *The New Oxford History of Music.* London, New York: Oxford Univ. Pr., 1954ff. 10 vols. planned.

1758. *The Oxford Companion to Music.* 10th ed. Ed. by John Owen Ward. London, New York: Oxford Univ. Pr., 1970. ix, 1189pp. illus.

1759. *The Oxford History of Music.* 8 vols. Ed. by Sir William Henry and Percy Carter Buck. London: Oxford Univ. Pr., 1929-1934.

1760. *The Pelican History of Music.* Ed. by Alec Robertson and Denis Stevens. 3 vols. Harmondsworth: Penguin, 1960-1969.

1761. Riemann, Hugo. *Dictionary of Music.* 2 vols. New York: Da Capo Pr., 1970. (Repr. of 1908 ed.)

1762. ———. *Musik-Lexikon.* Ed. by Willibald Gurlitt, Hans Heinrich Eggebrecht. 12th ed. 3 vols. New York: Schott, 1959-1967.

1763. Schering, Arnold. *Tabellen zur Musikgeschichte. Ein Hilfsmittel beim Studium der Musikgeschichte.* 5th ed. Wiesbaden: Breitkopf & Härtel, 1962. 174pp. ([1]1914)

1764. Seeger, Horst. *Musiklexikon in zwei Bänden.* Leipzig: Deutscher Verlag für Musik, 1966.

1765. Thompson, Oscar, ed. *The International Cyclopedia of Music and Musicians.* Ed. by Bruce Bohle. 10th ed. New York: Dodd, Mead, 1975. 2511pp.

1766. Wiora, Walter. *Die vier Weltalter der Musik.* Stuttgart: Kohlhammer, 1961. 185pp. English ed.: *The Four Ages of Music.* New York: Norton, 1965. 233pp. illus.

1767. Wörner, Karl Heinrich. *Geschichte der Musik. Ein Studien- und Nachschlagebuch.* 4th ed. Göttingen: Vandenhoeck & Ruprecht, 1965. 554pp. ([1]1954)

1768. ———. *History of Music. A Book for Study and Reference.* 5th ed. New York: Free Pr., 1973. xx, 712pp.

E. PHILOSOPHY

1769. Bréhier, Émile. *The History of Philosophy.* 7 vols. Chicago: Univ. of Chicago Pr., 1963-1969.

1770. Cassirer, Ernst. *Die Philosophie der Aufklärung.* Tübingen: Mohr, 1932. xviii, 491pp. English version: *The Philosophy of the Enlightenment.* Princeton: Princeton Univ. Pr., 1951. xiii, 366pp.

1771. Cole, George Douglas Howard. *A History of Socialist Thought.* 5 vols. in 7. New York: St. Martin's Pr., 1953-1960.

1772. *Contemporary Philosophy. A Survey.* ed. by Raymond Klibansky. 4 vols. Florence: La Nuova Italia, 1968-1971.

1773. Copleston, Frederick Charles. *A History of Philosophy.* 9 vols. Westminster, Md.: Newman Bookshop, 1946-1975.

1774. *The Encyclopedia of Philosophy.* Ed. by Paul Edwards. 8 vols. New York, London: Macmillan, 1967.

1775. Gardiner, Patrick L., ed. *Nineteenth Century Philosophy.* New York: Free Pr., 1969. 456pp.

1776. Glockner, Hermann. *Die europäische Philosophie von den Anfängen bis zur Gegenwart.* Stuttgart: Reclam, 1958. 1184pp.

1777. *Handbuch der philosophischen Grundbegriffe.* 3 vols. Ed. by Hermann Kringe, Hans Michael Baumgartner, and Christoph Wild. Munich: Kösel, 1973-1974.

1778. Heise, Robert. *Die Großen Dialektiker des 19. Jahrhunderts. Hegel, Kierkegaard, Marx.* Cologne, Berlin: Kiepenheuer & Witsch, 1963. 437pp. English version: *Hegel, Kierkegaard, Marx. Three Great Philosophers Whose Ideas Changed the Course of Civilization.* New York: Delacorte Pr./S. Lawrence, 1975. x, 438pp.

1779. *Historisches Wörterbuch der Philosophie. Völlig neubearbeitete Ausgabe des Wörterbuchs der philosophischen Begriffe von Rudolf Eisler.* Ed. by Joachim Ritter. Vol. 1ff. Basel, Stuttgart: Schwabe, 1971ff.

1780. Lehmann, Gerhard. *Die Philosophie des 19. Jahrhunderts.* 2 vols. Berlin: de Gruyter, 1953.

1781. *Philosophisches Wörterbuch.* Ed. by Georg Klaus and Manfred Buhr. 2 vols. 6th rev. and enl. ed. Berlin: Das europäische Buch, 1969.

1782. Reinhardt, Kurt F. *The Existentialist Revolt. The Main Themes and Phases of Existentialism. Kierkegaard, Nietzsche, Heidegger, Jaspers, Sartre, Marcel. With an Appendix on Existentialist Psychotherapy.* 2 vols. New York: Ungar, 1960.

1783. Schmidt, Heinrich. *Philosophisches Wörterbuch.* Ed. by Georgi Schischkoff. 18th ed. Stuttgart: Kröner, 1969. 656pp.

1784. Totok, Wilhelm. *Handbuch der Geschichte der Philosohpie.* Vols. 1-3ff. Frankfurt: Klostermann, 1964ff.

1785. Urmson, J.O., ed. *The Concise Encyclopedia of Western Philosophy and Philosophers.* New York: Hawthorn Books, 1960. 415pp.

1786. Überweg, Friedrich. *Grundriß der Geschichte der Philosophie.* 5 vols. 12th ed. Berlin: Mittler, 1924-1927.

1787. Vorländer, Karl. *Geschichte der Philosophie.* Ed. by Erwin Metzke, Hinrich Knittermeyer. 9th ed. 2 vols. Hamburg: Meiner, 1949-1955.

1788. Windelband, Wilhelm. *Lehrbuch der Geschichte der Philosophie. Mit einem Schlußkapitel: Die Philosophie im 20. Jahrhundert, und einer Übersicht über den Stand der philosophiegeschichtlichen Forschung.* Ed. by Heinz Heimsoeth. 15th ed. Tübingen: Mohr, 1957. 654pp. (^{1}1892)

F. CULTURAL HISTORY

1789. Adams, Marion, ed. *The German Tradition. Aspects of Art and Culture in German-Speaking Countries.* Sydney, London: Wiley, 1971. xi, 220pp.

1790. Barth, Ilse-Marie. *Literarisches Weimar. Kultur, Literatur, Sozialstruktur im 16.-20. Jahrhundert.* Stuttgart: Metzler, 1971. viii, 164pp.

1791. Bäuml, Franz. *Medieval Civilization in Germany 800-1273.* New York: Praeger, 1969. 230pp. illus.

1792. Boehn, Max von. *Die Mode. Menschen und Moden vom Mittelalter bis zur Gegenwart.* 8 vols. Munich: Bruckmann, 1923-1925.

1793. Bruford, Walter Horace. *Deutsche Kultur der Goethezeit.* Constance: Athenaion, 1965. 327pp. illus.

1794. Bruun, Geoffrey. *Nineteenth Century European Civilization, 1815-1914.* New York: Oxford Univ. Pr., 1960. 256pp. illus.

1795. Buchheim, Karl. *Deutsche Kultur zwischen 1830 und 1870.* Frankfurt: Athenaion, 1966. 261pp. illus.

1796. Ermatinger, Emil. *Deutsche Kultur im Zeitalter der Aufklärung.* Potsdam: Athenaion, 1935. 312pp. illus.

1797. ———. *Deutsche Kultur im Zeitalter der Aufklärung.* Rev. by Eugen Thurnher and Paul Stapf. Frankfurt: Athenaion, 1969. 381pp. illus.

1798. Fischer, Heinz. *Deutsche Kultur. Eine Einführung.* Berlin: Schmidt, 1973. 170pp.

1799. Flemming, Willi. *Deutsche Kultur im Zeitalter des Barock.* Potsdam: Athenaion, 1937. 329pp. illus. 2nd ed. Constance: Athenaion, 1960. 439pp. illus.

1800. Friedell, Egon. *Kulturgeschichte der Neuzeit. Die Krisis der europäischen Seele von der schwarzen Pest bis zum Weltkrieg.* 3 vols. Munich: Beck, 1930-1931. English version: *A Cultural History of the Modern Age. The Crisis of the European Soul from the Black Death to the World War.* 3 vols. New York: Knopf, 1930-1932.

1801. Fuchs, Eduard. *Illustrierte Sittengeschichte vom Mittelalter bis zur Gegenwart.* 3 vols. in 6. Munich: Lange, 1909-1912.

1802. Gay, Peter. *The Enlightenment. An Interpretation.* 2 vols. New York: Knopf, 1966-1969.

1803. ———. *Weimar Culture. The Outsider as Insider.* New York: Harper & Row, 1968. xv, 205pp.

1804. Gössmann, Wilhelm. *Deutsche Kulturgeschichte im Grundriß.* 4th rev. ed. Munich: Hueber, 1970. 171pp. illus.

1805. Gumbel, Hermann. *Deutsche Kultur von der Mystik bis zur Gegenreformation.* Potsdam: Athenaion, 1936. 259pp. illus.

1806. Hampson, Norman. *A Cultural History of the Enlightenment.* New York: Pantheon Books, 1968. 304pp.

1807. *History of Mankind. Cultural and Scientific Development.* Ed. by the International Commission for a History of the Scientific and Cultural Development of Mankind. 5 vols. in 13. London: Allen & Unwin, 1963-1976.

1808. Hofmann, Werner. *Ideengeschichte der sozialen Bewegung des 19. und 20. Jahrhunderts.* Berlin: de Gruyter, 1962. 243pp.

1809. Hollander, Hans. *Die Musik in der Kulturgeschichte des 19. und 20. Jahrhunderts*. Cologne: A. Volk, Gerig, 1967. 171pp.

1810. Johann, Ernst, and Jörg Junker. *Deutsche Kulturgeschichte der letzten hundert Jahre*. Munich: Nymphenburger Verlagshandlung, 1970. 400pp. illus.

1811. Johnston, William M. *The Austrian Mind. An Intellectual and Social History 1848-1938*. Berkeley, Los Angeles: Univ. of Calif. Pr., 1972. xvi, 515pp.

1812. Kelling, Hans-Wilhelm. *Deutsche Kulturgeschichte*. New York: Holt, Rinehart and Winston, 1974. 500pp.

1813. Kletler, Paul. *Deutsche Kultur zwischen Völkerwanderung und Kreuzzügen*. Potsdam: Athenaion, 1934. 194pp.

1814. Koch, Franz. *Deutsche Kultur des Idealismus*. Potsdam: Athenaion, 1935. 340pp. illus.

1815. Kohn, Hans. *The Mind of Germany. The Education of a Nation*. New York: Harper & Row, 1960. 370pp. illus.

1816. Kramer, Hans. *Deutsche Kultur zwischen 1871 und 1918*. Frankfurt: Athenaion, 1971. 323pp. illus.

1817. Lüdtke, Gerhard, and Lutz Mackensen. *Deutscher Kulturatlas*. 5 vols. Berlin: de Gruyter, 1928-1938. illus.

1818. Masur, Gerhard. *Prophets of Yesterday. Studies in European Culture 1890-1914*. New York: Macmillan, 1961. 481pp.

1819. Mildenberger, Gerhard. *Sozial- und Kulturgeschichte der Germanen. Von den Anfängen bis zur Völkerwanderungszeit*. Stuttgart: Kohlhammer, 1972. 147pp.

1820. Mönch, Walter. *Deutsche Kultur von der Aufklärung bis zur Gegenwart. Ereignisse, Gestalten, Strömungen*. Munich: Hueber, 1962. 536pp. illus.

1821. Mosse, George Lachmann. *The Crisis of German Ideology. Intellectual Origins of the Third Reich*. New York: Grosset & Dunlap, 1964. vi, 373pp.

1822. Naumann, Hans. *Deutsche Kultur im Zeitalter des Rittertums*. Potsdam: Athenaion, 1938. 203pp. illus.

1823. Neckel, Gustav. *Kultur der alten Germanen*. Potsdam: Athenaion, 1939. 177pp. illus.

1824. Neurohr, Jean Frederic. *Der Mythos vom Dritten Reich. Zur Geistesgeschichte des Nationalsozialismus*. Stuttgart: Cotta, 1957. 286pp.

1825. Pascal, Roy. *The Growth of Modern Germany*. New York: Russell & Russell, 1969. vi, 145pp. ([1]1946)

1826. Payne, J.P., ed. *Germany Today. Introductory Studies.* London: Methuen, 1971. xi, 183pp.

1827. Pinson, Koppel Shub. *Modern Germany. Its History and Civilization.* 2nd ed. New York: Macmillan, 1966. xv, 682pp.

1828. Reinhardt, Kurt F. *Germany: 2000 Years.* Rev. ed. 2 vols. New York: Ungar, 1961.

1829. Schallück, Paul, ed. *Deutschland. Kulturelle Entwicklungen seit 1945.* Munich: Hueber, 1969. 232pp. English version: *Germany. Cultural Developments since 1945.* Munich: Hueber, 1971. 216pp.

1830. Schwarz, Dietrich Wallo H. *Die Kultur der Schweiz.* Frankfurt: Akademische Verlagsgesellschaft Athenaion, 1967. viii, 408pp. illus.

1831. ———. *Sachgüter und Lebensformen. Einführung in die materielle Kulturgeschichte des Mittelalters und der Neuzeit.* Berlin: Schmidt, 1970. 244pp. illus.

1832. Steinhausen, Georg. *Geschichte der deutschen Kultur.* 4th ed. Leipzig: Bibliographisches Institut, 1936. 557pp. illus.

1833. Sydow, Eckart von. *Die Kultur des deutschen Klassizismus. Leben, Kunst, Weltanschauung.* Berlin: Grote, 1926. vii, 264pp. illus.

1834. Taylor, Henry Osborn. *The Medieval Mind.* 4th ed. 2 vols. Cambridge: Harvard Univ. Pr., 1959.

1835. Taylor, Jacob Leib. *Romanticism and Revolt. Europe, 1815-1848.* New York: Harcourt, Brace & World, 1967. 216pp.

1836. Zeeden, Ernst Walter. *Deutsche Kultur in der frühen Neuzeit.* Frankfurt: Athenaion, 1968. xv, 510pp. illus.

G. ECONOMIC AND POLITICAL HISTORY

1837. Aubin, Hermann, and Wolfgang Zorn, eds. *Handbuch der deutschen Wirtschafts- und Sozialgeschichte.* 2 vols. Stuttgart: Union, 1971-1976. 2nd rev. ed.

1838. Barraclough, Geoffrey. *The Origins of Modern Germany.* New York: Capricorn Books, 1962. 481pp.

1839. *Biographisches Wörterbuch zur deutschen Geschichte.* Ed. by Karl Bosl, Günther Franz, Hanns H. Hofmann. 2nd comp. rev. ed. 3 vols. Munich: Francke, 1973-1975.

1840. Bracher, Karl Dietrich. *Die Krise Europas, 1917-1975*. Frankfurt: Propyläen, 1976. 519pp. illus.

1841. Buchheim, Karl. *Das deutsche Kaiserreich 1871-1918. Vorgeschichte, Aufstieg, Niedergang*. Munich: Kösel, 1969. 303pp.

1842. *The Cambridge Economic History of Europe*. Ed. by H.J. Habakkuk and M.M. Postan. 2nd ed. Cambridge: Cambridge Univ. Pr., 1966ff.

1843. *The Cambridge Economic History of Europe from the Decline of the Roman Empire*. Ed. by J.H. Clapham et al. 5 vols. Cambridge: The Univ. Pr., 1941-1967.

1844. *The Cambridge Medieval History*. 2 vols. Cambridge: Cambridge Univ. Pr., 1966-1967. (1st ed. in 8 vols. New York: Macmillan, 1911-1936)

1845. Carr, William. *A History of Germany, 1815-1945*. London: Edward Arnold, 1969. xii, 462pp.

1846. Dahrendorf, Ralph. *Gesellschaft und Demokratie in Deutschland*. Munich: Piper, 1965. 516pp. English edition: *Society and Democracy in Germany*. Garden City, New York: Doubleday, 1967. xvi, 457pp.

1847. Dill, Marshall. *Germany. A Modern History*. Rev. and enl. ed. Ann Arbor: Univ. of Michigan Pr., 1970. x, 490pp.

1848. Diwald, Hellmut. *Anspruch auf Mündigkeit um 1400-1555*. Frankfurt: Propyläen, 1975. 485pp. illus.

1849. Eyck, Erich. *Bismarck and the German Empire*. London: Allen & Unwin, 1950. 327pp.

1850. ———. *Geschichte der Weimarer Republik*. 2 vols. Erlenbach-Zurich, Stuttgart: Rentsch, 1954-1956. English version: *A History of the Weimar Republic*. 2 vols. Cambridge: Harvard Univ. Pr., 1962-1963.

1851. *Fischer-Weltgeschichte*. Ed. by Jean Bollack. Vols. 1-34ff. Frankfurt: Fischer Bücherei, 1965ff.

1852. Gebhardt, Bruno. *Handbuch der deutschen Geschichte*. Ed. by Herbert Grundmann. 9th ed. 4 vols. Stuttgart: Union, 1970-1976.

1853. Görlich, Ernst Joseph, and Felix Romanik. *Geschichte Österreichs*. Innsbruck, Vienna, Munich: Tyrolia, 1970. 624pp.

1854. Grunberger, Richard. *The 12-Year Reich. A Social History of Nazi Germany, 1933-1945*. New York: Ballantine Books, 1971. 602pp. illus.

1855. Hamerow, Theodore S. *Restauration, Revolution, Reaction, Economics and Politics in Germany, 1815-1871*. Princeton, N.J.: Princeton Univ. Pr., 1958. 347pp.

1856. ———. *The Social Foundations of German Unification, 1858-1871*. 2 vols. Princeton, N.J.: Princeton Univ. Pr., 1969-1972.

1857. *Handbuch der deutschen Geschichte*. Ed. by Leo Just. 5 vols. in 6. Constance: Athenaion, 1956-1973.

1858. *Handbuch der Schweizer Geschichte*. 2 vols. Zurich: Verlag Berichthaus, 1972-1977.

1859. Holborn, Hajo. *A History of Modern Germany. The Reformation*. New York: Knopf, 1959. xvi, 374pp.

1860. ———. *A History of Modern Germany 1648-1840*. New York: Knopf, 1964. xii, 531pp.

1861. ———. *A History of Modern Germany 1840-1945*. New York: Knopf, 1969. xv, 818pp.

1862. Kersten, Kurt. *Die deutsche Revolution 1848-1849*. Frankfurt: Europäische Verlagsanstalt, 1955. 364pp.

1863. Kohn, Hans. *A History of the European Century*. 2 vols. Princeton: Van Nostrand, 1965-1968.

1864. Ludz, Peter Christian. *The German Democratic Republic from the Sixties to the Seventies. A Sociopolitical Analysis*. Cambridge: Harvard Center for International Affairs, 1970. 100pp.

1865. ———. *Soziologie und Marxismus in der Deutschen Demokratischen Republik*. 2 vols. Neuwied: Luchterhand, 1972.

1866. Lütge, Friedrich Karl. *Deutsche Sozial- und Wirtschaftsgeschichte. Ein Überblick*. 2nd ed. Berlin: Springer, 1960. 552pp. ([1]1952)

1867. Mandrou, Robert. *Staatsräson und Vernunft. 1649-1775*. Frankfurt: Propyläen, 1976. 472pp. illus.

1868. Mann, Golo. *Deutsche Geschichte des 19. und 20. Jahrhunderts*. Frankfurt: Fischer, 1966. 1063pp. ([1]1958)

1869. ———. *The History of Germany since 1789*. New York: Praeger, 1968. xii, 547pp.

1870. *The New Cambridge Modern History*. 14 vols. London: Cambridge Univ. Pr., 1957-1970. (1st ed. in 13 vols., 1907-1912)

1871. Ploetz, Karl. *Auszug aus der Geschichte*. 27th ed. Würzburg: Ploetz, 1968. Frequent editions. ([1]1863)

1872. *Propyläen Weltgeschichte. Eine Universalgeschichte*. Ed. by Alfred Heuß, Golo Mann, and August Nitschke. 12 vols. Berlin: Propyläen, 1960-1965.

1873. Ramm, Agatha. *Germany 1789-1919. A Political History.* London: Methuen, 1967. 517pp.

1874. Rössler, Hellmuth. *Europa im Zeitalter von Renaissance, Reformation und Gegenreformation, 1450-1650.* Munich: Bruckmann, 1956. xv, 719pp.

1875. ——— and Günther Franz. *Sachwörterbuch zur deutschen Geschichte.* Munich: Oldenbourg, 1958. 1472pp.

1876. *Saeculum Weltgeschichte.* Ed. by Herbert Franke et al. 7 vols. Freiburg, Basel, Vienna: Herder, 1961-1976.

1877. Schmidt, Ludwig. *Geschichte der deutschen Stämme bis zum Ausgang der Völkerwanderung.* 2nd comp. rev. ed. 2 vols. Munich: Beck, 1940-1941. (Repr. 1970)

1878. Schoeps, Hans Joachim. *Der Weg ins deutsche Kaiserreich.* Berlin: Propyläen, 1970. 322pp.

1879. Sethe, Paul. *Deutsche Geschichte im letzten Jahrhundert.* Frankfurt: Scheffler, 1966. 456pp. (^{1}1960)

1880. Sontheimer, Kurt. *Antidemokratisches Denken in der Weimarer Republik. Die politischen Ideen des deutschen Nationalismus zwischen 1918 und 1933.* Munich: Nymphenburger Verlagshandlung, 1962. 413pp.

1881. ——— and Wilhelm Bleek. *Die DDR, Politik, Gesellschaft, Wirtschaft.* Hamburg: Hoffmann und Campe, 1972. 259pp. English version: *The Government and Politics of East Germany.* London: Hutchinson, 1975. 205pp.

1882. ———. *Deutschland zwischen Demokratie und Antidemokratie. Studien zum politischen Bewußtsein der Deutschen.* Munich: Nymphenburger Verlagshandlung, 1973. 257pp. English version: *The Government and Politics of West Germany.* London: Hutchinson, 1972. 208pp.

1883. ———. *Grundzüge des politischen Systems der Bundesrepublik Deutschland.* Munich: Piper, 1971. 237pp.

1884. Stadelmann, Rudolf. *Soziale und politische Geschichte der Revolution von 1848.* Munich: Münchener Verlag, 1948. 216pp.

1885. Treue, Wilhelm. *Deutsche Geschichte. Von den Anfängen bis zur Gegenwart.* 3rd ed. Stuttgart: Kröner, 1965. xii, 828pp.

1886. ———. *Wirtschaftsgeschichte der Neuzeit. Im Zeitalter der industriellen Revolution 1700 bis 1960.* Stuttgart: Kröner, 1962. xv, 788pp.

1887. *Ullstein Weltgeschichte. Daten, Stichwörter. Bilder.* Ed. by Christfield Coler. 5 vols. Frankfurt: Ullstein, 1965.

1888. Vossler, Otto. *Die Revolution von 1848 in Deutschland.* 2nd ed. Frankfurt: Suhrkamp, 1967. 152pp.

1889. Weber, Hans Ulrich. *Bismarck und der Imperialismus.* Cologne, Berlin: Kiepenheuer & Witsch, 1969. 582pp.

1890. Zeeden, Ernst Walter. *Das Zeitalter der Gegenreformation.* Freiburg, Basel, Vienna: Herder, 1967. 302pp.

1891. Zeman, Zbyněk A.B. *The Break-up of the Hapsburg Empire. A Study in National and Social Revolution.* London, New York: Oxford Univ. Pr., 1961. 274pp.

1892. Zöllner, Erich. *Geschichte Österreichs. Von den Anfängen bis zur Gegenwart.* 5th ed. Munich: Oldenbourg, 1974. 694pp.

H. GEOGRAPHY

1893. Elkins, Thomas Henry. *Germany. An Introductory Geography.* Rev. ed. New York: Praeger, 1968. 334pp. illus.

1894. Schmitt, Eckart. *Deutschland.* 25th ed. Munich: List, 1970. 526pp.

1895. Sinnhuber, Karl A. *Germany--Its Geography and Growth.* 2nd ed. London: J. Murray, 1970. 132pp. illus.

I. ETHNOLOGY AND FOLKLORE

1896. Bach, Adolf. *Deutsche Volkskunde. Wege und Organisation, Probleme, System, Methoden, Ergebnisse und Aufgaben, Schrifttum. Mit 57 Skizzen und Karten.* 3rd ed. Heidelberg: Quelle & Meyer, 1960. 708pp.

1897. Bausinger, Hermann. *Volkskunde. Von der Altertumsforschung zur Kulturanalyse.* Berlin, Darmstadt: Habel, 1971. 303pp.

1898. Dünninger, Josef. "Brauchtum." *Dt. Phil. im Aufriß* (No. 1283), III, 2571-2640.

1899. Haberlandt, Arthur. *Taschenwörterbuch der Volkskunde Österreichs.* 2 vols. Vienna: Österreichischer Bundesverlag für Unterricht, Wissenschaft und Kunst, 1953-1959.

1900. Hain, Mathilde. "Die Volkskunde und ihre Methoden." *Dt. Phil. im Aufriß* (No. 1283), III, 2547-2570.

1901. *Handbuch der deutschen Volkskunde.* Ed. by Wilhelm Pessler. 3 vols. Potsdam: Akademische Verlagsgesellschaft Athenaion, 1934-1938.

1902. *Handwörterbuch des deutschen Aberglaubens.* Ed. by Hanns Bächthold-Stäubli, Eduard Hoffmann-Krayer. 10 vols. Berlin, Leipzig: de Gruyter, 1927-1942.

1903. Hoops, Johannes, ed. *Reallexikon der deutschen Altertumskunde.* 2nd rev. and enl. ed. by Heinrich Beck, Herbert Jankuhn, Hans Kuhn, Kurt Ranke, Reinhard Wenskus. Berlin, New York: de Gruyter, 1973ff. vol. 1ff.

1904. Kellermann, Volkmar. "Germanische Altertümer." *Dt. Phil. im Aufriß* (No. 1283), III, 1455-1546.

1905. ———. *Germanische Altertumskunde. Einführung in das Studium einer Kulturgeschichte der Vor- und Frühzeit.* Berlin: Schmidt, 1966. 132pp.

1906. Lutz, Gerhard, ed. *Volkskunde. Ein Handbuch zur Geschichte ihrer Probleme.* Berlin: Schmidt, 1958. 236pp.

1907. Naumann, Hans. *Grundlage der deutschen Volkskunde.* Leipzig: Quelle & Meyer, 1922. 158pp.

1908. Peuckert, Will-Erich, and Otto Lauffer. *Volkskunde. Quellen und Forschungen seit 1930.* Bern: Francke, 1951. 343pp.

1909. Spamer, Adolf, ed. *Die deutsche Volkskunde.* 2 vols. Leipzig: Bibliographisches Institut, 1934.

1910. Weber-Kellermann, Ingeborg. *Deutsche Volkskunde zwischen Germanistik und Sozialwissenschaft.* Stuttgart: Metzler, 1969. x, 113pp.

1911. *Wörterbuch der deutschen Volkskunde.* Ed. by Richard Beitl and Oswald A. Erich. 3rd ed. Stuttgart: Kröner, 1974. vii, 1005pp.

J. PHILOLOGY

1. Encyclopedias

1912. Agricola, Erhard, Wolfgang Fleischer et al. *Die deutsche Sprache.* 2 vols. Leipzig: Bibliographisches Institut, 1969-1970.

1913. Althaus, Hans Peter, Helmut Henne, and Herbert Ernst Wiegand. *Lexikon der germanistischen Linguistik.* Tübingen: Niemeyer, 1973. xvi, 675pp.

2. History of the Language

1914. Bach, Adolf. *Geschichte der deutschen Sprache*. 9th ed. Heidelberg: Quelle & Meyer, 1970. 534pp.

1915. Behagel, Otto. *Die deutsche Sprache*. 14th ed., ed. by Friedrich Maurer. Halle: Niemeyer, 1967. vii, 316pp.

1916. Chambers, W. Walker, and John R. Wilkie. *A Short History of the German Language*. London: Methuen, 1970. viii, 167pp.

1917. Eggers, Hans. *Deutsche Sprache im 20. Jahrhundert*. Munich: Piper, 1973. 135pp.

1918. ———. *Deutsche Sprachgeschichte*. 4 vols. Reinbek: Rowohlt, 1963-1977.

1919. Hirt, Hermann A. *Geschichte der deutschen Sprache*. 2nd ed. Munich: Beck, 1925. viii, 299pp.

1920. Krahe, Hans. *Sprache und Vorzeit. Europäische Vorgeschichte nach dem Zeugnis der Sprache*. Heidelberg: Quelle & Meyer, 1954. 180pp.

1921. Langen, August. "Deutsche Sprachgeschichte vom Barock bis zur Gegenwart." *Dt. Phil. im Aufriß* (No. 1283), I, 931-1396.

1922. Lockwood, William B. *An Informal History of the German Language. With Chapters on Dutch and Afrikaans, Frisian and Yiddish*. London: Deutsch, 1976. x, 265pp.

1923. Maurer, Friedrich, and Heinz Rupp, eds. *Deutsche Wortgeschichte*. 3rd ed. 5 vols. Berlin, New York: de Gruyter, 1974-1978.

1924. Moser, Hugo. *Annalen der deutschen Sprache von den Anfängen bis zur Gegenwart*. 4th ed. Stuttgart: Metzler, 1972. ix, 98pp.

1925. ———. *Deutsche Sprachgeschichte. Mit einer Einführung in die Fragen der Sprachbetrachtung*. 6th ed. Tübingen: Niemeyer, 1969. 228pp.

1926. ———. "Sprachgeschichte der älteren Zeit." *Dt. Phil. im Aufriß* (No. 1283), I, 621-854.

1927. Priebsch, Robert C., and William E. Collinson. *The German Language*. 6th ed. London: Faber, 1968. xx, 496pp.

1928. Schirmer, Alfred. *Deutsche Wortkunde. Kulturgeschichte des deutschen Wortschatzes*. 5th ed. by Walter Mitzka. Berlin: de Gruyter, 1965. 125pp. ([1]1925)

1929. Schirokauer, Arno. "Frühneuhochdeutsch." *Dt. Phil. im Aufriß* (No. 1283), I, 855-930.

1930. Sperber, Hans. *Geschichte der deutschen Sprache*. 8th comp. rev. ed., ed. by Peter von Polenz. Berlin, New York: de Gruyter, 1972. 219pp.

1931. Tschirch, Fritz. *Geschichte der deutschen Sprache*. 2nd ed. 2 vols. Berlin: Schmidt, 1971-1975.

1932. ———. *1200 Jahre deutsche Sprache. Die Entfaltung der deutschen Sprachgestalt in ausgewählten Stücken der Bibelübersetzung vom Ausgang des 8. Jahrhunderts bis in die Gegenwart*. Berlin: de Gruyter, 1955. xxiii, 127pp.

1933. Watermann, John T. *A History of the German Language. With Special Reference to the Cultural and Social Forces That Shaped the Standard Literary Language*. Seattle, London: Univ. of Washington Pr., 1966. xiii, 266pp.

3. Indo-European and Germanic

a. Grammars

1934. Brugmann, Karl. *Kurze vergleichende Grammatik der indogermanischen Sprachen*. Strasbourg: Trübner, 1904. 777pp. (Repr. 1970)

1935. ——— and Berthold Delbrueck. *Grundriß der vergleichenden Grammatik der indogermanischen Sprachen*. 5 vols. Berlin: de Gruyter, 1967. (Repr. of 1893 ed.)

1936. Fick, August, ed. *Vergleichendes Wörterbuch der indogermanischen Sprachen*. 3 vols. 4th ed. Göttingen: Vandenhoeck & Ruprecht, 1890-1909.

1937. Hirt, Hermann. *Handbuch des Urgermanischen*. 3 vols. Heidelberg: Winter, 1931-1935.

1938. ———. *Indogermanische Grammatik*. 7 vols. Heidelberg: Winter, 1921-1937.

1939. Hudson-Williams, Thomas. *A Short Introduction to the Study of Comparative Grammar (Indo-European)*. Cardiff: Univ. of Wales Pr., 1951. x, 78pp.

1940. Krahe, Hans. *Germanische Sprachwissenschaft*. 2 vols. 7th ed. Berlin: de Gruyter, 1969.

1941. ———. *Indogermanische Sprachwissenschaft*. 2 vols. 5th ed. Berlin: de Gruyter, 1966-1969.

1942. Lockwood, William B. *Indo-European Philology, Historical and Comparative*. London: Hutchinson, 1969. 193pp.

1943. Porzig, Walter. *Die Gliederung des indogermanischen Sprachgebietes*. 2nd ed. Heidelberg: Winter, 1974. 251pp.

1944. Streitberg, Wilhelm. *Urgermanische Grammatik.* 4th ed. Heidelberg: Winter, 1974. xx, 372pp. ([1]1896).

b. Dictionaries

1945. Buck, Carl Darling. *A Dictionary of Selected Synonyms in the Principal Indo-European Languages. A Contribution to the History of Ideas.* Chicago: Univ. of Chicago Pr., 1949. xix, 1515pp.

1946. Pokorny, Julius. *Indogermanisches etymologisches Wörterbuch.* 2 vols. Bern, Munich: Francke, 1959-1969.

1947. Prokosch, Eduard. *A Comparative Germanic Grammar.* Philadelphia: Linguistic Society of America, 1939. 353pp.

1948. Walde, Alois. *Vergleichendes Wörterbuch der indogermanischen Sprachen.* Ed. by Julius Pokorny. 3 vols. Berlin, Leipzig: de Gruyter, 1927-1932. (Repr. 1973)

4. Gothic

a. Grammars

1949. Braune, Theodor Wilhelm. *Gotische Grammatik. Mit Lesestücken und Wörterverzeichnis.* 18th rev. ed. Ernst Albrecht Ebbinghaus, ed. Tübingen: Niemeyer, 1973. xii, 201pp. ([1]1880)

1950. Hempel, Heinrich. *Gotisches Elementarbuch. Grammatik, Texte mit Übersetzung und Erläuterungen.* 4th ed. Berlin: de Gruyter, 1966. 169pp. ([1]1937)

1951. Krahe, Hans. *Historisches Laut- und Formenlehre des Gotischen. Zugleich eine Einführung in die germanische Sprachwissenschaft.* 2nd ed. Elmar Seebold, ed. Heidelberg: Winter, 1967. 151pp.

1952. Krause, Wolfgang. *Handbuch des Gotischen.* 3rd rev. ed. Munich: Beck, 1968. xx, 320pp. ([1]1953)

1953. Wright, Joseph. *Grammar of the Gothic Language, and the Gospel of St. Mark, Selections from the Other Gospels and the Second Epistle to Timothy with Notes and Glossary.* 2nd ed. O.L. Sayce, ed. Oxford: Clarendon Pr., 1954. ix, 383pp.

b. Dictionaries

1954. Feist, Sigmund. *Vergleichendes Wörterbuch der gotischen Sprache. Mit Einschluß des Krimgotischen und sonstiger zerstreuter Überreste des Gotischen.* 3rd rev. ed. Leiden: Brill, 1939. xxviii, 710pp. (Repr. 1961)

1955. Holthausen, Ferdinand. *Gotisches etymologisches Wörterbuch. Mit Einschluß der Eigennamen und der gotischen Lehnwörter im Romanischen.* Heidelberg: Winter, 1934. xxiv, 133pp.

1956. Streitberg, Wilhelm. *Gotisch-griechisch-deutsches Wörterbuch.* 2nd ed. Heidelberg: Winter, 1928. xii, 180pp. (Repr. 1960)

5. Old High German and Old Saxon

a. *Grammars*

1957. Armitage, Lionel. *An Introduction to the Study of Old High German.* Oxford: Clarendon Pr., 1911. 264pp.

1958. Baesecke, Georg. *Einführung in das Althochdeutsche. Laut- und Flexionslehre.* Munich: Beck, 1918. xi, 285pp.

1959. Braune, Theodor Wilhelm. *Abriß der althochdeutschen Grammatik mit Berücksichtigung des Altsächsischen.* 13th ed. Ernst Albrecht Ebbinghaus, ed. Tübingen: Niemeyer, 1970. 68pp. (^{1}1891)

1960. ———. *Althochdeutsche Grammatik.* 13th ed. Hans Egers, ed. Tübingen: Niemeyer, 1975. xv, 357pp. (^{1}1886)

1961. Ellis, Jeffrey. *An Elementary Old High German Grammar, Descriptive and Comparative.* Oxford: Clarendon Pr., 1953. xi, 106pp.

1962. Gallee, Johann Hendrik. *Altsächsische Grammatik.* 2nd ed. Johannes Lochner, ed. Halle: Niemeyer, 1910. xi, 352pp. (^{1}1891)

1963. Holthausen, Ferdinand. *Altsächsisches Elementarbuch.* 2nd ed. Heidelberg: Winter, 1921. xv, 240pp. (^{1}1900)

1964. Naumann, Hans. *Althochdeutsches Elementarbuch.* 4th ed. Rev. by Werner Betz. Berlin: de Gruyter, 1967. 183pp.

b. *Dictionaries*

1965. *Althochdeutsches Wörterbuch.* Rev. and ed. by Elisabeth Karg-Gasterstädt and Theodor Frings on the basis of papers left by Erwin von Steinmeyer; editing continued by Rudolf Grosse. Berlin: Akademie, 1968ff.

1966. Graff, Eberhard G. *Althochdeutscher Spracheschatz oder Wörterbuch der althochdeutschen Sprache.* 6 vols. Berlin: Nicolaische Buchhandlung, 1834-1846. (Repr. 1963)

1967. Holthausen, Ferdinand. *Altsächsisches Wörterbuch.* 2nd ed. Münster, Cologne: Böhlau, 1967. viii, 95pp. (^{1}1954)

1968. Schützeichel, Rudolf. *Althochdeutsches Wörterbuch.* 2nd ed. Tübingen: Niemeyer, 1974. xxxvi, 250pp.

1969. Sehrt, Edward H. *Vollständiges Wörterbuch zum Heliand und zur altsächsischen Genesis.* 2nd ed. Göttingen: Vandenhoeck & Ruprecht, 1966. viii, 738pp. ([1]1925)

6. Middle High German and Middle Low German

a. Grammars

1970. Asher, John A. *Short Descriptive Grammar of Middle High German. With Texts and Vocabulary.* Wellington: Oxford Univ. Pr., 1967. 64pp.

1971. de Boor, Helmut, and Roswitha Wisniewski. *Mittelhochdeutsche Grammatik.* 7th ed. Berlin: de Gruyter, 1973. 150pp. ([1]1956)

1972. Eis, Gerhard. *Historische Laut- und Formenlehre des Mittelhochdeutschen.* Heidelberg: Winter, 1950. 160pp.

1973. Lasch, Agathe. *Mittelniederdeutsche Grammatik.* Halle: Niemeyer, 1914. xi, 286pp.

1974. Paul, Hermann. *Mittelhochdeutsche Grammatik.* 20th ed. Hugo Moser and Ingeborg Schröbler, eds. Tübingen: Niemeyer, 1975. xlvii, 504pp. ([1]1881)

1975. Walshe, Maurice O'C. *A Middle High German Reader. With Grammar, Notes and Glossary.* Oxford: Clarendon Pr., 1974. xvi, 216pp.

1976. Weinhold, Karl. *Kleine mittelhochdeutsche Grammatik.* 6th ed. Hugo Moser, ed. Vienna, Stuttgart: Braumüller, 1972. viii, 179pp. ([1]1881)

1977. Wright, Joseph. *Middle High German Primer.* 5th ed. Maurice O'C. Walshe, ed. Oxford: Oxford Univ. Pr., 1955. 227pp.

1978. Zupitza, Julius, Franz Nobiling, and Fritz Tschirch. *Einführung in das Studium des Mittelhochdeutschen. Ein Lehr- und Lernbuch für die Studierenden der deutschen Philologie und zum Selbstunterricht.* 3rd ed. Jena: Gronan, 1963. xiii, 197pp. ([1]1868)

b. Dictionaries

1979. Benecke, Georg Friedrich, Wilhelm Müller, and Friedrich Zarncke. *Mittelhochdeutsches Wörterbuch.* 3 vols. Leipzig: Hirzel, 1854-1966. (Repr. 1963)

1980. Lasch, Agathe, Conrad Borchling, and Gerhard Cordes. *Mittelniederdeutsches Handwörterbuch.* Vol. 1ff. Neumünster: Wachholtz, 1956ff.

1981. Lexer, Matthias. *Mittelhochdeutsches Handwörterbuch.* 3 vols. Leipzig: Hirzel, 1872-1878. (Repr. 1974)

1982. ———. *Mittelhochdeutsches Taschenwörterbuch.* 34th ed. Additions by Ulrich Pretzel with the aid of Wolfgang Bachofer and Rena Leppin. Stuttgart: Hirzel, 1974. viii, 504pp.

1983. Schiller, Karl, and August Lübben. *Mittelniederdeutsches Wörterbuch.* 6 vols. Münster: Aschendorffsche Verlagsbuchhandlung, 1931. (Repr. 1969)

7. Early New High German

a. Grammars

1984. Brooke, Kenneth. *An Introduction to Early New High German.* Oxford: Blackwell, 1955. lxviii, 155pp.

1985. Moser, Hugo, and Hugo Stopp. *Grammatik des Frühneuhochdeutschen. Beiträge zur Laut- und Formenlehre.* 2 vols. Heidelberg: Winter, 1970-1973.

1986. Moser, Virgil. *Frühneuhochdeutsche Grammatik.* Vol. 1. Heidelberg: Winter, 1929-1951. Vol. 1. *Lautlehre.* pt. 1. *Orthographie, Betonung, Stammsilbenvokale.* 1929. xlv, 215pp. Vol. 1, pt. 3. *Konsonanten. 2. Hälfte.* 1951. xx, 332pp.

b. Dictionary

1987. Götze, Alfred. *Frühneuhochdeutsches Glossar.* 7th ed. Berlin: de Gruyter, 1967. xii, 240pp. ([1]1912)

8. New High German

a. Grammars

1988. Brinkmann, Hennig. *Die deutsche Sprache. Gestalt und Leistung.* 2nd rev. ed. Düsseldorf: Pädagogischer Verlag Schwann, 1971. xxxi, 939pp. ([1]1962)

1989. Curme, George O. *A Grammar of the German Language.* 2nd ed. New York: Ungar, 1952. xii, 623pp.

1990. *Duden. Grammatik der deutschen Gegenwartssprache.* 3rd rev. ed. Paul Grebe et al., eds. Mannheim, Vienna, Zurich: Bibliographisches Institut, 1973. 763pp.

1991. Erben, Johannes. *Deutsche Grammatik. Ein Abriß.* 11th rev. ed. Munich: Hueber, 1972. 392pp. ([1]1958)

1992. Grimm, Jacob. *Deutsche Grammatik.* 2nd ed. Vols. 1-2 ed. by Wilhelm Scherer, vols. 3-4 ed. by Gustav Roethe and Edward Schröder. Berlin: Dümmler, 1870-1898.

1993. Helbig, Gerhard, and Joachim Buscha. *Deutsche Grammatik. Ein Handbuch für Ausländerunterricht.* Leipzig: Verlag Enzyklopädie, 1974. 629pp.

1994. Lockwood, William Burley. *Historical German Syntax.* Oxford: Clarendon Pr., 1968. xiv, 279pp.

1995. Paul, Hermann. *Deutsche Grammatik.* 5 vols. 4-6th ed. Halle: Niemeyer, 1959. (Repr. 1968)

1996. Schulz, Dora, and Heinz Griesbach. *Grammatik der deutschen Sprache.* 8th ed. Munich: Hueber, 1970. xv, 475pp.

1997. Stolte, Heinz. *Kurze deutsche Grammatik auf Grund der fünfbändigen deutschen Grammatik von Hermann Paul.* 3rd ed. Tübingen: Niemeyer, 1962. 522pp.

1998. Wilmanns, Wilhelm. *Deutsche Grammatik. Gotisch, Alt-, Mittel,- und Neuhochdeutsch.* 3 vols. Straßburg: Trübner, 1897-1909.

1999. Wright, Joseph. *Historical German Grammar. Phonology, Word Formation and Accidence.* London: Cumberledge, 1952. xiv, 314pp.

b. General Dictionaries

2000. *Deutsches Fremdwörterbuch.* Ed. by Otto Basler. Vols. 1-3ff. Berlin, New York: de Gruyter, 1913-1977ff.

2001. *Duden. Bedeutungswörterbuch. 24 000 Wörter mit ihren Grundbedeutungen.* Ed. by Paul Grebe, Rudolf Köster, Wolfgang Müller, et al. Mannheim, Vienna, Zurich: Bibliographisches Institut, 1970. 815pp.

2002. *Duden. Fremdwörterbuch.* 3rd rev. ed. Wolfgang Müller et al., eds. Mannheim, Vienna, Zurich: Bibliographisches Institut, 1966. 781pp.

2003. *Duden. Das große Wörterbuch der deutschen Sprache in sechs Bänden.* Ed. by Günther Drosdowski. Mannheim, Vienna, Zurich: Bibliographisches Institut, 1976ff.

2004. *Duden. Rechtschreibung der deutschen Sprache und der Fremdwörter.* 17th rev. ed. Mannheim, Vienna, Zurich: Bibliographisches Institut, 1973. 793pp.

2005. *Duden. Zweifelsfälle der deutschen Sprache. Wörterbuch der sprachlichen Hauptschwierigkeiten.* 2nd rev. ed. Ed. by Dieter Berger, Günther Drosdowski, et al. Mannheim, Vienna, Zurich: Bibliographisches Institut, 1972. 784pp.

2006. Grimm, Jacob, and Wilhelm. *Deutsches Wörterbuch*. Ed. by the Deutsche Akademie der Wissenschaften zu Berlin. 16 vols. Leipzig: Hirzel, 1854-1960. Rev. ed.: *Deutsches Wörterbuch. Neubearbeitung*. Ed. by the Deutsche Akademie der Wissenschaften zu Berlin in cooperation with the Akademie der Wissenschaften zu Göttingen. Leipzig: Hirzel, 1965ff. Supplement: *Quellenverzeichnis zum Deutschen Wörterbuch von Jacob und Wilhelm Grimm*. Ed. by the Deutsche Akademie der Wissenschaften zu Berlin in cooperation with the Akademie der Wissenschaften zu Göttingen. Leipzig: Hirzel, 1966ff.

2007. Klappenbach, Ruth, and Wolfgang Steinitz, eds. *Wörterbuch der deutschen Gegenwartssprache*. 6 vols. Berlin: Akademie, 1964-1977.

2008. Küpper, Heinz. *Wörterbuch der deutschen Umgangssprache*. 6 vols. Hamburg: Claassen, 1963-1970.

2009. Paul, Hermann. *Deutsches Wörterbuch*. 7th ed. Werner Betz, ed. Tübingen: Niemeyer, 1976. x, 841pp.

2010. *Trübners Deutsches Wörterbuch*. Ed. by Walter Mitzka. 8 vols. Berlin: de Gruyter, 1939-1957.

2011. Wahrig, Gerhard. *Deutsches Wörterbuch*. Gütersloh: Bertelsmann, 1975. 1488pp.

c. Etymological Dictionaries

2012. *Duden. Das Herkunftswörterbuch. Die Etymologie der deutschen Sprache*. Ed. by Günther Drosdowski, Paul Grebe, et al. Mannheim, Vienna, Zurich: Bibliographisches Institut, 1975. 816pp.

2013. Kluge, Friedrich. *Etymologisches Wörterbuch der deutschen Sprache*. 21st ed. Walther Mitzka, ed. Berlin: de Gruyter, 1975. xvi, 915pp.

2014. Walshe, Maurice O'C. *A Concise German Etymological Dictionary. With a Supplement on the Etymology of Some Middle High German Words Extinct in Modern German, by Marianne Winder*. London: Routledge & K. Paul, 1951. xxiv, 275pp.

d. Dictionaries of Synonyms

2015. Dornseiff, Franz. *Der deutsche Wortschatz nach Sachgruppen*. 7th ed. Berlin: de Gruyter, 1970. 922pp.

2016. *Duden. Sinn- und sachverwandte Wörter und Wendungen. Wörterbuch der treffenden Ausdrücke*. Ed. by Wolfgang Müller, et. al. Mannheim, Vienna, Zurich: Bibliographisches Institut, 1972. 797pp.

2017. *Duden. Stilwörterbuch der deutschen Sprache*. 6th rev. ed. Mannheim, Vienna, Zurich: Bibliographisches Institut, 1971. xvi, 846pp.

2018. Görner, Herbert, and Günter Kempke. *Synonymwörterbuch. Sinnverwandte Ausdrücke der deutschen Sprache.* Leipzig: Bibliographisches Institut, 1973. 643pp.

2019. Meldau, Rudolf. *Schulsynomik der deutschen Sprache.* Heidelberg: Groos, 1972. 327pp.

2020. Peltzer, Karl. *Das treffende Wort. Wörterbuch sinnverwandter Ausdrücke.* 8th ed. Munich: Ott, 1964. 640pp.

2021. Wehrle-Eggers. *Deutscher Wortschatz. Ein Wegweiser zum treffenden Ausdruck.* 13th ed. Hans Eggers, ed. Stuttgart: Klett, 1967. xxxi, 821pp.

e. Bilingual (English, German) Dictionaries

2022. Eggeling, Hans F. *Dictionary of Modern German Prose Usage.* Oxford: Oxford Univ. Pr., 1961. ix, 418pp.

2023. Engeroff, Karl Wilhelm, and Cicely Lovelace-Käfer. *An English-German Dictionary of Idioms. Idiomatic and Figurative English Expressions with German Translations.* 5th ed. Munich: Hueber, 1975. 320pp.

2024. Farrell, Ralph Barstow. *Dictionary of German Synonyms.* 3rd ed. New York: Cambridge Univ. Pr., 1977. ix, 412pp. ([1]1953)

2025. Kremer, Edmund P. *German-American Handbook. A Collection of Current Idioms, Colloquialisms, Familiar Quotations, Localisms, Dialectical and Slang Expressions, and Words not Generally Found in German-English Dictionaries.* Chicago, Philadelphia, New York: Lippincott, 1939. xi, 390pp.

2026. *Langenscheidt's New Muret-Sanders Encyclopedic Dictionary of the English and German Languages.* Otto Springer, ed. 4 vols. New York: Barnes & Noble, 1962-1975.

2027. *The New Cassell's Dictionary. German-English, English-German.* Harold T. Betteridge, ed. New York: Funk & Wagnalls, 1971. xx, 646pp., 632pp.

2028. Spalding, Kenneth, and Kenneth Brooke. *An Historical Dictionary of German Figurative Usage.* Oxford: Blackwell, 1952ff.

2029. Taylor, Ronald J., and Walter Gottschalk. *A German-English Dictionary of Idioms. Idiomatic and Figurative German Expressions with English Translations.* 2nd rev. ed. Munich: Hueber, 1966. 598pp. ([1]1960)

f. Phonetics and Pronunciation

2030. Bithell, Jethro. *German Pronunciation and Phonology.* London: Methuen, 1952. xx, 514pp.

2031. *Duden. Ausspracheworterbuch. Der große Duden, vol. 6.* 2nd rev. ed. Max Meingold, ed. Mannheim, Vienna, Zurich: Bibliographisches Institut, 1974. 791pp.

2032. Isacenko, Alexander, and Hans-Joachim Schädlich. *Model of Standard German Intonation.* The Hague, Paris: Mouton, 1970. 66pp., 1 spoken record.

2033. Moulton, William G. *The Sounds of English and German.* Chicago: Univ. of Chicago Pr., 1962. 145pp.

2034. *Siebs. Deutsche Aussprache. Reine und gemäßigte Hochlautung mit Ausspracheworterbuch.* 19th rev. ed. of Theodor Siebs. *Deutsche Hochsprache. Bühnenaussprache.* Helmut de Boor, Hugo Moser, and Christian Winkler, eds. Berlin: de Gruyter, 1969. ix, 494pp. (^{1}1898)

2035. Wängler, Hans-Heinrich. *Grundriß einer Phonetik des Deutschen. Mit einer allgemeinen Einführung in die Phonetik.* 3rd ed. Marburg: Elwert, 1974. viii, 254pp.

g. Collections of Quotations

2036. Büchmann, Georg. *Geflügelte Worte. Der Zitatenschatz des deutschen Volkes.* 31st ed. G. Haupt and W. Rust, eds. Berlin: Haude & Spener, 1964. xii, 990pp. (^{1}1864)

A compendium of quotations of literary and historical origin. Does not include folk proverbs and sayings. Entries are listed by country of origin and include the original quotation, its meaning and later application. For specific quotations, see indexes: name, subject.

2037. Hellwig, Gerhard. *Zitate und Sprichwörter von A-Z. Ausgewählt und nach Schlagwörtern geordnet.* Gütersloh, Berlin: Bertelsmann, 1976. 543pp.

A collection of ca. 15,000 items arranged by key-word: aphorisms, sayings, proverbs, quotations, idiomatic expressions, commercial jingles, slogans, titles, etc. Unusual or archaic expressions annotated. Appendix: foreign language quotations. A quite successful attempt to update a collection of sayings.

2038. Moll, Otto E. *Sprichwörterbibliographie.* Frankfurt: Klostermann, 1958. xvi, 630pp.

A bibliography of bibliographies, collections, and various other sources, arranged by languages, which include African, Eastern, Semitic, etc. Chronological list of German collections, pp. 254-330. Information easily accessible.

2039. Puntsch, Eberhard. *Zitatenhandbuch.* 2nd ed. Munich: Moderne Verlags-GmbH, 1966. 1021pp. (^{1}1965)

Lists some 10,500 sayings, aphorisms, maxims, and proverbs, arranged according to 550 thematic categories in 42 cumulative chapters. Often juxtaposes contrasting subjects. International in scope. Readily accessible for finding quotations to suit special occasions.

K. BIBLIOGRAPHIES FOR FOREIGN-LANGUAGE TEACHING

2040. Boueke, Dietrich, Rüdiger Frommholz, Werner Psaar, Brigitte Röttger, and Jürgen O. Thöming, eds. *Bibliographie Deutschunterricht. Ein Auswahlverzeichnis.* 2nd rev. and enl. ed. Paderborn: Schöningh, 1974. 240pp.

Range: material published 1965-1974. Extensive bibliographical listings on all aspects of teaching German except teaching German as a foreign language; includes bibliographies, reference works, methodology, the mass media, teaching speech, spelling, composition, reading, literature. Lists both textbooks and secondary criticism. A good selection of titles for German literature. Index: authors.

2041. Buck, Kathryn, and Arthur Haase. *Textbooks in German 1942-1973. A Descriptive Bibliography.* New York: MLA, 1975. viii, 165pp.

An annotated list of 645 textbooks on the junior-high, high-school, and college level; each textbook, grammar, anthology extensively evaluated. Appendix A: supplementary material, workbooks, manuals for phonetics and pronunciation, word and idiom lists, books for self-instruction, dictionaries; appendix B: methodological and bibliographical references. Indexes: authors and editors, titles, publishers. Excellent for teachers.

2042. "Das gesprochene Wort. Jahresverzeichnis der literarischen Schallplatten." *Deutsche Nationalbibliographie.* Sonderheft. Ed. by the Deutsche Bücherei. Leipzig: Verlag für Buch- und Bibliothekswesen. 1959ff. (No. 55)

Appears annually as a supplement to *Deutsche Nationalbibliographie* (No. 55). Spoken records of East and West Germany listed in a genre and subject index. Indexes: author, subject, speaker.

2043. Gipper, Helmut, and Hans Schwarz, eds. *Bibliographisches Handbuch zur Sprachinhaltsforschung. Teil I. Schrifttum zur Sprachinhaltsforschung in alphabetischer Folge nach Verfassern mit Besprechungen und Inhaltshinweisen.* Cologne, Opladen: Westdeutscher Verlag.

I. *Buchstabe A-G.* 1966. ccvii, 774pp.
II. *Buchstabe H-K.* 1973. pp. 775-1902.
III. fasc. 17 (1974)-20 (1976)ff.

Beiheft I. Proberegister (zu Teil I. Bd. I-II, A-K). Auswahl aus der Ordnung nach Sinnbezirken und dem Namenregister nebst

Sprachverzeichnis und Anhang. 1974. 81pp. Indexes: subject, proper names; supplement to journals surveyed.

Range: 1920's-1974ff. An international, annotated review of books and articles. 17,687 items covering onomatology, semasiology, etymology, stylistics, synonymology, ethnolinguistics, etc. Not included: phonetics, phonology, historical phonology, grammar, morphology, histories of languages. Very complete coverage. Useful also for the student of literature and the language teacher.

2044. *A Language-Teaching Bibliography*. Publ. by the Centre for Information on Language-Teaching and the English-Teaching Information Centre of the British Council. 2nd ed. Cambridge: Univ. Pr., 1972. x, 242pp.

Guide to authoritative and useful works (books only) on the theory and practice of foreign language teaching. Each language section is divided into linguistic and methodological aspects of teaching. German material in Ch. 5, pp. 157-177, contains 837 items. Works are listed by titles A-Z and include reference and source materials, dictionaries, etc. All items are annotated. Volume quite useful.

2045. Littmann, Arnold. *Die deutschen Sprechplatten. Eine kritische Bibliographie*. Munich: Hueber, 1963. 271pp.

Comprehensive listing of German spoken records issued in Austria and Germany to July, 1963. Includes literary and documentary material. Extensive annotation on the contents, the performer, and the performances. Outdated but informative.

2046. Schmidt, Heiner, and F.J. Lützenkirchen, eds. *Bibliographie zur besonderen Unterrichtslehre. Teil 1. Deutsche Sprache, Literatur und Fremdsprachenunterricht. Zeitschriften-Nachweise 1947-1967*. Weinheim, Basel, Berlin: Beltz, 1971. xviii, 374pp.

Bibliography collated from pedagogical journals and arranged under 175 subject categories embracing German, literature, older and modern languages. Of primary interest to secondary school teachers in Germany.

Index

INDEX